in *Masks of difference* ... cultural
representation as a ... which embraces anthropo... ...rary
theory and colonial/postcolon... ...riginal
and informative readings of individua... ...s of colonisation in Europe, Africa and America from the sixteenth century to the twentieth century, 'naturalistic'
representations are revealed as textual practices which
betray their own subject positions. Together with
extended surveys, Richards discusses writers, artists
and anthropologists as diverse as Titian, Aphra Behn,
Walter Scott, James Frazer, T. S. Eliot, Matisse and
Clifford Geertz. *Masks of difference* also examines how
the historical discourses of cultural representation are
being challenged, adapted or redefined by contemporary critics, anthropologists and postcolonial writers.

Cultural Margins 2

Masks of difference
Cultural representations in literature, anthropology and art

Cultural Margins

General editor
Abdul JanMohamed
Department of English, University of California, Berkeley

The series **Cultural Margins** originates in response to the rapidly increasing interest in postcolonial and minority discourses among literary and humanist scholars in the US, Europe, and elsewhere. The aim of the series is to present books (both contributory and by single authors) which investigate the complex cultural zone within and through which dominant and minority societies interact and negotiate their differences.

Studies published in the series range from examinations of the debilitating effects of cultural marginalisation, to analyses of the forms of power found at the margins of culture, to books which map the varied and complex components involved in the relations of domination and subversion. The books engage with expressions of cultural marginalisation which might be literary (e.g. the novels of African or Caribbean or native American writers within a postcolonial context); or textual in a broader sense (e.g. legal or cultural documents relating to the subordination of groups under categories such as race and gender); or dramatic (e.g. subversive performance art by minority groups such as gays and lesbians); or in the sphere of popular culture (e.g. film, video, TV).

This is an international series, addressing questions crucial to the deconstruction and reconstruction of cultural identity in the late twentieth-century world.

1. Anna Marie Smith, *New Right discourse on race and sexuality: Britain, 1968–1990*
2. David Richards, *Masks of difference: Cultural representations in literature, anthropology and art*
3. Vincent J. Cheng, *Joyce, race and empire*

Masks of difference

Cultural representations in literature, anthropology and art

David Richards
University of Leeds

CAMBRIDGE
UNIVERSITY PRESS

Published by the Press Syndicate of the University of Cambridge
The Pitt Buildings, Trumpington Street, Cambridge CB2 1RP
40 West 20th Street, New York, NY 10011-4211, USA
10 Stamford Road, Oakleigh, Melbourne 3166, Australia

First published 1994

Printed in Great Britain by Woolnough Bookbinders Ltd,
Irthlingborough, Northants

A catalogue record for this book is available from the British Library

Library of Congress cataloguing in publication data applied for

ISBN 0 521 44458 6 hardback
ISBN 0 521 47972 X paperback

CE

For Sue, Tom and Kate
And in memory of my father

All images are partial but may masquerade
for an age as absolute or sovereign.

Wilson Harris

Contents

Illustrations

Note on the text

In writing this book I have attempted to place terms in their representational and historical contexts. Designations such as 'savage', 'primitive' (and related expressions), 'indian' and 'dwarf' are used in reference to forms of representation and are not descriptions of characteristics of individuals or peoples.

Preface

I would like to thank the Harold Hyam Wingate Foundation for a generous and well-timed grant which enabled me to continue work on this book. My thanks are due to the Librarian and Staff of the Brotherton Library, University of Leeds, the University Library, Birmingham University, and the Wren Library, Trinity College, Cambridge for their co-operation and courtesy. I am grateful to the Master and Fellows of Churchill College, Cambridge where I was both an undergraduate and postgraduate student and to the Master and Fellows of Trinity College, Cambridge for their generosity during visits to the Frazer archive held in the Wren Library.

My thanks also to colleagues in the School of English, the University of Leeds, and the English Department, University of Birmingham for answering my many queries without signs of irritation. To numerous members of the Universities of Ife, Lagos and Nsukka, and the people of Erin Osun, Nigeria, I owe thanks for their many acts of kindness and help. I am grateful to many individuals: Shirley Chew, Muraina Oyelami, Frank Kermode, Howard Erskine-Hill, Adrian Poole, Alistair Stead, Martin Butler, John Barnard, Martin Banham, Lynnette Hunter, David Lindley, Steve Watts, Steve Xerri, Lalage Bown, David Lodge, Ian Small, Mark Storey, Martin Pumphrey, Deirdre Burton, Alison West, Jenny Rice, Phil Rice, Karin Barber, John Pemberton III. I hope the impersonality of a list does not obscure the warmth of my gratitude.

My special thanks are due to Tim Cribb for his inspiration, erudition and friendship.

This book is dedicated to Sue, Tom and Kate Richards who helped, cajoled, sympathised, and made room for its awkward presence in their midst. And in memory of my father, who never saw its completion, but to whom my debt is beyond words.

1 E. Beck, *Africa* and *America*, 1740

Introduction

> In the most ancient languages, the words used to designate
> foreign peoples are drawn from two sources: either words that
> signify 'to stammer' 'to mumble' or words that signify 'mute'.
>
> *Ernest Renan*[1]

Much of what follows in this book is expressed emblematically by
the two illustrations drawn in 1740 by E. Beck (figure 1). They show a
double obsession: the representation of other more primitive cultures and the experimentation with perspective and lines of sight.
The coincidence is more than simply fortuitous, it is symptomatic.

To see these anamorphic images, one must break the conventions
of figurative art. It is necessary to lay the illustration on a flat surface
(not hang it on the wall) with the eye in the same plane as the figure
(not at 90°) and place a polished cylinder on the grey disc below the
figure. When the figure is turned through 180° and the beholder
looks into the cylinder (not at the drawing at all, but its reflection), a
perfectly proportioned figure representing Africa or America in
allegorical form can be seen. The images encode a knowledge which
is secret and which evokes the special expertise possessed by the
viewer. Ignorance of the drawings' technical brilliance will result in
the image remaining what it is: a gross, malformed distortion which
appears to melt on the page.

The images accomplish two goals simultaneously in fulfilling the
desire to see and in situating the primitive within the frame of
western representation. But, in order to see and to situate these
figures, one must apply to them a set of interpretive devices and
techniques. The image must be distorted, tilted, inverted and then
re-envisioned. To obtain that vision, one must not view the object
itself but its reflection in a distorting mirror. The figure only becomes

'known' to us through the transformation of an already encoded representation which is subject to the distortions of perspective. Equipped with the appropriate skills to render the object visible – just as an 'educated' reader brings to the literary or anthropological work the appropriate skills to decode it – the spectator is able to unlock the stylised depiction which has been imprisoned within a distorted representation.

'Africa' is an olive-skinned female, breast-plated, and dressed as a figure from the Roman carnival. She carries an indeterminate branch and the mythical unicorn is her heraldic beast. 'America' is a bare-breasted Amazon, darker skinned, barefooted, warlike with a heraldic parakeet. Now that the object has come into focus, the viewer can begin the work of interpretation as the 'primitive other' displays its mysterious and female nature. The viewer progresses from one kind of distortion (inchoate, malformed, undesirable, obscure, ugly) to another (allegorical, proportioned, aesthetic, desirable, orderly, known).

The images are an appropriate metaphor for the interpretive strategies and encoding processes, the 'tilting', 'inverting', 'applying of cylinders' kind of thing, which goes on in the making of representations of 'other peoples': the 'cylindrical' perspectives of their ways of seeing.

This book will begin with a familiar image from the High Renaissance of Italian art. My reading of Titian's *The Flaying of Marsyas* will emphasise how the picture represents ancient mythological figures of the wild, savage or primitive which are released from the painting, charged with new significances. The painting's underlying allegorical intentions shape the mass of associations into new narratives in new contexts. Central to this action of redistributing old images to new narratives is the attempt to fix, not a unique point of origins in 1570, but a primary boundary: that of the distinction between the wild, the primitive or the savage and the civilised which is focused upon the body of the primitive subject as both the vessel which contains these exemplary images and the site for the discovery of new forms of knowledge. It is upon this display of differences that my discussions of subsequent acts of cultural representation have their foundation.

The desire to make the representation of the savage fit into a narrative scheme is the subject of the next chapter, which deals with a first encounter between Europeans and other peoples in the late sixteenth century and recorded in the ethnographic illustrations of

Jacques Le Moyne de Morgue. The discovery narrative which these images set down also elaborated many of the models which shape the anthropological apprehension of its subject. Ancient mythical images of the wild are engaged and subjected to a romance narrative strategy, but the images also display a series of radical inversions of that romance narrative. The images fall under the pressure of external events which shape a counter discourse even in the act of representation. The pictures, in attempting to show the people of another land, succeed most successfully in presenting the contemporary religious and political obsessions of a European nation in conflict.

Similar conditions shape the texts discussed in chapter 3, where the romance conventions of representation of other peoples are similarly adapted to new historical conditions: those of slavery, 'race' and the growth of empire. But here the texts are fashioned as much by the conditions of authorship as by the perception of their savage subjects or external political forces. The first text, Aphra Behn's *Oroonoko*, makes implicit connections between the narratives of discovery and the discourses of sexuality. In the second text, which is situated in the same place but written by Captain John Stedman one hundred years later, romance tropes struggle to enunciate the facts of miscegenation, colonial violence and the crisis of male self-fashioning. The conventions of representation of other peoples begin to fragment as the allegorical images and narratives inherited from the Renaissance become insupportable or inadequate to the task of rendering the actuality of an imperial history.

Although many of the ancient images and romance themes persist in an altered form into the late eighteenth century, the next chapter examines how these transformations contribute to an emphasis upon the primitive's role in constructing historical narratives. Walter Scott's narratives are founded on the premise of the primitive's exemplary status both as a point of origin and as an anachronistic presence fated to imminent extinction. This theme is explored further in the next chapter which positions evolutionary and philological schemes of cultural history against the new 'narrative' constructions of the 'primitive'. James Frazer's research emphasised the necessity for the accumulation of 'facts' about other peoples. In this respect James Frazer, and the other Victorian evolutionists with whom he is compared, enacted a similar gathering of images to that examined in the Renaissance, not with allegorical intent, but in the spirit of scientific enquiry. The twentieth-century modernists and anthropologists discussed in the next chapter effectively stripped this endeavour of its scientific content and redirected the primitive materials towards new goals of definition of the self and art.

Thus far, this book will describe a narrative of sorts: a linear scheme of progressive accumulation, structuration and narration which is followed by a collapse or decay of narratives to allow a new process of accumulation, structuration, narration. There is an underlying historical rhythm: that of the *making* and *unmaking* of cultural representations. All these representations, however, are predicated upon a vision of a world which is indelibly divided: discourses obsessed with the assigning and demarcation of manichean boundaries between that which is savage and that which is 'cultured'.

In my discussion, I emphasise the ways in which the paintings, literary texts and ethnographies construct through their compositional strategies a structure for the processing and enunciation of the anomalous materials of otherness. The debt of literature and painting to anthropology is a major feature of that discussion, but my purpose in this book is not just to write about the well-documented theme of the savage in art and literature.[2] I hope also to demonstrate that the artistic, literary and anthropological rendering of the savage subject is constructed out of discourses of mutual dependence. Anthropology has provided literary texts with images, exotic colour, themes and theories about history, evolution and development but the literary and figurative have, in their turns, radically shaped anthropological discourses. Anthropology is every bit as heterogeneous in its representations as either literature or painting.

But Beck's illustrations afford us one further metaphorical insight: however we see them, either as perfectly proportioned cylindrical projections or as blurred smearings on the flat page, 'Africa' and 'America' cannot escape the force of their representation. They are forever rendered up to representation within this perspective. What act of will, violence or compassion will free 'Africa' and 'America' from the enclosing quotation marks?

The final chapters of this book will attempt to examine that question. The representation of other peoples can be maintained only so long as the subjects of study remain in that condition designated by Renan, as 'stammerers', 'mutterers' or, most likely, 'mutes'. Cultural representations in literature, art and anthropology have, historically, been founded upon the assumption that its discourse is unknown to the subjects of its analysis. Predicated upon, on the one hand, the illiteracy of its subjects and the remote and hidden nature of its work on the other, anthropology has been supremely and uniquely free to apply itself to an uncontested sphere of special, secret knowledge.[3] Much the same is true in the cases of both literary texts and paintings derived from or dependent upon anthropological insights.

The final chapters of this book will be concerned with postcolonial writings and anthropological and critical theories which have turned the discourse of representations against itself, to insist upon a new visibility, and to articulate, to repulse or to redefine the terms of discourses which are ostensibly 'about them'. The final chapters will discuss the work of writers from Africa and America who have laboured under the shadow cast by Beck's anamorphs and it will focus upon their deconstructions of cultural representations: Soyinka, Achebe, Okri, Marlene Nourbese Philip, Neil Bissoondath and others.

My discussion here focuses on two related but distinct movements. Both challenge the compulsion to see other peoples within the charmed circle of western cultural representations; both challenge the history of western cultural representations' capacities to misrepresent. In the first, contemporary critics and writers are engaged in unravelling, not only those falsifications, but the very premises of identity, language and culture upon which they are based; the hegemonic constructions are met with the deconstruction of their codes, 'presence' is confronted by 'absence', language by silence. These writers step out of the orders of discourse made for them by others into the incalculable space of the ellipsis.

The second theme of the final chapters examines the ways in which contemporary writers work – to a degree – within constructed models of representation in order to repossess the cultural materials they contain and to re-present them in different terms. In this discussion, cultural materials are made to function according to different criteria, given new meanings, new histories, new identities. The conclusion is firmly optimistic, although its material is often horrific, because these writers offer an alternative vision to that hegemonic cycle of accumulation, structuration and narration: a new construction outside the history of misrepresentations.

I have called this book *Masks of difference* because the mask seems to me to have exemplary qualities as a conceit or metaphor for discourses which attempt to characterise the cultural identities and differences which epitomise the representation of savage or primitive peoples. But the mask has other more potent and challenging

2 *Egungun face mask* in wood, from Oyo, Nigeria

possibilities; particularly so in view of the African writers under discussion in the final chapters.

This book is an extended meditation, speculation or conceit on the image reproduced above (figure 2) which acts as an insistent alternative to Beck's anamorphic drawings. The mask is made of wood and is a little over seven inches in length. It comes from south-west Nigeria, from the district of Oyo in the Yoruba homelands. This mask is of a type less commonly found than the more widespread *idan* or *paaka* types, in that it is made to fit very snugly over a person's face rather than on top of the head. It is ancient and shows signs which situate it as having been made at a place close to Oyo, the Yoruba king's (the Alafin's) capital city, since the facial marks and incisions which the mask bears are those of an ancient Oyo lineage. The mask is associated with the *egungun* cult. *Egungun* refers to ancestors who control human destinies on earth. Remembrance of the ancestors is vital to the success of human endeavours; to ignore them will result in witchcraft, plagues and social dissolution. *Egungun* masks are made by the Yoruba to participate in festivals which remember and celebrate the ancestors. The *egungun* masked festivals are still the most widespread of the many masked festivals the Yoruba enjoy but the cult with which this mask is associated dates from the end of the sixteenth century and evolved out of a massive dislocation of peoples. The *Igboho*, or exile, saw the forced removal of peoples from Ife, Nupe and other areas of Yorubaland and their gathering at old Oyo under the dominion of the Alafin. These diverse groups and lineages required a homogenising influence to which they could demonstrate their shared allegiance and *egungun* provided such a sense of collective identity. The mask is therefore a powerful source of Yoruba cultural identity and cohesion linking an ancestral past with a contemporary circumstance of dislocation.[4]

We have already crossed the threshold into ethnography. How rapidly the mask's enigmatic presence unravels. It spills its meanings at the merest touch.

Throughout the history of the *egungun* mask's existence as an object of exegesis, which is roughly the timespan covered in this book, its remarkable clarity has been utterly obfuscated. Not allowed to be what it most clearly *is*, its expressiveness has been covered by another mask which renders it invisible. Nor is it 'mute', on the contrary, the mask 'speaks' clearly enough what it is. A great deal of this book will document the failure to see the mask 'at face value' as it were; to see, not the thing itself, but a kind of portrait of otherness; that the true, challenging, productive and beautiful difference of the *Ara Orun*, who control human destinies on earth, is masked by other differences which have been contrived to express all manner of theories, obsessions, wishes, desires and hatreds.

The book has three main ambitions: to describe those 'masks of difference'; to document the historical conditions which produced the cultural representations of other peoples; to discuss responses to those cultural representations by the peoples whose identities the masks of difference 'masked'. This book will attempt to uncover how the mask has itself been masked and, finally, to see how the mask is reclaimed and remade by those to whom it properly belongs.

Chapter 1

The satyr anatomised: Venice 1570

Lear: I'll teach you differences![1]

The painting shows the moment of the satyr's death. Seven figures in a sylvan setting with two dogs. Marsyas hangs inverted from a tree while two figures begin the work of flaying. To the left another figure holds the *lira da braccio*; to the right a satyr carries a pail, an older man contemplates the action and a faun looks out of the painting at the viewer.

The Flaying of Marsyas (figure 3) was one of Titian's late works, possibly from the 1570s although critics have disputed that the painting may also be the work of Palma il Giovane.[2] His source for the painting was Ovid's myth and a fresco on the subject by Giulio Romano in the Sala delle Metamorfosi in Mantua.[3] Ovid in his *Metamorphoses* tells the myth of the Phrygian satyr Marsyas, an accomplished musician who challenged the god Apollo to a musical duel for supremacy in the art.[4] Marsyas played the pipes, whereas Apollo played the lyre; the agreement was that whoever won the contest would be able to do whatever he wished to the other. Marsyas lost the contest and his skin, as the penalty Apollo inflicted upon the satyr was that he should be flayed alive.

The identification of the figures in Titian's painting is no easy task since Apollo would seem to appear twice in the painting, both holding the lyre and flaying the satyr.[5] Alternative identifications point to the figure with the lyre being either Olympus, Marsyas' pupil, or Orpheus, the chief practitioner of Apollonian art.[6] The seated contemplative figure is less problematic since most critics agree that this is Midas. But here again, another identity is offered for this figure, that the figure is Titian's self-portrait. The identifica-

3 Titian, *The Flaying of Marsyas*, c. 1570

tion of Midas with Titian himself is founded on the similarity of this figure and the *Self-Portrait* in the Prado.[7] Certainly, Titian frequently showed himself in his paintings, in the *Pieta* and in the *Allegory of Time Governed by Prudence*.[8] In these respects, the painting offers a multiplicity of identifications in its presentation of its figures; identity is masked and plural.

Interpretation of the painting centres upon its allegorical significances in Christian–platonic terms. Within those doctrines the painting symbolises variously but consistently a set of triumphant humanist ideologies. The victory of Apollo 'represents the triumph of divine art', a personification of a 'state of divine harmony', of 'the soul liberated from earthly bonds' by the rhapsodic power of Apollonian music and of the 'redemption of the sufferer' through ecstatic agonies.[9] Interpretation emphasises the terms of neoplatonic allegory and the benign and redemptive qualities of the image; its exaltation of a spiritualised essence which, like the *auto da fé*, attempts to recuperate in the realm of the spirit what Marsyas lost (quite literally) in the world of the flesh.

The painting expresses this 'spiritualisation' in depicting space in an orderly composition. The picture has a classical composition which is almost architectural, as the figures would fit under one half of a pediment. An ascending diagonal line dissects the canvas from the child to the enrapt player. The line terminates in the eyes of the singing youth, but his gaze deflects its trajectory, turns it and projects it to an unseen ethereal destination beyond the picture's limits. His figure seems to mark the side of a triangle which is formed from the child, to the left-hand ground, to his eyes which are the apex. Beneath, but within and inside the 'half-pediment' is another full 'pediment' formed from Apollo's back to the body of Marsyas to the right-hand ground. The painting seems to show an interior space *within*, an inner sanctum within the temple, a dark secret place where Apollo crouches, searching Marsyas' bodily interior.

Arms, bent in right-angled shapes, repeat themselves across the canvas. Such repetitions make for an insistent 'rhythm'. The satyr who carries the pail uses his left arm as a counterweight to the load he carries, but it repeats the gesture of the youth as if he, too, is playing an invisible violin. Apollo's bent right arm is repeated in his helper's; both are mirrored in the gesture of the seated man. The picture's developed sense of rhythmical movement echoes the musical theme of the myth in an inaudible 'musical' rhythm, a kind of pictorial counterpoint.

Marsyas is the exception to the organisation of these spaces. Only his arms are not engaged in making music, flaying or contemplation, and his goat's legs and human torso break the orderliness of these lines. Who (in paintings) adopts this posture? Women in a horizontal pose to hide their modesty? In this inverted vertical posture it is the opposite of that elegant shapeliness. It is the very model of awkwardness; wry, askew, unheroic, exposed. A creature in this condition is lost. His body is almost an abstract shape – a dark abstraction – a great forked slash down the centre of the canvas. His shape pulls sight away from the ascending trajectory of the diagonal line and the gaze of the youth in his rapture and downwards to the woodland floor. The picture's composition divides in two antagonistic directions: out beyond the canvas to an ethereal and unrepresentable vision located somewhere above the middle top of the picture, and diametrically below that point to the middle bottom where a pool of blood is forming. Between these points hangs the body of Marsyas and this place smells of blood even at the moment of exaltation.

Titian's Apollo would seem to revise the Christian–platonic reconstruction of classical myth. Botticelli's Venus, for example, transforms the mythical to a Christian form of platonic beatitude and Venus' naked beauty becomes interchangeable with an ideal, essential virtue. Apollo, too, is beautiful and in that he is clearly related to Botticelli's Venus, but he is *cruelly* beautiful. The platonic equations of truth, beauty and virtue are not wholly sustained by Titian, as the nature of the platonic forms which the classical deities represented has been recapitulated. The image seems both to record and also to resist the platonising of the classical myth. Unlike Botticelli's treatment of classical myth, Titian's handling of the Marsyas myth perpetuates a double reading in 'splitting sight' along the axis of exaltation/blood which Marsyas' body describes.

The body in this posture recalls a scene of martyrdom but never so completely as actually *to be* that scene. While the picture evokes the inverted crucifixion of St Peter, or the *Isenheim Crucifixion* in its violence, Marsyas' death leads not to an ascension but plunges downwards into the darkness of the forest floor where a dog laps up the blood. The painting, although engaging with those familiar and elevated images, nonetheless also evokes a low subject: meat hanging in a kitchen still life, Rembrandt's carcass of beef.

The myth still retains its darkness, it is still unrevised, unreconstituted, its messiness remains unrefined; while the youth may 'see' a platonic vision of the ethereal (*à la* Botticelli) the painting does not show this although it records its possible presence outside. For all the platonic visions which emanate from beyond its borders, the painting remains a brutal image. A half-human, half-animal body strung up by its fetlocks and sliced into while barely restrained dogs try to lap up its blood. The neoplatonic reading of the image is sustained by passing over what the painting most brutally shows: a body in torment. To look at this image and see only the glorification of the power of Apollo is to ignore, in part, Apollo's depiction as a figure of conquest and cruelty, absorbed in his task of vivisection. In its concentration upon the spiritual codes of the painting, the body, its actual subject, is somehow lost from view.

12

The painting is paradigmatic of a recurrent 'crisis' of representation which lies deep in the platonic tradition of European art and
interpretation. Western art is constructed upon this problem of
representing that which it cannot, while effectively dismissing the
actual body as an inconsequential means to the end of an impossible
representation.[10] Its substantial presence fades into a shadow in the
contemplation of the inherent or immanent spirituality of its depic-
tions. Critical interpretation merely compounds art's intentions by
supplying the 'spiritual' gloss to an act of impossible representation;
thus the body is doubly dismissed, doubly masked behind a spiritualised essence. But the painting seems to resist this transformation
of the body of the wild creature into its ethereal 'non-presence' just
as the disputed presence of Palma il Giovane's hand in the painting
leaves the question of attribution open, the identification of the
figures of Apollo/Olympus/Orpheus and of Midas/Titian unsettles
the moral and narrative ascriptions of the image and the extraordinary disruptions of the strategies of composition and the
'rhythm' of gestures challenges a sublime aesthetic interpretation of
the canvas.

Titian's painting is undoubtedly steeped in the visual language of
neoplatonic interpretation but out of that vocabulary emerge other
challenging presences which demand that the viewer pay attention
to what the painting does actually show – the body – and not simply
the spiritualisation of its values. Consistently, the image seems to
present a series of analogical, parallel, inverted statements – 'double
visions' or a set of masked presences. In this view of the image, the
painting encodes a double 'moment': the suppression of and victory
over the wild by Apollonian civilisation and the insatiable curiosity
that civilisation feels for an investigation of the flayed wild creature
it has overwhelmed. The painting expresses this paradox: wild
Marsyas has been overpowered by civilised Apollo, but Marsyas is
still the most powerful presence in this painting. His power is that of
the victim of Apollo, of the wild creature which, even in its subjugation, continues to enunciate a disturbing and unremitting
potency. The picture's composition draws the viewer's sight along
two contradictory lines of vision, 'ascending' and 'descending' tra-
jectories each expressing divergent narrative significations. In
viewing again the body of Marsyas, a complementary set of interpretations becomes available, more partial, elusive and problematic than
those which attend on the figures of Apollo and Orpheus, but which
gestures to a field of representations and discourses which frame

and comment upon this body's representation. 'Moral and cosmological' allegories of the victorious Apollonian spirit lie behind and inform Apollo's depiction, but equally, what other allegories lie behind this traumatic image of an animal/human body, trussed and cut open?

The compositional strategy of the picture would seem, therefore, to register an inherent manicheism; a radical dialogism whereby the Apollonian ascendency is subverted (literally *inverted*) by its other, an insistent descent into the pain of the sylvan killing floor. In this reading of *The Flaying of Marsyas* the picture represents a meditation on a familiar manicheism which forms around a set of binary 'differences': 'ascendent' and 'descendent', animal and human, human and divine, body and spirit, civilised and wild. The world is divided along an immutable axis of difference. Yet this reading of the image is also a simplification of Titian's design just as the neoplatonic reading simplified the painting's recalcitrant subject, and just as the manichean impulse is a reduction of the world it aspires to describe into the binarism of wild/civilised. Titian's project is much more ambitious and some sense of the painting's ambition can be gained by reference to another enigmatic canvas and one which reiterates many of the elements of *The Flaying of Marsyas*.

The Allegory of Time Governed by Prudence (figure 4) shows three male heads in right and left profile and full face, above three animal heads, respectively, a wolf, a dog and a lion. The iconographic features of this image have also been the subject of a great number of interpretations. In the eighteenth century the painting was thought to be a portrait of Pope Julius II (left), Duke Alfonso d'Este (centre) and Emperor Charles V (right) and this interpretation held throughout the nineteenth century, except that the left-hand portrait was thought to be of Pope Paul III. The picture's allegorical meanings began to be interpreted in the 1950s as an allegory of the three ages of man; a reading which was expanded upon by Panofsky and Saxl who focused attention upon the inscriptions above the heads: Ex PRAETERITO PRAESENS PRUDENTER AGIT NI FUTURU[M] ACTIONE[M] DETURPET. For Panofsky, the iconography of the image recalls the three-headed serpent of Serapis–Apollo–Sol described in the *Saturnalia* of Macrobius and rededicated in Pierio Valeriano's *Hieroglyphica* as ambiguously both an image of Time and Prudence. Panofsky drew together the disparate elements of the painting in a reading which sees prudence governing time through memory, intelligence and foresight in its different aspects of the past (the

4 Titian, *The Allegory of Time Governed by Prudence*, c. 1565

wolf) 'which devours', the present (the lion) 'which acts' and the future (the dog) 'which flatters'. As was the case with *The Flaying of Marsyas*, however, Panofsky went on to make further indentifications: the portrait on the left is that of Titian himself, his son Orazio is in the centre and his nephew Marco on the right.[11]

Again, as with *The Flaying of Marsyas*, the picture can be interpreted as a neoplatonic meditation. In reading the image as recalling the esoteric figure of Serapis–Apollo–Sol, neoplatonic interpretation emphasises its vertical or ascendent axis. The picture appears in this light like an architectural or sculptural feature: a monument or column. The viewer's eye moves as the spirit ascends from the animal to the human to the Word which hovers above in dominant abstraction. Such an interpretation gives access to readings similar to those available for *The Flaying of Marsyas* in which suffering is transmuted by art into rapture through the domains of the subjugated wild, human and divine levels of being.

As with *The Flaying of Marsyas*, however, *The Allegory of Time* can be read as possessing an alternative compositional strategy which becomes available by reversing the ascendent tendency of the neoplatonic reading. Jurgis Baltrusaitis argues that the human portraits have a close physiological similarity to the animals beneath them and that Titian's picture expresses a connection between the animal and human physiognomies. In this Titian was following Leonardo Da Vinci, Della Porta, and a number of written sources in showing that each animal corresponds to a particular passion, that these passions become expressed by the animal's physiognomy, and that traces of these passions in human nature produce a human physiognomy appropriate to both animal and passion. Thus, strength, virility and courage anthropomorphically seen in the lion produce the leonine features of the human portrait in the middle of the *Allegory*. The shared geometry of the human and animal face – angles of eyes, nose, chin – display the assumed characteristics and it is this artistic technique which lies in a direct line of descent to nineteenth-century racial theories encoded in the anthropometry of Petrus Camper's 'facial angle'.[12] The *Allegory* contains a further allegory or secret: that the human body contains an animal presence which can be read in the dimensions of the 'plummet-measured face'. In this reading, the ascendent humanist doctrine is challenged, as in *The Flaying of Marsyas*, by a contrary trajectory: one which reverses the immanent divinity of the human face and redirects attention to its animal characteristics and origins.

Thus far, however, both paintings would seem to extemporise on the structures of the representation along the scale of manichean difference in a dialogue of binary oppositions. Both paintings are meditations upon the primary boundary between the animal and the human, the civil and the wild, engaged for different ends. However, where the *Allegory* helps with a reading of *The Flaying of Marsyas* is in a recognition of the painting's overall structural patterning. The *Allegory* shows an extraordinarily complex 'geometry' of relationships of forms between each of the levels of the canvas. Reading the picture requires not just a movement along a vertical ascending or descending axis, but horizontally and diagonally across the canvas comparing the different texts, faces and animals each with the other. If the painting were reduced to a simple diagramatical form it would closely resemble the points of a compass, the direction of vision radiating out from a centre, sweeping the entire canvas and pulled in all directions. Time is not unilinear; time emanates out from the present (represented by Titian's beloved son) but it is multidirectional. Thus, for example, *Providentia* can be read through the present as emanating from the ravening wolf of the past, just as the past will take us to the artist himself and to *Memoria*. Vision endlessly circulates around time's multiple coordinates.

The difference such a reading makes is to direct attention not to the immanent meaning or meanings of the painting, but to its *arrangement of meanings*. What is being articulated is not a narrative (ascendent or descendent) but a pattern, a structure or a 'map' of routes, directions, ways of seeing and thinking about time. The present has an insistent priority – in full face and in the centre – but it is as our necessary route of access to the contemplation of a whole network of connections and homologies. The painting demands that we think of time not as an analogical and linear destiny, but as a field or pattern of associations. Time has no *meaning*, and hence the allegory of time is not an allegory at all since no single meaning will suffice, but time does have a structure – or at least it has the structure we make for it from Titian's map of homologies. The allegory of time is the allegory of the structure of our understanding.

The value of *The Allegory of Time Governed by Prudence* for a reading of *The Flaying of Marsyas* resides in the apprehension of similar reading strategies. In both pictures an 'ascendent' spiritualising movement is countered by a 'descendent' bodily trajectory; out of that sense of opposition of manichean differences a larger pattern can be perceived. *The Flaying of Marsyas* is similarly composed around the three levels which characterised *The Allegory of Time* except that here the homologies are even more complex. The patterns of animal/human/disembodied essence, past/present/future, youth/maturity/age and high/middle/low, which structured *The Allegory of Time*, are replicated in *The Flaying of Marsyas* where gods, demi-gods and humans are projected onto an equally elaborate series. The figures are similarly arranged on the canvas as a reorganisation of the forms of the *Allegory*: the animal satyr is above the aging Midas who is above the faun; the rhapsodic youth is above the god's assistant who is above the god. Marsyas' own figure seems to demand that we pay particular attention to the painting's inherent composition: in his inverted position, the animal half is at the top, the human at the bottom as if the *Allegory* had been turned upside down.

The picture redistributes the categorical terms of the *Allegory* in its play upon types of beings, yet the composition still allows the same kind of horizontal, vertical and diagonal relationships to be read. Reading the composition of *The Flaying of Marsyas* in the light of the *Allegory* envisages the painting as a structural paradigm or 'map' of the domestication through subjugation of the wild. In many respects, Titian's painting is precisely that structuralist product – a field of differences articulated as sets of binary oppositions reducible to an irreducible code of culture's action upon nature. But it is also infinitely more than that sterile anodyne. Having made the structure of representations, Titian then begins to dissent from the object he has made.

As in the *Allegory*, the painting radiates from a centre, but in *The Flaying of Marsyas* that centre is an inanimate object: the knife Apollo uses to cut into the satyr's flesh. All connections must be made through the agency of this knife; we 'enter' the picture through the undisputed fact of its existence. All the creatures (gods, humans, animals) have congregated because of this cruel instrument. All kinds of life focus upon its presence and it is the pivot upon which the compass points of the picture turn. All the homologies are distributed around the presence of the knife in a map or structure which brings the varieties of created nature into sharp focus.

The god seems to cut the human half of the satyr from his animal half as his art 'cuts' the human from animal nature and the civil from the sylvan. It is through the agency of the knife that the child may gain the rhapsody of the youth; it is the knife which separates the active and unthinking assistant from the static and contemplative Midas; it is the knife which liberates the youth's rhapsody from the satyr's pain. We can follow any 'route' but the knife will not be denied its clarifying role as that which separates and divides, once and for all, the Apollonian from its other. In terms of the *Allegory*, the bloody knife is the picture's present tense. It is the instrument with which Apollo makes his triumphant acts of designation; acts which in themselves contain a paradox in that Apollo is 'made' by those he 'unmakes'.[13] The structure cannot *be* without the destructuring of Marsyas. The knife is the divine *caesura*, the image of an absolute separation, it makes all the *difference*.

But Titian insists that we look to the composition of the *whole* canvas to see this structuring/destructuring at work, not just to the immanent meanings of its parts. *The Flaying of Marsyas* is extraordinarily insistent that the viewer pay attention to the arrangement of its figures and none more so than the figure of Titian himself, represented as Midas. Midas/Titian is inactive; he plays no part in the Apollonian triumph, his art does not come, as does the youth's, from the celebration of Apollonian triumph but from the recording of the structure which the triumph articulates. In the articulation of the system of differences, Midas/Titian appears, most definitely on 'the other side' of the body of Marsyas to Apollo, on 'the other side' of the knife's *caesura*, a contemplative 'Marsyan' figure by choice. In the *Allegory* Titian participated in the structuration of the representation as the emblem of a decaying past, but one which had given us the present in his own son and the future in his nephew. Titian and his heirs are the very essence of time. Such is not the case in *The Flaying of Marsyas*, where he places himself in the scene as a sceptical and mournful figure while this great work of flaying, rapture and structuration goes on around him.

The painting's allegory shows how the refined Apollonian world of humanist and platonic Europe deals with those it has designated as its wild, savage other. But the painting itself is both the product and producer of the same allegories and structures of difference. Midas' dilemma is how to think himself out of this conundrum; how to conceive of a structure which is other than the Apollonian map of designations, triumphs and blood-lettings, when his very presence is made by that pattern. Titian, masked by his disguise as Midas, marks an important and unique dissenting presence in the picture, a presence which questions every confident and triumphant act of designation which Apollo wills into being. The system of differences of the civilised and its others is made ambiguous and contingent upon this brooding presence. Inevitably the picture 'turns' around its central point, the knife with which Apollo slices into Marsyas' flesh, but to read only the Apollonian narrative and not the Marsyan narrative is to miss the point. Apollo 'makes' the world – as a great manichean division of 'kinds of beings' – at the very moment of a mythical 'unmaking' of the body of the other. But Midas' scepticism also unmakes that making; a reading which becomes available by 'turning' the picture around one of its many compositional axes – a literal and metaphorical 'tilt' of the head to reveal alternative Marsyan and Apollonian centres of gravity.

The knife in the god's hand in the painting is the focus of attention of the assembled group of figures; its presence clarifies, simplifies and structures the world. In Ovid's *Metamorphoses*, Marsyas' crime was to have the effrontery to challenge Apollo's superiority; a simple matter of the tyrannical justice of an offended deity. Mythology teems with such disasters arbitrarily called down upon an individual, city or people for the offence of preferring the beauty of one goddess over another, or of giving to men what belongs to the gods. In an Ovidian sense the knife's presence underscores the fact of Apollonian power.

In a similarly Ovidian sense, it demonstrates that, of all these beings, only gods cannot bleed, only gods feel no pain. Apollo here is the antithesis of the Christian image of the divine as the suffering sacrifice. Apollo seems intrigued by the fact – unknowable to him, unimaginable to him – of a body in torment. The knife is Apollo's unknowable pain objectified just as it is the object of Marsyas' known pain. Apollo's lack is Marsyas' surfeit; the absence of one causes the existence of the other.

How can pain be visualised for those who do not know what it is? In the Ovidian sense of mythology as the display of divine might, the answer is simple: Apollo does this because he can. Elaine Scarry (in a different context) observes that 'objectified pain is denied as pain and read as power': 'the larger the prisoner's pain the larger the torturer's world'. Apollonian art is therefore the realisation, objectification and transformation of pain into the 'insignia of the regime'.[14]

There is a second question which is closely related to that of the problematic 'visualisation' of pain: what kind of a scene is this which the knife calls into being? Again following the Ovidian sense, Marsyas is put to the use of Apollo in this process of metamorphosis from pain to power and the scene we witness is a process of Apollonian aggrandisement through sacrifice.

Familiar humanist themes are repeated in the Ovidian answers to these questions; the knife is not seen as an object but as an instrument in the sacrificial process which accomplishes its transcendent goal and thus allows Marsyas to be seen in the same light as the flayed Christian martyrs SS Savin, Cyprian and Simonino. The 'thingness' of the knife is substituted by its role in a sacrificial drama. Its load of pain is obliterated as abjection becomes subjection to a higher power. But Titian's image goes beyond the narrative of a creature who did not know his proper place, and beyond, also, the Ovidian tragic vision of mythology as the narratives of divine power.

The presence of the sceptical figure of Midas acts in the same way as did the body of Marsyas in disrupting the transcendent composition of the image. Midas' mournful presence insists that the knife is *still* a knife, however Apollo may try to make it into an 'insignia of the regime'. Midas' sceptical resistance to the Apollonian signification of the knife challenges the integrity of the scene of redemption. Is this a sacrifice or an execution?

The question is posed as if these were irreconcilable opposites when in the Renaissance city–states the two were inseparably intertwined. It was precisely when the victim signalled his 'acceptance of the execution' as Marsyas does in the Ovidian myth that the death of a felon became a part of the *ars moriendi* and was 'transfigured into sacrifice'.[15] Contemporary events in the Venetian Republic would have supplied Titian with plenty of examples of the intertwining of the notion of sacrifice with the practice of state power, since Venice prided itself on staging some of the most elaborately ritualised executions in Europe. The living bodies of the victims were towed down the Grand Canal, displayed in their torments (often flayed with red-hot tongs) and strung up from the column of St Mark.[16]

Some critics feel that one particular event in the course of Venice's imperial contest with the Turks may have deeply influenced Titian in his study of Marsyas: in August 1571, the Venetian Marcantonio Bragadin was flayed in Famagosta by order of Pasha Mustapha and Titian may have recorded his anger in his choice of mythical subject matter.[17] But this event produces either a very unlikely allegory or a very sceptical reading of the painting indeed, since Titian would have had to bestow Venetian citizenship upon the satyr and depict Apollo as the Islamic despot.

Nonetheless, the arrangement of the figures on the canvas does bear a striking resemblance to the ritualised scene of execution as it was practised throughout continental Europe during Titian's lifetime. Like Titian's canvas, the execution stage was crowded with people fulfilling one particular function or another: the victim, the executioner, the executioner's servants, the magistrate's substitute, the confessor, the clerks and secretaries who recorded the event.[18] Most of these roles can be identified in the figures in the canvas: Marsyas/victim; Midas/confessor; Orpheus/clerk; Apollo's assistants/executioner's servants.

Where the ascriptions begin to falter is in designating Apollo's role. He seems to follow two very distinct occupations, as both magisterial legislator and executioner. This marks a particularly significant conjunction of roles on a number of counts. Apollo's intimate involvement in the execution is an outrageous breach not only of divine dignity but of the decorum of the execution scene since the highest authority of the state was conspicuously absent at executions, his place being supplied by his deputy. The actual execution of the legal sanction was considered beneath the dignity of high office.[19] How much more demeaning, therefore, that he should break not only this taboo but that the god should be involved in the physical act of flaying?

The office of executioner represented an absolute denial of the Renaissance codes of honour which brought shame on an individual who slew a defenceless person. Indeed, the executioner was often a condemned man himself, reprieved on the condition that he execute his fellow criminals. He was considered to be so polluted by his grisly duties that a host of superstitions surrounded him: he was thought to be immune from sorcery and a sorcerer himself, it was said that his purse never emptied of money, that he could exorcise demons. In the Empire executioners were deemed to be *unehrliche leute* (infamous persons), untouchable by decent men. He was the individual who was given the task of supervising prostitutes, emptying the public latrines and chasing away lepers. Only one class was more *unehrliche* than the executioner, and that was the skinner – and Apollo would seem to be a skinner of kinds also. When an imperial decree abolished *unehrliche leute* status for executioners in 1731, the skinners had to wait until 1772 for similar relief.[20]

Apollo's conduct (as magistrate, as executioner and – ultimate pollution – as skinner) can be seen in this light to be utterly despicable by the standards of Renaissance decorum since it affords neither dignity to his 'office' nor the required sanctity to enable the execution to be transformed into sacrifice. Far from establishing the 'terrible omnipotence of the *merum imperium*'[21] the painting depicts Apollo's role as a travesty of the *ars moriendi* and, consequently, of the intertwined powers, the sacred and the juridical, which the travesty evokes.

The narrative which ends in this travesty of redemptive punishment begins in music. What inherent connection exists, or by what logic do we move from a musical contest to flaying? What dictates that flaying is a suitable penalty for defeat in a musical contest?

The contest was a dispute between *kinds* of music. Within neoplatonic doctrine, of course, music carried an immense philosophical burden. For the neoplatonists, music was the spirit of a universal harmony and its notation embodied the mathematical relationship of all created matter. In such a context, the myth's significance lies in the imposition of Apollonian harmony upon nature. The wild is identified by its sound, its 'rude musicke'. Marsyas' instrumental music was played on the pipes which hang from the tree alongside Marsyas and which robbed him of a 'voice', of poetry. Marsyas' 'muteness' was opposed by the sophisticated song of Apollo with lyre accompaniment. For Kaufmann, the dispute was 'a foregone conclusion' as it expressed the 'moral power of music' and the triumph of the superior Apollonian form over the Dionysian passion of the wild.[22] It would be difficult to discover a more eloquent example of an interpretation which conjures the spirit by displacing the matter of the body, but clearly the myth articulates very significant attitudes to the importance of music as an index of Apollonian civilisation's triumph over the wild.

Ovid, however, is clear about the origin of the pipes which Marsyas played and hence the kind of music which was eclipsed by Apollo's triumph of divine art. He interjects into his brief account the important information that the pipes were Minerva's invention. If the picture truly does explore the myth of the origin of lyric poetry in the triumph of Apollonian and Orphic art over the roughly instrumental, an origin which contains an explicit moral content, then the proper myth of origin for the defeated pipes is Minerva, not Dionysus. The distinction is important in that Ovid is evoking an ancient mythological past, much older than Dionysus. The pipes may come to be associated with Dionysus, but Ovid explicitly evokes Minerva in this context of origins. Ovid's placing of Marsyas in a line of descent from Minerva associates Marsyas with the goddess' embodiment of wisdom, warlike prowess and skill in the arts of life, rather than Dionysian revelry and disorder. The figure of the satyr is so clearly connected to the figure of Dionysus in classical mythology that Titian's image must be read in that light also, but the Ovidian context of the image opens the prospect of the contest as not simply that of the familiar and often repeated rivalry between an anarchic and wild Dionysus and a civilising Apollo, but between two aspects of the same civility. One is male, one is female; both express aspects of the same spiritualised civic code and both represent 'divine art'.

The painting's engagement with the Ovidian context and with the contemporary neoplatonic debate on the moral power of music has the effect of greatly increasing and sceptically interrogating the system of differences which that debate engenders. Indeed, the myth gains a further, additional dimension in the context of the belief, often reported in the sixteenth century, of the addiction of savages to music and their fatal fascination for the higher Apollonian musical art of the Europeans. Hakluyt has it that native Americans 'delight in musicke above measure and will keep and stroke to any tune which you shall sing the same time aptly after you.' He goes on to state emphatically that the presence of musicians is essential on any expedition 'for the solace of our people, and [the] allurement of the savages'.[23] William Browne also expressed the same widely held notion that the savage was easily won over to the higher merits of Apollonian lyric:

> An Indian rude that never heard one sing
> A heavenly sonnet to a silver string,
> Nor other sounds, but what confused herds
> In pathless deserts make, or brooks or birds,
> Should he hear one the sweet pandora touch,
> And lose his hearing straight; he would as much
> Lament his knowledge as I do my chance,
> And wish he still had liv'd in ignorance.[24]

Browne's poem draws extensively on the discourse of the 'moral power of music' but reverses the platonic doctrine in his representation of the tragic consequences for the 'Indian rude'. Both Browne and Titian question the easy ascriptions of a simplistic neoplatonic doctrine of differences. They infiltrate into their representations of the satyr and the native American a sense of the rapacious nature of the culture which captivates and destroys, which moves from music to flaying.

But the fascinating aspect of Browne's poem and Hakluyt's testimony is the slippage which occurs from the platonic doctrine of the relative moral and aesthetic merits of Apollonian/Marsyan music expressed in myth and allegorical images, to its application to contemporary encounters with savage peoples. In the sixteenth century the Marsyas myth would appear to have gained new currency because it articulated the new condition of Apollonian, European civilisation's role in a world suddenly enlarged to encompass new forms of wildness. These ancient myths have a revived relevance as expressing the European's concern to represent a world occupied for the most part by Marsyan figures; one in which the naked power of European superiority over the savage and the dire consequences of that 'superiority' are expressed through the available Ovidian myths and images of Apollonian triumph. The figure of Marsyas in Titian's painting can be read as a response to that *new* condition, but through the mask of *ancient* narrative structures and representations of classical myth, where there occurs a distillation and a transformation of a range of discourses on the nature of otherness derived from a history of speculations about the wild.

By the time Titian painted Marsyas, the satyr in Renaissance art had become a fairly familiar presence, but it had only relatively recently become so. His painting gathers in the mythological figures of the wild in order to direct them to achieving new significances, new narratives. The satyr made his reappearance in European art at roughly the same time (c.1450) as artists began to extend their commitment to the full range of classical forms and content. When the satyr was revived he fitted into the extensive moral and aesthetic discourses of neoplatonism, as indeed did all the other elements of classical myth, but the revived satyr returned to fulfil a unique role as the exemplary figure of speculations concerning historical and cultural evolution and the relationship of contemporary civilisation to the savage, wild or animal world which it constructed as its original state.

Piero di Cosimo's *The Discovery of Honey* (1498) (figure 5), for example, for all its jollity and seeming 'cuteness', makes some significant additional emphases to the representation of the satyr. The image shows a large group of satyrs, humans and gods around a dead tree in a realistically rendered landscape with a town in the background. As with Titian's much more sombre image, all three levels of beings consort together: gods, humans, satyrs of a range of ages and states of nakedness. But here the group appears not as competing individuals, but as a primitive horde. The male gods, humans and satyrs are accompanied by human, divine and satyr women, and they make distinct family groupings within the horde. The central figure is not the deity – an attractive but understated Bacchus is seen to one side of the canvas – but an event, the discovery of honey in the tree. Mead will be made from the honey; another family group has discovered grapes in the woods to the left. The narrative seems to project from this event the development of a civic culture, glimpsed in the town in the distance. Piero does not transform his jovial satyrs into dramatic historical or revealed mythical presences, but sees them as symbolic of an initiatory moment in a collective evolutionary history, a moment which begins in the undifferentiated primitive horde of humans, gods and beings who are half-human, half-animal demi-gods, but which will end in the civil society of the town.[25] The satyr marks a key liminal phase in

5 Piero di Cosimo, *The Discovery of Honey*, 1498

such an evolutionary development, as the point at which the animal begins to change into a human.

Similar contexts were made for the satyr in the works of Dürer, Cranach and Altdorfer where the satyr became expressive of the German artists' reclamation of a primitive northern cultural origin, an intermediate state between man and beast, and finally a way of representing the contemporary discoveries of the primitives of America. The satyr in the Renaissance expressed an admiration for the primitive, an exploration of cultural origins and a meditation upon the nature of New World 'savages'.[26] On this last point, the satyr's closest relative, and his chief point of contact with savage peoples, was the wildman of classical myth and medieval romance. The satyr and the wildman are domestic European products, savage races who reside at home in pictures, friezes and poems. The wildman's pedigree was ancient, enduring and closely intertwined with the history of the satyr, to which he is related. When the two tropes meet, the resulting conjunction of attendant themes and images is immensely instructive for the history of representation of primitive peoples. Both Pausanias and Strabo had attempted to link living peoples with satyr and wildman myths and this was repeated by St Jerome who added *pilosi, incubi* and *hommes silvestres* to his list of living 'demons of the wilderness'.[27] But the wildman was similarly the subject of a divided response; he was identified according to a strict manichean duality, as either Orcus or Silvanus, as Bernheimer explains: 'To the wildman Silvanus, benefactor of fields and woods, there corresponds the wildman Orcus, enemy of living things and of man himself.'[28]

The wildman has an ambiguous and changing nature, as would be expected of a figure who marks a boundary between the human and the wild. As Silvanus, he is a benign woodland spirit assisting animals and humans with his forest lore and a chief participant in the pageants and processions of the civic state, the guardian of secular authority or the king's bodyguard. He is the saviour of ladies lost in the forest as in the case of Sir Satyrane in Spenser's *The Faerie Queen*. His image could indicate ascetic saintliness as in the images of St John Chrysostom and St Anthony. As Orcus, however, he engages with a much more savage aspect as a cannibal, as a rapist, as the prime mover of the wild horde in its destructive rampage through human society. His presence is used to evoke the consequences of defying divine will, as in the representation of Nebuchadnezzar as a wildman.

Both the wildman and the satyr underwent some radical changes in their representation and the direction of these changes is indicative of a wider current in adapting ancient European motifs to fit the new conditions of the discovery of other, savage peoples. The ancient figure of the wildman was habitually 'incoherent or mute'[29] as an indication of his social isolation. The Silvanus aspect of the wildman's representation emerged in a series of Northern Renaissance images by Master b α 8 and Master B ⚓ R in the fifteenth century. These images represented the wildman as a *pater familias* and a 'noble incarnation of what humans might strive for'. As Kaufmann further argues, in showing the wildman *en famille* the connection was undeniably made to the representations of the Holy Family.[30] The revivified images of the wildman and the satyr depicted in a harmonious family unit resituates them in a condition of minimal, though immensely significant, social organisation where he is equipped with language (in Spenser and Sachs) of a most elegant and poetic kind. The wildman as Silvanus loses his significance as the primal, pre-social, pre-linguistic being but he gains a newer relevance as an articulate figure in the evolutionary development of mankind.

This reconstructed wildman represents a denial, ultimately, of total wildness. The distance between the wild and the non-wild is reduced to the point where it can be accommodated as part of the vision of what constitutes *dominium,* the capacity to exercise the right to 'private property, actions, liberty and their own bodies',[31] even in its most minimal features. If *dominium* is a part even of wildness, the traffic between wildness and civilisation authenticates European social orders by accommodating what, by its nature, was conceived of as unaccommodated and its opponent. Hayden White writes of the medieval conception of the wildman as representing:

> [a] degraded nature, a nature fallen into corruption and decay. And one could speak of a fallen humanity, the state from which Christ had come to release those enthralled by Adam's sin. But to speak of a wild man was to speak of a man with the soul of an animal, a man so degraded that he could not be saved by God's grace itself. [32]

The reinvention of the wildman figure involved a major adaptation of this model. The spiritual condition of the wildman had become, in Kaufmann's term, 'mutable'.[33] The spiritual nature of the wildman was transformable and 'improvable' into the recognisable human contours of civility and polity. These patterns of distinction become the essential template for the representation of savage peoples, for the 'indian rude' inherited this melange or *bricolage* of symbolically significant mythical elements structured into binary sets of differences. What emerges can, perhaps, be best symbolised by the manichean designation of primitive peoples commented upon by Stephen Horigan when he distinguishes two kinds of 'primitives'. The imaginary, perpetually undiscovered races were 'soft' and led leisured lives of comfort and plenty, whereas the actual, observed peoples were always constructed as 'hard', leading a deprived, harsh, brutish existence, unclean, violent or immoral.[34] If mutable, 'soft' Silvanus was redeemable by Apollonian civility, what of unreconstructed 'hard' Orcus, the animal spirit of the wildman?

The Orcus aspect of the satyr/wildman conjunction of tropes draws most heavily on Europe's oldest myth of other peoples. Whereas Silvanus finds an accommodation in the schemes of an emerging notion of evolutionary history, Orcus is associated with the much looser speculations and accounts of travellers and scholars of the pseudo-anthropological field of 'teratology', the study of monstrous races.[35] Reports of the existence of monstrous races exhibited a remarkable fluidity as their discovery followed the voyages of exploration and they moved their location from India to Africa to the New World.[36] Yet despite their mobility the monstrous races could be invested with stable moral and allegorical meanings, as Wittkower puts it:

> the pygmy stands for humility, the giant for pride, the cynoce-phali [dogheaded men] for quarrelsome persons and the people who cover themselves with the lower lip are the mis-chievous, according to the word of the psalm: 'Let the mischief of their own lip cover them.'[37]

The significance of the monstrous races extends to a bodily repre-sentation of moral and behavioural states. As a symbolic order, they encode the principles of a nascent psychology of human types reminiscent of Galenic theories of 'humours' in physiology. They represent a kind of *speculum mentis* of the human condition, an improvisation upon the categories of created nature evoked by the ordering principles of the chain of being. The human body is seen as possessing the potential for radical genetic transformation. As sym-bolic forms with an extraordinary resilience, they seem to articulate a bizarre collective 'dream'. The dog-headed, crane-billed, headless or single-footed men of other lands issue from a desire to construct images of other peoples in surreal blurrings of the animal and human domains, domains which the neoplatonists, with their sublime characterisation of human anatomy, attempted to hold as definitively separate. The discourse of the monstrous races, therefore, can be read as a sceptical challenge to orthodox humanist representations of the human body as an index of harmonious and aesthetic proportion.

The prospect of the sublime form of the humanist image of the human body invaded by the animal and partaking of an animal 'uncivil' nature, becomes expressive of a sceptical interrogation of the *vanitas* of a European homocentric universe.

> We are faced with the curious paradox that the superstitious Middle Ages pleaded in a broadminded spirit for the monsters as belonging to God's inexplicable plan for the world, while the 'enlightened' period of humanism returned to Varro's *contra naturam* and regarded them as creations of God's wrath.[38]

As a sceptical discourse the monstrous races could be turned to interrogate the humanist reconstruction of values in a way which had the consequence of provoking a hardening of those attitudes to other peoples. If monstrosity questioned humanist visions of man as microcosmic nature, then humanism responded by branding other peoples with the stigma of *contra naturam*. The discourse of the monstrous races recapitulated other peoples as living denials of the sublime form of nature, as travesties of a perverted nature, but in a way which also conjured the surreal imaging of the human form conjoined with the animal as possessing a 'miraculous' potential to escape the normal limits of the human body.

A sense of the lines of transmission from the study of monstrosity to the apprehension of contemporary savages can be seen from three illustrations which show a progressive structuring of the representation of the primitive which grows out of ancient mythical types. The first (figure 6), from the *Liber Chronicarum* of 1493, shows a collection of extemporisations upon the theme of alternative human kinds. The second (figure 7) comes from Sebastian Munster's *Description of the World* of 1543 and shows a 'monstrous child', born in either Cracow or the Netherlands (Munster is unsure), a being with dogs' heads on all its limbs, a cat's head on its stomach, webbed feet and a horn for a nose. Although this image purports to show an actual monstrous birth, its iconographic features and its presence in a book describing the varieties of strange beings which occupy the world places it firmly in the tradition of the monstrous races. The third illustration (figure 8) marks a key moment in the transition of these

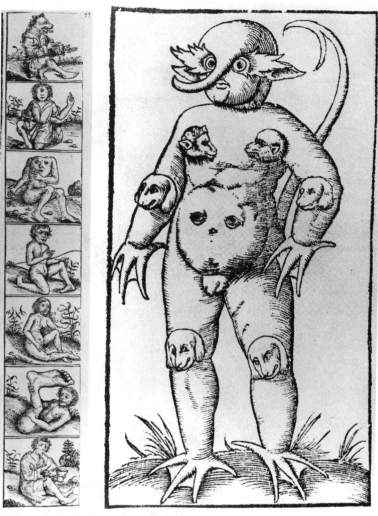

6 Edgings from *Liber Chronicarum*, 1493 (*left*) and   7 A 'monstrous child', from Sebastian Munster, *Description of the World*, 1543 (*right*)

mythical images from the discourse of the monstrous races into the domain of savage description. The picture is by John White and dates from c. 1580; it shows a *Pictish Man Holding a Human Head*. The 'Pict's' stance is heroic and the modelling of his body indicates a sublime form of masculinity. In this aspect he seems a model of the

8 John White, *Pictish Man Holding a Human Head*, c. 1580

Silvanus type, yet his heroic splendour is rendered conditional by the presence of the severed head of his enemy. Clearly, the indices of monstrosity have, in this image, been rededicated: the 'Pict's' body shows a remarkable similarity to that of the 'monstrous child' with painted animal forms in the same positions on the body, at the shoulders, chest and limb joints. The image is a *bricolage* of historical, cultural and mythological traces where the speculative reconstruction of a British ancestral tribesman consorts with the oriental (the shield and scimitar which the 'Pict' holds) and the monstrous. In representing the 'Pict' as a violent painted savage bearing the marks of the myth of monstrosity, the image engages that speculation about prehistory and primitive origins of the European past with both the myth of monstrous races and the contemporary 'savage'.

The relationship of Silvanus to Orcus takes on spatial and historical significances. Orcus inhabits the *exterior* spaces beyond Europe or he is a part of a prehistorical past. He is projected onto other contemporary primitive peoples, as if the European savage of speculative pre-history is visible in the present condition of other peoples. That savagery is perceived and recognised by the extraordinary skin of the savage which recalls the discourse of monstrosity. Silvanus inhabits a world of civic *interior* spaces; his presence can be displayed inhabiting an imitation of the European polis in the primitive society of the horde or evolutionary nuclear family.

The Flaying of Marsyas represents just such a complex discourse incorporating a range of speculative theories about satyrs, wildmen, monstrous races and native societies. The painting evokes a sense of the nature of wildness, of the animal which is also human; it evokes, as John Berger puts it in his reading of the picture, what it may be like to have animal fur instead of human skin.[39]

What is depicted in *The Flaying of Marsyas* is a representation of types or kinds of men engaged in a bloody scene of masculine violence: males alone, god, humans and satyrs; men, also, of all ages, a complete range from the child to the old man; men in different degrees of dress and nakedness. The satyrs show their lack of civility by their absolute nakedness, while the enrapt youth shows his cultured condition by his full dress. A 'spectrum' of male types seems to structure the picture around the coordinates of kinds of being (divine, human, satyr), age and clothing. But Apollo's position on this spectrum is consistently that of the middle range. His flimsy wrap places him midway between satyr and youth, both clothed and naked. He is midway also in the spectrum of age. He is not the enrapt minstrel nor the labouring satyr but the skinner – not an essential – quintessential – presence, but the mean, middle ground *between* men and satyr.

Titian would also seem to render his satyr ambiguously between the categories of the evolutionary, moral and civic debates. Marsyas embodies both aspects of the manichean division of tropes, or at least, his figure seems indeterminately between them. This indeterminacy results from the double context of Marsyas' pedigree as both a 'Minervan' and a 'Dionysian' being, as Silvanus and Orcus. In his Minervan–Silvanus aspect he can attain Christian–platonic redemption through suffering and the agency of divine art and thus gain access to the *polis* of European civility as a sacrificial icon of the benign mutability of essential human nature. In his Dionysian–Orcus aspect he is the unredeemably wild and dangerous creature subject to and executed by the destructive discipline of the Apollonian order which is satisfied with nothing less than the flaying of the monstrous skin of the creature. Marsyas is punished as much for his *difference* as for his *hubris*; a difference which is constructed upon his residence in the intermediate domain between animal and human differences. Whatever is perceived of as existing between discrete and oppositional categories, in the marginal interstices of manicheism, invites the attention and judgement of Apollo. Marsyas' designation as Varronian *contra naturam* returns us again to the fact of the knife as the symbol of that manichean 'division' of beings.

The Renaissance had a further use for the Marsyas myth, as it became a conventional trope in the illustrations of anatomical texts for the depiction of the dissected body.[40] In these illustrations the viewer is placed in the position of Apollo himself, unmediated by the sceptical presence of Midas/Titian; what Apollo 'sees' in Titian's image is, here, the privilege of the viewer/reader of the anatomical text. Here the knife has another purpose: knowledge is made in unmaking Marsyas since the reader/viewer is initiated into the science of the human body. The human body hides some secret core, the human animal or the human soul, a hidden centre which is elusive to representation, but from which essential humanity emerges. In 'making' that knowledge Apollo 'unmakes' the body which comes under his power. Titian's painting records but dissents from Apollo's obsessive searching in the body of the satyr for the object of his quest for knowledge.

Palma il Giovane, Titian's pupil and the disputed painter of or contributor to *The Flaying of Marsyas*, described in his diary how

Titian painted his pictures. He would hang the canvases in his studio facing the wall and each day he would turn them over and add a little more paint to each before turning them back again:

> When he wanted to apply his brush again he would examine them [his paintings] with the utmost rigour, as if they were his mortal enemies, to see if he could find any faults; and if he discovered anything that did not fully conform to his intentions he would treat his picture like a good surgeon would his patient, reducing if necessary some swelling or excess of flesh, straightening an arm if the bone structure was not exactly right, and if a foot had initially been misplaced correcting it without thinking of the pain it might cost him, and so on ... Thus he gradually covered those quintessential forms with living flesh, bringing them by many stages to a state in which they lacked only the breath of life.[41]

This is the opposite of the Apollonian and Vesalian 'making' which makes its object – its knowledge of differences – by unmaking its subject. Ultimately, Titian's art denies the knife. He bends, twists and breaks the body, but in order to make it whole and like 'living flesh'.

We may now be able to begin to answer the question, by what logic does *The Flaying of Marsyas* connect music to flaying? The original contest was of kinds of music, the Apollonian lyric opposed to Marsyan 'rude musicke'. The discourse of musical kinds also enunciated another set of differences of divine, human and animal types. These distinctions of types are gathered together in the forest grove as both exemplars and witnesses to Apollo's great act of differentiation. Out of the making of that structure of differences Apollo subjects the body of the satyr to a redemptive ritual of sacrifice transforming his suffering into the art of civilisation. The scene has other analogues which it draws into its compass – the revived representations of satyrs, wildmen and monstrous races, each of which act their parts in the construction of a discourse of otherness. That discourse in its turn functions in a wider world where living beings, not mythical tropes, are processed by similar structures of difference and deprived of their *dominium*, of their lives. Like Marsyas, they are unmade in the very act of another's making. In the Renaissance, those categorical boundaries between the wild and the civil, between the human and the animal, constitute the logic by which the myth unfolds the narrative of a musical contest which ends in flaying.

But the painting develops a counter-logic to the Apollonian orthodoxy: that of the Minervan origins of the 'rude musicke', the evolution of satyr *dominium*, Apollo's travesty of the rituals of the *ars moriendi* of sacrifice and execution, his presence not as a god but as *unehrliche leute*, his unchristian ignorance of bodily pain. At each stage in the logic of the myth of otherness, its procession from music to flaying, there is always the sceptical presence of Titian/Midas and the object of his contemplation: above all there is the body of Marsyas, the great forked slash down the canvas whose presence will not be dismissed. *The Flaying of Marsyas* is the dialogism of cultural representations rendered into an image; an image which includes both Apollonian structuration and Midas' scepticism.

The image presents us with a construction, a making of the world of the other which forms around the body of the wild creature. The body is subjected to a violence which creates art, music, rapture, aggrandisement, sacrifice, triumph, moral order, evolutionary schemes and knowledge, all of which are produced by the Apollonian designation of difference. But through the figure of Midas/Titian, the image also sceptically interrogates that fashioning, ultimately through Titian's own art – the opposite of Apollo's – which lacks 'only the breath of life'.

Chapter 2

Identity and its others: Florida 1564–91

> In a primeval forest . . . a large ape-man, bear or cave-man
> threatens to attack the dreamer with a club. Suddenly, the
> 'man with the pointed beard' appears and stares at the
> aggressor so that he is spellbound. But the dreamer is
> terrified. The voice says, 'Everything must be ruled by the
> light.'   *C. Jung*[1]

In 1550, the French royal household, on its progress to the city of
Rouen, was treated to the spectacle of a recreated Brazilian jungle
complete with parrots, marmots and apes loose in the trees of a
meadow by the Seine. Two Brazilian villages had been erected and
populated by fifty 'Tabbagerres' and 'Toupinaboux', specially
imported for the occasion, and two hundred and fifty Frenchmen in
costume. In a performance which lasted two days, one village
attacked the other in mock warfare. After the spectacle, Henri II
performed his *entrée* into the city where he was presented with 'a
complete re-enactment of a Roman Imperial triumph'.[2]

The symbolic 'mock combat' was a familiar feature of royal entertainments, and often featured the wildman, as in Henry VIII's
Twelfth Night celebrations of 1515.[3] Significantly, the Tupis had
displaced the wildman in the Rouen spectacle as the symbolic figure
of savage nature. Moreover, the combat was between 'savages', or
Frenchmen disguised as 'savages', and not between members of the
court. The royal household and its chivalric guardians retired from
the scene and assumed the role of spectators, looking in on a savage
tableau vivant. The site of the spectacle is also of ceremonial and
symbolic significance. Although it would have been difficult to stage
such a display within the city, a semiotics of imperial spaces is

expressed in a violent tableau of wildness *outside* the city walls, from which the king progresses to an imperial triumph *within*.

In the royal entertainments, processions and *entrées* of the sixteenth century, the savage increasingly figured as a sign of imperial domination. In 1539, when Eleanor of Toledo entered Florence as the future duchess it was through an arch which depicted Charles V in Roman garb resplendent as the conqueror of the savage peoples of Mexico and Africa. A statue of Charles erected in Milan in 1541 not only showed Charles on horseback, the equestrian statue being reserved for the emperor in classical Roman statuary, but depicted a vanquished Moor, a native American and a Turk. Charles IX's festivals at Bayonne in 1564 had knights dressed for the tournament as Trojans, Spanish, Roman and Greek heroes in typical and traditional style, but the festival also contained individuals dressed as 'wild Scotsmen, Turks and demons'. A German visitor to the court of Elizabeth I, who attended the tournaments in 1584 to celebrate the anniversary of the queen's accession commented that some of the servants 'were disguised like savages, or like Irishmen, with their hair hanging down to the girdle like women, others had their horses equipped like elephants'.[4]

Sixteenth- and seventeenth-century monarchs used the pageants and entertainments for very specific ends: to reinforce their claims to political control by the stimulation of cultural codes of 'magnificence'. The Habsburgs, the Valois and the Tudors and Stuarts all promoted in their cultural propaganda their claims to being the *Rex Christianissimus* or the titular head of a *sacrum imperium*[5] which increasingly turned upon the figure of the vanquished savage as an index of princely domination in the complex semiotics of monarchical display and government.

The royal entertainments, however, demonstrate an emergent and highly potent form of structuration of the loose agglomeration of myths, symbols and codes which shape and affect the perception of savage peoples. That emergent imperial semiology processed the representation of the savage into narrative form in ways which recall Titian's meditations upon the mythical tropes of wildness contained in the Marsyas myth. In Titian's *The Flaying of Marsyas* the exemplary myths and tropes of a wild, savage and primitive nature were recorded to express and dissent from a manichean model of representation; in the royal *entrées*, however, the sceptical presence of the observing artist is obliterated by a narrative of regal power. The key terms of that narrative structuring are to be found in the semiotic representation of space (to be inside or outside the city; in the wild or in the *polis* of the *citta ideale* of monarchical government) the relationship of 'savage nations' to the *sacrum imperium* and of identity (plural savage selves and the singular imperial self). But the *truly* powerful invention, for anthropology, literature and art, is the narrative form itself as a process of textualisation and representation which shapes anomalous and 'unruly' materials into a theatre of power.

Information about other peoples, and particularly about New World peoples, was largely conveyed to Europeans in the form of illustration. Wittkower traces modern 'photo-reportage' back to the fifteenth century, to the point when Gentile Bellini first 'reliably depicted' oriental people. Costume books, travellers' tales and texts provided a well-established set of conventions for the illustration of savage life in the New World which proliferated in the sixteenth and seventeenth centuries.[6]

Illustration lies between Titian's 'high art' and the 'low art' of the emerging popular press; its capacity for multiple copying places it within the reach of a popular media culture as text for the illiterate, yet the languages of gesture and iconography which the illustrations depict owe much to the conventions of figurative painting. Illustration is 'news' in the sense that it purports to describe recent events and encounters, yet the limitations of engravure circumscribe illustration's potential as a means of 'photographic' mimesis. The absence of colour, chiaroscuro, the reduced range of textures, the density of shade and the predominance of line are all features which determine illustration's representative capacities and mark it as different from – less than – painting. Yet painting, which has none of these limitations, was little used for the representation of these subjects since the conventions of representation dictated that these subjects should be shrouded in the allegories of classical myth. The primitive was a suitable subject for illustration – not for painting – midway between the classical pose and the political or sectarian broadside or pamphlet. Its subject was actual not allegorical, yet so fantastical as to go beyond the capacity for wonder which even fables possessed. These early illustrations of primitive life were, from the outset, expressive of an anomalous condition betrayed by both their medium and their subject, a subject which could only dubiously be represented by high art but which demanded visualisation as an image. Illustration as a medium for representing other peoples marks the entry of savage peoples into European culture at a particular level appropriate to the esteem of its medium of representation. Illustration, as art transformed to print, is the decorous solution to the problem of the liminality of savages.

Among the first illustrations of New World peoples were those published as engravings by the German publisher Theodore de Bry from pictures made in America by John White and Jacques Le Moyne de Morgues. The illustrations by Le Moyne are part of a series which records the daily life, religious rites and conduct in war of the Timucuas of Florida. Le Moyne was a French artist, botanical illustrator and cartographer. As both a Calvinist and a draughtsman with some reputation at the French court he was enlisted as a member of the Huguenot expedition to Florida under the leadership of René de Laudonnière in 1564. Although relations with the native peoples were, at first, amicable, the expedition ended in disaster just as a previous expedition to Florida, led by Ribault in 1562 ended in mutiny, starvation and cannibalism by the French of their fellow settlers. The second expedition became embroiled in the inter-tribal enmity of the Timucuas and suffered, as the first had done, from a series of mutinies. But it was an imported European rivalry which finally ended their colonisation. The Spanish Adelantando Menendez de Avilas could not tolerate a French Protestant settlement so close to the shipping lanes of Mexico and the South where his *flota*, loaded with silver, would have been easy pickings. The Spaniard sacked the French fort and massacred the Huguenots and in a shocking display of ruthlessness, murdered his prisoners. Le Moyne escaped, with his watercolours. Only one of the originals exists but the forty-two engravings represent an important copy of these early acts of representation.[7] The Timucuas are also lost, but without any copies.

The first encounter with the native Americans is described by Le Moyne in his *Narratio* in this description of the Timucuan chief Satouriwa's greeting of Laudonnière:

> He [Satouriwa] was preceded by fifty youths carrying their javelins or spears in their hands. Nearer to him were twenty pipers who were playing some primitive thing discordantly and raggedly, merely blowing the pipes as hard as they could. These pipes are no more than extremely thick reeds with two holes, an upper one where they blow and a lower one where the breath comes out, as with the pipes or tubes of organs. Flanking the chief on the right was the sorcerer and on his left his leading counsellor, for he undertakes nothing without these two. Going alone into the place which had been made ready, he

sat down in indian fashion, that is, on the ground itself, like a monkey or other animal.[8]

Le Moyne's description of this first encounter evokes a range of subtexts. Satouriwa's train begins by resembling a regal *entrée* complete with musicians and warriors, as if they have stepped out of one of the Medici tapestries commemorating Charles IX's Bayonne festivals. But the description begins to change with the evocation of the 'rude musicke' of the Marsyan pipes and the chief's regality descends to a display of another, animal nature as being 'like a monkey or other animal'. The written text of Le Moyne's *Narratio* constantly and indecisively shifts between these contradictory attitudes. The images of savage life similarly encode Le Moyne's uncertain apprehension.

Number 34 in the series of engravings (figure 9) depicts René de Laudonnière, the leader of the second expedition, and the Timucuan chief Outina seated on a rustic bench flanked by armed Huguenot arquebusiers while Timucuan women perform a ritual dance. In the background is a group of Timucuan warriors and a stump of a large tree before which a woman crouches in supplication.

Space is dynamically organised around two sharp divisions. The foreground, where the European observers are placed, is higher than the dancing space and divided from the women and warriors by a steep decline – a line drawn diagonally across the illustration separating the natives from the Europeans and creating the effect of a theatre. The illustration privileges the act of seeing; the women are on a stage, as performers, as if this meeting of European and savage emphasises the specular nature of the encounter. It is this theatrical and visual aspect of Le Moyne's 'representations of events and figures taken from life' that De Bry emphasises in his introduction to the plates when he writes: 'We have published them out of regard for intelligent people so that the story should not just be told but should *seem to be enacted vividly before their eyes.*'[9]

Only the presence of Outina in the 'audience' breaks the spell; but his gaze is turned not to the dancing women, but towards his guests. With a classical gesture of disclosure, his hand holds back an invisible curtain, revealing what is 'inside' his state. Laudonnière is depicted in the act of observation as a welcome guest and witness to a culture's secret spectacle. While the arquebusiers stand well-armed and fascinated, Laudonnière seems apprehensive. His body recoils from the sight, his right hand poised in surprise, his left clutches his sword, his legs are awkwardly placed as if about to leap to his feet.

9 Jacques Le Moyne de Morgues, 'They Sacrifice First-Born Sons to the Chief in Solemn Rituals', 1591

Outina, by contrast, is relaxed. His right hand is on his guest's shoulder in a gesture of familiarity, friendship and reassurance. His elegant form is draped across the bench in contrast to his guest's rigid posture. He is a model of attractive classical form: athletic, muscular, nearly nude, clear-eyed, beautiful. Laudonnière's clothing distorts his physique: his ruffs, pleats and paddings seem a mimicry of the natural grace of the chief's beauty. Le Moyne himself called attention to this contrast when he writes that the native Americans were 'splendid-looking men, strong, hardy' and were 'astonished when they noticed the difference between the smoothness and softness of our bodies and theirs, and the unfamiliar clothing we wore'.[10] In contrasting the ostentation of Laudonnière's clothing with Outina's near-nakedness the image evokes European evolutionary hypotheses which gained expression through codes of civility in dress. Yet there is also much in their appearances to link these two figures. The chief's tattoos, which cover his body, seem to merge with and continue the lines of slashes, pleats and embroidery of

Laudonnière's dress. Cuffs, collars and chains find an echo in the natives' beads and necklaces. Their headgear of feathers and topknots similarly replicate each other. Outina, turning towards Laudonnière, appears a close mirror image of the European, and only the sword – like Apollo's knife – marks a significant and stark caesura between the two men. The sword is the mark of Laudonnière's uncertainty: an uncertainty which the image also shares.

Space is further divided, from top to bottom along the middle of the engraving. The world here is a series of flat surfaces laid one behind the other. The mirror effect of the first surface where Laudonnière and Outina share the opulence, in body and clothing, of a mutual nobility, gives way to the haughty manhood and sexual compliance of the native's inner world. Everything to the viewer's right is spectacle; the left is the spectator's domain. This play upon the act of seeing is also gendered: the spectators are male, native or European; the gazed upon are female. The women bare all, freely cavorting with loose hair and even looser grass aprons. The 'outside' specular image of gazing males reveals an 'inner' reality of female rituals fraught with the dangers of sexuality and heresy. At the point of transition from viewer to viewed is the lone figure of the suppliant woman who crouches in front of the altar, but, in relation to the male spectators, she is immediately beneath the imperious figure of the warrior and directly, though in a different plane, in front of the chief and the European males. The world which we see Outina inviting Laudonnière to see is a world of female paganism and feminine supplication to male authority.

At the centre of the circle is a child, displayed or being carried to the altar for some unknown female rite, and here interpretation begins to falter. What does this image depict? Is this child a symbol of benign maternity and female fecundity offered to the phallic herm and celebrated by the circling women? Or is it to be a blood sacrifice in some 'unspeakable' ceremony which causes the Huguenot to reach for his sword? The image is titled by Le Moyne as 'They Sacrifice First-Born Sons to the Chief in Solemn Rituals' but the illustration ambiguously encodes both possibilities.

The women appear like classical nymphs from a painting, or like the illustrations of Marguerite de Valois' famous ballet in the Tuilleries gardens in 1573, dancing out of the high art of the Renaissance and into this New World relationship of male power, authority and colonisation. But similar compositional strategies, albeit more crudely executed, can also be seen in seventeenth-century political

10 'The Adamites Sermon', 1641

pamphlets and broadsides attacking religious sects such as the Brownites, Adamites or Ranters (figure 10). The linking of native custom and heretical activity was a part of the popular print's agenda in stigmatising both the savage and the politically suspect. There are the same figures of authority foregrounded and displaying the sect's activities in a theatrical 'sylvan' setting: heretical religious practices, sexual licence or acts of violence.

The 'theatrical' nature of the image also links the Le Moyne–De Bry print with the conventions of Renaissance stage design, since Laudonnière's prospect of the Timucuas conforms in spirit to the revived *scenographia* of the humanist theatre learned from Vitruvius. Vitruvius identified only 'three kinds of scenes':

> one called tragic, second, the comic, third, the satyric. Their decorations are different and unlike each other in scheme. Tragic scenes are delineated with columns, pediments, statues, and other objects suited to kings; comic scenes exhibit private dwellings, with balconies and views representing rows of windows, after the manner of ordinary dwellings; satyric

scenes are decorated with trees, caverns, mountains, and other rustic objects delineated in landscape style.[11]

The Vitruvian stage settings provide an important key to the Renaissance organisation of space and its significances. Henri II's Rouen *entrée* marked out space in both Apollonian manichean dualities and in Vitruvian fashion: a 'satyric' scene, outside the city, was followed by an imperial procession of Vitruvian 'tragic' signs through a city of 'comic' actuality. Space is 'politicised' in the sense that the arrangement of the stage expressed clear attitudes to the nature of power; 'tragic' space is concerned with the socially significant individual, a seriousness which the classical and imperial architecture emulate. 'Tragic' space is 'patrician' space reflected in a civic style which betokens clarity of perspective, order and dignity. An ideal city is envisaged by the Vitruvian tragic stage which focuses the audience's aspirations upon the ruler as a mirror of an ideal prince. The 'comic' scene is nonetheless 'civic', although 'private' and 'ordinary'; this is an inverse analogue of the 'tragic' scene with its emphasis upon the mundane, the suburb rather than the forum, low plebeian rather than high patrician. The two 'scenes' complement each other in their play of public and private, civic ideal against the actuality of citizenship.

But what is described by Vitruvius and enacted at Rouen is not, essentially, three scenes, but two. Civility and citizenship, either 'tragic' or 'comic', carry their own moral connotations of duty, sociability and altruism as well as an assumption of a 'higher' form of governmental organisation and political sophistication absent from the 'satyric' scene. The Timucuan 'satyric' scene of 'rustic objects delineated in landscape style' lies outside the civic world of the twinned 'tragic' and 'comic' domains. Yet this early illustration proclaims that there is *something* to be revealed by Outina's gesture of disclosure. However confusing or threatening Laudonnière finds what is revealed to him, there is a *polis* here. The key iconographic feature of Laudonnière's prospect is that the Timucuas are accorded a role in representation which can be accommodated ambiguously to both the 'satyric' and the civic contexts of the Vitruvian scene.

Within the terms of sixteenth-century moral and political philosophy, the revelation of Outina's gesture is of immense significance. For jurists, schoolmen and political theorists the New World natives posed a moral and philosophical dilemma about the European's place in the New World and involved a complex and conscience-laden search for justification. The crucial issue turned on the nature and status of native American *dominium*, which Anthony Pagden broadly defines as the right to 'private property, actions, liberty and their own bodies':

> By the terms of the social contract, men had renounced their primitive freedom in exchange for the security and the possibility of moral understanding which only civil society could provide; but they retained certain natural and hence inalienable rights of which *dominium* is the most fundamental.[12]

The Spanish invasion of the New World could only be justified and made legitimate if it could be shown that the native Americans had forfeited their natural rights to *dominium*, or, indeed, if it could be shown that they never actually possessed them in the first place. Le Moyne's image, coming from a thoroughly Protestant provenance, represents a negation of the Catholic denial of native *dominium*. Outina's *dominium* does exist and it is a complex interweaving of social codes and structures. Male and female articulate a set of structural ranks and demarcations which the engraving displays as a complex social order. As significantly, Laudonnière must also play his role in Outina's *mise en scène* since this illustration testifies to his presence in the play of differences between noble native and noble Frenchman, between arquebusiers and warriors, and their relations to the authority which Outina as savage king, and Laudonnière, as a 'friend' of Charles IX, represent.[13]

Outina's gesture of revelation, the delicately unfolding hand which reveals the primitive scene, is also a gesture of gift. Outina appears to bequeath 'all of this', his patrimony of girls and warriors, to the Frenchman. In their likeness, one resembling (but not quite) the other, they seem interchangeable as rulers of this state. Within the politics of Huguenot propaganda, which this illustration also refers us to, the message is clear. The French Protestants are greeted as friends and recognised as suitable rulers by the indigenes themselves, unlike the natives of Spanish colonies. The French gaze with surprise, even alarm, on the savage state but they, unlike the Spanish, recognise them for what they are – a people to be ruled. The significance is clear in relation to the French Protestants' desire to establish colonies in Florida, an ambition which is thwarted, not by the natives, who welcome them into their world, but by the Spanish Catholics who murder both Huguenots and natives without mercy. It would seem that these illustrations, then, acquire new meanings as both anti-Spanish and anti-Catholic, Protestant propaganda.

Le Moyne's ethnographic illustrations record that *dominium*, however, as a collection of identifiable, specialised roles and activities: king, chief, wives, widows, priests, conjurors, warriors which tie the savage to a social function. Le Moyne's Timucuan world is, as T. S. Eliot once said of Milton's Heaven, very sparsely furnished. The horizon which is so sharply drawn marks the end of their world; there is nothing beyond or outside these frames. They possess a *polis* but it is a world of social functions. They are what Marcel Mauss termed 'personas', in his discussion of the evolution of the modern notion of the self, individuals identified by the 'masks' of their social roles.[14] They lack 'character' and are different from and less than the European's ability to exist as a 'self' above and beyond his social role. They appear content to be so greatly reduced to these few acts of representation. 'Complexity', 'personality', 'profundity' or 'depth' are terms which seem inappropriate here. What we see, frankly displayed, are 'contentless' people. But the Le Moyne–De Bry print contains not only the representation of the Timucuan *polis*, but also the explorer–colonist–ethnographer. His presence as witness or audience to Outina's theatrical scene causes the scene to exist; it is Laudonnière, not the natives, who is the *raison d'être* of this image. The depiction of Laudonnière is the only one which goes beyond the representation of people as masks or personas. He is more than just his role. The uncertainty of his response, his awkwardness, fear or apprehension, give him a 'human' texture. But Laudonnière's individuality is achieved by stressing the 'non'-individuality of those who surround him and who appear as so many 'masks' in comparison. As Mauss wrote of the self in Ancient Rome: 'only the slave is excluded from it [possession of selfhood]. *Servus non habet personam*. He has no "personality". He does not own his own body, nor has he ancestors, name, cognomen, or personal belongings.'[15] Laudonnière extends his mastery over native *dominium* because his selfhood, his personality, eclipses those who are like Roman slaves, and with whom he shares this ethnographic space.

Whereas the savage has only a public function of display of socialisation, the European has a private dimension of selfhood which exceeds his role and which constitutes his 'true' significance. Dislocation, the voluntary removal of the European from his customary environment, both threatens and strengthens this sense of his unique individuality.

The illustration functions according to a remarkable ambiguity: the Timucuas are identified by a recognition of certain social roles which 'our' society shares with theirs, seen through the filters of the conventions of representation, whereas Laudonnière's individuality is recognised by his 'difference'. But if, as the illustrations seem to proclaim, savage identity consists of specialised social roles, then it follows that the European has no place here since he has no social 'persona', unless and until he makes one for himself by reorganising and recategorising the social roles and identities of those around him to enable him to have a presence. Laudonnière adds one more 'role' to the catalogue of specialisms, but it is a role which only the outsider can fulfil, that of the observer, the 'European-who-sits-on-the-edges-of-our-dances-who-does-not-participate-but-who-organises-our-world-into-inspectable-form'. All the other categories of savage social identity are known by their function in that society, but Laudonnière's role serves a function outside that world, in another. The sense of Laudonnière's more complex and individual identity descends in part from this extremely ambiguous position. The savage is both actor and witness to the social formation in which he assumes his role; Laudonnière appears as a witness to the savage world but he never participates in its action. His 'personality' rests upon his belief in his *substantia individua rationalis*[16] as 'different', as a being superior to the mere masks he sees around him, yet he is a presence without social substance. He is a ghost, both more and less than 'human'. In this context, therefore, contrary to Burkhardt, Dilthey and Greenblatt, the Renaissance self is not a new self, but a self made newly evident by the discovered presence of others and by the fear of extinction. Laudonnière's representation by Le Moyne–De Bry marks the entry of the dislocated European into a set of constructed generic locations which he has made, but within which he is depicted as a spectator.

The Huguenot/Timucuan division of identities could be endlessly replayed in the different disguises of Renaissance manicheism. The Timucuas are the masked personas of Ciceronian civic humanism who see their lives as a *negotium*, an engagement with social role and duty, opposed to Laudonnière and the *otium* of the contemplative individualist.[17] Or the image embodies the conceptual polarities of the *duplex interpretatio* of civil science, the intellectual habits of division enshrined in the opposition of key terms: *imperium* and *iurisdictio*, *potestas* and *auctoritas*, *princeps* and *populus*.[18] Sir Thomas Browne writes of the doubleness of European man and his fear of his 'primitive inner' nature:

> But it is the corruption that I feare within me, not the contagion of commerce without me. 'Tis that unruly regiment within me

that will destroy me, 'tis that I doe infect my selfe, the man without a Navell yet lives in me; I feele that originall canker corode and devoure me, and therefore *defenda me dios de me*, Lord deliver me from my self, is a point of my Letany, and the first voyce of my retired imaginations.[19]

European man is a *homo duplex*[20] cut by Apollo from the natural world; only the 'man without a Navell', Adam, 'natural' man or animals escape the contests of his divided nature. Calvin summarises the essence of the whole procedure: 'Il y a double régime en l'homme. L'un est spirituel ... L'autre est politic ou civil, par lequel l'homme est apprins des offices d'humanité et civilité.'[21]

For the Calvinist, the doubleness of man's calling constitutes a key to the nature of human history. Man's seeking after righteousness involves the transformation of his political or civil nature into the 'spiritual'; '... the whole field will be unified, holism will have vanished from ideology, and life in the world will be thought of as entirely conformable to the supreme value ...'.[22] The Christian mission is complete, for the Calvinist, when the outer world of Browneian 'commerce' is indistinguishable from the inner world of Christian spirituality. 'Calvin marks a conclusion: his church is the last form that the church could possibly take without disappearing.'[23]

For the Huguenot Laudonnière, described by Le Moyne as a person 'outstanding for his sense of Christian duty',[24] the savage world represented a special kind of challenge in relation to the 'double régime' of man and his Christian mission. The substance of the Timucuan world, its roles and artifacts are gathered in these illustrations into declarations of a messianic intention. The Le Moyne–De Bry illustrations strongly suggest that human identity has a history which is unfolding as a narrative. The Timucuas are the opening chapters of that narrative. In primeval society and contemporary primitive cultures identity is constrained and constructed by social role, but the narrative will evolve from this minimal identity towards a complex modern identity represented by Laudonnière himself.[25] Savage society will emerge from its socially orientated notions of identity-as-role towards a conception of different individualities endowed with the rights of the European. This narrative process is intimately entwined with notions of citizenship and the idea of the growth of the nation–state[26] but it is also a historical process in which ambiguity will be overcome as Laudonnière's individuality (constructed as inherent 'differences' between people) overwhelms and becomes the model for a society previously recognised solely by its social roles. The narrative will end in the future Calvinist nation–state in which all Timucuas are indistinguishable from Laudonnière and the public role of identity has been eclipsed by the private and sovereign individual. Laudonnière and Le Moyne are sifting the Timucuan world to identify its primitive social orders, but also to see its future potential; the beginning and the end of the narrative of history gaze at each other in this illustration. That history has already begun to advance with the rendering of the 'savage'. In seeing a putative prehistoric past, the future development is also discerned in which, as the Moravian Comenius wrote in the 1650s, 'there will be one Lord and his name one, and all the land shall be turned into a plain'.[27]

Laudonnière begins to situate himself on his rustic throne, becomes aware of himself and becomes self-possessed in his vision of other people who are seen as actors or poses in a spectacle or *scenographia*. Laudonnière's own identity is what is at stake, and it can only exist when it is tied to this arrangement – to the Timucuas as figures in a known representation – as a prelude to Laudonnière's self-possessed identity taking hold of the Timucuas as possessions. Laudonnière and his arquebusiers seem to be completely alone in this place, like Cortés and Pizarro and the *conquistadors* before him and upon whom he is both modelled but also (in the subtext of European religious rivalries) to whom he is contrasted. That sense of aloneness is the spur to empathetic emotions of isolation, fear, alienation, but also of freedom, individuality, triumph, exultation. If exultant individuality is to win over alienation and Laudonnière is to triumph as the viceroy of America, then the destructured world of the Timucuas must be compelled to take the shape of a known reality.

The illustration represents an early attempt to organise the reality of the European experience of the savage state into an influential form of ethnographic representation, but although these forms of representation of other peoples became the foundations for a 'grammar' of ethnographic representation and narrative, they were not newly invented by the artists and engravers of the late sixteenth century to accommodate the New World 'savage'. The *bricolage* of Renaissance anthropological attitudes to the savage attempted to accommodate the mythical beliefs and sensitivities of Europeans which, in turn, organised the content of that representational space. Although the factual content of that representation was exceedingly sparse, the ethnographic information was powerfully overdetermined by the structure of representation. The terms of that process of narrativisation are constructed around formal manichean categories of high/low, male/female, noble/commoner, interior/exterior, powerful/powerless, civil/wild as they were also in Titian's painting. The combination of weak data and strong form meant that available myths could be rapidly and easily accommodated in pictorial narration and turned to articulate 'metropolitan' European concerns.

The savage space depicted in this image is subjected in the grammar of ethnographic representation to a systematic set of narrative demarcations and dissections. The foreground is elevated and affords a specular advantage over the theatrically arranged scene which represents the native *polis*. This position becomes the projected site of the authority which is vested in the European. At the boundary between the foreground and the stage is the native informant, Outina, who, as 'king' or mirror image of the European, has sufficient authority for his testimony to be trusted. The scene itself is entered through the intermediary gestures of the informant and its protective circle is breached wherein is discovered, to the European's discomfort, the alien practices of native custom. These compositional or diagrammatic formulae and requirements of the illustrator's conventions of reportage establish, at a very early date, the essential characteristics of the anthropological encounter with other peoples. The scene is entered through a specular relationship established on a firm and authoritative foreground; the compliance of an informed intermediary, a native informant, is necessary to substantiate the representation; the substance of the native state is enclosed in a mysterious circle which must be entered, its contents viewed and evaluated.

Le Moyne's illustration structures apprehension into known forms of representation: the popular print, the revived Vitruvian staging, the royal display. Le Moyne's ethnographic illustration is the first stage in a process of identification. It engages with a sense of progressive disclosure in its 'showing the other' – a movement – from *terra incognita*, to a *place*, to a *scene*, and ultimately, to a *narrative*. The narrative which it most strongly evokes is that of the chivalric romance.

The romance is an extremely formulaic narrative genre, that is, the success of an individual text is gauged, to a large degree, by the extent to which certain narrative prerequisites and expectations are satisfied in the reader who is initiated into the codes of the genre's realisation. The 'standard plot' of romance, as Ker, Loomis, Hibbard, Abrams and Babcock[28] have variously defined it, consists of the manipulation of a number of repeated narrative events and characterisations. Characters are clearly identifiable types who have little psychological depth but are of immense significance as representatives of social orders: the King, the Queen, the Knight, the Maiden, the Squire, the Magician. The Le Moyne–De Bry prints similarly show the same figures or 'characters' in Timucuan society, identified solely by their role (presented theatrically) or social position.

In the romance, these 'personas' of social identity act out, in a world of fabulous, magical or exotic unfamiliarity, certain preordained narrative functions. Typically in romance, the young knight leaves the security of a known or familiar social world to endure exile in another place: 'Fairyland', the 'wandering wood', the wilderness, the Vitruvian satyric scene. These other places reflect the mundane world in sets of direct correspondences. The 'wandering wood' is not an escape from the world and its religious, political or moral strifes; the romance world is not a place 'outside' but a projection of the mundane onto the exotic. Those exotic other places are both more complex and simpler environments than the world of normal sociability. More complex because it is in these worlds apart that the knight encounters the 'savages', monstrous races, and demonic villains which radically expand the possibilities of created nature beyond the boundaries of what is possible in the mundane world. Simpler because the intellectual and moral world which this otherness describes is sharply manichean in its radical distinction of good and bad. Moral chiaroscuro is expressed through iridian forms.

The noble figure of the knight is engaged, in this land, on a quest to discover a significant object or 'truth' and he is beset by a number of tasks (usually three) which test his moral fibre, his courage and his intelligence. Having killed the beast, solved the riddle and defended the lady he returns from the other world endowed with special gifts, powers or insight and he wins the hand of the princess and re-emerges into the mundane world equipped with a higher-level persona, as prince or king. Thus restored to the world as a recognisable mask or persona, the knight-made-king can now reinitiate the whole cycle, as the authority figure who sets further tasks to future knights. Individual romance narratives are linear and bound for a specific destination as one might expect of a quest narrative, but collectively romances describe a perpetual circularity of ejection, quest and reincorporation motifs. The named 'individuals' – barely individuals since the knights are homogeneous – may change as the cycle of stories revolves, but the masked social types, the personas of romance, never change. The romance mirrors a social hierarchy in timeless contemplation of its own endless, fixed and unchanging replication.

The Huguenot spectator and the savages of the Le Moyne–De Bry print are just such romance characters reworked into the 'wandering wood' of the New World. Their pictorial and narrative functions are as types, personas in the Maussian/Roman sense of being 'masks' of projected European role models, and as social types they are identifiable by role and not by their 'individuality'. Similarly, like the knight of romance, Laudonnière is exiled from his world, engaged in a quest to penetrate and colonise the 'wandering wood' of the exotic and charmed circle of the Timucuas' *dominium*. What he sees there in the multicoloured display of the Timucuas, is a moral chiaroscuro which reflects back at him the controversies of European religious, moral and philosophical debates. The savage space is a test of Laudonnière's courage, morality and intelligence. His goal and his prize is the ethnographic knowledge which will enable him to proclaim his *dominium* over savagery in a replicated version of European kingship. The strangeness of his vision is simply superficial since he, nonetheless, discovers there a mirror of his own *polis* in the shape of a king and his subjects. He is incorporated into Timucuan society as its potential lord, just as the knight is reincorporated into his society as king. Ethnographic illustration reflects a rediscovered social hierarchy in the New World, undisturbed by its geographic relocation as the narrative nuclei of romance re-emerge in the conventions of ethnographic illustration.

At the same time that De Bry published his illustrations of savage life, Edmund Spenser published *The Faerie Queene*. Book VI of *The Faerie Queene* is set, like all the others, in 'Faeryland' and concerns the 'legende of Sir Calidore the Knight of Courtesie'. As its subject is civility, the poem makes extensive use of 'salvage' men and 'salvage nations' which exhibit, again, the Silvanus/Orcus division of tamed or naturally virtuous wildness against rapacious and violent 'savagery'. In Cantos viii and ix, Sir Calidore and his barely distinguishable companion Sir Calepine are the witnesses, in very much the style of Laudonnière, of two extraordinary rituals. The first is that of the 'salvage nation' who, having captured the beautiful Serena, strip her and tie her to an altar. Calepine chances upon the scene:

... the Priest with naked armes full net
Approching nigh, and murderous knife well whet,
Gan mutter close a certaine secret charme,
With other divelish ceremonies met:
Which doen he gan aloft t'advance his arme,
Whereat they shouted all, and made a loud alarme.

Then gan the bagpypes and the hornes to shrill,
And shreike aloud, that with the peoples voyce
Confused, did the ayre with terror fill,
And made the wood to tremble at the noyce:
The whyles she wayld, the more they did rejoyce.[29]

This is a widely acknowledged representation of savagery written by Spenser out of the codes of representation offered by the voyagers' literature of the late sixteenth century of which Le Moyne–De Bry is a significant part. The signs of wildness abound in the Marsyan 'rude musicke' of horns and pipes, the heathenism, and violence. Most significant is the way in which space is organised in this prospect of the 'salvage nation'. Sir Calepine, situated on the boundary or edge of the stage, voyeuristically peers into a circums-cribed space containing the savage secret in a scenario which is repeated in Le Moyne's image.

A major structuring principle of Spenserian romance is his use of parallel images, symbols and episodes; moral comparisons are con-stantly evoked by the juxtaposition of two narrative events. Thus, very shortly after Sir Calepine's prospect of savagery comes another, similar prospect, seen this time by his *doppelgänger*, Sir Calidore. The Knight, in his quest to suppress the Blatant Beast of discourtesy, comes upon a landscape arranged like a Vitruvian satyric scene of the theatrical stage:

It was an hill plaste in an open plaine,
The round about was bordered with a wood
Of matchlesse hight, that seem'd th'earth to
            disdaine,
[....]
And on the top thereof a spacious plaine
Did spred it selfe, to serve to all delight,
Either to daunce, when daunce would faine,
Or else to course about their bases light[30]

As the knight approaches he hears the sound of pipes and of feet 'thumping the hollow ground' and discovers 'a troupe of Ladies':

He durst not enter into th'open greene,
For dread of them unwares to be descryde,
For breaking of their daunce, if he were seene;
But in the covert of the wood did byde,
Beholding all, yet of them unespyde.
There he did see, that pleased much his sight,
That even he him selfe his eyes envyde,
An hundred naked maidens lilly white,
All raunged in a ring, and dauncing in delight.

All they without were raunged in a ring,
And daunced round; but in the midst of them
Three other Ladies did both daunce and sing,
The whilest the rest them round about did hemme,
And like a girlond did in compasse stemme:
And in the middest of those same three, was placed
Another Damzell, as a precious gemme,
Amidst a ring most richly well enchaced,
With her goodly presence all the rest much graced.[31]

The source of this image is the mythological representation of the classical Graces and must be read alongside the text's appeal to the magnificent displays and ballets of the Renaissance court and to Spenser's other similar presentations of female classical figures such as Diana (III. vi. 19), Amoret (IV. x. 52) and Pastorella (VI. ix. 8). But the close proximity of the two episodes of the 'salvage nation' and the Graces invites comparison in the ways which they, also, mirror each other. Both episodes are the result of a surprise encounter since both knights are engaged on other quests but chance upon their visions. Both knights voyeuristically peer into the theatrical display arranged as a circle of ritualists. The texts also invite comparison by the nature of their polarised differences since both texts present opposite visions of the pastoral; one shows the pastoral world as barbaric, lustful and violent (anti-pastoral), the other as courtly, refined and essential nature. Similarly, the texts are 'gendered' in the sense that the first is a 'male scene', the second a female world.

When these poetic texts are juxtaposed to the Le Moyne–De Bry prints, the similar semiotic and narrative strategies emerge there also: of quest, noble outsiders, voyeurs, male and female, the classical dancing nymphs as a major iconographic source, strange ritual. Laudonnière's surprised response to the women's ritual descends from the fact that he is unsure which of the Spenserian romance visions he is witnessing – the dance of the Graces or the ritual sacrifices of a 'salvage nation' – since elements of both are present in

11 Jacques Le Moyne de Morgues, 'The Treatment of the Enemy Dead', 1591

the image's representation and, as in Titian's *The Flaying of Marsyas*, vision is split between an elevated and transcendent vision and its opposite. His uncertainty typifies a major element of the image: the European's 'shock of the other' experienced when the material ambiguously fits the frame of representation. But less significant than which of the readings of the scene strictly applies is that a narrative formulation has occurred. Both Spenser's poem and the ethnographic illustration partake of the same semiotic and narrative moves and the source of those moves is the romance.

Laudonnière's prospect does not so much increase the viewer's understanding of Timucuan culture, as assimilate the other into known structures of representation. The image proclaims itself to be presenting 'new' materials, 'new' peoples, 'new' or shocking subjects for representation but, on the contrary, offers only repeated acts of structuration hidden in the cloak of reportage, illustration and the romance. The 'structure' which is constantly and repeatedly 'restructured' is the Apollonian manichean process of 'othering'.

*

The shocking image in figure 11, entitled 'The Treatment of the Enemy Dead', was not new in the sixteenth century. De Bry had already published a similar plate depicting a cannibal barbecue and extensive descriptions of native American warfare and the treatment of the dead, as food or as trophies (as in this case), had been available in descriptions of the Brazilian natives. Thevet and Léry had described the Tupinamba's cannibal practices with considerable and quite surprising understanding of the role ritual and social cohesion play in cannibalism.[32] But Le Moyne's illustration of the 'savage butchers' gains part of its shock value from its fracturing of the frames of representation displayed in the previous illustration. Here, the terms of the apprehension of the savage scene must be reorientated and reconsidered since this image radically challenges the pictorial, narrative and ideological constructions of the savage subject.

This image, unlike the previous image, depicts a 'male' scene of brutality as in Titian's *The Flaying of Marsyas*. There are no women, and there is no *polis* either. There is nothing for Outina to gesture at, inviting us into the charming circle of dancing women. What is candidly displayed is male brutality, male genitals and a vicious parody of the act of buggery. In the position occupied by the supplant woman in the first illustration there is now a dismembered and scalped male torso with a long arrow inserted in his rectum. The female world, so reminiscent of the courtly festival and the iconography of the classical myth of the Graces, gives way here to the male aspect of savagery redefined as violence, display and sexual violation.

This image is above all instrumental in demarking the other extreme from the previous image of savage life; the manicheism of the Silvanus/Orcus split is repeated here in a comparison of these two illustrations. The Orcus aspect of the wildman is refigured as 'cannibal', whereas the Silvanus aspect of the domesticated and socialised wildman is refigured as the Outina theatrical image. The images display the polarised contents of the native scene, occupying spaces at opposite ends of the spectrum of primitive society. Outina is the refigured Silvanus of the first illustration; the haughty native with the scalp reigns as Orcus and throws the carefully laid strategies of incorporation of the savage into disarray.

Although the contents and subject-matter of the two illustrations are thus polarised around familiar manichean tropes, the organisation of pictorial space in both images is comparable if not remarkably similar. Again, the composition of this scene recalls a theatrical performance: a stage set for the audience. The foreground is raised above the scene enacted below. The circle described by the women's dance is repeated in the line from the raised club to the savages disappearing over the very sharply defined horizon. Each circle contains a secret rite: the child offered to the phallic herm in the women's image, the defiled and mutilated corpse in the men's image.

The illustrator's conventional illusion of a secret circle which is visualised and penetrated recurs in this representation and the sexual metaphor of male penetration of secret circles seems deeply inscribed in both the illustrations. From the staged foreground we enter a theatrical world of horrors circumscribing a dreadful secret. In the second it is clearly presented in a shocking act of violation. With each breaching of the conventional circle of culture these illustrations appear to bring us to a secret aspect of nature. From one image to the other, we 'move' further into that essence of wildness, and closer to the savage animality which 'truly' represents the life of primitives.

We progress through the circles by regressing into man's savage nature. The imperious figure of haughty savagery has moved closer to his viewer but still stands in the same classical pose of relaxed arrogance. But this time he displays his victim's scalp while looking directly at the viewer, increasing the sense that the viewer is confronted by what he/she sees. He adopts the familiar pose of a classical warrior. All mortality is like this. Nothing further can be revealed. This is the last scene, the heart of darkness.

But this illusion that the secret circle of savage custom has been breached and entered is created solely by the formal and narrative actions of the conventions of illustration. What is manifested by those conventions is not a matter of 'nature', nor is it a boundary or border of any kind except that made by the conventions of representation, of illustration, of the manifestations of western power.

Although the first image of the savage *dominium* under the 'kingship' of Outina–Silvanus has been posed as opposite to that of the second image of butcher–Orcus, the structure of their representations is consistent. The same compositional patterns apply in both illustrations, although the second is an inversion of the first: they are the same but opposite. The two images are contradictory in terms of content but share a compositional affinity.

The first image expressed in pictorial form some of the narrative strategies which, I have argued, are analogous to the romance; the second image similarly reworks conventions reminiscent of the romance but in an inverted form. The second image could be described as the 'inverted double' of the first, in that it retains the same pictorial 'shape' but offers contrary messages about the politics of its representation. The degree to which the second image inverts the codes of the first image can be gauged by the use of a further literary analogy, because the romance has itself a 'double' in the narrative form of the picaresque.

As Barbara Babcock has shown, each social persona of the romance character-type and each romance narrative event finds an inverted 'double' in the types and events of the picaresque.[33] The chivalrous knight of the romance is ejected from the picaresque to be replaced by the *picaro*, the anti-authority, low-life figure. Similarly, his 'quest' is neither heroic nor determined by any goal, but becomes instead a rambling peregrination, not through 'faeryland' or other such green world, but through the wilder landscapes of European cities. The maiden becomes a courtesan or prostitute and instead of tests of morality, courage and intelligence, the *picaro* is expected to win through by cunning, deceit and violence.

Thomas Nashe's *The Unfortunate Traveller*, published in 1594 and therefore contemporary with Spenser's poem, displays a perfectly inverted congruence with *The Faerie Queene*. Jack Wilton's adventures parallel those of the knight whose destiny he invertedly parodies. Jack begins well enough, like his knightly double, in the world of Henry VIII's court, at the Field of the Cloth of Gold. But Jack is an 'appendix or page', 'sole King of the Cans and Black-jacks, Prince of the Pigmies, County Palatine of Clean Straw and Provant, and, to conclude, Lord High Regent of Rashers of the Coals and Red-Herring Cobs';[34] a savage of the cities. Jack's parody of social roles and statuses is a 'radical desacramentalisation' of the glorification of hierarchy in a prose which owes more to 'Billingsgate, slang and argot' than to the courtly decorum of romance poetry.[35]

Jack too, like his knightly double, is ejected from his (low) position in the mundane world and journeys through the wild cities of Italy and France; he also achieves a higher social status – through wealth not position – by cheating the savage Italians. He marries his courtesan and returns to the king's court. The romance rites of passage, narrative motifs of expulsion, quest and reintegration are reinscribed in Jack's tale, as are the thematic and image contrasts and parallels. *The Unfortunate Traveller* embodies the structure of romance at the

same time that it inverts it, with the consequence that the didactic
moral messages of the romance are similarly embodied and challenged. The fixed certainties of form, social order and morality
depicted in the romance are unmade by Jack's Midas touch,
rendered compromised, contingent and problematic by the picaresque's dislocation of its generic typologies.

Spenser, in his letter to Raleigh (who was also, coincidentally, Le
Moyne's patron in England when he fled France in 1580 'for religion') famously 'discover[ed] ... the general intention and meaning'
of his poem: 'to fashion a gentleman or noble person in vertuous and
gentle discipline'.[36] Jack's tale similarly has a lengthy preamble in the
shape of, characteristically, two dedications, the first to the Earl of
Southampton, the second to 'the dapper Monsieur Pages of the
Court'. Southampton is described as an 'ingenuous [ingenious]
honourable lord', yet in the following preamble to the pages Nashe
proclaims 'marry, the tavern is honourable'. Like Falstaff, a character
with whom Jack shares many affinities, Nashe subjects 'honour', the
keyword of chivalric conduct, to a process of 'bisociation', which
Arthur Koestler defines as the 'effect of perceiving an idea or event,
simultaneously or in quick alternation, in two habitually incompatible frames of reference'.[37] Entry to Jack's text is, therefore, through a
double portal, one high, one low. Anything which Jack states in his
text is subjected to 'bisociation' and the evocation of simultaneous
contradictory states. Systems of signs and meanings conjoin, interact
and are opposed, denying the possibility of ever 'fashioning a
gentleman' or anything else, since all forms of knowledge are sceptically interrogated.

The romance, in the examples cited from Spenser's text, used
mirrored imagery and the representation of 'doubles' as a device to
point up a single moral truth about the 'natural' conceived as
opposed states of either divine civility or savage turpitude conditional upon the state of grace of the participants. Both offer lessons
which will fashion the gentlemanly voyeurs who witness them. The
picaresque engages with the same narrative codes but as an inversion of their intentions: 'doubling' is used in this context to point to
the contingent and fabricated nature of perceptions and the sceptical
dissolving of certainties about language, morality and social hierarchy. Ethnographic illustration, as a narrative and representational
model for the fashioning of other peoples, exhibits the same
grammar of images, spatial organisation and 'doubled' and inverted
narratives. The two Le Moyne–De Bry illustrations, as exemplary

types, are similarly twin doorways through to the romance–picaresque worlds of 'bisociated' Graces and 'salvage nations' and which
evoke the voyeur's perception as constantly shifting between the
ambiguities of the scene he witnesses.

But where the 'savage butchers' illustration is closest to the picaresque is in the similarity of their subject matter. The romance is
singularly incapable of dealing with the graphic detail of this image:
Spenser's depiction of the 'salvage nations'' sacrificial rites falls far
short of the intensity of Le Moyne–De Bry's depiction of the mutilated and mangled bodies. Such 'detail' is, however, the essential
feature of the picaresque. The picaresque answers, as it were, the
romance's adherence to elevated expression by a constant affirmation of the popular print's fascination with the prose 'detail' of
public executions, just as the 'savage butchers' image undercuts the
noble allusions of the first image.

Jack Wilton, at one stage of his adventures, falls into the hands of
Jews, Zacharie and Zardoche. Zardoche sells Jack to Zacharie for use
in an anatomy lesson but after a detailed description of what
happens in an 'anatomy' and by a truly picaresque twist to the plot
involving a fair amount of sex and violence, Jack is freed and
Zardoche goes to the stake. Further details of the action of fire upon
human flesh are followed almost immediately by yet another execution. The last event of *The Unfortunate Traveller* is the execution of the
'wearish dwarfish writhen-faced' criminal Cutwolfe and recalls
Marsyas and the anatomy lesson in the 'expertise' displayed by the
savant executioner.

'Away with him, away with him! Executioner, torture him, tear
him, or we will tear thee in pieces if thou spare him!'
The executioner needed no such exhortation hereunto, for of
his own nature was he hackster good enough. Old excellent he
was at a boneache. At the first chop with his wood-knife would
he fish for a man's heart and fetch it out as easily as a plum from
the bottom of a porridge pot. He would crack necks as fast as a
cook cracks eggs; a fiddler cannot turn his pin so soon as he
would turn a man off the ladder. Bravely did he drum on this
Cutwolfe's bones, not breaking them outright but, like a
saddler knocking in of tacks, jarring on them quaveringly with
his hammer a great while together. No joint about him but with
a hatchet he had for the nonce he disjointed half, and then with
boiling lead soldered up the wounds from bleeding. His tongue
pulled out, lest he should blaspheme in his torment. Venemous
stinging worms he thrust into his ears to keep his head ravingly
occupied. With cankers scruzed to pieces he rubbed his mouth

and his gums. No limb of his but was lingeringly splintered in shivers. In this horror left they him on the wheel as in hell, where, yet living, he might behold his flesh legacied amongst the fowls of the air.[38]

The Unfortunate Traveller, with its conjunction of demonised (Jewish) 'others', anatomy lessons and the savagery of the public stage of executions inhabits territory similar to both *The Flaying of Marsyas* and the Le Moyne ethnographic illustration. The picaresque offers a context within which to make the image of the 'savage butchers' readable. But Cutwolfe's execution is prefaced by a long speech of justification which ends with Cutwolfe proclaiming:

> Revenge is the glory of arms and the highest performance of valour; revenge is whatsoever we call law or justice. The farther we wade in revenge, the nearer come we to the throne of the Almighty. To His sceptre it is properly ascribed; His sceptre He lends unto man when He lets one man scourge another.[39]

The irony of Cutwolfe's last words is perfectly in keeping with the sceptical doubleness of Nashe's text. Cutwolfe's self-justification is precisely the justification of the judicial powers which are about to execute him and there is, at this point, no moral distance between the two; only mercy from the crowd and a pardon from the bench would prove him to be wrong. As it is, his death proves to justify his claim that justice is revenge. Cutwolfe's death leads us into a moral maze where all categorical boundaries and certainties are dissolved. The butcher image's derivation is from a similar source and produces the same moral complexes, sceptical effects and culturally relativistic conclusion. Just as the picaresque challenges the certainties of the romance world of structured apprehensions, so too the 'savage butchers' image renders contingent all those confident and refined ascriptions of the first image by insisting that the viewer look closely at the image of the savage body in torment.

A reading of the Le Moyne illustration in the light of the bisociated nature of the picaresque also renders the other associations of the image contingent upon the 'doubleness' of its treatment. For example, a relation which this illustration makes is also, as in Titian's *The Flaying of Marsyas*, to the illustrated books of physiology and anatomy. I have already discussed how those anatomical illustrations are intimately entwined with the apprehension of the savage through the paradigmatic figure of Marsyas and the use of the satyr as both anatomical material and as a trope representing colonial contact with savage peoples. There is more than a little of Vesalius in the Le Moyne–De Bry illustration.

The raised bank in the foreground becomes a kind of dissecting table upon which the savage anatomist, delicately slicing into his victim, with his assistants hacking at the limbs, performs his version of a Vesalian anatomy lesson. The 'specialist' qualities required of the 'savage anatomists' are indicated by Le Moyne in his explanatory text to the image:

> In these skirmishes those who fall are immediately dragged out of the camp by *those entrusted with this responsibility* who cut the scalp down to the skull, in a circle from front to back, with pieces of reed sharper than any steel blade ... Even in the course of a battle they will cut off with these same reed knives the arms of corpses below the shoulder, and legs below the hip, break the bared bones with a piece of wood and then dry out the mutilated and blood drenched parts of the bodies by roasting them over the ... fire. Then they will carry them home triumphantly, with the scalps hanging from their spear points.[40]

Incidentally, the complex European response to the Vesalian images of the anatomised body is projected upon this text which describes native custom, but native custom becomes a metaphor for European concerns. In questioning the morality of the Vesalian image the savage becomes the projection of Europe's moral panics about its own dilemmas in distinguishing the place of scientific investigation in a moral universe. The association of the savage with a brutally dissected body is becoming habitual and we will return again to this image of the violated body of the primitive.

The image of the savage as a devoted cannibal and butcher of his own kind could only be pronounced by the French in a fit of absent-mindedness or as a remarkable act of sublimation of the Huguenots' own conduct in Florida. The first Huguenot expedition had ended in disaster when their leader Ribault had left a small contingent of men in Florida under the command of the tyrannical Albert della Pierria. The remnants rebelled and killed their oppressive captain and took to the high seas in a homemade boat under the command of their new chief, Barré. They were soon lost at sea and started to starve. Barré made his men draw lots, and they killed and ate the unlucky loser.[41]

In the graphic moral questioning of this image, culpability is again transferred from the Huguenots to the natives in a way which will become a model of western representation of the savage scene. The unspeakable torments of the European conscience are projected upon the native as ethnographic truth. The Timucuas are the means by which European morality deals with its darkest taboos and disguises the reality of the unspeakable fact. European anthropophagy becomes the discourse of native cannibalism, and the confident moral condemnation of the savage butchers dissolves in the historical actuality of Frenchmen eating Frenchman.

But these sleights of hand also have a practical utility in assisting the Huguenots' colonial project. The scene also seems to support the justification, in Protestant ideology, for colonisation, already established in the previous image. The Timucuan atrocity seals them off from the action of divine grace, which is the central tenet of Lutheranism and which (for the Protestants) overrides the Catholic concern with *dominium*. This graphic image of scalping, mutilation and broiling is of barbarity unrestrained by authority. The viewer alone sees this, unmediated and unprotected by the sanctioning gesture of the chief or his guest. Where there is no Laudonnière/ Outina there is no authority and the presence of the heroic observer in a state of higher Grace would seem to be the only bulwark against the Graceless 'savage'.

In this respect, Laudonnière presents himself as the deputy of the French king and therefore the proper authority to restrain the violence of the savages; but a 'picaresque' or 'bisociated' reading of the image begs the question, *which king?* Both Ribault and Laudonnière had gone to Florida with the direct support of the Valois king, Charles IX, and thus Laudonnière is depicted in the previous image as a loyal royal deputy. Charles had pursued a pragmatic policy of involvement of Huguenot grandees in Catholic court enterprises, but the rivalry between Catholic and Protestant interests intensified in the 1560s into open hostility.

As was the case with the previous image, the 'savage butchers' also has a political or propaganda subtext. An indication of the ideological utility of this image and the part it plays in the complex political and religious conflicts of sixteenth-century France, can be gauged from the date of publication. Le Moyne drew the scenes 'from life' in the 1560s but they were not reproduced and published as engravings by De Bry until 1591. In the intervening years France had been traumatised by the violent anti-Protestant campaign of the Duc de Guise, the St Bartholomew's Day massacre of Huguenots in Paris in 1572, the Wars of Religion and the extinction of the Valois dynasty and the rise to power of the erstwhile Protestant Henri IV in

1589. Concurrently, the last decades of the sixteenth century witnessed a proliferation in the number of accounts by Protestants of
the Huguenot settlements and their termination at the hands of
Catholics. Publications by Ribault (1563), Le Challeux (1566), Laudonnière himself (1586) and Le Moyne (1591)[42] served the purpose of
keeping the aspirations of the Protestants and the events of the 1560s
alive throughout a thirty-year period. In the context of the Protestant cause in an age of uncertain and bloody turmoil the illustrations are a subtle but effective political stratagem for metropolitan
consumption. The Huguenot Laudonnière of the first illustration,
seated on his wooden throne in Florida, the survivor of Catholic
plots and massacres and friend to affectionate colonial subjects,
emerges as a type of alternative to the Catholic Valois king, a
Protestant *imperator*, King Henri IV.

Furthermore, in the context of the Catholic massacre of Protestants
and the Huguenot vindication of their rights as proper colonial
masters and kingly figures, this illustration graphically demonstrates
what it is like to bear witness to a massacre by native Americans in
Florida, or Spaniards in Florida, or (perhaps more significantly) by
French Catholics in Paris. The foreground, which was occupied by
the sanctifying presence of the authority figures of Outina and his
Huguenot guests, is invaded by the savage – an affront to ethnographic knowledge and to colonial authority in that it usurps the site
of visualisation and intellectual authority.

In omitting the figures of restraining authority from their customary place, the illustration foregrounds the king's deputy as an absent
presence required for the restraint of violent barbarity. Figured as
the Protestant Laudonnière, that absent presence is paralleled in
French metropolitan terms as Henri IV, without whom European
savagery will flourish. Le Moyne's *Narratio* recounts the massacre of
the Huguenots by the Spanish which is not only as graphic as that
recorded in the image of native American butchery and its related
text, but is also very close to it in detail:

> He fell on his knees, pleading for his life; but seized with fury
> they hacked him to pieces and transfixed the dismembered
> parts on the points of their pikes and spears.

> Men were detailed to kill the rest who had been tied up by
> striking them on the head with clubs and axes which they did
> without any delay, repeatedly calling them Lutherans and
> enemies of God and of the Virgin Mary.[43]

The subtexts of this illustration cannot escape the propaganda of

12 Antoine Caron, *Massacre of the Triumvirs*, 1566

European religious schisms and political struggle. The illustration acts in a similar capacity in 'low art' to Antoine Caron's 'high art' image *Massacre of the Triumvirs* (figure 12) which uses a Vitruvian civic space and classical form to allude to the murder of Protestants. In a corresponding fashion, the illustration indirectly recalls both the terrible history of the Laudonnière expedition and the Protestant subjugation in Counter-Reformation Europe by projecting those events onto native American cultural practice.

The invention of a narrative form for the textualisation and representational shaping of the anomalous and unruly materials of the savage is itself the most significant feature of this illustration. Except, of course, that nothing has really been 'invented', merely redirected, reused, or reinvented, just as Orcus, Silvanus, Marsyas and the other myths were reinvented for different ends.

Ethnographic illustration as a prototypical form of anthropological representation encodes several discursive and generic features which resemble the literary forms of the romance, particularly romance's pastoral interludes. Renaissance ethnographic illustration is also comparable to the royal festivals and *entrées* and to theatrical *scenographia* in their organisation of spatial representation and symbolic figuration. The Le Moyne–De Bry prints, as the first comprehensive set of illustrations of primitive peoples in the New World, embrace a manichean discourse of differences and identities which typically depict the savage as a 'functional being' identified by role, lacking human 'texture' and devoid of the characteristics of European individuality. The European is thus marked as 'different' and as possessing a superior purposefulness and an individualistic representation. In holding up the savage to scrutiny that world is seemingly recorded, totally catalogued, revealed, its secret circles penetrated and thus 'textualised' and known, rendered ripe for the transforming effects of a future trajectory towards the destination of 'civility'.

The Le Moyne–De Bry prints accomplish these effects but if that was all that they did they would be imperialist images, not ethnography. In many respects they *are* imperialist images, but there is much else in them, much of the anomalous condition of the 'other', which will not simply conform to the imperial project.

The examples and analogies conjure two contradictory movements. The first movement assimilated the material of savage life to the representational strategies of the romance; the second discovers a textual form in popular descriptions of public executions and the picaresque. The second image's inverted relation to romance narrative and its interrogation of the hierarchical values and certainties of the romance world enables the accommodation of a sceptical apprehension. That disruption of the romance ascriptions of the savage enables metropolitan concerns and covert political issues to permeate the image of otherness. Although the first 'movement' keeps its enunciating categories distinct and meaningful, and the second 'blurs' or confuses all distinction and interrogates all 'meaningful' statements, both, nonetheless, mark the arrival of articulate media for the 'showing' of other peoples. That otherness, however formally presented in ethnographic illustration or poem, is always shown as 'difference'; but 'difference' which disguises the identity – the inherent familiarity – of its enunciation as pastoral, romance, picaresque, execution scene. The early ethnographic texts such as Le Moyne–De Bry's indelibly mark anthropology as a divided subject: Midas' gaze is again split between the making and unmaking of a world of representations – the world of the savage in the image of the Graces or in the image of a massacre. The Le Moyne–De Bry prints sequentially present images of 'arrest', of 'closure', of 'narratable' subjects identified as social 'functions' against images whose 'function' is to remain 'open', 'unnarratable' and 'uncertain'.

One final point: the Timucuas of the second illustration give expression to a kind of liberation, violent, bloody and questionable though it is. The savages are freed from the kinds of social roles which the romance/Outina image imposed upon them. They riot. In both the literary and ethnographic contexts, 'rioting' means that categorical judgements – manichean designations – are made ambiguous and perfidious. In the historical contexts of these illustrations' production, their message seems to be that there is little *real* 'difference' between 'savage butchers' and 'European butchers', the Duc de Guise and Spanish colonialists. And that is a point of view which both Le Moyne and Jack Wilton would have shared.

Chapter 3

The lovers of Paramaribo: Surinam 1663–1777

Man differs more from Man than Man from beast.   *Rochester*[1]

In 1650 Francis Willoughby, Earl of Parham, established the first English colony in Guiana. This was considered a courageous, if not foolhardy, action given the country's remoteness, its torrid climate, the impenetrable forests of the interior and, not least, the reputation of the Carib natives for violence and cannibalism. But it was none of these dangers which terminated the English project. A little more than seventeen years after the earl founded the capital city of Parham the Dutch invaded the colony and split off the province of Surinam from the rest of Guiana. The Dutch hanged or expelled most of the English colonists and took *de facto* control of the territory until the Treaty of Breda in 1684 confirmed their ownership in a deal with England which exchanged Surinam for New Amsterdam.[2] Aphra Behn's visit to Surinam in 1663 and the subsequent novella, *Oroonoko or the Royal Slave*[3] of 1688 which recorded her impressions of the colony, bridge most of the turbulent early history of the territory.

In her introductory remarks to *Oroonoko*, Behn's narrator promises an absolute veracity in representing that past:

> I do not pretend, in giving you the History of this ROYAL SLAVE, to entertain my Reader with the Adventures of a feign'd Hero … there being enough of Reality to support it, and to render it diverting, without the Addition of Invention. I was myself an Eye-witness to a great Part of what you will find here set down.
> (*Oroonoko*, p. 129)

For Behn, reality relies upon a moralised notion of the role of the author who must be 'true' to the rendering. The key figure of Behn's text, as her introduction establishes, is not therefore Oroonoko, the hero of the novella, but the author and her ability to show this reality. Just as De Bry emphasised the truthfulness of Le Moyne's images because they depicted 'figures taken from life ... enacted vividly before their [the viewers'] eyes', Behn lays claim to the reader's confidence by the same means: she 'was [her]self an Eye-witness to a great Part of what you will find set down'. The reality is guaranteed by an authorial presence in the text and, more impor-tantly, in Surinam. Behn hangs her tale upon the cardinal tests of ethnographic narrative: of presence, visualisation and represen-tation. Behn's own autobiography as a participant observer under-writes the reality she shows, which existed because she existed; the authorial self is the guarantee of a reality constructed essentially as presence.[4] Moreover, that presence is established upon the corrobor-ation of observation, endorsed by the Lockean paradigm that 'the perception of the mind is most aptly explained by words relating to sight'.[5] But as Behn's novella unfolds so too does an awareness that being an 'Eye-witness' entails much more than a naturalistic repre-sentation of 'reality'. What will be shown the reader, the narrator claims, is 'reality'. But her rendering of the 'reality' of *Oroonoko* comprises a variety of meanings beyond that simply of recording a neutral or colourless representation of an actuality devoid of prefer-ences, decoration or authorial intentions. Without apparent contra-diction, the showing of reality also involves an act of sincerity or loyalty; her preamble is a token of a purity of intention, a sincerity or honesty of purpose. For Behn being an 'Eye-witness' or participant observer entailed a negotiation between the various meanings of the 'reality' she will show. What is required of a tale to make it 'real' is the sincerity of its telling.

Behn's first eye-witness account of the native people of Surinam is given as a 'holiday' excursion into native American territory. After eight days in a boat, the tourists approach a native village at which point 'the Hearts of some of our Company fail'd, and they would not venture on shore'. Only Behn's narrator, her maid, her brother and Oroonoko disembarked but they were at first concerned: 'none of us speaking the Language of the People, and imagining we should have a half Diversion in gazing only'.[6] A translator is found among the crew but the narrator's initial apprehensions signal the nature of the encounter. The concern is less for the dangers of the meeting with the natives than for a 'half diversion' which would leave the Europeans dissatisfied. Behn's language is of desire and the gratification which the native Americans can offer. 'Gazing only' is insufficient; more must be attempted.

The purpose of the encounter is to view the natives in their habitat, but for the narrator and her party of tourists, simply looking is insufficient. Behn's narrator hides her coloured companions in a thicket while she, her brother and 'her woman' pass on towards the village: 'We had a mind to surprize 'em ... making them see something they never had seen (that is, White People).' The narrator teasingly reverses the object of the gaze so that the narrator's sudden appearance out of the forest transforms the viewers into the viewed and the Europeans become the objects of the savages' gaze. 'Eye-witnessing' is thus displaced onto the objects of the gaze as the narrator watches the natives watching her. In this text, being an eye-witness involves the scrutiny of one's own reflection in the eyes of others. The encounter very rapidly escalates from this play of identity, desire and the gaze:

> They had no sooner spy'd us, but they set up a loud Cry, that frighted us at first; we thought it had been for those that should kill us, but it seems it was of Wonder and Amazement. They were all naked; and we were dress'd, so as is most commode for the hot Countries, very glittering and rich; so that we appear'd extremely fine; my own Hair was cut short, and I had a Taffety Cap, with black Feathers on my Head; my Brother was in a Stuff-Suit, with Silver Loops and Buttons, and abundance of green Ribbon. This was all infinitely surprising to them; and because we saw them stand still till we approached 'em ... and offer'd 'em our Hands; which they took, and look'd on us round about, calling still for more Company; who came swarming out, all wondering, and crying out *Tepeeme*; taking their Hair up in their Hands, and spreading it wide to those they call'd out to; as if they would say (as indeed it signify'd) *Numberless Wonders*, or not to be recounted, no more than to number the Hair of their Heads. By Degrees they grew more bold, and from gazing upon us round, they touch'd us, laying their Hands upon all the Features of our Faces, feeling our Breasts, and Arms, taking up one Petticoat, then wondering to see another; admiring our Shoes and Stockings, but more our Garters, which we gave 'em, and they ty'd about their Legs, being lac'd with Silver Lace at the Ends; for they much esteem any shining Things. In fine, we suffer'd 'em to survey us as they pleas'd, and we thought they would never have done admiring us.   (p. 185)

The native Americans' response to the English is figured as innocence; their fumblings and gropings are simply the curiosity of naked people for the clothed.[7] Behn's narrator's response is less innocent and she is remarkably frank about the pleasures of contact with her native subjects: 'frighted', surrounded by naked natives, touched, caressed, her clothing intimately explored and her garter taken, but above all 'surveyed' as an object of wonder and amazement. Just as the natives are constructed by the Europeans' gaze, so too the Europeans are remade by the looks and touches of the natives and it is thus that the Europeans become truly 'very glittering and rich', 'extrem'ly fine'.

Behn's text reverses the narrative strategies of disclosure of the primitive in that it is initially the *English* who lack an identity for the *native Americans* and appear alien to this scene but are made into objects of desire by the savages' touch. Behn seems to be reproducing the scopophilia of the male scrutiny of women: female identity is the reflected perception of the gazing male. But here the scopophilia of gender exchanges is projected onto an encounter with the primitive other. The narrator resituates herself in her encounter with the natives in the role of the woman subjected to the patriarchal gaze and she is as concerned to see her image reflected back at her from their eyes as she is to see them. In a similar reversal of the drama of encounters with the savage, it is the Europeans not the natives who are described as 'things'; 'astonishment', 'surprise' and curiosity are the reactions of the natives, not of the Europeans.

This language of glances, touches, reversal, mirroring, reading the gaze of the gazed upon and fabricating a self-image out of the reaction of those who are both spectators and 'spectated', encodes, as in Le Moyne's ethnographic illustrations, the 'grammar' of a psychology of 'othering' as projection, eroticism, self-fashioning. The text is always ripe with this potential for reversal; the capacity to see oneself and one's own culture reflected back in the mirror of the primitive:

> They are extreme modest and bashful, very shy, and nice of being touch'd. And tho' they are all thus naked, if one lives for ever among 'em, there is not to be seen an indecent Action, or Glance: and being continually us'd to see one another so unadorn'd, so like our first Parents before the Fall, it seems as if they had no wishes, there being nothing to heighten Curiosity: but all you can see, you see at once, and every Moment see; and where there is no Novelty, there can be no Curiosity.[8]

Although critics of Behn's novella invariably identify these people as the Caribs, Behn's narrator is nowhere so specific.[9] Indeed, she never identifies any of the native peoples by name; they remain throughout simply 'the indians', a nameless, undifferentiated mass of admiring looks, naked bodies and roving hands. Behn's purpose here is not wholly to depict the native Americans as pre-lapsarian 'soft' primitives but to use the natives as an inverted reflection of her own culture which is the natives' manichean double. Behn is, here, commenting again upon the relative 'civility' of naked natives and clothed Europeans: clothing engenders hypocrisy, deceit and lust, from which the native is free and hence more civil than the European who is by comparison, 'adorn'd', immodest, forward, easily touched, indecent, as Behn's narrator herself shows. But Behn extends the comparison beyond the civility debate to encompass the nature of the noble savagery of 'our first Parents before the Fall'.

All the world is visible to the natives: 'all you can see, you see at once, and every moment see'. The natives exist in an antinominalist unmediated 'reality', unlike the English 'eye-witness' who sees 'reality' and herself only as a reflected image of another's gaze. Whereas the Englishwoman's descriptions mark her as a desiring subject, desire is unknown to the natives; they have 'no wishes', there is 'nothing to heighten Curiosity' because there is 'no Novelty'. Behn's discourse of noble savagery is less a description of native peoples than a critique of European corrupted desires: 'And these People represented to me an absolute Idea of the first state of Innocence, before Man knew how to Sin: And 'tis most evident and plain, that Simple Nature is the most harmless, inoffensive and virtuous Mistress'.[10]

In the light of Pufendorf's Hobbesian maxim that 'men float in a whole Tide of Affections and Desires, utterly unknown to Beastes',[11] these natives, being outside the defining qualification of desire, would take up the position of an animal in the order of created nature. But for Behn the natives possess a sense of natural justice. They 'know no fraud', vice or 'cunning' 'but when they are taught by *White* Men'.[12] There is a poignant and polemical significance in designating the Surinam natives as edenic peoples in a context of cultural representations which had typified the Caribs as unregenerated cannibals.

Behn's text is polemical in another sense also; her unrestrained nostalgia for native American primitivism expresses an essentially degenerative view of history. Late seventeenth- and eighteenth-century theorists of history regarded the exposition of the 'universal' history of mankind as being central to their inquiry; ethnographic data were of significance not in their own right, but only so far as they illuminated the general question of human social development. The nature of historical progress was central, for example, in the Battle of the Books controversy which focused upon the relative merits of ancient and modern learning and conveyed a wider concern for ideas of progress and degeneration. In the various expressions of the controversy, the comparison of discrete historical epochs, classical and modern, extended the range of comparative historical method.[13]

Locke saw something of the emerging 'pattern' of history when he wrote that 'in the beginning all the world was America', and 'America ... is still a Pattern of the First Ages in Asia and Europe'.[14] Thomas Blackwell's *Inquiry into the Life and Writings of Homer*, 1735, followed Locke's lead, by claiming that a cultural typology is available by observation of 'the state of the country', 'the common manners of the inhabitants', 'their constitution, civil and religious', 'their ordinary way of living ... as it happens to be polite or barbarous, luxurious or simple', 'the Manners of the Times', 'the Private Education', and finally, 'the particular way of life we choose and pursue'.[15] The particular situation of a society can be observed in these features, as it is borne along by the stream of history. At the very source is the revivified figure of the medieval and Renaissance wildman, the 'solitary savage' or American native.

Behn is openly hostile to an evolutionary vision of progress, seeing the world pessimistically, embarked on a decaying and declining historical trajectory. The natives of Behn's depiction are, therefore, of use to her in her general project to represent her critique of modernity. Their role as an edenic and historical *parousia*, a 'zero degree',[16] lies in their function, not as historical subjects in their own right, but as an illumination of an English historical context.

In this context, Behn touches on the 'rude musicke' debate and revivifies the Apollo–Marsyas image:

> When we had eat, my Brother and I took out our Flutes, and Play'd to 'em, which gave 'em new Wonder; and I soon perceiv'd, by an Admiration that is natural to these People, and by the extreme Ignorance and Simplicity of 'em, it were not difficult to establish any unknown or extravagant Religion among them, and to impose any Notions or Fictions upon 'em.
>
> (p. 186)

Music is again the agency by which the Apollonian European accomplishes a complete victory over the Marsyan savage in a perfectly reconstructed Vitruvian *scenographia* of the satyric scene. Wonder and admiration for western achievement eclipses ignorance and simplicity, rendering them susceptible to 'Religion'. Yet Behn gives the allegory a further twist because the Apollonian knowledge which the narrator and her brother lay the natives open to receiving is not viewed as a higher form of enlightenment but as 'extravagant Religion', 'Notions' and 'Fictions'. Apollo's gift to Marsyas, which is also Marsyas' destruction, his 'Fall' from edenic grace, is the corruption of decayed religion and fanatical political lies. In the 'double narrative' of Behn's design, where the depiction of native Americans invertedly reflects and corresponds to a European context, the Apollo–Marsyas image comments not only upon the future corruption of native peoples, but also upon the past imposition of 'extravagant Religion', 'Notions' and 'Fictions' upon the 'ignorant' and 'simple' people of England. In this reading of the Marsyas myth, the moral debate about music reflects an ideology of degenerative historical decline; the 'Fall' which awaits the natives is the same pollution of dissenting ministries and radical theories which have afflicted England.

The Marsyas myth is not the only mythical trope which Behn employs in her representation of the Surinam natives. Oroonoko expresses a wish to meet the native American war-captains, who, when they appear, give the narrator a fright:

> So frightful a vision it was to see 'em, no Fancy can create; no sad Dreams can represent so dreadful a Spectacle. For my Part, I took 'em for Hobgoblins, or Fiends, rather than Men; But however their Shapes appear'd, their Souls were very humane and noble; but some wanted their Noses, some their Lips, some both Noses and Lips, some their Ears, and others cut through each Cheek, with long slashes, through which their teeth appear'd: They had several other formidable Wounds and Scars, or rather Dismembrings. (p. 187)

The narrator's reaction to the war-captains runs through the gamut of images and associations which also clustered around the Renaissance representation of the savage. Vision is now 'frightful'. They are unrepresentable, beyond fancy and nightmares, they are creatures of hellish myth, monstrous races, demonic essences; the marks of their savagery are inscribed, cut upon their bodies in mutilations and anatomical 'dismemberings'. The narrator records that their bodies were mutilated by themselves as a demonstration of their courage and victory over pain. The war-captains, in contrast to the other natives, recall the distinctions between 'hard' and 'soft' primitives and the attendant opposed tropes of Silvanus and Orcus, the two aspects of the wildman. They open their own bodies as a sign of their savagery.

The narrator, despite her insistence that for all their savage mutilations, their souls are humane and noble, nonetheless represents the 'unrepresentable' savage in the terms of bodily excision and mythical tropes. Oroonoko's response to the war-captains, brief though it is, is immensely instructive for the system of differences which the text elaborates. 'It's by a passive Valour they shew and prove their Activity; a sort of Courage too brutal to be applauded by our Black Hero; nevertheless, he express'd his Esteem of 'em.'[17]

Oroonoko will not applaud their 'brutality', but he understands and esteems its significance and does not reorder the war-captains' self-display into the mythical tropes of an absolute difference, as the narrator does. Native American and European exist at opposite extremes in terms of civility and the natures of their desires and practices; 'our Black Hero' completes the spectrum of racial differences as an intermediary figure.

It is symbolically significant that Behn, in this test of Oroonoko's reactions to the savages, typifies him as black, as if the variety of cultural practices and differences is directly relative to the spectrum of skin colour. Race and culture are implicitly coterminous elements in her tale. For Le Moyne, social function identified savage personas, but for Behn, colour and culture are inseparably intertwined symbols which identify others for the purposes of comparison. Most insistently the comparison is made between the black (African) or 'reddish yellow' (native American) and the reader's white culture. In Behn's emphasis upon sight and upon the play of visualisations, colour is immensely significant in the 'eye-witnessing' which is the primary justification of the novel since colour is not just form, it is content also. Colour – coloured skin – contains cultural practices. The semiotic system of colour–culture renders others not only visible to the eye-witness, but explicable and representable in the shorthand of racial differences.

Colour is significant in another related sense, since colour and culture are intertwined, colour signifies and conditions character and the structure of events in the novel. Men and women act in Behn's text, not as 'personas' or social functions of the savage *polis*, nor out of their own sense of themselves as *substantia individua rationalis*, but as presences determined by their colour–culture. In many respects, Behn substitutes the role-playing character types of the romance for the colour–culture nexus in that there is an inevitability about Behn's plot which descends from visualisations which identify colours with cultures, which determine actions, which shape the text, just as the orders of romance fiction determined the characters' actions.

Behn's text, in structure, content and representation, is profoundly embedded in an emerging and increasingly articulate racism. Behn's text does not espouse a doctrine of racial supremacy or of racial hatred, but the text could not exist without the acceptance of the cultural significance of 'race'. Indeed, the correlatives of colour and culture most evidently engage with the semiotics of race when the novella attempts to present positive images of the '*Black* Hero'. This famous description of Oroonoko, for example, constructs character and identifies culture solely out of the recognition and specification of the visual signs and physiological symbols of racial difference:

> He was pretty tall, but of a Shape the most exact that can be fancy'd: The most famous statuary could not form the Figure of a Man more admirably turn'd from Head to Foot. His face was not of that brown rusty Black which most of that Nation are, but a perfect Ebony, or polished Jet. His Eyes were the most aweful that could be seen, and very piercing; the White of 'em being like Snow, as were his Teeth. His nose was rising and *Roman*, instead of *African* and flat: His Mouth the finest shaped that could be seen; far from those great turn'd Lips, which are so natural to the rest of the Negroes. The whole Proportion and Air of his Face was so nobly and exactly form'd, that bating his Colour, there could be nothing in Nature more beautiful, agreeable and handsome. There was no one Grace wanting, that bears the Standard of true Beauty. His Hair came down to his shoulders, by the Aids of Art, which was by pulling it out with a Quill, and keeping it comb'd; of which he took particular Care. Nor did the Perfections of his Mind come short of those of his Person; for his Discourse was admirable upon almost any Subject: and whoever heard him speak, would have been convinced of their Errors, that all fine Wit is confined to the white Men, especially those of Christendom; and would have confess'd that *Oroonoko* was as capable even of reigning well, and of governing wisely, had as great a Soul, as politick Maxims, and was as sensible of Power, as any Prince civiliz'd in the most refined Schools of Humanity and Learning, or the most illustrious Courts.   (p. 136)

The description delineates Oroonoko against a set of assumptions about black physiology and culture. It is, most certainly, a positive image, but its positive qualities are asserted as the distinguishing features of one individual against a backdrop of negative racial values. Oroonoko's description far from annulling or denying the racial stereotype of black colour–culture operates within and assumes those racist constructions as a valid means of description. Oroonoko's singularity as an extraordinary individual is achieved by reinforcing the degraded nature of the typical.

As the eye wanders over Oroonoko's physique, praising his beauty, gazing at the statuesque modelling of his features in intimate detail, the text replicates the narrator's encounter with the Surinam natives. Oroonoko is subjected to the same scrutiny by the narrator's gaze as the Englishwoman and her maid were subjected to by the curious natives. The narrator comments that:

> He was adorn'd with a native Beauty, so transcending all those of his gloomy Race, that he struck an Awe and Reverence, even into those that know not his Quality; as he did into me, who beheld him with Surprize and Wonder, when afterwards he arrived in our World. (p. 134)

The narrator's 'Surprize and Wonder' mirrors the 'Wonder and Amazement' which she read in the eyes of the admiring savages as they rummaged in her petticoats. Colour–cultural differences, the semiotics of race, are also in this complex relationship of mirrorings and substitutions, articulating an eroticism of gazes. The racial spectrum is superimposed upon by an erotic spectrum: natives 'wonder' at and fondle Europeans; Europeans explore the contours of the African body; the African sexual–racial nature seems by contrast to be intrinsic to itself, hardly participating in this play of touch and sight.

Behn's ethnographic narrative is powerfully engaged with the exploration of racial, cultural and sexual differences and desires in a context of colonial hegemony. The erotic gaze, centred upon the Europeans' unrestrained ability to 'see' the naked bodies of others while their own bodies remain clothed, enunciates the unequal power relations of the Surinam colony which is predicated upon racial difference. Part of Oroonoko's erotic 'wonder' derives from his physical presence as a figure of power and potency, yet however powerful and potent an image is made for him to inhabit, the novella demonstrates how that power is less than the power of those who own him.

Oroonko and Imoinda, Oroonoko's beloved, mark out two further parameters of the text: absolute masculinity and absolute femininity. Imoinda is:

> A Beauty, that to describe her truly, one need say only, she was Female to the noble Male; the beautiful Black *Venus* to our young *Mars*; as charming in her person as he, and of delicate Virtues. I have seen a hundred White Men sighing after her, and making a thousand Vows at her Feet, all in vain and unsuccessful. And she was indeed too great for any but a Prince of her Nation to adore. (p. 137)

Just as all 'wonder' at Oroonoko, all 'adore' Imoinda, who behaves, utterly incongruously given her situation as a slave on a Surinam plantation, like Petrarch's Laura or Sidney's Stella, all 'cold fire', the object of adoration in a lover's sonnet: ' . . . 'tis a Miracle to see, that she who can give such eternal Desires should herself be all Ice and Unconcern'.[18]

'Eye-witnessing', the complex ethnography of gazes, becomes voyeurism and assumes a different context of conventions and representations. Behn resituates her narrative of cultural, racial and sexual differences in another kind of text. Imoinda emerges, not as a violated, dispossessed slave of historical actuality, but as a petrarchan literary trope where author and reader seek refuge in a furtive eroticism.

Her owner, Trefry, comes closer to the actuality of plantation life when he confesses to the narrator that:

> I have, against her Will, entertained her with Love so long, as to be transported with my Passion even above Decency, I have been ready to make Use of those Advantages of Strength and Force Nature has given to me: But Oh! she disarms me with that Modesty and Weeping, so tender and so moving that I retire, and thank my Stars she overcame me. (p. 172)

The narrator, the lusting colonist and the reader are compelled to assume the stance of a petrarchan lover whose advances are rebuffed while the beloved beds down with another man:

> I believe she was not long resisting those Arms where she so longed to be; and having Opportunity, Night, and Silence, Youth, Love and Desire, he [Oroonoko] soon prevail'd, and ravished in a Moment . . . (p. 152)

Behn's description of Imoinda's body also begins in the ethnographic gaze but ends rather differently:

> One may imagine then we paid her a treble Respect: and tho' from her being carved in fine Flowers and Birds all over her Body, we took her to be Quality before, yet when we knew Clemene was Imoinda we could not enough admire her.

> I had forgot to tell you, that those who are nobly born of that Country, are so delicately cut and raised all over the Fore-part of the Trunk of their Bodies, that it looks as if it were japan'd, the works being raised like high Point round the Edges of the Flowers. Some are only carved with a little Flower, or Bird, at the Sides of the Temples, as was *Caesar* [Oroonoko's slave name]; and those who are so carved over the Body, resemble our antient Picts that are figured in the Chronicles, but these *Carvings* are more delicate.   (p. 174)

Within the ethnographic range of the novella, the only image comparable to Imoinda's 'carved' torso is the native war-captains' mutilations. But although this is of a similar kind, Behn transforms the image from 'so dreadful a Spectacle' into one of 'delicacy'. Imoinda is compared to an ornate object, a cabinet or table, which might adorn a fashionable drawing room ('japan'd'), or as embroidery or lace-work ('high Point'). Or, most tellingly, Imoinda is compared to the illustrations in the 'Chronicles' in a direct reference to Theodore De Bry's *America* (part I, 1591) which contained an engraving of Jacques Le Moyne's miniature watercolour 'A Young Daughter of the Picts' (figure 13). The engraving depicts a young naked girl painted with flowers in a sylvan landscape containing a large dwelling. The image gains an emblematic status in De Bry's text on the Virginia colony although it is an anomalous, beautiful object. It purports to represent ancient British peoples yet the flowers which decorate the girl's body were recent discoveries from America and Asia Minor (garden tulip, the marvel of Peru, the mourning iris).[19] Behn alludes to the figure for the same reason that De Bry includes it in his text on America: native Americans and Africans are viewed as if they were the ancient Picts. The other is accommodated within a representational frame which enables recognition by affirming cultural and historical difference.

Behn softens the presence of Imoinda's body. Her erotic strangeness, sensuous and patterned, is domesticated; her exotic and erotic threat is redefined as virginal purity. Imoinda's presence is one of heightened sexual excitement transformed in the process of Behn's narrative into the chaste image of petrarchan poets and artists. Behn's text transforms Imoinda's cultural and sexual difference into the model of European artistic production. There is no contradiction, for Behn, between 'reality' and 'invention'; art structures ethnography into inspectable, recognisable form as a petrarchan figure or chronicle icon. As the text unfolds, her role is increasingly redefined – away from cultural strangeness and eroticism to a repository

13 Jacques Le Moyne de Morgues, 'A Young Daughter of the Picts', 1591

of honour, virtue and the chaste marriage. She adopts the status, not of the exotically unfamiliar, but of an archetypal heroine of romance whose virtue is assailed but unbroken. The text turns repeatedly upon the prospect of Imoinda's possible violation: 'Perhaps,' Oroonoko thinks, imagining a scenario reminiscent of the assault on Serena in *The Faerie Queene*, 'she may be first ravish'd by every Brute; expos'd first to their nasty Lusts, and then a shameful Death.'[20] It is this possibility which leads Oroonoko finally to resolve to kill her himself:

> He, with a hand resolved, and a Heart-breaking within, gave the fatal Stroke, first cutting her Throat, and then severing her yet smiling Face from that delicate Body, pregnant as it was with the Fruits of Tenderest Love. As soon as he had done, he laid the Body decently on Leaves and Flowers, of which he made a Bed and conceal'd it under the same Cover-lid of nature; only her Face he left yet bare to look on. (p. 203)

As seventeenth-century literary deaths go, this is unique. There are precedents, of course, in Titian and Le Moyne, and in Behn's own text, in the war-captains' physical mutilations and in Imoinda's own decorative bodily 'carvings', but these are accommodated in the symbolic and artistic criteria the text establishes. The shockingness of this image seems to relate, again, more to the fantastical episodes of romance; to the assault on Parthenia by Demogorus in Sidney's *New Arcadia* (I, 5) and Quarles' *Argolus and Parthenia*. (But although Parthenia's face is horribly disfigured the effect is temporary and she survives.) The ghastly uniqueness of Imoinda's death derives from Behn's combining opposed strands of imagery: romance emblems of heroic love, the petrarchan symbolism of the beloved and the chronicle icon, and the explicit sight of the mutilated body of the mythical creature and the savage. 'Eye-witnessing', the viewer viewing Oroonoko gazing upon the severed, but 'still smiling' fleshy mask of his beloved, forces together the two elements of Behn's textual strategy of 'reality' and 'invention'.

Yet Behn runs enormous risks in the literary strategy she adopts. The Le Moyne prints gained their power from the radical alternation of the *duplex* imagery from which flowed statements about the propriety of the European presence, the nature of the experience of the alien *polis*, and the European political and religious contexts which frame them. They have a startling, if divided, clarity of purpose. Behn's infiltration of what was juxtaposed in the prints conceals the historical and ethnographic conditions of Surinam in 1663 behind the mask of romance registers.

Oroonoko's killing of Imoinda is explained *away* by the romance contextualisation of the event. Behn disguises male violence as 'honour' or Othello-like 'greatness of soul' by her adherence to the elevated values of the codes of noble conduct with which she has coloured Oroonoko's portrait. Similarly, the African's 'esteem' for the native American's barbaric courage seems to presage his own capacity for racially determined acts of violence fulfilled in his killing Imoinda. Most pertinently, however, Behn shows a murder of a black woman by a black man, when in colonial Surinam killings of black men and women were habitually committed by white men and women. Imoinda's death may be unique in literary representation but it was far from unique in the Surinam slave colony. Events such as this, and worse, were an everyday event, a historical fact of life for slave women. Ethnography rewritten as romance displaces the sociology and history of slavery by an adherence to the values of aristocratic virtues. Such displacements project the culpability for acts of brutality onto the black victims of colonial violence rather than the white colonists, underpinning the deception by the appeal to the inherent violence of racially determined 'ethnographic' subjects. Behn's ethnography reconstructed as romance depicts its characters as essential types, symbols of the variety of 'natural' man. In 'seeing' native American or African primitives, ethnographic romance becomes blind to its ethnographic subjects as being, also, colonial subjects. The primitive world, thus constructed around the moral universe of romance typologies, is filled with symbolic power but a power which is a transformation of other forms of power. Political, economic and imperial power is transfigured, misrecognised and legitimated by ethnographic romance.

Yet Behn's text also makes a symptomatic reading possible. Her novella also contains elements which go against the grain of the transfiguring action of romance, calling into question the colonial misrecognition of the slave as a romance figure. This is achieved, paradoxically, by the text's reference to the very values enshrined in romance. Oroonoko, for example, in the descriptive portrait, is likened to classical statuary and repeatedly linked to classical references. 'His nose was rising and Roman instead of African and flat.' His slave name is Caesar and 'he wanted no Part of the personal courage of that *Caesar*, and acted Things as memorable'.

The insistent classical references of the text invite further comparisons between ancient and modern empires. Compare, for example, this Roman African's commemorative inscription with Oroonoko/Caesar's biography:

> To Quintus Lollius Urbicus, son of Marcus, of the tribe Quirina, consul, legate of Augustus for the province of Lower Germany, *fetial* [priest], legate of the Emperor Hadrian in the campaign in Judea, in which he was presented with the spear of honour and a golden crown, legate of the 10th Legion *Gemina*, praetor as Caesar's candidate, tribune of the *plebs* as Caesar's candidate, legate of the proconsul of Asia, urban quaestor, tribune with the broad stripe of the 22nd Legion *Primigenia*, member of the Commission of Four for the maintenance of roads, patron [of Tiddis], by decree of the town councillors [*decurions*] at the public expense.[21]

Quintus Lollius would, of course, have been utterly unknown to Behn and her contemporaries, but the contrast of Quintus Lollius' career with Oroonoko's illustrates an insistent theme in Behn's text. The Roman African of antiquity finds a glorious place in the conduct of the empire; the 'Roman' African of modernity cuts sugar cane. Africans, like Europeans, are also fallen men, desiring subjects whose vision is refracted and distorted by the compulsion to see and be seen through the reflected light of 'curiosity'. Only the native Americans are beyond/before desire; only they can 'see'. Behn's constant resort to the images of classical imperialism articulates the degenerative historical model which informs her writing. Modern empires waste the talents and nobility of their subjects; contemporary neoclassicism and Augustanism is a hollow and brutal diminution of imperial Rome.

It is through the evocation of ancient empires and superior ages of praetorian nobility and honour, therefore, that Behn elaborates a reactionary critique of modern colonialism. Behn's *Oroonoko* attempted to reimpose the romance codes and all that they signified in terms of a moral and symbolic universe of didactic, aristocratic and imperial ideals upon a historical situation of contemporary colonialism and slave-owning states which denied such representations. Colonial authority in Surinam is in the hands of 'notorious Villains' who 'understood neither the Laws of God nor Man, and had no principles to make them worthy of the Name of Men'.[22] The colony is remote and isolated. The empire lacks a centre; in many ways it lacks an emperor who, in antiquity, overwhelmed the parochial tendencies of the colonies. Such an imperial model would be unworkable in the modern world of factions, 'extravagant Religion', 'Notions' and 'Fictions'. The modern empire which the example of

Surinam represents is one of materialist accumulation and ecological plunder. Surinam is a warehouse of bourgeois commodities.[23]

Only Oroonoko/Caesar represents the true aristocratic, romance values of honour and valour appropriate to that other, ancient vision of the empire. For some critics, *Oroonoko* is Behn's elegy to Charles I, since the same powers of bourgeois acquisitiveness which destroyed Oroonoko also destroyed Charles:[24]

> He desir'd they would give him a Pipe in his Mouth, ready lighted; which they did: And the Executioner came, and first cut off his members, and threw them into the Fire; after that, with an ill-favour'd Knife, they cut off his Ears and his Nose, and burn'd them; he still smoak'd on, as if nothing has touched him; then they hacked off one of his Arms, and still he bore up and held his Pipe; but at the cutting off of his other Arm, his Head sunk, and his pipe dropt, and he gave up the Ghost, without a Groan or a Reproach ... They cut Caesar into Quarters and sent them to several of the chief plantations: One Quarter was sent to Colonel Martin who refus'd it, and swore, he had rather seen the Quarters of *Bannister*, and the Governor himself, than those of *Caesar*, on his Plantations; and that he could govern his negroes, without terrifying and grieving them with frightful Spectacles of a mangled King.   (p. 208)

Certainly this execution scene, the last image of the text, which again combines the Le Moyne *duplex* of heroic romance values and savage butchery, ends with a plangent symbol of a murdered king. Ethnographic romance ends in a radical critique of modern imperialism and the image of the savage body in torment. Yet the romance values Behn espouses and her heroic and symbolic figures belonged more to the masque spectacles of a Renaissance court than to the pragmatic era of the bourgeois revolution and the subsequent Whig supremacy.[25]

The period between Behn's ethnographic romance and my second major Surinam text, written one hundred years later, is characterised by a proliferation of data about non-European peoples embraced with an interpretative zeal, as Shaftesbury was to complain:

> [B]arbarian customs, savage manners, indian wars and wonders of the *terra incognita*, employ our leisure hours and are the chief materials to furnish out a library. These are in our present days what books of chivalry were in those of our forefathers.[26]

Shaftesbury acknowledges the eclipse of the romance by the contemporary passion for a different kind of cultural representation: the construction of narratives out of conjectural histories, racial theories, and classificatory systems rather than the ancient orders of romance. Yet from an English colonial point of view, Behn described a world which had already passed, in that part of the globe at least. English imperial ambitions had been thwarted and abandoned and Behn looked back on a lost world over an intervening period of twenty-five years. The pre-lapsarian native Americans were defiled by modernity, Oroonoko was executed, Surinam surrendered to the Dutch, the Roman imperial past has expired. The images, narrative and language of romance struggle to describe the conditions in Surinam, always aware that the harsh brutalities of the colonial regime challenge and deny romance's moral orders and attempted figural transformations. As the romance patterns begin to break down, a new system of differences is articulated in Behn's novella, where erotic, economic and imperial themes are subjected to the new 'rigours' of cultural and racial classification and subjugation. Traces of ethnographic romance and its attendant imagery of monstrous races, satyrs, wildmen and the beautifully eloquent Marsyas persist, but these images are fading from the 'reality' of the colonial regime.

*

> Stedman, your gentle melancholy Art
> Distills the Loyal chaos of your heart,
> Weeps over the victims of a barb'rous Age,
> But distances to Elegance, Outrage;
> You could not murder Style to match their Life;
> You saw not Slaves but Men and a dear Wife.
>
> Landeg White[27]

John Gabriel Stedman was born at Dendermonde in Holland in 1744. His father was an officer in the Scots Brigade, as later was Stedman, a regiment of mercenary troops established in the sixteenth century for the protection of the Protestant Netherlands. There was a great deal of work for his father to do during the incessant European wars which tore across the Low Countries during the middle decades of the century. Stedman adored his father and often accompanied him on his furloughs. Such holiday trips invariably involved a visit to some past battlefield or other, indeed one of Stedman's earliest memories is of an excursion to Fontenoy where a battle had been fought five years earlier and where his father had picked up 'a strong human jaw-bone with fine teeth'. His father declared that it belonged to an English soldier and kept it out of 'partiality for the English Nation'.[28] When his father died in 1770, Stedman inherited the relic and little else. Quarrels with his peevish mother and uncaring brother had denied him what little was due to him from his father's estate. But a soldier's jawbone seemed a fitting legacy to Stedman.

By the time of his father's death, John Stedman's life had been filled with such images of mortality. He attended public executions frequently ('This morning I saw twenty people hanged'),[29] and on a brief and unhappy visit to Scotland as a child, to further his education but also to put him out of the reach of his mother, he shared his lodgings with a small open closet containing the 'skull, ribs, arms, legs etc., of a man who had been hanged' and 'which my uncle had begun with wire to joyn, intending to make a moving skeleton'.[30] In 1772, impoverished, despised by his family and impatient for adventure, John Stedman took up a commission with Fourgeoud's corps bound for Surinam. At twenty-eight he was the oldest officer in the company except for Fourgeoud. However grim the experiences of the first three decades of his life had been they proved to be a good training for what he discovered in Surinam.

Stedman produced two texts which record his life and his Surinam experiences. In 1796, the year before he died, he produced a handsome two-volume work, with engravings taken from his own sketches by William Blake, Bartoluzzi and others, entitled *A Narrative of a five years expedition against the revolted negroes, in Surinam, Guiana, on the wild coast of South America, from the year 1772–1777, elucidating the history of that country, and describing its productions, viz: quadrupeds, birds, fishes, reptiles, trees, shrubs, fruits and roots, with an account of the Indians of Guiana, and negroes of Guiana* (referred to hereafter as *A Narrative*). The other text, unpublished until 1962, has been given a more restrained title by its editor, *The Journal of John Gabriel Stedman 1744–1797: Soldier and Author* (hereafter *The Journal*) although Stedman called it *The Progress of Modern Ambition or Outlines of a Military Life (being a genuine narrative founded on facts)*. Stedman's two texts, one public, the other private, nonetheless respond to each other: *The Journal* is the sourcework for *A Narrative*. *The Journal* is the almost daily-recorded actions and thoughts of an eighteenth-century soldier, its pages are crowded with his opinions, hopes, resentments, hatreds. It records his eating habits, his health, the progress of his paltry exchequer, his sexual exploits, his duels and quarrels, his journeys and his obscenities. *A Narrative* is both a diminution and a reordering of this vast chaotic autobiography. The existence of *The Journal* gives another and often contradictory dimension to 'eye-witnessing': 'participant observation' is split between the private and public functions of the two texts. Two 'realities' exist in the two texts.[31]

The different natures of the two texts can be seen from the prefaced 'apologies' of each work. *A Narrative* pleads, Behn-like, for its acceptance as an authentic text: 'However trifling, and like the style of romance, this relation may appear to some, it is nevertheless a genuine account, and on that score I flatter myself may not entirely be uninteresting to others.'[32]

Stedman is a model of decorum and humility. The apology begs for acceptance of the authenticity of the text in spite, almost, of itself. It is 'genuine' non-fiction even if it appears fictional. The guarantor of that authenticity is, again, the experiencing authorial self. *The Journal* begins very differently: 'D-mn spelling, d-mn writing, and d-mn everything overdone. I am above you all, and which trifles I will leave, to be corrected by Samuel Johnson, while native genius, naked truth, and simple nature, without disguise or artifice, are throughout this journal, to be the guides of my untutored pen.'[33]

There is, of course, the same appeal to the authenticity of the experiences described, guaranteed by the authorial self. But the authorial self is wholly changed from the decorous apologist to the strident common man, 'untutored' but possessing 'native genius, naked truth, and simple nature'. The effect of the two apologies is, in many respects, similar to the two introductions to *The Unfortunate Traveller*, where Jack Wilton's picaresque tale is rendered sceptically uncertain by the textual doubleness of his persona. Stedman's two texts similarly introduce a picaresque model, not merely in the nature of their subject-matters (travels), but in the transgressive figure of the 'damning' author, split between the writer of *A Narrative* and the more explosive self of *The Journal*. If both accounts are 'genuine' then authenticity is an experience relative to each of these different voices and they record an, at least, double 'reality'.

There are other, more direct connections between Jack Wilton and the author of *The Journal*. *A Narrative* apologises that the work is like a romance, although it never specifies what that might mean. *The Journal* makes it clear. Filled with delight and admiration for the modern novel, Stedman throws 'aside Plutarch's *Lives*, Flavius Josephus, *Spectator* etc., I read romance, setting out with *Joseph Andrews*, *Tom Jones*, and *Roderick Random* which heroes I resolved for my models from this date.'[34]

For Behn, the romance would have conjured Spenser and Sidney and the Latin writers of the Caroline court; she would have described Stedman's preferred models as 'picaresque'. For Stedman and a late eighteenth-century readership, romance is redefined as the adventures of the rakish dashing blade let loose on a tempestuous world of sinful urban pleasures. Literary history had accomplished an inversion worthy of Jack Wilton himself.

Stedman, nicknamed 'Desperate Jack' by his fellow officers, was a 'spendthrift' of his meagre income from the Scots Brigade, 'an incessant drinker', a gambler and 'a lover of no mean character'.[35] *The Journal* records his exploits with a bravado and, often, an explicitness:

> I had a *Je ne se que* about me, of the fascinating kind, which attracted the girls as the eyes of the rattlesnake attracts squirrels, and unaccountably persuaded them to submission. I had besides a gaiety about me, and even made them hear me in the night-time; when the sweet creatures lay sighing and twisting in their pillows   (p. 107)

Stedman was, if he is to be credited, 'much beloved of the girls', but, as he writes, 'of a certain sort, not the best of them'.[36] He falls in love with Narcissa but she is unattainable; he falls out of love with Narcissa, and into love with Cornelia Cornel, a seaman's daughter 'whose breath was like violets', but 'abominates to debauch her' and fights a bulldog in her presence instead 'to give proof of my courage'.[37] He goes absent without leave to Amsterdam where the picaresque riots of Desperate Jack are carried to carnivalesque heights:

> I sleeped in a bawdy-house, in the *Kermesse Haagh* where I met a poor Englishman dying with the p-x. I saw the *Stadthouse*, the *Exchange*, and the wild beasts at *Blauwjan* etc., then left the town of Amsterdam, whose canals are abominably stinking, and escorted the wh-res, like a wild man, to Rotterdam, to which place they are sent, with whole waggon fulls, to remain during the week at the fair at Rotterdam. I wore a sailor's dress, play'd the devil in the *Spielhuysen*, and drew my knife on two officers ... kept dancing, drinking etc., etc., till the last day of Rotterdam *kermis*.   (*The Journal*, p. 83)

> Another time, Fritz [Wagrel, Stedman's companion] introduced a gang of us to a *bawdy-house*, where, shocking to relate, made her appearance, a wretch just at the down-lying. Such brutality I detested, and in place of allowing such a creature to be

prostituted, I made a contribution for her in my hat, with which, and my good advice, she got leave to decamp out of the way without being touched by one in the company. I have seen a mother take the bed-cloaths from her dying daughter, spread them on the floor, and prostitute herself in her presence. We have often had one mistress between us, particularly at the Craan-port guard, when Fritz and I stood sentinel by turns. Tables and chairs have often been broke by our manoeuvres in such sad places; as not a bed or mattress could be met with. I have seen this Wagrel pick up a ragged tatterdemalion from the soldiers, and cohabit with her on a publick country road.

(*The Journal*, p. 70)

For all Stedman's effort to live up to his nickname, however, 'Desperate Jack' does not seem to have been either much liked or trusted by his fellows: '*Milord*, my dog, was my next greatest resource, I not caring a damn for any officer in the regiment at this time, who indeed cared as little for me since I was continually drunk or in one dog scrape or other; being exceedingly vicious in my *cups*.'[38]

Clearly, much of Stedman's account of Desperate Jack's exploits is shaped and influenced by his reading of the picaresque/romance. The episode, for example, where Gauteman's servant girl 'rapes' Stedman and then mistakes her master for Jack when she attempts it again is worthy of Fielding. But *The Journal* also combines with its picaresque/romance aspirations a steely and unremitting tone and a remarkable factual clarity. The entries record few, if any, moralisings; just a relentless documentation of a culture in moral crisis. The early years of *The Journal* describe with intimate and often painfully self-aware honesty the detailed lives of the military; its features are humour and some generosity, but above all a sense that European culture is fragmenting into chaos, displayed by its constant wars, its sexual predations and its violent obsessions. It is this riven culture, exported to South America, which Stedman is sent to protect from the 'revolted negroes' of Surinam.

Since the writing of *Oroonoko*, the Dutch in Surinam had acquired the reputation of being the cruellest slave-owners in the Americas. The whites had domestic jurisdiction over their black slaves and were permitted to perform any act of punishment except mutilation and the death penalty, and even in those cases charges against a slave owner were dropped on the payment of a small fine. No slave was permitted to bear witness against a white person; the only status a slave had before the law and the only time the law recognised his/her existence, was as a felon.[39]

The Dutch took their slaves opportunistically, from Cape Verde to Angola, and as a result, the slave population was heterogeneous with few common cultural or linguistic bonds. Even so, runaway slaves formed cohesive groups in the Surinam interior and although there was never a single general slave rebellion, these 'tribes', the Owca and Sarameca, were a sufficient thorn in the side of the colonial government to merit peace treaties in 1749, 1760 and 1762. Finally, in 1772, the Dutch government sent Fourgeoud's troops to secure the colony from further harassment.[40]

Fourgeoud's ships dropped anchor in Surinam after an uneventful voyage to a sight which *A Narrative* describes in elysian terms:

> Our ships' crews now were in the highest flow of spirits, seeing themselves surrounded by the most delightful verdure, while the river seemed alive by the many boats and barges passing and re-passing to see us, while groups of naked boys and girls were promiscuously playing and flouncing, like so many *Tritons* and *Mermaids*, in the water ... Nothing could equal the delicious sensations with which we seemed intoxicated by the fragrance of the lemons, limes, oranges, and flowers, wafted over from the adjoining plantations.   (pp. 11–12)

Gilded tent boats, with flags flying and musicians playing, plied the rivers and harbours of Paramaribo, the colony's capital (renamed by the Dutch after the English were evicted from Parham). Stedman's description is all sights and smells of delight as Surinam assaults his senses. But the keyword in his description is 'seemed'; the text alerts the reader to a deception which will be unravelled as the 'seeming' beauty of Surinam is uncloaked.

Stedman is billeted at the house of a plantation owner, Lolkens, who is away from town inspecting his plantations, and there he has his first close encounter with a slave. *A Narrative* records that he is greeted by a 'mulatto' girl whose pidgin he cannot comprehend. She wears nothing but a thin petticoat. She feeds him and he drinks a bottle of Madeira. He then gestures that he wishes to sleep whereupon she gives him an 'ardent kiss' and proceeds to accompany him to bed. Stedman is 'heartily provoked at this unexpected and (from one of her colour) unwelcome salutation' and retires alone having extricated himself from her embrace.[41] But *The Journal* records another version of Stedman's first encounter on Surinam soil: one which is more reminiscent of 'Desperate Jack' than Captain Stedman. 'I got fuddled at a tavern. Go to sleep at Mr Lolkens, who was in the country. I – one of his negro maids.'[42] Captain Stedman censors 'Desperate Jack's' graphically blunt ellipsis. Stedman is struggling to fashion an identity for his narrator of *A Narrative* which is different from that of *The Journal*. Although this identity is falsified and untrue, Captain Stedman must be seen to be exceptional: a moral voice in a colony filled with 'Desperate Jacks'. The whole nature of Captain Stedman's representation of Surinam depends upon that sense of difference: difference from his other, *Journal* identity and from the other white colonists. That difference is first identified in the descriptions of the sexual mores of the colonists.

Surinam is, according to Captain Stedman, a cesspit of perverse sexual practices which the slave women are forced to endure at the hands of the white colonists. 'The Tropical ladies' as he calls the white women, are 'like mosquitoes' in having 'an instinctive preference for a newly-landed European'.[43] Surinam is a world-upside-down where women ('Amazons') fight duels for the sexual favours of men.

> Dissipation and luxury appear to be congenial to the inhabitants of this climate ... [the men] appear withered and enervated in the extreme, nor do the Creole females exhibit a more alluring appearance; they are languid, their complexions are sallow, and the skin even of the young ladies is frequently shrivelled. (*A Narrative*, p. 18)

The men die early of sexual exhaustion; they never survive their second marriage, whereas it is quite common to find a woman on her fourth or fifth husband.

Stedman's Surinam is a state where Mandeville's pleasure principle has been transformed by hedonism into the violence of luxury.[44] Stedman carefully documents a society where the pursuit of sexual gratification is enmeshed with slave ownership and violence. At Goed Accord plantation the dinner guests were waited on by 'young negro women ... all stark naked'.[45] A jealous white woman murdered a young 'mulatto' girl by inserting a hot iron into her vagina because her husband slept with her too often. Miss Spaan, the daughter of a plantation owner, had a 'negro woman whipped most barbarously' over the breasts 'and nowhere else'. Miss Spaan 'seemed to enjoy a peculiar satisfaction'.[46]

Both *A Narrative* and *The Journal* record the daily sufferings of the black population. Whippings and executions are a constant spectacle: Mrs Stoner drowns a baby with her own hand for crying; a slave is forced to jump into a vat of boiling sugar; a woman is given two hundred lashes and a chain of 'several yards in length' is attached to her ankle and to a weight which she is forced to drag around behind her; a man is hanged from a hook through his ribs; slaves are pulled apart by horses; men are 'broken' with iron bars; women are slow roasted; a slave girl who was eight months pregnant was whipped until her 'intestines appeared' for 'breaking a tumbler'; at one execution eleven people were killed, one hanged from the gibbet with an iron hook through his ribs, two chained to stakes and slow roasted, six women were broken alive on the rack, and two girls were beheaded; a 'poor half-starved mulatto woman' is stripped naked and whipped until no skin is left on her thighs and legs. The daily toll grows, reflecting the hideous incongruity of colonial life:

> During my absence three negroes were hang'd on the boat and two whipt below the gallows. On the eighth, being the Prince of Orange, his birthday, Col. Fourgeoud gave a genteel supper and ball to the ladies and gentlemen, *la salle de danse* [was in the] officers' guardroom. (*The Journal*, p. 122)

> Nothing happened worth mentioning except the cruelty; of which Mr Matthew and Vischer took pleasure, of letting a cook, with his throat half cut, cripple up and down the post, to excite the laughter of the other beasts. (*The Journal*, p. 192)

> The Colony of Surinam ... is reeking and dyed with the blood of the African Negroes. (*A Narrative*, p. xvii)

Behn's description of the execution of Oroonoko recorded many of the same details: the same recognitions that the black body is the object of the white gaze, to be fucked or flogged, but the differences are immense. Behn's Oroonoko achieved the status of a symbolic enunciation which Stedman's figures can never do. There is no textual form, no narration which can 'account' for, render, or make eloquent these figures in the same way. Stedman's point of reference is neither the romance nor the Renaissance images of martyrdom, but another kind of text which is, as yet, unwritten: Conrad's *Heart of Darkness*.

After 1771 and yet another peace treaty with the escaped slaves, a new threat emerged from another group. The rebels under the leadership of three men, Bonni, Joli Coeur and Baron, were encamped around the Cottica River. One Lieutenant Lepper was ordered to take a party of men to investigate and probe the Cottica rebels' settlements. When he did not return a larger expedition was launched and Stedman was sent in a gunboat up the Cottica to safeguard an important branch in the river. The force made contact with Bonni's rebels and drove them from their homes, destroying their rice fields, where they discovered the heads of Lepper and six of his men, mouldering on stakes.[47] A revenge attack on the rebels followed and Stedman witnessed the colony's soldiers playing bowls with the heads of the executed captives. Most of the rebels escaped further into the forests and Stedman was ordered to resume his station on his gunboat on the Cottica.

Stedman and his company of fifty-four soldiers and an assortment of slaves sat for months on their gunboat at Casseepore Creek. 'The sick groan, the negroes beg, the Jew prays, the soldiers swear, the child cries, the mother sings, the fire smokes, the rain beats, and the whole stinks confounded.'[48] Prone to sickness, the bites of vampire bats and the taunts of the rebels who called out after one battle that the soldiers were to be pitied more than they since they were 'white slaves',[49] Stedman barely held his corps together. Fourgeoud let it be known amongst the soldiers that he had sent to Holland for a hangman and would hang any who disobeyed him.[50] The whole military adventure threatened to collapse or end in mutiny. During this period, Fourgeoud's troops were dying at the rate of six or seven men each day, with very little to show in terms of victories over the rebels. Eventually the whole escapade simply petered out, as the rebels either moved on from Cottica or adopted more pacific behaviour. Stedman's company was recalled to Paramaribo; only nine of the original fifty-four had survived, most killed by disease. Stedman estimated that of the twelve hundred Dutch troops sent out to Surinam with Fourgeoud in 1772, only a hundred returned to Holland in 1777.[51]

Surinam and the months on the Cottica had an extraordinary effect on the narrative voice of *A Narrative*. 'Desperate Jack' was partly exorcised from Stedman. In later life he would reflect upon his past personas.

> What is remarkable is, that in all places, I have been beloved by the inhabitants, when known, but at first called mad, in Scotland, hated in England, ... [called] *gek* or *dol* by the Dutch, and *laws* by the negroes in Surinam, owing entirely to my studying to be singular, in as much as can be so.   (*The Journal*, p. 269)

Stedman recoils from the Jack Wilton figure who whored, fought and visited executions because he witnessed in Surinam exactly what the 'wildman' of the Rotterdam *kermis* does in the carnival of colonisation. If the hideous reality of Surinam is not to cause his text to collapse into the nihilistic despair of a precursory *Heart of Darkness* then the 'singular' figure of *The Journal*, Stedman's 'identity' created out of his version of 'romance/picaresque', must be made in *A Narrative* to give way to other narrations which could effectively validate and structure the experience. The self-fashioned voices of *A Narrative* proliferate, pushing 'Desperate Jack' to the margins; other forms of narrative compel meanings out of the meaninglessness of colonial Surinam.

For Stedman, the native peoples of Surinam represented an anti-dote to the violence of the Cottica and colonial Paramaribo. He inserts into his history of the wars between black and white a description of the 'copper-coloured' natives who are outside conflict.

> Happy people I call them still, whose peace and genuine morals have not been contaminated with European vices; and whose errors are only the errors of ignorance, and not the rooted depravity of a pretended civilisation, and a spurious and mock Christianity ... For my part I must say, with Socrates, that this kind of poverty is alone the truest felt of riches; as those who want least approach nearest to the gods, who want nothing. (*A Narrative*, p. 206–7)

Stedman makes his 'Socratic' natives an untouched culture in a state of primal purity. Outside the colonial war and the horrors of Paramaribo, they, like Behn's natives, are free from history and desire. Yet these 'happiest creatures under the sun' are not, as in Behn, an undifferentiated mass of humanity, because Stedman proceeds to name and distinguish their tribes. The 'Accawaus' (Ackawai, a Carib people) are 'few in number', are distant from European settlements and are 'treacherous', 'distrustful' and given a repu-tation as accomplished 'poisoners'. The 'Worrows' (Warraws) are 'cruel and dispicable', 'dark coloured and extremely ugly', 'strong but pusillanimous', 'lazy and indolent', they go about naked and 'stinkingly dirty'. The 'Taiiras' (another Carib people) are numerous and 'peaceable' but very 'indolent'. The 'Piannacotaus' (Pianakoto) live far inland and are irreconcilable enemies to all Europeans and 'would murder all the Christians in Guiana if they had an oppor-tunity'. The 'Caribbees' (Caribs) fare somewhat better in Stedman's identifications, but even they carry an enormous stigma; the ancient curse of Deuteronomy:[52]

> Among all the indian nations, the Caribs are the most numer-ous, active and brave. These reside in great numbers near the Spanish settlements, which they often harass, in immortal revenge for the inhuman cruelties inflicted on their forefathers at Mexico and Peru ... [B]ut what disgraces them above all others in Terra Firmis is, that however unnatural it may seem,

and however much it is has been contradicted, they are anthro-
pophagi, or cannibals; at least they most certainly feast on their
enemies, whose flesh they tear and devour with the avidity of
wolves, though this is generally supposed to be more from a
spirit of revenge than from depravity in their taste.

(*A Narrative*, p. 218)

Stedman gives the Caribs a spurious historical justification, that of
'immortal revenge', before he revivifies the myths of Carib cannibalism. Of the six native cultures he (often erroneously) identifies, only
one exhibits any of the socratic qualities he applied to them all. His
ethnographic sketches begin in ecstatic praise but end, in the process
of articulating their differences, in qualification, except in the case of
the 'Arrowouks [Arawaks], my favourites':

> [H]appy people, who with the distinctions of rank or land (the
> causes of contention in more enlightened states) are unac-
> quainted; who know no evil but pain and want, with which
> they are very seldom afflicted in this ever-verdant, this ever-
> blooming climate; who while their wishes are so very limited,
> possess all that they desire in this world: and thus, while they
> expect a future state, never give their minds the smallest unea-
> siness, but die in peace; nay who seldom think upon tomorrow.
> (*A Narrative*, p. 219)

Stedman recalls the Abbé Reynal when he observes that 'happiness is more frequently found in a pure state of nature, than in that
of the most refined civilisation'.[53] The 'Arrowouks' live in a condition
of 'negative happiness',[54] a state of unawareness of desire, they are
ignorant of a division of labour or the accumulative acquisitiveness
of European modernity: the living embodiment of Pufendorf's and
Rousseau's speculative natural man.

Stedman's cultural identifications attempt to lend an air of categorical certainty to his representations. By thus distinguishing the
peoples of South America he vastly extends the crude colour–culture
typologies of Aphra Behn with sophisticated categorical distinctions.
Yet these are of a largely spurious nature, since many of the peoples
he distinguishes were in fact of the same linguistic and cultural
groups. The favoured 'Arrowouks' are a case in point since they
belonged to the much wider cultural orbit which extended
throughout the Caribbean and Guianas. As 'Arrowouks' this larger
group is not only fragmented into smaller units split off from its
wider area of influence, in effect already placed in reservations, but
the wider connotations of that history – their enslavement and near

extinction by the colonists – is ignored and falsified. Written as 'Arrowouks' they are a self-contained, separate and ahistorical 'natural' society when in reality they were a people whose history had reached a stage of terminal devastation.

Once wrenched from their historical context, the natives are reconstructed in ethnographic textual form replete with cross-cultural allusions to the mythologies of European representations. They fight their wars by night, scalp male prisoners, bringing home their war trophies of limbs and bones just as the Timacuas did. 'The best archers at Cressy, Poictiers and Agincourt, must have yielded to their superiority', Stedman writes.[55] Most natives die of old age and are buried naked in a cotton bag. One year later the body is exhumed and the bones distributed among the relatives in a 'practice [which] bears some affinity to Dr Smollett's description of a burial in the Highlands of Scotland'.[56] The women are married at twelve and deliver their children without apparent pain as 'they seem to be exempt from the curse of Eve'.[57] The native females are 'naturally disagreeable in their shapes', a situation not helped much by their addiction to flattening their foreheads 'like Choctaws', binding their knees and ankles into swollen shapes and cutting holes in their ears and lips. They paint their bodies and hair to look like 'a boiled lobster' and, recollecting the image of Pict/Virginia/Imoinda, 'they make figures on their faces and all over their bodies, resembling hieroglyphicks'.[58] The natives are by tradition polygamous but rarely take more than one wife; they never beat their children nor educate them in anything but hunting; they never use abusive language; their language resembles Italian in pronunciation; they have no calculation of time; their 'government' is a gerontocracy by elders called *Pen*.

Stedman's description is a heterogeneous amalgamation of information lent a structure by the myths of European represen-tation. 'Arrowouks', for example, are 'extremely sociable people' and sociability is reinforced by dances which consist of 'stamping on the ground, balancing on one foot, and staggering round in different attitudes for many hours, as if intoxicated'.[59] All of this is done in a perfectly Vitruvian sylvan scene to the incessant rhythm of Marsyan 'rude musicke', the sound of the *too-too* which Stedman compares to the 'lowing of an ox', and to the 'warbling of clear but discordant sounds' of the *quarta* called 'by Ovid a *sirinx*, by some poets *Pan's chaunter*'. 'Nor have I seen a better representation of the god Pan playing on his chaunter than a naked indian among the verdant foliage playing upon one of those reedy pipes.'[60]

In their rather different ways, both Behn and Stedman ultimately arrive at this similar terminus of containing the native in the conventions of representation, and the language of ethnography 'slips' into the familiar *bricolage* of myths. However, Stedman extends his thirst for categorisation of human types from the native peoples he encounters to the colonial situation. The 'national character' of the Africans in Surinam, Stedman generalises, is 'as in Africa':

> perfectly savage; the twenty thousand Ouca and Seramica free negroes have lived separately and under no control of Europeans, for a number of years, and yet I have never seen any marks of civilisation, order or government among them, but, on the contrary, many examples of ungovernable passion, debauchery, and indolence. (*A Narrative*, p. 112)

Savagery and the lack of 'marks of civilisation' are radically redefined here. The same features which constituted the natives' claim to 'negative happiness' and their condition as Rousseauesque natural creatures in a Vitruvian *scenographia* are employed here to demonstrate the Africans' 'ungovernability'. Against that image of the native American Silvanus is juxtaposed the blacks' Orcus-aspect, where the same 'lack' is negatively distinguished.

As with his designations of indian tribal types, Stedman articulates differences along a spectrum of colour–culture: White, Mestico, Quadroon, Mulatto, Samboe, Mongroo, Black. There is a rage for the absoluteness of these categories of colour in Stedman's writings, the minute gradations of shade representing precise identifications, just as the distinction of indian tribes specified qualitative traits in their behaviour. Behn's rather simple (by comparison) designations of 'black', 'white' and 'reddish yellow' societies are arranged upon a historical spectrum superimposed upon the greatly expanded colour–culture spectrum. The codes of history and of geography and the codes of colour and of culture increasingly come to coincide. All societies began in prehistory as savage and 'coloured' but gradually achieved civilisation and 'whiteness': history bleaches the 'cultural' skin.

Just as ethnic categorisations supersede Stedman's version of ethnographic romance, so too Stedman's textual personas successively 'peel back', one from another. 'Desperate Jack' of the picaresque is replaced by Captain Stedman the conjectural historian of racial differences. 'Desperate Jack', the wildman of the picaresque, decribes a world of undying racial conflict which gives rise in *A Narrative* to a neutralisation of that conflict in the enlightenment classification of human types. In *A Narrative* the various strands of narration and their attendant personas weave and slip between codes. The text's propensity for 'slipping' from one kind of narrative to another takes a final twist. In one episode which Stedman recounts, he stumbles upon two naked girls bathing in a pool:

> Peeping through the foliage, I soon discovered two most elegant female figures after bathing, the one a fine young *Samboe*, the other a *blooming-Quadroon*, which last was so very fair complexioned, that she might have passed for a native of Greece, while the roses that glowed in her cheeks were equal to those that blossomed in the shrubbery. They were walking hand in hand, and conversing with smiles near a flowery bank that adorned the side of the crystal brook, in which they plunged the instant they heard me rustling amongst the verdure, like two mermaids.

> Then to the flood they rush'd; the parted flood
> Its lovely guests with closing waves received,
> And every beauty soft'ning, every grace
> Flushing anew, a mellow lustre shed.   (*A Narrative*, p. 336)

The 'slippage' of the text is evident from the bathing girls extract. In this instance, the precision with which he distinguishes the girls by their colours is embedded in a remarkable cluster of associations which, again, hark back to historically earlier forms of representation. The voyeuristic gaze of the viewer recalls Behn's insistence upon pleasurable sight as her narrator's eye lingers over the bodies of her native Americans, and of Oroonoko and Imoinda. Stedman's flight into verse recalls also Spenser's heroes 'peeping' upon the sylvan scene from their concealed positions. The reference to Spenser is further strengthened by some close textual similarities between this extract and Book II of *The Faerie Queene* where Sir Guyon, the knight of Temperance, is enraptured by the sight of two naked beauties bathing:

> Two naked Damzelles he therein espyde,
> Which therein, bathing, seemed to contend,
> And wrestle wantonly, ne car'd to hyde,
> Their dainty parts from vew of any, which them eyde.[61]

Spenser explores a complex moral dilemma through the virtuous Sir Guyon's increasingly aroused apprehension of the naked girls; but no such moral tension exists in Stedman's text since he shrouds its voyeuristic sexual arousal in the language of racial difference – Greek/ Quadroon/ Samboe. The girls 'fit' into a spectrum of colour and romance narrative onto which is also mapped a 'spectrum' of Stedman's sexual desire. The sexually charged pastoral interlude engages racial classification with eroticism.

At the centre, the apex, of Stedman's diagram of racial–sexual types is the *mulatto*, combining in equal measure 'white' civilisation and 'black' savage physique. The *quadroon* girl comes close to this sexually preferred racial type, but the *mulatto* is the ideal. *A Narrative* contains the last of his narrative slippages or metamorphoses, the tale of Stedman's love for Joanna, the *mulatto* slave, which transforms Stedman the ethnographer into Stedman the lover.

Less than three weeks after Stedman's ship had docked in Surinam, *A Narrative* records how an elderly woman entered his apartment, and presented him with her daughter, a 'black girl about fourteen' 'to become what she was pleased to term my wife'.[62] As with the episode of Lolkens' servant, *A Narrative* and *The Journal* carry slightly different accounts of what ensued. *A Narrative* has Stedman finding it 'difficult to express my astonishment' and politely rejecting the girl with the explanation that many of 'the sable beauties ... follow their own *penchant* without any restraint whatever ... Bestowing their favours for a dram or a broken tobacco-pipe, if not for nothing'.[63] In *A Narrative* Stedman again separates his own conduct from that of the generality of black and white colonists, but *The Journal*'s briefer account shows rather different motives from those of the higher moral standing of the author: 'A negro woman offers me the use of her daughter while here, for a certain sum. We don't agree about the price.'[64]

Barely a week later, Stedman had another offer, this time from a 'beautiful *mulatto* girl' called Joanna, again of fourteen years of age. Stedman was twenty-nine.

> [Joanna was] rather taller than the middle size, she was possessed of the most elegant shape that nature can exhibit, moving her well-formed limbs with more than common gracefulness. Her face was full of native modesty, and the most distinguished sweetness; her eyes, as black as ebony, were large and full of expression, bespeaking the goodness of her heart; with cheeks through which glowed, in spite of the darkness of her complexion, a beautiful tinge of vermillion, when gazed upon. Her nose was perfectly formed, rather small; her lips a little prominent, which, when she spoke, discovered two regular rows of tooth, as white as mountain snow; her hair was

dark brown inclining to black, forming a beautiful globe of
small ringlets, ornamented with flowers and gold spangles.
Round her neck, her arms, and her ancles, she wore gold
chains, rings, and medals: while a shawl of indian muslin, the
end of which was negligently thrown over her polished
shoulders, gracefully covered part of her lovely bosom: a petticoat of rich chintz alone completed her apparel. Bare-headed
and bare-footed, she shone with double lustre, as she carried in
her delicate hand a beaver hat, the crown trimmed with silver.

(*A Narrative*, p. 52)

Joanna's clothing and appearance depict her function and her
colour. Her colour is euphemised by Stedman, as Oroonoko's
'ebony' skin was euphemised by Behn, into 'vermillion'. Colour is
not an inherent quality, it is not in her skin, but emanates from it as
she shines with 'a double lustre'. The key physical marks of her racial
identity, colour, hair, lips, teeth, eye-colour are again, as with Oroonoko, denied or reinscribed as close imitations of European models
of beauty in order to make Joanna 'an ornament to civilised society'.

Joanna was the daughter of a rich Dutch planter called Kruythoff
and Cery, a slave woman on the Fauconburg estate. Kruythoff had
attempted to buy Cery and her daughter from Fauconburg but had
been refused. As the localised slave rebellions erupted, Joanna had
been placed in increasing danger and came under the protection of
two men. The first was her uncle Cojo, a slave whose fidelity was
demonstrated by a silver armband bearing the inscription 'Loyal to
the Europeans'. The other had a history much more discomforting to
the Dutch. When the slaves rebelled on the Fauconburg estate and
caused the director to flee for his life, Joanna was taken in by Joli
Coeur. At that time Joli Coeur was a slave owned by a Dutch Jew
called Schultz. At a later date Schultz raped Joli Coeur's mother and
flogged his father. Joli Coeur's response to the outrage was to hang
up his master, behead and flay him and flee to the forests leaving
Schultz's skin to dry on a cannon. Joli Coeur joined Bonni and Baron,
the rebel leaders, and became one of their most feared captains. It
was this rebel band which led to the colony requesting the Dutch
authorities to send Fourgeoud's troops and, hence, Stedman's presence in Surinam.[65]

It is against this background that Stedman's account of his
relationship with Joanna is told. By April 1773 Joanna and Stedman
were openly living together. Stedman gave Joanna presents to the
value of £10 which she promptly returned to the store because, as
she is reported in *A Narrative*:

'Your generous intentions alone, Sir (she said) were sufficient: but allow me to tell you, that I cannot help considering your superfluous expence on my account as a diminution of that good opinion which I hope you have and will ever entertain, of my disinterested disposition.'

Such was the language of a slave, who had simple nature for her instructor . . .   (*A Narrative*, p. 62)

Quite, but hers is also the language of the eighteenth-century epistolary novel. Stedman's sexual conduct in Surinam is moralised by *A Narrative* into the shape of a tragic love story. His goal is to present his sexual activities in the best possible light, one which ignores the essential determinants of power, violence and money which conditioned all relationships between white men and black women in the colony, in favour of a sentimentalisation of the progress of love and his depiction of Joanna as an ornament to the civilised society of a European ladies' salon. Stedman recasts his love story as a decorous affair but one which is constantly undermined and desentimentalised by the historical conditions of colonial Surinam. Stedman becomes, in *A Narrative*, acutely aware of the climate of decorum of his readership. The affair with Joanna was made, as much as it was possible to make it, as inoffensive and as like the conduct of a drawing-room romance as possible.

Stedman gives Joanna 'a decent wedding' to sanctify the match, not in church, but in their hut, but at which 'many of our respectable friends made their appearance'.[66] When the Fauconburg estate is put into receivership Joanna is sold. The event, according to *A Narrative*, throws the lovers into a flurry of Richardsonian proportions and accomplishes the transformation of Joanna into the textual form of eighteenth-century sentimentalism:

Good God! – I flew to the spot in search of poor Joanna: I found her bathed in tears – she gave me such a look ah! such a look! From that moment I determined to be her protector against every insult, and persevered, as shall be seen in the sequel. – Here, reader let my youth [Stedman was thirty], blended with extreme sensibility, plead my excuse; yet assuredly my feelings will be forgiven me – by those few excepted – who delight in the prudent conduct of Mr Incle to the hapless and much injured Yarico at Barbadoes.

I next ran to the home of my friend Lolkens who happened to be the administrator of Fauconberg estate; and asking his assistance, I intimated to him my strange determination of purchasing and educating Joanna. Having recovered from his surprise, after gazing at me silently for some time, an interview at once was proposed, and the beauteous slave, accompanied by a female relation, was produced trembling in my presence.

Reader, if you have perused the tale of *Lavinia* with pleasure, and though the scene admits of no comparison, reject not the history of Joanna with contempt. (*A Narrative*, p. 59)

When it became clear that Stedman could not afford to buy his beloved, the *mulatto* begins to speak like Pamela or Clarissa:

'I am born a low contemptible slave. Were you to treat me with too much attention, you must degrade yourself with all your friends and relations; while the purchase of my freedom you will find expensive, difficult, and apparently impossible. Yet though a slave, I have a soul, I hope, not inferior to that of all Europeans; and blush not to avow the regard I retain for you, who have distinguished me so much above all others of my unhappy birth. You have, Sir, pitied me; and now independent of every thought, I shall have pride at throwing myself at your feet, till fate shall part us, or my conduct become such as give you cause to banish me from your presence.'

This she uttered with a down-cast look, and tears dropping on her heaving bosom ... From that instant this excellent creature was mine. (*A Narrative*, p. 61)

An arrangement is made with Joanna's new owners, who were moved by this scene of devotion, and the couple return to their hut with the utmost propriety, to continue their lives of domestic bliss. Only the small matter of the Cottica disturbs their ecstasy.

The textual devices employed here are all too obvious. Joanna is prepared for consumption in the guise of 'Lavinia', just as Imoinda was presented as the chronicle icon and petrarchan lover's object of desire. Lavinia's love for Palemon also expressed the sentimental anguish of relations between two socially unequal partners. But in typically blunt entries, *The Journal* describes it all very differently. Barely one month after his 'marriage' to her, Stedman proclaims in his diary that he 'resolves to lie with her no more for certain good reasons'.[67] The 'good reasons' are never stated, but repeatedly he intends to 'put her off'. 'Joanna [is] a good-for-nothing': 'She makes me an odd discovery which makes me think'.[68] The melodrama over the sale is also handled differently: 'Crawl out to see the selling of my dear Joanna, and the whole plantation.' 'I hire her from her master, for ten bits a week, and set her to doing for myself.'[69]

The affair is brought to an end by Stedman's return to Holland after five years in the colony, and again the sentimental mode of narration fills *A Narrative*.

> The unfortunate Joanna (now but nineteen) gazing on me, and holding me by the hand, with a look ten thousand times more dejected than Sterne's Maria, was unable to utter one word. I perceived she was distracted – the hour had come. I exchanged a ringlet of . . . hair . . . The power of speech also forsook me, and my heart tacitly invoked the Protection of Providence . . . Joanna now shut her beauteous eyes. Her lips turned the pale colour of death. She bowed her head, and motionless sunk into the arms of her adopted mother.　　(*A Narrative*, p. 197)

Her 'adopted mother' was Mrs Godefrooy, a matronly figure who appears often in Stedman's texts and who had refused him a loan to buy Joanna but who became, instead, not her adopted mother, but her new mistress. Clearly, the history of Joanna demonstrates the Europeans' desire to reconfigure and misrepresent the brutal sexuality of colonialism within an acceptable frame of sentimental novels. Indeed, three further texts did precisely that: in 1804 a play by Franz Kratter, *Die Slaven in Surinam*, an anonymous novel of 1824 entitled *Joanna or The Female Slave*, and a novel by Eugene Sue, *Adventures d'Hercule Hardi* (1840), each extracted from Stedman's *A Narrative* the episodes describing their affair and reproduced its sentimental style.[70]

After his return Stedman married (this time legitimately, and in a church) the highly respectable Adriana Wierts van Coehorn, a descendant of the great Dutch engineer.[71] Adriana had five children by Stedman at their new home in Tiverton, Devon, and the Stedman children provide a remarkable insight into the degree to which the British imperial enterprise had entered so completely into the lives of English families at the beginning of the nineteenth century. Sophia Charlotte married into the Cotton family of East India entrepreneurs and Maria Joanna married Captain Horace John Aylward of the Royal Artillery. George William was a lieutenant in the Navy and was killed boarding a French ship off Cuba in 1803. Adrian fought in the Indian war of 1846 and was honoured after the Battle of Aliwal against the Sikhs. He also died at sea in 1849. John Cambridge was a captain of the 34th Light Infantry, East India Company, and was killed in the attack on Rangoon in 1824.[72]

But Stedman's marriage to Adriana almost certainly caused Joanna's death. She died of poisoning shortly after she heard of it, either self-administered or, which is more likely, poisoned by a jealous slave who, seeing her protector elsewhere engaged, took revenge for the favours shown Joanna by the whites. And Stedman's affair with Joanna had further consequences. She had had a child by him, a boy named Johnny, whom Stedman had managed to buy out of slavery but had left with his mother. When Joanna died, Mrs Godefrooy packed off young Johnny Stedman, the manumitted slave, to his father's new house and family. Stedman publicly acknowledged Johnny, educated him and often defended him against Adriana's displeasure. What the local population of Tiverton thought of Johnny can be gauged from an incident when Johnny was sent to buy some oranges: 'he was absolutely taken for the Devil, and drove from the turnpike road two men and a woman, who all fled'.[73]

The Journal seems almost to ignore the rest of his children and Adriana in favour of recounting the progress of Stedman's beloved Johnny. Johnny enlisted in the British Navy, Stedman having secured a berth for him as midshipman on a good ship with a decent and humane captain. Ironically, his ship was sent on patrol to the Caribbean where Johnny was drowned at the age of seventeen. Stedman had written a letter to his son to be read after Stedman's own death but, events turning out as they did, the letter and an elegy he composed to Johnny's memory were published instead in the *Gentleman's Magazine* and *The Weekly Entertainer*.[74] The letter is filled with admonition to Johnny to bear up manfully to his loss, but also with clear signs of Stedman's affection. The elegy is a poor imitation of *Lycidas* but it contains these lines:

> No more thy olive-beauties on the waves,
> Shall be the scorn of such European slaves,
> Whose optics, blind to merit, ne'er could spy
> That sterling worth could bloom beneath a western sky.
> Now soar, my angel! to thy Maker's shrine,
> There meet that prize due to such worth as thine.
> Fly gentle shade, fly to that blest abode,
> There view thy mother – and adore thy God.
> There, O my boy!, on that celestial shore,
> O may we gladly meet, and part no more. (*The Journal*, p. 375)

Stedman obtained £500 from the publisher for *A Narrative* and had hopes of making a further £1,000: a sizeable income from his new persona as author. That role brought Stedman into contact with the most radical and dissident members of British society. Joseph Johnson, Stedman's publisher, was jailed for nine months in 1797 for publishing Gilbert Wakefield's political works. Johnson commissioned William Blake and Bartolozzi to engrave the eighty plates from Stedman's drawings which illustrate the text and Stedman became a close friend of Blake's, staying with him on numerous occasions; and Blake undertook to do business for Stedman when Stedman was not in London.[75] The plates show with uncompromising directness the violence of the imperial regime in the colony. The eyes of the victims stare directly out of the page, more in reproach than in agony.

Yet Stedman's own position was much more compromised and contingent than these images suggest. In 1778, when he returned to Holland from Surinam, Stedman was offered the deputy-governorship of Berbicé, a district of Surinam. Stedman declined the offer not for reasons of conscience but because the terms of his pension were unsuitable. Similarly, he had boasted of the harmony of his 'multicultural' family consisting of 'four people only, yet four nations, viz; Scotch, Dutch, English and American – who speak no less than 6 different languages'[76] and of the Europeans and Africans, he wrote, 'the first were the greater barbarians of the two'.[77] 'I love the African negroes,' Stedman also wrote, but not without a caveat: 'I wish from the bottom of my heart ... to prevent the fatal decision of a total abolition of slavery 'till 1800, or the beginning of the next century.'[78] His reasoning was that 'LIBERTY, nay even too much lenity, when *suddenly* granted to illiterate and unprincipled men, must be to all parties dangerous, if not pernicious.'[79] Stedman refused to put his name to Sampson's abolitionist petition.[80] Stedman was himself a slave-owner from the first days of his stay in Surinam. He had bought a young black boy, Quaco, 'to carry my umbrella' and had returned to Europe with him. Quaco continued as Stedman's slave for a further year and six weeks until finally given his freedom.[81]

Stedman, in all probability, would see no contradiction in any of these positions, indeed, Stedman's texts are filled with such dissociations: 'Desperate Jack' and Captain Stedman; the anti-slavery slave-owner; the soldier/ethnographer, killing and describing by turns; Joanna's lover and the cartographer of a racial geography; the survivor of the Cottica and the ethnographer of a sublime savagery which he saw existing *in that same place*; the critic of the colonial psyche and the prospective governor of Berbicé; romance imagist, epistolary novelist, picaresque/romance stylist. None of these contradictions seem to offer a perceptible challenge to Stedman's moral authority.

The incongruities of Stedman's self-fashionings, multiple personas and textual representations demonstrate the contemporary ability to construct an 'otherness', plural and complex, while simultaneously denying its power. The testimony of the self or selves, in the 'field', in Surinam, is finally subordinated to the structures of knowledge which prevail outside that place, in a European imperial centre. It is not that the individual testimony of the observer is now 'unreal' or falsified or untrue or, even, untrustworthy, but that that testimony is subjugated to the strictures of a racial ideology claiming universality. 'Eye-witnessing' is as essential to Stedman's works as it was to Behn's, but only in so far as bearing witness can be reconciled with pre-existing representational and epistemological allegiances. All else is incongruous, insignificant, subjective, 'personal' and supplementary.

Yet it is precisely the incongruous awkwardness of Stedman's constant shifts and reconstructions of personas which constitutes the vital interest of his texts. His disrupted narrations attempt, often desperately, to make these data, these sights, these feelings fit a scheme of narration or pattern of known categories. His biography and the biographies of those he loved continue to question the universal biography of race of which they are all victims. Ultimately, Stedman resigns himself and them to a lesser significance besides the 'reality' of that universal human condition, that 'No one is *perfectly free in this world.'*[82]

14 José Conrado Roza, *Wedding Masquerade*, 1778

Chapter 4

Making history: Scotland 1814

For ethnology to live, its object must die.   *Baudrillard*[1]

José Conrado Roza's painting *Wedding Masquerade*, 1778 (figure 14), depicts eight figures in a landscape celebrating a marriage. The happy couple stand on a fashionable phaeton, dressed in the fine style of a lady and gentleman – silks, embroidery, scarlet, pink, silver-tipped walking stick, fan. A bishop obligingly blesses their nuptials with his presence. In the immediate foreground are the witnesses, revellers, musicians, servants, each in their appropriate garb: a steward, a lady in waiting, a page, a footman. It is an ancient scene, reminiscent of a royal *entrée*, depicting the perpetuation of a pyramidal social order through the holy office of the marriage ceremony. Time is stilled to this essential representation of social hierarchy; a sturdy interdependence of social rank which produces an icon of an *ancien régime*.

But these are not Europeans, although they assume the orders of European social ranking. Seven of these people are slaves, given as gifts to the court of the Portuguese monarch by the governors of the provinces of Brazil. Nor is this a marriage, since slaves are not free to marry as they choose, but must seek the permission of their masters who retain the right of ownership of any offspring of such a marriage, as they retain the right to have sex with any of their female slaves. These people are other than they may seem to be in another sense; seven 'court dwarfs' and a boy suffering from Harlequinism, a genetic disorder of the melanin in his skin. Queen Maria I, before she went insane, liked to have such 'human curiosities' around her at court.

The clothes they wear depicting their various social stations are not theirs but their masters'. To emphasise this sense of ownership, Roza has written the slaves' personal histories on the hems of their garments: Dona Anna (with the tambourine) originated from Rio de Sena, sent to the court by the governor general of Mecabique; Don José from Moruide (in the turban), thirty years of age, sent by the viceroy of Brazil; Siriaco from Cotingingba, twelve years, sent by Don Rodrigo de Menezes e Noronoha because of the marvel of his skin; Sebastien from Sena (with the flute), aged thirty-one, a gift from Antonio de Mello e Castro. Only one individual is not enslaved. He is also a court dwarf and is dressed, not in the mimicry of a freeman's costume, but in native American gear. He raises his miniature bow and arrow to shoot the symbolic dove of peace.[2]

How to read this remarkable painting? This colonial masquerade embodies the historical vision of a placid and orderly civic community while simultaneously and at every level it denies the ideology of that hierarchy. The painting ironises the notion that to understand a social structure one must understand its authority systems, yet each statement, about authority, opulence, rank, sanctity, marriage, bodily presence, is 'cancelled' through and rendered contingent and unsatisfactory as it is confidently declared, while the unremitting eyes of the enslaved gaze directly out of the canvas at the viewer. The *Masquerade*'s mode of representation of the colonial economy of late eighteenth-century Portugal and Brazil is wholly within the hierarchies of the society, yet it also seems to challenge, to parody or mock that order.

Only one figure does not turn his accusing gaze at the spectator; the 'freeborn' native American mimic shoots at the dove (or is his target the 'bishop'?). Roza may be recording in symbolic mode, the resistance of the native Americans to colonial rule, and to the enslavement which had afflicted the Africans in the scene. The year in which this painting was made had witnessed one of the most violent defeats of Europeans by natives in Brazil – the Guaikuru attack on Fort Coimbra which left the Portuguese outwitted and with forty-five dead.[3] The native is mimicked, therefore, as a figure of unaccommodated violence, outside the pyramidal structure of colonial society.

At the same time that the painting records its ambivalence to its subject, it also records the limits of its representation of the historical conditions which have created this social order. Roza's critique of colonialism is expressed (but how expressed!) by the inversion of an expected imaging of a social whole and by the plangent, unfathomable gaze of its subjects. The violent dynamism of the native American mimic can only be conceived of as external to that hierarchy. The painting reproduces the historical conditions in the pyramidal hierarchy of the conventional image of social stasis which it parodies.

The only narrative available in the image would appear to be that of the immutable stasis of colonial history whereby the colonies themselves 'mimic' European social and historical order. It is not so much that Roza lacks the skill to articulate his subject, but that that subject lacks a representation save in the borrowed clothes of colonial replication. It is colonial history itself which lacks a narrative representation, other than that of the endless repetition and inversion of the stasis which it already knows. The violence of radical action, the unaccommodated native, is hustled to the margins of social order as an aberrant and destructive force.

John Singleton Copley lived, for a large part of his life, on a different border. Copley was born in Boston, Massachusetts in 1737 where he made his living as a portrait painter. As colonial America increasingly divided itself over the issue of independence, Copley found his clientele among the wealthy Bostonians who exercised their patronage according to political affiliations, demanding that he choose which side of the conflict he supported. In 1774 Copley made his choice and left America for London.

The 1770s was a thoroughly bad decade for British imperialism. The demand for American independence occurred concurrently with the threat to West Indian and Canadian possessions by the French. Patriotic art depicted an imperial enterprise under stress: noble and heroic struggles to the death, where victory is snatched from the jaws of defeat and the imperial ambition hangs on by the fingertips. In 1778 France made an alliance with the American rebels and, as a consequence, the British army found itself fighting yet another rearguard action much closer to home.

England's reply to the alliance was to do what she had always done in similar circumstances, which was to turn loose her privateers on French shipping. The centre of privateering activity was the island of Jersey and the French commander in Cherbourg, General Dumouriez, described the Jersey privateers as the 'despair' of French trade. By the end of 1778 over 150 prizes had been taken and 1500 French seamen were held captive on Jersey. The French court ordered the intrepid Prince of Nassau, who had sailed around the

15 John Singleton Copley, *The Death of Major Peirson, 6 January 1781*, 1784

world collecting botanical and ethnographic data with Bougainville, to invade the island, but bad weather frustrated his intention and the English fleet picked off five of his vessels. The Chevalier de Luxembourg tried again, this time with a force of 950 Normandy militia and convicts released from the chain-gangs. The force, depleted to 600 men because of the sudden turning of the tide which prevented a full landing, bluffed their way into St Helier and demanded the surrender of a garrison of a thousand regulars and three thousand militiamen. Under threats that the French would burn the town, the commander-in-chief surrendered.

On hearing of the surrender of St Helier the commander of the Highland regiment stationed in Westmount refused to accept it. He, and a young major, Francis Peirson, in charge of the 95th Foot while his superiors were away on Christmas leave, marched on St Helier. The opposing forces met in Royal Square in front of the Old Court buildings. The French were hopelessly outnumbered, and fighting lasted less than ten minutes. Both Peirson and the French commander were killed and Peirson became a posthumous national hero as much for his saving England from a humiliating defeat as for his heroic action and self-sacrifice.[4]

The incident aroused Copley's intense interest as here was an imperial struggle which offered an oblique view of the American conflict. The link with the Jersey merchants and part-time privateers was particularly strong since Jersey had extensive trading links with his native Boston, and Copley had painted the portraits of many Massachusetts entrepreneurs. In painting the event Copley was able to display his commitment to his new country's heroic struggle without entering the personally fraught and politically sensitive theme of the American Revolution. Significantly, Copley chose this subject to explore the subtleties of historical representation in an age which had rediscovered the genre of history painting in order to explore the increasingly complex matter of imperialism. The result was a huge canvas, *The Death of Major Peirson, 6 January 1781*, exhibited in 1784 (figure 15).

The scene of the painting is St Helier's Royal Square in front of the Old Court and statue of George II. Four main groups fill the foreground. The central group shows the officers of the militia and the 95th supporting the dead major beneath the (pre-1801) Union flag. To the left is a dying drummer boy and a group of reinforcements; to the immediate right is the French enemy where the scene of a dying commander is mirrored. At the extreme right of the painting is a

dead soldier and the fleeing figures of two women and a boy; one of
the women carries a second child. In the distance, the Highland
regiment fire down onto the town from a hill. Gunsmoke and dust
swirl through the picture, figures are caught in the actions of
moving, falling, running, flags flying. The family which flees the
cataclysm is Copley's own wife and children. The boy, the only
figure who looks out of the canvas, caught in an expression of terror,
frozen in a scream, is Copley's eldest son, John Singleton Copley Jr,
who was in later life to become the Lord Chancellor of England.
Copley takes this event seriously enough to depict his own family as
being at the mercy of the enemy.

Prown asserts that Copley had four models for this painting, all of
which were paintings or engravings of the Massacre of the Innocents.[5] Clearly the reference has propaganda value, depicting the
French invasion as a war crime. Of those models, Copley's chief
influence was Rubens' *The Massacre of the Innocents*, where Rubens
introduces into his image the touching innovation of the figure of a
loyal black servant defending her mistress. Copley takes from
Rubens both the stylisation of the distressed figures of his own
family refigured as the Innocents and the theme of the loyal black
servant and shows Peirson's own black servant avenging his
master's death. In doing so, Copley invites his viewer to see the
painting on two levels simultaneously: as the authentic historical
record of an event and as an artifice composed of references to other
paintings and representations.

Copley's is the only image of the Battle of Jersey to represent
Peirson's servant in this key role. In fact, it is the only image to
depict the black man at all, since the illustrations of the event made
immediately afterwards and Copley's preliminary drawings show
no black figure. Even in a much later oil sketch by Copley the
figure of revenge is quite clearly another, white regular soldier.
When the painting was first exhibited it was shown together with a
key printed on the admission ticket which named all the figures in
the painting: Captain Clophane, Captain Macneil, Captain Corbot
and so on. The key acts as a historical authentication, in naming, of
a historical event depicted in paint. It makes the subject 'real'. In
the key, the black figure is simply called 'Major Peirson's Black
Servant' and has not, therefore, the historical authentication of a
name; he lacks that reality. In truth the nameless individual shown
was certainly not Peirson's servant, if indeed he had one, because
the portrait of the romantic black is that of one of Copley's

neighbour's servants who lived across from Copley in Leicester Square.[6]

Copley's depiction of the role of Peirson's servant serves a number of functions important to the picture's political and historical contention. He is a reverential 'intertextual' footnote to Rubens' depiction of the touching bond of human loyalties but he also serves the same purpose as his children's inauthentic presence – not as historical presences but as allegorical motif; as a means of directing the viewer to a reading of the painting as a representation of wider historical concerns.

In the political contexts of the painting, which always has one eye on the wider issues of British colonialism and the American problem, the black figure is immensely significant. The black servant is the chief and central figure of action; other people are shooting their muskets in the painting, but only he is shown killing someone, indeed, he seems to be carrying on the battle almost singlehanded while the others tend to the fallen hero. The allegorical message would seem clear, that in the war between the opposing nations for imperial domination, the black man's best course is to actively join with Britain against her upstart rivals.

Copley's painting also shows an extraordinary degree of colonial mimicry. The painting by Roza expressed some considerable ambiguity about the enforced assumption of colonial behaviour, dress and social order by an enslaved underclass. Copley has no such doubts. Not only are American blacks – in fact, all colonised people – better served by British rule, Copley's new dynamic narrative of history forms itself *around* the alien other, accommodating his perceived violence as the essence of the historical machine of progress, change and development. The colonial mimic is authenticated, not as a 'real' named individual but as the central spirit of this new historical moment. This is a grand deception, for having made the colonial mimic, that subject is re-made as the object of history, its *zeitgeist*. British imperialism is being effectively, energetically promoted by its subject peoples against rival claims, to the degree that the ambition of imperialism is shown to be at one with the loyalties and aspirations of its subjected peoples. In a telling image from the painting, Captain Macneil points at the target which the nameless black then shoots.

In contrast to Roza's painting, Copley has found a new vocabulary for the representation of the event in a time of imperial struggle. The new historical moment is not that of Roza's pyramid of interconnec-

ting social forces which are self-justifying in their internal equi-
libriums, leaving the acculturated slave to gaze questioningly but
hopelessly at the viewer out of an image which effectively margina-
lises the threat of violent transformation to a position outside its
social borders, on the wild side of historical irrelevance. Copley's
'history painting' envisages history as a vortex of violent eruptions.
It represents the historical moment as a dynamic, cataclysmic event
which draws the peripheral figure of an alien forcefulness into its
centre where it may usefully commit its act of terror in the cause of
progress. Roza's and Copley's paintings are, respectively, icons of
stasis and change which meditate upon the changing roles of the
other in the representation of a new world of colonial history.

There is another moral to be learned from Copley's national
parable of the glory of self-sacrifice. Four nations, cultures, 'races' are
shown in conflict under the gaze of the statue of the Hanoverian
monarch on the very borders of his kingdom: English, French,
African and Scottish. The Battle of Jersey becomes a miniature of the
world's peoples in conflict. John Singleton Copley Jr, in his bid to flee
the scene of conflict, strides over the body of a dead soldier. The
soldier is easily identifiable, not by name because he, like the black
servant, has no name and is not mentioned in the key, but he is
identified like the black servant by his 'race', and his significance as
both nameless and 'racially' identifiable signals his presence as an
allegorical figure. He is a Highlander, as his claymore, plaid and
bonnet proclaim. There are echoes here of another kind of conflict,
that of the Highland rebellions of 1715 and 1745. The moral power of
the image cannot be lost on an audience viewing this scene only
forty years after the Highlanders threatened the very existence of
the power which is so triumphantly in evidence under its Union
flag. The fallen Highlander was once a rebellious subject, like the
American colonists, but tamed and defeated by English power; his
violence is also, now, like the black's, put to use by and spent for the
cause of the British crown. But the Highlander's symbolic presence is
as a corpse, over which the tide of history's violence sweeps. A victim
of the past, who must be seen to have paid for his past, the Highlander is one of history's expendables.

Benjamin West's *Colonel Guy Johnson and Karonghyontye*, 1775–6
(figure 16), gathers together the various strands of national determination, narration, ethnography and portraiture. Native American
material culture is discovered in the detail of Karonghyontye's

16 Benjamin West, *Colonel Guy Johnson and Karonghyontye*, 1775–6

clothing and in the decorations appended to Johnson's redcoat uniform: the native American blanket, moccasins, garters and belts. In the background, viewed from within the cave where the painting seems to be painted is a typical warriors' encampment.

The narrative this painting records is expressed through the play of light on Johnson's face. The light seems not to fall on Johnson, but to emanate from within him to create a halo. Oddly, it has the effect of casting Karonghyontye into a greater darkness, since his features barely catch the light at all and he risks slipping deeper into the cave's gloom. Johnson's gaze is fixed on an object to the left and in front of the canvas. Karonghyontye gazes upon Johnson alone, attempting to distract his visionary gaze to a world which he represents and which is seen outside the cave. Karonghyontye seems about to speak, but what he has to say is irrelevant to Johnson who has eyes only for his source of enlightenment. Johnson's beauty transcends his savage trappings. Karonghyontye's role is as a foil to this portrait of a supreme national selfhood; he is, quite literally, eclipsed by the light of imperial civilisation exemplified by Johnson's beautiful *Englishness*.

Portraiture's emergence and flowering coincided with the development of history painting to which it is closely allied: 'What the antique statues and bas-reliefs which Italy enjoys are to the history painters, the beautiful and noble faces with which England is confessed to abound, are to the face-painters.'[7]

For Richard Steele, portraiture's predominance among the plastic arts was because of its pre-eminently *English* quality. Whereas Italy could supply the models of historical representation, England could supply the physical types for portraiture which bespoke a national quality of beauty. The rise of portraiture is, therefore, intimately connected to a sense of a uniquely national contribution to the arts and the recording of the beautiful nobility of the English face amounts to a patriotic duty no less than the historical record of the nation's achievements.

All these threads converge in West's image, but the revival of interest in England in the portrait disguises the importance of those very Italian models which Steele was eager to use as a foil to the English achievement. The models for English portraiture were a 'handful of portraits produced in the Italian High Renaissance' and almost all derived from a set of poses shown in the paintings of Titian and Van Dyck.[8] English imperial portraiture is thus seen to be neither very English nor is it wholly comfortable in its imperial certainty.

The glorification of 'Englishness' which West's painting expresses acts as a way of distracting our attention from the savage actor. The native Americans make this picture as they made Johnson's triumphant career; they are the reason for his success and for the painting which records that success, but in their representation they are masked by other concerns. West directs onto Johnson the light which overshadows Karonghyontye and in that contest of light, to render the native decorative but subservient and ultimately irrelevant to his mission. Yet in banishing Karonghyontye to the margins, the painting makes him assume a new centrality. The portrait of Karonghyontye fascinates by what it does not reveal. When this painting is viewed alongside others by West, *The Death of General Wolfe* for example, or alongside Copley's *Watson and the Shark*, the 'otherness' is revealed as an extraordinary fascination for death: the black and the native American are mysterious harbingers or connoisseurs of death. Similarly, Karonghyontye's portrait functions as a kind of anti-portrait to Johnson's portrayed 'Englishness': a darker *alter ego*, a romantic shadow, a mysterious and secretive anti-self to Johnson's triumphant clarity. The painting accomplishes the creation of a totally other world filled with the secret allure of the peripheral.

The three paintings offer three conceptions and representations of the historical progress of the savage or alien subject. Roza's image functions within the orders of a known social hierarchy with its severe delimitations of rank and 'race'. The potential disordering of that fixity can only be conceived of as a cruel parody or irrelevance to its static reticulations. Copley's image offers more direct support to a particular historical process but does so by recruiting the danger of the perceived violence of the other as the spirit of mighty historical change. West's image of Karonghyontye depicts a scene when that violence has been spent and the 'career' it promoted has been successfully made (to the degree of having a portrait to record it). The savage enters a darker, more mysterious but ultimately tamed and safer historical presence as his appearance is shaded by the romantic silhouette of an ethnic historical decoration.

In the autumn of 1786, Walter Scott spent a working holiday with one of his father's numerous Highland clients. Scott was only fifteen and already bored with his work as a clerk at his father's office.[9] He was to recall the journey he made into the Highlands a number of times in later life. In remembering the landscape of the Wicks of

Baiglie he wrote, in *The Fair Maid of Perth*, that he was so overcome by the scene that he had 'to convince himself that what he saw was real'.[10] But the journey was not all sight-seeing; he was given the task of evicting a sept of the clan MacLaren from the lands of Stewart of Appin.

> An escort of a sergeant and six men was obtained from a Highland regiment lying in Sterling, and the author, then a writer's apprentice, equivalent to the honourable situation of attorney's clerk, was invested with the superintendence of the expedition, with directions to see that the messenger discharged his duty fully, and that the gallant sergeant did not exceed his part by committing violence and plunder. And thus it happened, oddly enough, that the author first entered the romantic scenery of Loch Katrine, of which he may perhaps say he has somewhat extended the reputation, riding in all the dignity of danger, with a front and rear guard, and loaded arms. The sergeant was absolutely a Highland Sergeant Kite, full of stories of Rob Roy and of himself, and a very good companion. We experienced no interruption whatever, and when we came to Invernenty, found the house deserted. We took up our quarters for the night, and used some of the victuals which we found there. The MacLarens, who probably had never thought of any serious opposition, went to America, where, having had some slight share in removing them from their *paupera regna*, I sincerely hope they prospered.[11]

Scott's reminiscences of a Highland eviction is an evocation of the border scene. This journey across the frontier to claim the land of the indigenous population is retold in ways which glance at the historical conditions of colonialism. A potentially vindictive and unrestrained militia is held in check by Scott's presence, not only as a minor representative of the law – a law which is doubly recorded as the institution which both evicts and protects the Highlanders – but also as the representative of a higher (professional) class keeping the lower (military) orders in check. Scott's youthful excitement at the display of military might, gently self-ironised, plays against the real possibilities of an unleashed vindictive militia. The 'romantic scenery' is viewed as an escape, a holiday, from the impersonal and claustrophobic environment of his father's chambers, but Loch Katrine is a depopulated scene, emptied of its threatening inhabitants. The Highlands are, here, being prepared for new owners: Appin, certainly, who evokes his right under the law, but also the new generation of travellers who can now take possession of the landscape as unmolested tourists, and readers, for whom this landscape is being prepared as 'romantic scenery' and as the scene of historical novels. Loch Katrine is 'colonised' as a legal possession which places a prohibition on the native population, as accessible territory and as romantic narrative. Scott the lawyer helps clear the ground so that Scott the novelist may gain access to a subject he can write about. The novelist weeps over the Highlanders' removal from their *'paupera regna'* but the lawyer had a hand in their going.

The transformation of the Highlands, in Scott's writings, from dangerous territory into written text is a key landmark in the process of 'accommodating' the primitive to codes and discourses of representation. The 'textualised' Highlander's entry into narrative occurs precisely at the moment when the Highlander *per se* is sufficiently subdued or 'evicted' as to be invisible. There is no 'danger' and therefore no 'dignity' (key terms in Scott's lexicon) in the failed encounter with the absent MacLarens, because the house is empty; 'danger' and 'dignity' must be made to reoccupy the house, not as historical subjects (the law has evicted those) but as historical narratives. Scott's novels are about absent subjects; it is only when the Highlanders are constructed as *historically* invisible that they can re-emerge as textually visible and capable of bearing the burden of a historical discourse from which they are excluded as an extinct species. Scott is, in this respect, a precursor of later ethnographic strategies of hiding behind a cloak of invisibility the ostensible subject of analysis and textualisation.

The decay of the Highland clan system throughout the eighteenth century allowed access to territory which had previously been perilous to the outsider. A series of 'descriptions', 'tours' and 'sketches' followed which dealt with the Highlanders in ways which were similar to the treatment of other, more geographically remote, societies. In its demise the Highland social order was widely reconstructed as a primitive society.

Dalrymple (Lord Hailes), in his *Memoirs*, comments upon the 'civility' of the Highlanders and indicates an evolutionary context: 'The Highlander, whom more savage nations called savage, carried in the outward expression of their manners the politeness of courts without their vices, and in their bosoms the high point of honour without its follies.'[12] Likewise, Adams in his *Curious Thoughts on the History of Man*, writes: 'No people lived more innocently than the ancient Germans, though men and women lived together without reserve. They slept promiscuously around the walls of their houses; and yet we never read of adultery among them. The Scotch Highlanders to this day live in the same manner.'[13]

'Manners' here refers to both the Highlanders' level of civility and to a stage of social evolution comparable to the ancient Germans indicated by their similar practices of restrained sexual behaviour. Robertson in a sermon entitled *The Situation of the World at the Time of Christ's Appearance* comments that the Highlands and Islands of Scotland contain a 'society which still appears in its rudest and most imperfect form'.[14] The most renowned of all Scottish tours was Dr Johnson's and here too the emphasis is on the primitive state of Highland life: 'That the primitive manners are continued where the primitive language is spoken, no notion will desire me to suppose, for the manners of mountaineers are commonly savage, but they are rather produced by their situation than derived from their ancestors.'[15]

For Dr Johnson, it is the (undefined) 'situation' which determines Highland life rather than heredity, and in that context the Highlander is comparable with other peoples in similar 'situations' of civility. 'Their tables were as coarse as the feasts of Esquimaux, and their houses as filthy as the cottages of Hottentots.'[16] In this application of a comparative method, Johnson emphasises and greatly extends the geographical remoteness of the Highlands by an analogy with other peoples:

> To the southern inhabitants of Scotland, the state of the mountains and the islands is equally unknown with that of Borneo or Sumatra: of both they have only heard a little and guess the rest. They are strangers to the language and manners, to the advantages and wants of the people, whose life they would model, and whose evils they would remedy.[17]

This is particularly interesting in the light of a similar comment made by Scott:

> The more intelligent, when they thought about them [the Highlanders] by any chance, considered them as complete barbarians; and the mass of the people cared no more about them than the merchants of New York about the Indians who dwell beyond the Alleghany mountains.[18]

By the time Mrs Grant of Laggan wrote her *Essays on the Superstitions of the Highlanders* in 1811, theories of the progressive development of Scottish society had fully entered her writings:

> When nations, in the progress of knowledge and refinement, have arrived at a high state of cultivation, and are thus enabled to take extensive views of life and manners, from the heights to which they have attained, they begin to look with a mixture of

contempt and self-congratulation on those wider regions still inhabited by tribes, as rude and barbarous as their own ancestors have been at a remoter period.[19]

Mrs Grant, who was an acquaintance of Scott's, proceeds to forge an unmistakable link between the Highlander and her particular prejudices against the uncivil primitive world, which comes to a head over the matter of the Highland risings:

> The solitary, cruel, selfish and capricious savage, far from forming an object of amusing speculation, fills us with sensations of mingled horror and disgust, such as we feel at the Yahoo pictures of Swift; and makes us, like his reader, shudder at owning our fellow nature with a being so degraded ... Parental affection renders it necessary for us in cases of obstinate continuance in error, or determined disobedience to a known command, to inflict correction where it may be required.[20]

Mrs Grant's lack of self-doubt is amplified and lent a racial bias by John Pinkerton's *Dissertation on the Goths*, and *An Enquiry into the History of Scotland*, where he divides the population of Europe into four races, the Celts being the most ancient and 'to the others what the savages of America are to the European settlers there'.

> The Celts of Ireland, Wales and the Highlands of Scotland are savages since the world began, while a separate people, that is, while themselves and of unmixed blood.
>
> The Celts of Scotland always are, and continue to be, a dishonoured, timid, filthy, ignorant, and degraded race.
>
> Characters of nations change – characters of savage RACES never.[21]

These contemporary outbursts act as a sobering historical corrective to Redfield's and Toynbee's assertions that the Highlander was one of the three primitive peoples accepted as equal partners by the western world.[22]

Yet not all writers on the Highland savage saw him in the same terms as Grant or Pinkerton and many attempted to present a more reasoned and detailed ethnography of Highland culture. Scott, himself, was provoked to a spirited defence of the Highlanders, and by implication all primitive peoples, in his condemnation of Pinkerton's racist slurs: 'To lay such excessive weight upon the innate or inherited qualities of any peculiar race of Adam seems to us equally unauthorised by moral theory or by physical experience.'[23]

It was in much the same vein that General David Stewart of

Garth's *Sketches of the Highlanders* attempted to lend some substance to the defence of Highland culture. He did so by tracing the pre-history of the Celtic tribes, attempting to relate Gaelic to Hebrew, and describing a social order of patriarchal authority based on consanguinity and possessing an oral culture preserved in the tradi-tional lore of the bards and senachie. His is an extensive and fasci-nating ethnography; he describes the 'kearnachs' or warrior bands, their diet, religious beliefs and their legal system of hereditary jurisdiction.

Stewart's text bears more than a passing resemblance to the American Jesuit ethnographies. Lafitau's *Mœurs des sauvages Amer-iquains, comparées aux mœurs des premiers temps* of 1724 is an exemplary text for Stewart in many respects. Lafitau's central argument is to refute an assumed atheistical claim that man has no need of God by showing that native American paganism contains the light of true religion despite its heretical appearance. Lafitau's text leans towards both Behn's ethnographic romance and the ancient chronicles in discovering the 'virtuous savages' and in tracing North American natives back to an origin in antiquity, in Ancient Greece (a belief he shared with Fénelon, Bufier and Charlevoix).[24] But, most sig-nificantly, the connections he makes are not done wholly through a system of symbolic likenesses and preferences for notions of civility, but through ethnographic categorisation of the modes of subsistence and behaviour.

For Lafitau, the primitive world is infinitely more complex than his symbols will allow or can enunciate. His book marks off, in turn, the world according to its orders: religion, political government, mar-riage, education, occupations of men, of women, warfare, commerce, games, death, burial, mourning, sickness, medicines, language, classificatory kinship terminology. Lafitau's native culture presents a world of categorical entries, a prototypical pattern of segments of knowledge. After Lafitau, ethnography could no longer be about 'showing' another world, as Le Moyne showed Outina showing his world to Laudonnière: ethnography was encyclopaedic in imitation of the European enlightenment mind or it was nothing. Lafitau invented ethnography's most persistent myth, the myth of omni-science. Stewart's text similarly defended the 'virtuous Highlander' by a catalogue of Highland culture as if it were the ethnography of a savage people, open and available to rational categorisation of its social and cultural forms. The rational categorisation of primitive societies is achieved in a blizzard of identifications, the

the appearance of total disclosure: the conviction that the worlds of others are utterly transparent to us. What God was to Lafitau the Jesuit, Lafitau the ethnographer was to the Mohawks. In both cases, no secret could be hidden, since God and Lafitau could see all.

The effect of Stewart's text, and the others like it, was to preserve the context of the Highlander's representation as a 'savage', yet invest that representation with the recuperative agency of empirical data. The Highlander emerges as an anachronism, killed off not so much by the Redcoats as by the progressive movement of history leaving them behind. Thus identified as a complex historical 'stage', a savage anomaly, or a racial remnant, rather than as a social entity, Highland culture could be safely and favourably redefined.

Scott's fullest inquiry into Highland culture outside the novels appeared in an article for the *Quarterly Review* in 1816. Working from the papers of Lord President Forbes, who was largely responsible for the mobilisation of the anti-Jacobite clans in the '45, he described the Highland social structure in a way which makes use of a comparative method of considerable sophistication:

> Evidently it must have been a matter of astonishment to the subjects of the complicated and combined constitution of Great Britain, to find they were living next door to tribes whose government and manners were simply and purely patriarchal, and who, in the structure of their social system, much more resembled the inhabitants of the mountains of India than those of the plains of England.[25]

The 'matter of astonishment' Scott refers to is deeply informed by the philosophers of the Scottish Enlightenment, since 'astonishment' comes from the juxtaposition of two discrete epochs of social development, the barbaric and the commercial. Adam Smith fixed history into a drama with four acts: the first stage of society, the savage epoch, has hunting as its dominant mode of subsistence; the second, barbarism, is predominantly pastoral; the third is agricultural; the fourth, civilisation proper, is dominated by commerce.[26] The stadial theorists' conviction that societies developed according to the regulating principles of history uncovered by the categorisations of ethnography was an immensely powerful philosophical construction which profoundly shaped the representation of other peoples. Since the European 'past' could be seen in the lives of contemporary primitives who lived nonetheless in a 'previous' epoch of human development, travel to those peoples involved not only a geographical journey, but a voyage in time.[27]

The comparative material in Scott's account is taken from Elphin-stone's *Account of the Caubal*, which Scott had reviewed for the *Quarterly Review* and to which he frequently returned: 'The gene-alogies of Afgauni tribes may be parallelled with those of the clans; the nature of their favourite sports, their love of their native land, their hospitality, their address, their simplicity of manners exactly correspond.'[28]

Such superficial comparisons are, for Scott, sanctioned nonethe-less by an even deeper level of structural similarity of the two cultures. The Highlanders, for Scott:

> resembled these oriental mountaineers in their feuds, in their adoption of auxiliary tribes, in their laws, in their modes of conduct in war, in their arms, and, in some respects, even in their dress ... Our limits do not permit us farther to pursue a parallel which serves strikingly to show how the same state of society and civilisation produces similar manners, laws and customs, even at the most remote period of time, and in the most distant quarters of the world.[29]

The limits Scott refers to are empirical rather than methodological; the stadial theory outstrips the data. Central to Scott's theoretical orientation is the denial of any genetic linkage in favour of a generic identification: Afghan and Clansman are comparable peoples because 'produced' by the same 'state of society' and they are of the same order, not the same kind. Scott identifies and categorises the peoples of the world according to how those societies display their significant signs; the degree of significance is determined, with complete circularity of argument, by the very mode of categori-sation. Furthermore, it is a generic link which exists 'even at the most remote period of time and in the most distant quarters of the world', regardless of time or place. Highlanders would be like Afghans even if the Afghans were as historically remote as they are geographically distant. This comparative method depends entirely upon the evo-cation of time (the comparison of present primitives with those of the past to determine their relative status) and space (the com-parison of disparate peoples) in order to make its comparative connections and assimilations. Yet time and space are evoked only to be abolished as significant features in determining generic, stadial, social types and orders; the greatest historical novelist abolished history in speculating about history, abolished place in celebrating his nation.

The Highlander as a reconstructed Afghani tribesman is thus

identified as a remote and alien being whose purpose is not simply to satisfy a desire to understand other cultures, but to articulate an alternative social world for a European readership to occupy imaginatively. The relative ease with which Scott made these comparative observations may also have had an ideological and political subtext if, as Perry Anderson argues, British society had begun to fear the kinds of political and historical generalisations and conjectures of the Enlightenment as being a major contributory factor in causing the French Revolution: 'British Imperial society exported its totalisations onto its subject peoples. There, and there only, it could afford scientific study of the social whole. "Primitive" societies became the surrogate object of the theory proscribed at home.'[30]

Yet those conjectures about the development of European culture had to be applied elsewhere if their application 'at home' was ideologically troublesome. In these contexts, therefore, Scott's creation of an alterior culture and his linking of the Highlanders with others allowed him to neutralise the Highland threat by projecting it as extrinsic and alien. Thus 'neutralised' the Highlander could be safely used as a geographically close but historically and culturally remote example in a philosophical and literary inquiry which, otherwise, would have been tainted by sedition.

Behind Scott's portrait of the 'state of society' of Highland 'barbarism' there exists an extensive range of material which acts as 'covert' ethnography and which supplied him with the data required to overcome the limits of empirical data he had complained of in his review of Elphinstone. Scott was the first major literary figure to enter the field of 'antiquities' with any firm conviction or dedication. Firstly in *The Minstrelsy of the Scottish Border* and later in *The Border Antiquities of England and Scotland* and *Letters on Demonology and Witchcraft*, he refers to antiquarians as scholars researching into a definable corpus of material which will elucidate a 'social situation' through the systematic and comparative treatment and interpretation of traditional materials. Scott assembled his extensive textual and oral sources with meticulous care: Gervase of Tilbury, Gough, Reginald Scot, Aubrey, Hone, Brand, Pennant, Roby, Croker, Douce, Hailes, Stewart, Pennant, Pitcairn, Pinkerton, Keithley, Dalyell, Rich, Ellis, Glanville, Delrius and Grimm which he combined with the materials he garnered from Sinclair's *Statistical Accounts* of Scottish parishes made by incumbents.[31]

Scott, in his different guises as novelist and antiquarian, brings the 'unconscious' schemes of folklore to a state of explicitness. In so doing he foregrounds a major element in cultural representations since his researches play upon the relationship between a *verstehen* or *emic* approach which engages in a description from the point of view of the subject, and an *etic*, positivist approach which 'uncovers' the objective truth lying behind behaviour and beliefs.[32] An example he cites at length in *The Minstrelsy of the Scottish Border* is that of neolithic shards which are encoded by folklore as 'elf-bolts', the arrows used by the fairies to stun cattle. As an antiquarian Scott acted as a rationalist peeling back the layers of accumulated myth which cling to the object of study. In his antiquarian researches, Scott enters into the contemporary debate, which focused on Panlus' *Life of Jesus*, on the relative merits of myth and history.[33] For Scott, myth and history are not contradictory but complementary categories. Scott unravels the belief system which so encodes the object and thereby accumulates data for the description of the Highland habitus. In the novels, history and myth again correspond but here the rationalist exegesis is reversed and the object, practice or belief is reinvested with its mythical significances. 'Folklore' often forms a major part of the novels' structure and whole episodes are constructed around a folkloric centre. The explanation, for example, of the failure of Redgauntlet's rebellion is given, simultaneously, both a historical and a mythical context in that the evocation of the family curse colours the historical inevitability with the shades of a folkloric mystery. Scott effectively 'unmakes' folklore in his antiquarian researches only to 'remake' it in his novels and his representation of Highland culture is evoked, Titian-like, as a negotiation between these activities.

The effect of conjoining folklore with history is to offer various modes of interpretation of a history doomed to the foregone conclusion which endows the novel – particularly in the case of *Redgauntlet* – with a sense of the darkness and frustration of historical destiny. The interest is in the unfolding of the historically *and* mythically inevitable, the closing-off of all courses of action until the climax is stifled by thwarted, suppressed and eventually strangled energies. As an antiquarian, Scott presents his mission as being to untangle myth from history and to unpick the knots of contradictory and irrational folk belief; as a novelist, his mission was rather the reverse, to introduce the 'folk' as a complementary means of articulating and exploring the dialectical nature of a confrontational and often contradictory historical process.

Scott was fully aware of his method of making historical narratives out of this conjunction of folkloric data and enlightenment philosophies of stadial changes. His 'matter of astonishment' encountered at the meeting of one kind of barbarian world with another kind of commercial civilisation was fully expressed in universal terms in a letter to Southey who had, himself, published in 1810 a highly acclaimed history of the colonisation of Brazil (in which he summarised the native Brazilians' predicament as being either 'to remain and be treated like slaves or to fly to the woods and take their chances like savages').[34]

> The history of colonies has some points of peculiar interest as illustrating human nature. On occasions the extremes of civilised and savage are suddenly and strangely brought into contact with each other and the results are as interesting to the moral observer as those which take place on the mixture of chemical substances to the physical investigator.[35]

The Highlands are to be seen as a historical test case for a world 'experiment' with history which can subsequently become the structuring principles of narrative. In the 'General Preface to the Waverley Novels', Scott relates how he collected his material from the Highland 'veterans' of the '45 when,

> it naturally occurred to me that the ancient traditions and high spirit of a people who, living in a civilised age and country, retained so strong a tincture of manners belonging to an early period of society, must afford a subject favourable for romance...[36]

In the archetypal text, *Rob Roy*, the evocation of the 'matter of astonishment' is immediately followed by a series of geographically and culturally far-reaching comparisons.

> An interesting chapter, not on Highland manners alone, but on every stage of society in which the people of a primitive and half-civilised tribe are brought into close contact with a nation, in which civilisation and polity have attained a complete superiority.

> Thus a character like his, blending the wild virtues, the subtle policy, and unrestrained licence of an American Indian, was flourishing in Scotland during the Augustan age of Queen Anne and George I.

> His ideas of morality were those of an Arab chief, being such as naturally arose out of his wild education.[37]

Robin Oig, Rob Roy's son, is described as 'a good-looking young savage'; the city of Glasgow is seen as a frontier post 'frequented by the wilder tribes'; a gaoler, one of Rob Roy's clan, is a 'wild shockheaded animal', an 'uncouth, wild and ugly savage, adoring the idol of his tribe'.[38] Such savage subjects are legion in Scott's novels: from the 'old smoke-dried Highlander', a shaman who cures Edward's injuries after a hunting accident in *Waverley*,[39] to the 'half-savage' clans of *The Legend of Montrose* who make war like 'ancient Scythians or the salvage indians of America'.[40] In *The Chronicles of the Cannongate*, Chrystal Croftangry questions Mrs Bethune Baliol about the Highlands:

> 'The Highlands,' I suggested, 'should furnish you with ample subjects of recollection. You have witnessed the complete change of that primeval country, and have seen a race not far removed from the earliest period of society, melted down into the great mass of civilisation; and that could not happen without incidents striking in themselves, and curious as chapters in the history of the human race.'[41]

Yet Scott's 'primeval' Highlander lives neither in chaos nor savage anarchy; all action, no matter how violent or extreme, has a rational status *within* the culture of patriarchal barbarism – a rationality which he has uncovered in his antiquarian researches. In *Waverley*, for example, the feast at Glennaquoich displays the Chief at the centre of a benign feudal order:

> At the head of the table was the Chief himself, with Edward, and two or three Highland visitors of neighbouring clans; the elders of his own tribe, wadsetters, and tacksmen, as they were called, who occupied portions of his estate as mortgagees or lessees, sat next in rank; beneath them, their sons, and nephews, and foster-bretheren; then the officers of the Chief's household according to their order; and lowest of all, the tenants who actually cultivated the ground. Even beyond this long perspective, Edward might see upon the green, to which a huge pair of folding doors opened, a multitude of Highlanders of a yet inferior description, who, nevertheless, were considered as guests, and had their share both of the countenance of the entertainer, and of the cheer of the day.[42]

This vision of Highland society arises, as did Roza's image, as a pyramidal model of society which has several qualities to recommend it to Scott and his readership. The image is of a society of Maussian personas, of identities made by their social roles. It is also one of history stilled and immobile, and invested with the sacramental symbols of communion. The chief exists as the centre of benevolence and generosity in a society dominated by kinship ties and feudal orders. It is, above all, an image of social ranking which appears to be without any internal conflict; everyone knows his place, there are no under classes striving to usurp the power which does not belong to them. Glennaquoich reflects the ancient orders of the European pyramidal social hierarchy before the vortex of history destroyed them. In 1814, the image of the Highland world before the '45 offers the reader an alternative vision of a society untouched by the corrosive effects of commercial civilisation, social mobility and demographic change affecting civilised Britain.

But Scott's narratives embrace the historical vortex. His illustrations of Highland society are not born out of an intention to create discrete, hermetically sealed societies, but to place the Highlander in a relationship of conflict with other social forms and to see him break. In *The Heart of Midlothian*, one such confrontation occurs in microcosm:

> One, the same who had afforded such timely assistance, stood upright before them, a tall, lathy young savage; his dress a tattered plaid and philabeg, no shoes, no stockings, no hat or bonnet, the place of the last being supplied by his hair, twisted and matted like the *glibbe* of the ancient wild Irish, and, like theirs, forming a natural thickset, stout enough to bear off the cut of a sword. Yet the eyes of the lad were keen and sparkling; his gestures free and noble, like that of all savages.[43]

The Whistler, as this figure is called, escapes from the Redcoats who pursue him, is kidnapped, sold into slavery in America, escapes again and joins the natives with whom he shares a compatible level of culture, and he eventually dies a fully fledged 'wild Indian'.[44] The description of the Whistler represents a repertoire of Rousseauesque devices through which the savage world is represented. The culturally compatible Highlander, native American and 'ancient wild Irish' show the gulf which divides the world in the early nineteenth century; the Whistler could be any kind of savage antithetical to the other half of the world, the fourth stage of commercial civilisation.

This division is not racially determined since Jeannie Deans, the dour, respectable Lowlander of Covenanting stock, is also the Whistler's aunt and his parents are English aristocrats, Sir George and Lady Staunton. Jeannie attempts to read in the Whistler's face some of his parents' characteristics, but fails. Environment is all. In microcosm, the encounter shows two cultures, genetically linked but generically incompatible, which meet and fail to comprehend each other. This failure runs like a rift through time, emerging at points of conflict and historical crisis. Scott draws a world divided, and divided so deeply that the rift achieves the status of a historical law.

The Whistler episode is instructive in another sense also, that of Scott's narrative strategies. All of Scott's novels are deeply indebted to his voracious reading of romances and his reinscription of romance conventions in modern historical novels. The Whistler episode is one of those romance narrative story-types which frequently occur in Scott's novels – the foundling child. The romance convention, however, dictates a very different conclusion to that accomplished in Scott's novel. In the romance, the waif or foundling has a regal or noble bearing and demeanour which is confirmed as the plot unravels and it is discovered that the strange child has aristocratic or royal blood. Having been further ennobled by his/her sojourn in the liminal wilderness, the foundling is recovered and reincorporated into society at its very pinnacle, as its prince or king. In Scott's reworking of the romance story-type all the conventions of expulsion to the wilderness and subsequent detection are followed, the Whistler even has a 'free and noble' air, but romance cannot recuperate and reincorporate him. Indeed, the Whistler's departure from Scotland into even deeper savagery in America represents a travesty of the romance tradition. For Scott, the cultural and historical divisions are so deep, so extreme, that the older narratives of reconciliation cannot be made to function in the modern world, *except in an inverted form.* Romance is still of use to Scott as an articulate narrative medium, but this instance is an inversion of the conventions of romance since the trajectory of the Whistler's narrative is 'away' from culture and into deeper savagery. Scott is both unwilling and unable to make the recuperative strategies of romance fit with a modern history of displacement and eradication of cultural difference save by turning those articulate and recuperative narratives on their heads.

In *Waverley* the division emerges on a much grander scale and in terms which anticipate a Weberian distinction of bureaucratic and charismatic authority systems. The Hanoverians invest power in ruling cabals who operate a network of patronage through the control of offices. Their kinship structure is fragmented into small, nuclear groups, often jostling for power. Individualism is promoted over collective action, communication is by letter, commission, or formalised prescriptions. The Highlanders hold rights through blood ties and extended kinship networks as the universal cyphers of authority. Collective action under patriarchal leadership, warfare for booty and glory and the charismatic authority of the chief curtail individualism. Communication is oral. In every respect the charismatic Highlander is the inverse mirror of the bureaucratic Hanoverian.

Nineteenth-century readers of Scott's novels undoubtedly chose to take the side of the Highlander against their own 'Hanoverian' culture. The Victorian cult of the Highlands was inspired in large part by Scott's representation of the Highlander as the *alter ego* of the hegemony of Hanoverian commercial civilisation, which Scott represents as being fundamentally repressive. Power is the power of prohibition; nothing is produced, made or created by the Hanoverians other than denial.

Taken as a body of material, the Highland novels portray a process of repression of dissident ethnicities which borders on genocide. Ranald MacEagh, Vich Ian Vohr, Evan Dhu, Eachin MacIan, the son of *The Highland Widow*, the Whistler, are all victims of the opening of a tragic and exterminating vein in history when ethnic identities clash. History is seen as a field of struggles between orthodoxy and heterodoxy. What is remarkable, however, is the degree to which Scott's 'non-heroic' heroes not only survive the tragedies, but prosper from them. Menteith wins the love of Annot Lyle and high office, Waverley marries Rose and gains a wealthy inheritance, Frank Osbaldistone gains Die and his father's fortune, and even the despised Dalgetty wins back his family estate. Although each is in the centre of the historical vortex none is substantially harmed by its destructive forces. The 'middling' hero is unharmed because he remains detached from the warring ethnicities; he is not, as the Whistler is, an enculturated Highlander. But his role in the text is crucial as a narrative device of social exploration, the chief instrument for the accumulation of cultural information, passively to illuminate the social forms which constitute the historical confrontation from a position of objective 'neutrality'. Yet the goal of objectivity in the matter of cultural investigation is, Scott constantly demonstrates, an impossible condition and the quest for neutrality constitutes the 'crisis' of the middling hero.

Scott's 'middling' heroes are in a situation which is reminiscent of Scott's researches as an antiquarian. Scott as a researcher into cultural behaviour, and Waverley as a narrative device of cultural disclosure, unmask and make familiar the strange conduct of others; yet to be truly 'familiar' with the lives of others it is necessary to participate in that life, to be active. As observers, they are necessarily excluded from participation in social action and they exist, like the Huguenots of Le Moyne's illustrations, on the borders of a theatrical scene of social practices looking in. Their goal, to bring to their readers' eyes the 'truth' of this observed social world, to penetrate its masks of unfamiliarity and to make it narratable, redefines social practice as that and only that which is *visible*.

Scott is unsurpassed in his ability to make his cultures visible, but this ability to visualise has its negative aspect in that behaviour, activity, praxis is diminished to spectacle which turns everything into an object of observation, exegesis and representation. Scott's narrative descriptions reduce social relations to what is visible as spectacle and active familiarity as the praxis of social intercourse is substituted for spectacle masked as objectivity. Laudonnière's, Behn's and Stedman's particular emphasis upon the significance of 'eye-witnessing', the transformation of culture into spectacle, is also profoundly a part of Scott's narrative technique, but in Scott, the observer's inability to penetrate beyond the spectacle of social practices constitutes his crisis.[45]

In his particularly potent form of history-making, therefore, Scott recapitulates the social form envisaged in Roza's painting of a highly structured pyramidal historical order of ascending stages of social organisation derived from Enlightenment conjectural histories. The world is held together by its divisions and conflicts which his 'heroes' fail to render except as spectacle. The legalist formulae of rational political philosophies and the compromised objectivity of his observers deny the possibility of a primary experience of the cultures he describes. Scott's solution to this dilemma is to engage the reader's attention with an overriding, dynamic narrative technique which leads us out of a world which is both unknowable and at war with itself. The stadial theories of historical development showed a world unfolding in a prescribed pattern, but into this process Scott also introduces a narrative counterpoint which is similar in very many respects to Copley's reworking of the genre of 'history painting'.

As with Copley's images of historical conflict, Scott's dynamic narrative of history focuses upon the alien other, depicting his perceived savagery as the essence of the historical narrative. Again, having constructed the Highlander as a savage subject, the novels depict that subject as being expended by history so that history may continue. Scott's new narrative vocabulary creates the savage subject out of the rationalist theories only to see his violence and vigour expended and exhausted in the process of enunciation. There is a kind of economy of the savage in Scott's novels, whereby the savage is 'spent' by the narrative of history. Like Copley's black servant, his usefulness is in fulfilling his historical role of violent determination and then disappearing into contemporary anonymity or oblivion. Scott's novels and Copley's 'history painting' usher in a vision of history as a series of convulsions which pitch the marginal savage into its centre to be 'used up' in the interests of historical and narrative progress. The stasis and rigidity of rationalism give birth to a violent tempo in which the expendable marginal other is both key actant and first victim, the surplus value of historical narrative.

Something of the expendable nature of the Highlander has already been seen in Scott's reminiscences of his activities as a legal apprentice. Central to that reminiscence is an emphasis on the land of the Highlanders and Scott pays tribute to the beauties of 'the romantic scenery' and to himself as a central figure in making the Highlands visible and opening up that area to the gaze of the civilised. Scott's fictional treatment of landscape similarly discloses the Highlands as a spectacle for 'narrative tourists' but one which also contains historical inscriptions and the crucial role of the savage 'past' in the creation of the present. The landscape, and the picturesque precipice in particular, is an apt historical symbol for Scott's dynamic historical presentation of Highland culture since the Highlanders fell, were pushed or jumped to destruction. Precipices abound in Scott's novels: 'a huge precipice which barred all further passage' is the scene which typifies the Lowlander's contact with the Highlanders; Waverley meets the Highland cateran Donald Lean Bean on the edge of one precipice and loses his heart to Flora MacIvor on the edge of another; Baillie Nicol Jarvie dangles over another while a party of grenadiers is massacred below by Rob Roy. Campsie Abbey is the scene of the dramatic end of Eachin MacIan in *The Fair Maid of Perth*, and there too is the ubiquitous precipice: 'It arose on the summit of a precipitous rock, which descends on the princely river, there rendered peculiarly remarkable by the cataract called Campsie Linn, where its waters rush tumultuously over a range of basaltic rock which intercepts the current like a dike erected by human hands.'[46]

Eachin as the representative of Highland culture leaps from the falls and into the realms of antiquarian folklore since, Scott relates, he may have survived to become a hermit, or was snatched by the *daione shie* to become an 'elf-knight', although 'aught but thistledown must have been dashed to pieces'.[47] At the moment of extinction, Highland culture is ambiguously re-encoded by Scott in the veils of folkloric footnotes, doubly removed from history. The precipice is evidently a powerful trope of historical representation depicting the historical rift in geological terms. Yet the Highlander dies, falling into the chasm and into (possibly) myth, so that the new world of historical reality may be born; in *The Fair Maid of Perth*, the centralised Scottish state is left with a cleared historical landscape after Eachin's leap. Collectively, the novels depict the multiple births of the modern at the expense of the 'savage'. In every century, from the thirteenth to the eighteenth, Scott repeatedly shows the creation of modernity out of the catastrophe of the 'savage'.

Earlier in *The Fair Maid of Perth* and before Eachin's fall, Simon Glover is left to his own devices while the Highland clan with whom he is seeking refuge attend the funeral of their chief, the Captain of Clan Quhele. He climbs a hill and stretched beneath him is the Highland world in a microcosmic landscape. After a brief description of the lake, attention is focused on the ruins of the island abbey. It is a picturesque and antiquated spot which contains the remains of Sibilla, daughter of Henry I and consort of Alexander I. A paragraph later Scott recounts the approach of the funeral flotilla from out of the remote glen where the Dochart and Lochy enter Loch Tay, 'a wild and inaccessible spot, where the Campbells at a subsequent period founded their strong fortress of Finlayriggs',[48] the 'subsequent period' being, of course, after Culloden. The buildings testify to history's presence: a history of deaths, conquests and invasions over a six-hundred-year period of interminable conflicts. The narrative is set in the fourteenth century, but we 'see' the burial place of a twelfth-century queen and, in the same sentence, the future fortress of Finlayriggs, viewed from Scott's nineteenth-century viewpoint. The vision is subjected to prismatic deflections and varying perspectives: we see Simon looking, he is part of what we see, we see through his eyes, but above all, we see what Scott sees. What 'we' collectively (Simon, reader, Scott) 'see' is equally plural: twelfth-, fourteenth- and nineteenth-century landscapes, cemetery, funeral, fortress, Culloden. The history of death collapses time and identity in this landscape and the land is a text to be read synchronously by Scott. Simon, the reader, Scott see, in Fabian's phrase, a *monde commenté*[49] which establishes the prospect as a complex of historical and social discourses. This historical landscape, which is also an ethnographic landscape, is subjected to a double vision, at least. Scott's representation, his 'making history', plays on the difference between an attempted objective apprehension of history and another, more subjective and reflexive perspective which actively reveals the observer. In placing himself on the hillside with Simon (as omniscient viewer of the scene) *and* as writer of the text (as omnipotent maker of the scene), Scott attempts to present the scene to the imperious eye but succeeds only in recapitulating in his own textual identity the crisis of objectivity which he shows in his observers.

Scott's novels perpetually repeat similar images, narrative formulae, historical subjects, romance conventions. The narrational devices link novels together in chains of increasing complexity predicated upon a savage subject whose destruction leads to the birth of the 'modern'. These repeated patterns of history engage with the structures of romance and annotations frame and expand the fictional dimensions of the text, directing the reader to the correct apprehension of the historical narrative. History can be entered through romance; a narrative strategy of penetration of historical surfaces. Romance and historical structures are both aesthetic and moral as they conspire to produce symbolic and emblematic systems and signs which purport to be utterly expressive of the pleasures and pains of the historical past. The proper reading of these signs *should*, therefore, lead to a fuller comprehension of the twists and turns of history by reducing them to formulaic narratives. But instead of this desired state of enunciation, and instead of certainty in the emblematic structures, he describes the collapsing of cultures made of emblems and signs. Having made a kind of 'narrative machine' for the processing of history into narrative, Scott seems unwilling to make actuality fit an aesthetic and moral structure of history or romance, and the 'middling' hero is marked as much by his deep inability to 'see' things as they are, as he is by his ability to draw out the culture for examination. The uneasy relationship between history and romance, as if the narration is struggling with its own narrative, denies full validation to the historical processes described. Metaphorically stated, the precipice as an aesthetic and moral symbol, as both scenery and historical sign, would be a grand and instructive image if it were not for the Highland bodies falling from the cliffs.

Baron Bradwardine in *Waverley* gives the young and gullible eponymous hero a brief lesson on the state of the Highlands on the very 'precipice' of the '45:

'It did not, indeed,' he said, 'become them [the Highlanders], as had occurred in late instances, to propone their *prosapia*, a lineage which rested for the most part on the vain and fond rhymes of their Seannachies or Bhairds, as aequiponderate with the evidence of ancient charters and royal grants of antiquity, conferred upon distinguished houses in the Low Country by divers Scottish monarchs; nevertheless, such was their *outrecuidance* and presumption as to undervalue those who possessed such evidents, as if they held their lands in a sheep skin.'[50]

The Baron is, in his eccentric manner, drawing the distinction between Highland land tenure, founded on oral chronicles, and the antique charters of ownership issued by the monarchy; his disquisition depicts two kinds of *ancien régime*. Into this lesson erupts Evan Dhu in full Highland regalia. Edward 'thought the intrusion hostile' and 'started at the sight of what he had not yet happened to see'; the 'matter of astonishment' is here open to detailed examination as the figure of the Highlander is closely scrutinised and he is seen almost to coincide with John White's engraving of an ancient Pict. 'Stout', 'dark', 'young', 'strong', 'sinewy clean-made limbs', girt about with firearms and swords, Evan Dhu is handsome and violent. His speech is as alien as the Baron's is verbose:

'Fergus MacIvor Vich Ian Vohr,' said the ambassador in good English, 'greets you well, Baron of Bradwardine and Tully-Veolan, and is sorry there has been a thick cloud interposed between you and him, which has kept you from seeing and considering the friendship and alliances that have been heretofore between your houses and forebears of old; and he prays you that the cloud may pass away, and that things may be as they have been between the clan Ivor and the house of Bradwardine, when there was an egg between them for a flint, and a knife for a sword. And he expects you will say, you are sorry for the cloud, and no man shall hereafter ask whether it descended from the hill to the valley, or rose from the valley to the hill; for they never struck with the scabbard who did not receive with the sword; and woe to him who would lose his friend for the stormy cloud of a spring morning.'[51]

Evan's complex and rich language is, nonetheless, obedient to a strict pattern of stereotypical metaphors devised by Scott for the representation of primitive speech. Scott's Highlanders are always slipping into metaphorical speech, indeed the extended metaphors of arms, warfare and nature circumscribe the primitive worldview as being that of nature and violence.

The Baron's opening remarks, the references to 'the vain and fond rhymes of their Seannachies or Bhairds' compared to the 'ancient charters and royal grants of antiquity', express the differences between oral and literate cultures which are further explored in their relative speech patterns. Scott attempts in this passage to encompass the varieties of ways of expressing and thinking about the past; the myths and legends of the Highlands are contrasted with the literate forms of Lowland historiography and each conforms to either side of the historico-narrative cultural divide. A different kind of narrative enters along with Evan Dhu, one in which everything unfolds immediately before the 'hero' as Waverley and the speaking savage journey into the Highlands. Literacy and literate history is left in the Baron's dining room; in the Highlands, Edward and his companion talk their way into the landscape, halting and changing direction as speech and walking stop and start in new ways.

The dynamic of the narrative focuses attention on the single narrative event and oral exegesis. On their journey to Glennaquoich and the meeting with MacIvor, Evan and Edward come to the edge of a precipice and look down to the landscape below. Evan points out barely distinguishable marks in the moorland which were the graves of the Donnochie killed in a previous skirmish:

> 'If your eyes are good you may see the green specks among the heather' – He then immediately points upwards:
> 'See, there is an earn, which you Southrons call an eagle.'[52]

Vision shifts from extreme to extreme, top to bottom, to create a vertiginous effect in which space is dynamised, decomposed. The narrative momentarily follows the eagle, guiding the reader along a giddy and exhilarating progression of locations which leap into illumination. 'Looking' at this version of the Highland landscape is wholly unlike 'looking' at Simon Glover's scene. The landscape of Loch Tay presented the eye with a historical continuum through its multiple perspectives; this sublime landscape diffuses sight, the periphery forces itself into the centre of vision. Sight is liberated, here, from the compulsion to own or deny what it sees and is reinscribed as an experiencing subject's powerless but invigorated apprehension. Simon sees what many others have and will see as a historical fact; Edward sees for the first time and the primitive world is remarkably 'new' because it is beyond his capacity to 'own' it as a historical text; it is also beyond the sovereignty of the law of prohibition and denial. This is the timbre for the Highland narrative as a whole, as it twists and turns through a succession of narrative subjects: a progressive narrative sweep under the direction and control of the native's tongue.

The journey of Edward and Evan is a journey across the border and into the landscape. Simon Glover's landscape held the viewer distinct from the scene; this landscape encloses its figures who enter the vortex of the unknown. Although accompanied by Evan, Edward is alone as the alien figure in the landscape (Simon's hill, on the contrary, is rather crowded). This solitariness is as profoundly challenging to the Hanoverian notion of individualism and selfhood as Florida was to Laudonnière's Calvinist sensibilities, since identity must now become open and vulnerable to what it perceives as antithetical to its identity. Edward's journey captures the paradoxical situation of the explorer as exploration confirms the uniqueness and integrity of the male self alone, while simultaneously that identity must be the impotent subject of an uncertain environment. As if to underscore this jeopardy, Edward enters a gigantic landscape of mythological dangers:

> A thousand birds of prey, hawks, kites, carrion-crows, and ravens, disturbed from their lodgings which they had just taken up for the evening, rose at the report of the gun, and mingled their hoarse and discordant notes with the echoes which replied to it, and with the roar of the mountain cataracts.[53]

The frantic clamour of the Highland Pandemonium evokes a Miltonic epic subtext. At one point they cross a marsh traversed by tracks 'which none but a Highlander could have followed' and which is described by Scott as 'Serbonian' which refers us again to Milton:

> A gulf profound as that Serbonian bog
> Betwixt Damiata and Mount Casius old
> Where armies whole have sunk.[54]

The Serbonian bog has multiple significances: as a mythical and epic resonance which fits the scene; as the textual reference to the place where Typhon was overwhelmed and imprisoned for his rebellion against Heaven which presages the fall of the Highland cause and the Battle of Culloden; as an ill-omen, as the place where whole armies sink without trace.

These epic connotations are further underscored by the Dante-esque quality of the language and by linking Edward's trek to Dante's journey with his guide:

It was towards the evening as they entered one of the tremendous passes which afforded communication between the
High and the Low Country; the path, which was extremely
steep and rugged, winded up a chasm between two tremendous rocks, following the passage which foaming stream,
that brawled far below, appeared to have worn itself in the
course of ages. A few slanting beams of the sun, which was now
setting, reached the water in its darksome bed, and showed it
partially, chafed by a hundred rocks, and broken by a hundred
falls. The descent from the path to the stream was a mere
precipice, with here and there a projecting fragment of granite,
or a scathed tree, which had warped its twisted roots into the
fissures of the rock. On the right hand the mountain rose above
the path with almost equal inaccessibility; but the hill on the
opposite side displayed a shroud of copsewood, with which
some pines were intermingled.[55]

The landscape here is a symbolic condensation of the tortuous
history of the Highlands and one which carries echoes of Canto xii of
The Inferno:

The shelving path our cautious steps pursue;
When lo! another gulph appears in view;
Th' astonish'd eye starts back, our feet recoil.
Not with such fearful view the Trentian steep
Looks dizzy down upon the circling deep
    Where slow invasion mines the mould'ring soil.
There oft the thundering rain smites the plain;
The flood recoils, and leads her humid train
    Far, far aslope! the riv'n rock disjoins.[56]

The circle of Hell which Dante and Virgil approach is that
inhabited by the sons of violence, and of tyrants, oppressors and
conquerors, which is again a symbolic prognosis of the Stuart cause.
At the end of this first journey of 'th' astonish'd eye' into the
Highlands in Scott's first novel, though, another kind of landscape is
glimpsed, one which leaves behind the epic connotations.

The moon, which now began to rise, showed obscurely the
expanse of water which spread before them, and the shapeless
and indistinct forms of mountains with which it seemed to be
surrounded. The cool and yet mild air of the summer night
refreshed Waverley after his rapid and toilsome walk; and the
perfume which it wafted from the birch trees, bathed in the
evening dew, was exquisitely fragrant.[57]

The natural world is dissolving. The novel is passing into Karonghyontye's primitive penumbra. Obscurely, shapeless, and indistinct,
the epic mountains are resolving into formlessness, their power

spent. From the harsh, angular and violent world of the pass, which was a stone world, this is now a twilight of mists and water. The trees, 'bathed in the evening dew', pass into essence, fragrance which registers an invisible presence. The narrative has led to this ethereal but extinguishing perception. A different kind of knowledge, an intuitive vision of 'romantic scenery' is all that is left of Edward's expedition across the Highland border, riding, as Scott himself had done, 'in all the dignity of danger, with a front and rear guard, and loaded arms'. The Highlanders' and the landscape's violence having been spent, there is time, now, and safety enough – until the maelstrom – for the romance of making history.

John Richardson lived on a different border. Richardson was a major in the British army in Canada who followed the advice Scott offered to his own brother Thomas, then serving in the army in Canada, that he should write novels about the native Americans:

> He [Thomas] being familiarly acquainted with the manners of the native Indians, of the old French settlers in Canada, and of the Brulés or Woodsmen ... his brother would have made himself distinguished in that striking field, in which, since that period, Mr Cooper has achieved so many triumphs.[58]

Richardson's own biography is inscribed in the fictions *Wacousta!* (1832) and *The Canadian Brothers* (1840). His father had been heir to a younger branch of the Annandale family attainted in the Rebellion of 1745. Richardson's presence on the Canadian border can be accounted for by the actions of lawyers like the young Walter Scott. Both novelists describe the comparable historical situations of their own borders; Scott's fictionalisations of the '15 and '45 structure and inform Richardson's representations of the raids and indian wars and the American–British–Canadian War of 1812–14.

Richardson learned from Scott the potency of the conjectural or universal historian's account of human development in representing the narrative of the British Army sealed in their fastnesses against a sea of savagery. The narrative of *Wacousta!* is embedded in the style of the 'northern gothick' or 'wilderness romance' which was heavily indebted to Scott. Set in the forests of the Great Lakes in the period of Pontiac's wars against the British in 1763, the novel has as its main protagonists de Haldimar, the commander of the beseiged garrison, and Wacousta, a murderous and rapacious leader of a band of indian guerrillas. More extreme than his fellow savages, Wacousta is revealed to be (like the Whistler) a 'voluntary', as seventeenth-century writers might have described him, a European turned 'savage'. The Indian wars form the backcloth to the terrible revenge of Wacousta upon de Haldimar and his family. De Haldimar stole away and married Wacousta's beloved and Wacousta has his revenge on de Haldimar's children. *Wacousta!* gives full rein to the violence of the savage as brains are lapped up by 'wolf-dogs', dishevelled female victims are done to death (but not before they have bared their breasts); in fact, the only apparent motives the natives seem to have in waging war is to knock out brains and unhook bodices.

But there are points where something else filters through. De Haldimar's daughter's boudoir is a veritable Smithsonian Institution of native American domestic artifacts and *objets d'art*. But these are glimpsed only in passing, as the reader follows the victims' flight from the savages who are beating down the bedroom door. Richardson engages momentarily with these fascinating objects only to turn from them in horror or revulsion: 'This was too uneuropean – too much reversing the established order of things.'[59]

Clustering around his representation of the indian is a series of images combining to produce the *habitus* of native American culture. Richardson read his Scott well; Pontiac speaks like Evan Dhu, in the extended metaphors of war and nature. There is much also of the native American as a *speculum mentis* of the darker imaginations of a repressed, civilised psychology. Cleanly made limbs, strong bodies, naked breasts, secret kisses and hidden sexual encounters by night mark Richardson's representations of savagery and owe something at least to Scott's.

The ramparts of the fort are protection against the dark image of the forest. Again and again, the nature/culture division is inscribed onto the Canadian landscape in ways reminiscent of Scott, as Richardson shows civilisation under siege. Nowhere is this more emphatically shown than in the story of how Wacousta became a 'savage'. He tells how he was pursuing a stag to the edge of a precipice when the stag disappeared through a crevice in the rock. Wacousta followed to discover a secret garden, the home of a recluse and his beautiful daughter. Having fallen in love with the girl, 'the child of nature', he steals her away from this idyllic setting only to have her in turn stolen by de Haldimar. The play of binary opposites gradually reveals that this central narrative within the novel occurs, not in Canada, but in the Scottish Highlands, and Wacousta's real name is Reginald Morton, an officer in a British regiment suppressing and evicting the Highlanders.[60]

Richardson seems to have had few optimistic hopes for the providential historical plan. As one of his editors expressed it, Richardson seems to see man 'lured towards the rational conquest of the human and natural world only to prove its absolute meaninglessness'. The precipice in the dark is the dominant landscape motif of the civilised man cut adrift in wild nature. But it is not only the savage who leaps to his destruction; he is joined in his descent by the colonialist and finally by the historical romance itself. There is no capacity, no time, for Richardson to make history on a more elegant or subtle scale; his novels exist in a kind of permanent present tense of action without historical motivation. For Richardson, 'difference' means war. The rift in time cannot be healed nor theorised; Richardson can only put his faith in the discipline of the army or retreat to the fort. For Scott, a form of resolution of past conflict existed, however unsatisfactorily, in the pragmatic compromises of his own present, in the evocations of the timeless mists of the romantic landscape. In any case, by 1814 the savage threat of the Highlander was a spent force. Canadian literary culture in the 1830s offers no satisfactory alternative aesthetic to the horror (real or gothick) of cultural confrontation and destruction. Richardson's present can offer no coherence, resolution or independence. He may have learned the 'matter of astonishment' and much else to do with the 'colonial novel' from Scott, but there was little to be seen in the killing fields of nineteenth-century Canada to support a belief in the solace of 'romantic scenery'.

Chapter 5

'Do they eat their enemies or their friends?': Cambridge and Buganda 1887–1932

Keeping magic out has itself the character of magic.
Wittgenstein[1]

Two familiar vignettes: in volume I, chapter 3 of the first edition of *The Golden Bough*, 'Killing the God', there is a section dealing with the sacrifice of first-born children.[2] Frazer's examples are typically eclectic, ranging from Carthage, to Rhodes, to New South Wales, to East Africa, to the 'heathen Russians' in a single page – a completely undifferentiated geographic, cultural and historical mass. 'The Indians of Florida' are there also, one sentence stating simply that they 'sacrificed their first born male children' and acknowledging Strachey's *Historie of Travaille into Virginia Britannia* as his source. In a recent reprint of the first edition, this reference is the cue for an illustration by an anonymous contemporary of Frazer's, reworked from the Le Moyne–De Bry engraving (figure 17).[3]

The Golden Bough's illustration of the Timucuas is transformed from the Le Moyne original in many significant features. The scene has been reversed: the dancing women have been moved from the right to the left; the men have similarly moved across the page. *The Golden Bough's* image is a reflection of Le Moyne's. Outina, moved from left to right, no longer occupies the foreground, the stage of the imperial gaze, and he looks not away from the women, but directly at them, absorbed in their rites of supplication. His figure is diminished and solitary on his rustic throne as Laudonnière and his arquebusiers are absent from the scene. Outina's diminished scale makes the rendering of the detail of his body imperceptible; his tattoos, his decoration, his beauty have all disappeared. The viewer

17 Anonymous illustration of the Florida Indians, in James Frazer, *The Golden Bough*, 1890

now looks, not along the line of Outina's gesture as in Le Moyne's image, but from a right angle, to the side, the viewer's place concealed behind some bushes.

The Vitruvian stage has also given way to a natural landscape. The demarcations of audience and stage are dissolved into a landscape which continues to a vanishing point in picturesque mountains, precipices and the setting sun. It is all farther away, more distant, and lacking the dramatic immediacy of the original.

The sun casts an unnatural light on the landscape, setting as it is to the right, behind Outina, who casts a shadow towards the left, but the precipice casts a shadow towards the right, in the direction of the sun, shrouding half the women and all of Outina's warriors in darkness. The scene is not illuminated but darkened by the light. The supplicant women bow equally to the sun and to their king.

The Golden Bough illustration is an evocation but also a denial of many of the features of Le Moyne's original. The historical moment of the Laudonnière–Outina encounter is lost to be replaced and reconstructed as absolute difference between primitive and civilised. The Timucuas lose their name and become, instead, the 'Florida Indians'. This illustration's content of information is supplementary to its representational substance since the need to 'see' the primitive is less pressing at the turn of the nineteenth century than it was at the turn of the sixteenth. Chiaroscuro, the reduced range of colours and textures, is moralised in that the use of light uncovers the visible darkness of benighted savagery. Space is consequently also transformed from the Le Moyne original. The dynamically organised divisions of foreground and stage give way to one single threshold comprising the frame of the image as a whole. The viewer is now outside the image. The theatrical effect is still evoked, but this is the nineteenth-century stage of the proscenium rather than the festival stage of the royal *entrée* or masque. *The Golden Bough* illustration still privileges the act of seeing, but this is a private spectacle for the voyeuristic onlooker; the whole society, not just the women, are on stage and the viewer does not share his sight with Outina as Laudonnière did. The viewer is not implicated in this scene: 'we' are not there, nor is our representative; 'we' are not 'them'.

Outina's gaze is turned to the dancing women, not to his guests. He no longer invites us in with his gesture of disclosure, his hand holds back no invisible curtain revealing what is 'inside' his state. We steal this vision. The colonist–ethnographer is not depicted in the act of observation, nor is he a welcome guest and witness to a culture's

secret spectacle. Our apprehension goes unseen. There are no gestures of familiarity, friendship and reassurance. Outina's form is
remote, powerless to touch us. We are not mirrored in Outina's gaze.

Everything is now spectacle, frozen by the gaze or obscured by
shadow. Here are secrets. The world of the Timucuas is shaded by
the Romantic penumbra. Their *polis* which featured as the chief
subject of interest to Le Moyne, now has to compete with the
splendid scenery. Outina's *dominium* exists but it is of lesser significance than the Nature which qualifies it. The European vision is
not a part of that social whole, except perhaps as landlord. Where
the European gaze has no part of the image's representation, the
savage can have no part of the European's concerns. The Timucuan
state has nothing to say with respect to European political obsessions. The Timucuas cannot, in *The Golden Bough*'s image, be made to
participate in European propaganda; such things are above them.
They are denied access to our world, even in the misrepresented
form of our ambitions.

Ethnographic representation is abolished in favour of the narrativisation of absolute difference. The constructed formal boundaries
dissolve into one: us and them. The savage space is deadeningly
simple. But just as with Le Moyne's *bricolage* of Renaissance myths
and politics, this image also encodes its era's assumptions. The
viewer still enters the scene through his/her specular authority but
that authority does not require the compliance of an informed
intermediary. The 'grammar' of this illustration still encodes the
linking of native custom and heretical activity but 'heresy' is less
actively a part of this image's concern: Laudonnière does not reach
for his sword. 'Heresy' is tolerated as cultural relativity neutralises
behaviour into 'custom'. This is an example (alongside Carthage and
Uganda) less of belief or conviction than of primitive 'magic'. The
European viewer is not here, not because he does not participate in
this rite or this scene, but because he does not participate in this
savage epistemology.

Little remains of the romance connotations of this image save,
perhaps, for the voyeuristic situation of its spectator. The lingering
traces of the social orders of romance are, quite literally, overshadowed by the gloomy air of primitive ritual which occludes their
expressive capacities. Outina the king is less a social functionary
than a 'divine' heathen posing as the sun's representative. Their
existence as 'personas', individuals identified by the 'masks' of their
social roles, gives way to their depiction as subjects of a tyrant who

rules through their shared mental error. In this image, unlike the romance, the world of fabulous, magical or exotic unfamiliarity is transformed to the ubiquitous brutality of savagery, felt less as cruelty than as an example of defective thinking.

Romance is extinguished as Outina is diminished. The extinction of romance means that the spectator, as surrogate quester, can have no role as hero of the 'wandering wood' of the New World. The Renaissance perception of man as *homo duplex* is here redefined. Man's nature is still divided, but the lesser half worships Outina out there in the darkening grove. Outina and his people have been diminished to the status of a case study in the science of the evolution of human mentalities.

The second vignette is of Sir James and Lady Frazer, he exhausted and she ill, who spent the summer of 1915 away from Cambridge to recuperate in Perthshire, from where Frazer wrote to an old friend with information about Rivers' expedition to the New Hebrides and with advice for his friend's own planned expedition to Uganda. The letter then describes the Frazers' own situation:

> This is a very beautiful place at the lower end of Loch Tay, where the river flows out of it. The hills are high and some of them are well wooded. In the distance we see big Ben Lawers towering above the lake. The steamers are now running, and we hope to make expeditions in them.[4]

The rather flat tone disguises an unintentional irony. Frazer uses the same term to describe the Uganda and New Hebrides expeditions and his own 'expeditions' – trips on a Loch steamer. The Uganda expedition would also end beside a lake, Victoria–Nyanza, and the passage seems to recall, obliquely, that other lake.

Frazer 'stands' in his letter in the exact position in which Simon Glover 'stood' in *The Fair Maid of Perth*, and when Grant first stood on the shores of Lake Victoria, he sketched the scene in watercolours, but added steamers plying their trade across the Lake, depicting what, to his eye, Victoria–Nyanza would become.[5]

Frazer depicts a post-Culloden scene, neither 'wild' nor 'inaccessible', emptied of danger, emptied of content. Frazer depicts and Grant predicts a time after the history of deaths, when the loch and the lake have been or will be subdued and made accessible. In Scotland, Frazer shows Uganda's future when Lake Victoria would become an African Loch Tay. As Scotland was, Uganda is; as Scotland is, Uganda shall be; past, present and future glimpsed in transformed and transforming landscapes: the undeniable and irresistible coming of civilisation to the 'wild and inaccessible places' of the world. Making history, particularly the kind of history which Scott practised, is all but eradicated from these places; Frazer sees none of Glover's sights.

Frazer invented a new kind of master narrative to replace Scott's historical novel, one which emptied, ransacked that other world, and filled it again with new forms and structures. That process of remaking of the representation of the primitive world begins in the gathering of ethnographic data, and here Frazer encountered an immediate and pressing problem which the vignette also discloses. Rivers and his friend travel to Oceania and Africa to do their anthropology; Frazer stays in his rooms at Trinity College or makes 'expeditions' on the Loch Tay ferryboat.

How is it possible for an anthropologist to write anthropology without ever leaving his college? How does the 'armchair anthropologist' gather information without 'eye-witnessing'?

Frazer's solution to this seemingly intractable problem was to devise a series of questionnaires for distribution to travellers, government officials, missionaries and merchants and to request that they supply him with information on the primitive peoples they encountered. The *Questions on the Manners, Customs, Religion, Superstitions, etc. of Uncivilized or Semi-Civilized Peoples* began in 1887 as a privately published pamphlet of thirteen pages. Frazer's intention in 1887 was to distribute the *Questions* through every agency available to him and, as the titlepage requests, 'answers to all or any of the following questions will be gratefully received by J. G. Frazer, MA, FRGS, Trinity College, Cambridge, England'. 'Mr Frazer proposes to publish the results of his inquiries. Full acknowledgment will be made of those who have favoured him with answers, and printed copies will be forwarded to them.'

The original document of 1887 contained a caveat, however, that 'as the questions have been drawn up to elicit information about a large range of people, it is probable that many of them will not apply to the particular people with which you are acquainted'. Frazer's assumption seems to have been that the document should cover every eventuality of 'uncivilised' life, and that the questions asked would, if fully answered, constitute a complete ethnographic description and that it would not be the *Questions* which were inadequate to the task but the uncivilised society itself which would be exhausted by inquiry, thus rendering some questions redundant.

The questionnaires and the replies he received formed a significant body of data which he included in his works, but it would be misleading to represent Frazer as simply a conduit transferring the raw substance of observation to a reading public. On the contrary, the questionnaires are an integral part of a systematic method which arose from this undifferentiated mass of 'facts', and which shaped them into significant patterns of inquiry and structures of representation and discourse. The whole project, from observer to textual artifact, represented a radical reshaping of the discourse of cultural representation. Frazer's *Questions* represent an attempt to construct a template, a schema for the description of primitive peoples, and as such offer insights into the nature of the anthropological project as it was envisioned at the end of the nineteenth century.

What is remarkable, therefore, is the small number of questions which Frazer felt it was necessary to ask; the 1887 *Questions* consisted, in fact, of only eleven pages of text, excluding introductory material, and 187 questions in total. Admittedly, some questions contained multiple or supplementary questions, but even so, the range of inquiry – reminiscent in many ways of Lafitau's categorisations of savage society – is remarkably narrow, shaped by Frazer's research interests and by his own preconceptions of the uncivilised state.

The 187 questions are distributed among 32 named sections, which themselves form larger unnamed generic patterns.[6] In the 1887 *Questions*, Frazer refashioned the eighteenth-century ethnographic project by shifting attention away from the material subsistance of primitive societies and towards a number of specific and defining concerns. He would seem to have been most concerned to elicit information on 'Tribes; Birth, Descent, Adoption; Puberty; Marriage; Food; Agriculture; Measurement of Time; Magic and Divination; Superstitions' since all of these sections contain more than ten questions (including supplementary questions). The rest contain fewer questions, 'Salutations', 'Government' and 'Religious and Political Associations' being the fewest; 'Marriage' contains the most at 31 questions.

The emphasis of Frazer's questioning is also indicative of the relative importance he ascribed to certain activities: 'Property and Inheritance' gets remarkably short shrift, 'Government' is barely represented and little inquired into, and 'Religious and Political

Associations' are indistinguishably connected. The 187 questions and 32 sections could be further reduced to a very few topics which return repeatedly to Frazer's own presuppositions of the nature of uncivilised existence. The section concerned with 'Birth, Descent, Adoption', for example, asks questions of his informant which are almost entirely to do with ceremonial or ritual behaviour. Economic, educational or political issues are wholly ignored in favour of loosely defined 'rites'. Thus the ceremonies (which are assumed to exist) controlling 'uncleanness in pregnancy' or rituals concerning the appointment of 'god-fathers' and the Timucuan theme of 'the custom of killing the first-born at birth' predominate in his questioning. The shade of the Timucuas is seen again in the section concerned with 'War' since he asks if 'they mutilate their slain enemies?' 'War' is ritual by another means: an extension of ceremonial behaviour, without recourse either to its political or economic causation. 'Puberty' is similarly ritualised by Frazer's request for information on the 'ceremonies performed on lads'. Do they ritually 'kill the lad' and restore him to life? Do they (shades of the Surinam warchiefs and De Bry's chronicle icon) 'circumcise, knock out, chip or file the teeth, bore the nose, distend the ears, insert rings in the lips, etc.? do they tattoo or raise cicatrices on their bodies at puberty? what patterns?' Clearly, Frazer is anxious to gather material to substantiate his own theories on the ceremonial rites of the dying and reviving god, but in ways which vividly recall the ancient image of the culturally mutilated body of the savage. Frazer's interest in female puberty rites limits his informant's description to those concerned only with the onset of menstruation, so whereas men are permitted access to the rituals of Adonis, women are circumscribed within a physiological function.

The section on 'Murder', is a further telling example, since murder is only very loosely defined as criminality carrying a legal sanction; Frazer pitches his questions towards 'pollution, vendetta, bloodgeld, purification of the murderer'. Similarly, 'Death and Disease' frames the uncivilised notion of disease in the assumption that they already perceive disease as spirit possession or the effects of malevolent demons. 'Death' for the uncivilised is another round of ceremonies of purification, fear of ghosts and superstitions about the dead. Likewise, 'Agriculture' obliterates production in favour of the ceremonial activities required to make the harvest abundant. 'Food' is not about the production and preparation of food, but ritualised prohibitions on what can be consumed and cannibalism: 'do they eat their enemies or their friends? do they ever drink the blood of men or animals? do they think that by eating the flesh of certain animals or persons they acquire the qualities of the animal or person eaten?'

Certainly, some of the *Questions'* sections are distorted by Frazer's immediate research interests. The opening section on 'Tribes' begins with a simple request to 'enumerate the tribes' and to show how the tribes are 'distinguished', but very rapidly the questioning embarks upon a series of inquiries about totemism as Frazer rides his own particular hobby-horse through the questions. The lengthy section on 'Scapegoats' and 'Fire', or those on 'Men as women, women as men' and 'Oaths and ordeals', show Frazer asking for information to pursue theories he had already evolved. The 'Doctrine of Souls', for example, pitches the inquiry towards beliefs in the transmigration of the soul into animals and plants and asks for information on whether they believe animals possess a language of their own, all of which supplies him with data for work already undertaken.

Few of Frazer's questions are unalloyed requests for information; most are subjected to the torsions and inflections inherent in the question itself. The 'Measurement of Time' assumes that 'time' means 'natural' or 'seasonal' time rather than a 'western' notion of temporal progression. The uncivilised are assumed not to be able to count, or if they can, only to a limited value; illiteracy is a *sine qua non* of the uncivilised. The section on 'Marriage' asks for details of prohibitions on marriage, yet this, too, assumes that companionate marriage is an institution incompatible with uncivilised life with its emphasis upon 'purchase' or 'capture'.

The *Questions* of 1887, then, advance an extraordinarily limited area of research interests, essentially to do with 'totemism' and ritual, coloured by the assumed characteristics of the uncivilised. The subsequent publication and reissues of the *Questions* built upon the presumptions of the first edition, but they also attempted to include questions which reflected information he had received from the 1887 issue. *The Journal of the Anthropological Institute* published a supplement in 1889 which expanded the questionnaire by a further eight pages from 187 to 213 questions. The additional sections, although not entirely new, do represent Frazer's attempt to come to terms with the information he had already received. He expanded the section on 'Agriculture', included one on 'pastoral life' and lengthened his 'Miscellaneous' section, dropping 'superstitions' from the title. But even so, his new-found interest in economic subsistence very quickly gives way to established habits of mind.

From asking if 'they keep cattle?' the questions soon turn to 'is there any special sanctity attached to the dairy, and to the dairyman or dairywoman?' The 'Miscellaneous' section seems to include all those questions which do not fit elsewhere and the eccentric and frivolous mingle with rather more significant matters, such as 'have the natives any kind of money, or anything which passes as money . . .?' or 'how is the succession to the chieftainship or kingdom determined?'

In 1907 Cambridge University Press undertook to print, free of charge to Frazer, a revised version and Frazer radically overhauled and expanded the *Questions* of 1887 and the *JAI* supplement. The pamphlet more than doubled its length to fifty-one pages and from 213 questions to 507. Further reprintings by CUP in 1910 and 1916 replicated this 1907 version. But more than just the number of questions had been revised; Frazer had changed the title in a small but significant fashion. The Questions were now known as *Questions on the Customs, Beliefs and Languages of Savages*.

Other changes were also clearly at work. Frazer had persuaded the Press Syndics to keep the type of the *Questions* standing so that changes and additions could be made as the information shaped requirements. The rather presumptuous and dogmatic tone of the first edition was relieved by a greater flexibility of approach. Also, Frazer's introductory remarks had been extended into a short essay on the most efficacious means for the correspondent to act as participant observer. The questions 'should not be put directly to the savage' but should be used 'to indicate to a civilized enquirer in the field those subjects on which investigators at home would be glad to have information'.[7] The 'judicious enquirer himself should choose the exact form' of question. Nonetheless, the demarcation of terms is absolute, despite the flexible role Frazer envisages for his questionnaire; the savage is confronted by his opposite, the 'civilized' and 'judicious enquirer' with one eye on his fellow 'investigators' at 'home'. A loosening of the method of inquiry is accompanied by a tightening of the terms of the encounter.

Frazer cautions against the use of leading questions for, he writes, 'the savage is commonly quick enough to perceive the drift of such enquiries and polite enough to give the answers which he believes will be most acceptable'. But the savage's readiness to please, 'a fertile source of error', derives ultimately from his 'indifference to . . . abstract truth'; the 'best way to proceed' Frazer claims is to let the savage 'run on until he has exhausted himself' and then to double check his veracity by asking him points he has 'imperfectly explained'. Above all, it is important 'to let them speak as much and himself as little as possible' so as not to give away what the 'judicious enquirer' wishes to hear and to keep 'a pointed set of questions beside him' 'to recall the wandering attention of his interlocutor'.[8] Having instructed the informant on how to guard against the lies of savages, Frazer then goes on to specify the kind of information required:

> General answers to the questions are of little value: it is the details ... which are important to science. No facts should be neglected as too trivial to be investigated and recorded; for facts which, taken by themselves, appear to be wholly insignificant may be of the highest importance in their relation to others which are unknown to the enquirer.[9]

The 1907 *Questions* arranged its 507 questions through 34 sections. Many of the sections remain the same or only slightly changed from 1887/9 but many were omitted: Oaths and Ordeals; Salutations; Measurement of Time; Games and Dances; Religious and Political Associations; Scapegoats; Resurrection; Men as Women, Women as Men; Sleep Forbidden; Guardian Spirits. Many sections, although retaining the overall shape of 1887/9 had new additions: Clans and Totemism was added to Tribes; Infancy to Birth, Descent, Adoption; Intercourse of the Sexes to Marriage; Slaves to Property and Inheritance; Messages and Records replaced Writing and so on. Some wholly new categories were introduced, however: Relationship; Clothing, Implements, Houses, Industries; Trade and Commerce; Social Intercourse; Astronomy, Meteorology, the Calendar; Earth, Stones, Trees, Plants, Water, Animals; Traditions; Folktales and Riddles; Names; Language; Vocabulary.

The 1907 *Questions* shows some relative shifts of interest. In 1887/9, the section concerned with Government was thinly represented with only four printed questions, but in 1907 the number of questions had risen to 63. Agriculture rose from 15 in 1887 to 46 in 1907; questions relating to marriage almost doubled; those concerned with birth and descent rose from 18 to 42. But this should not be seen simply as Frazer discovering a new materialism in this emphasis upon the nature of kinship, property, subsistence and politics, because the familiar Frazerian fascination with non-material culture persists: Ceremonial Uncleanness, Sacrifices, the Doctrine of Souls and Demons and Spirits all show a similar extensive expansion. Nonetheless, Frazer's inclusion of new topics (for him) does go some way to redressing the non-materialist bias of his earlier collection, even to the extent of acknowledging that 'Trade and Commerce' or 'Industries' may be relevant terminologies to apply to savage societies.

The interest in ritual and ceremony again predominates, but newer and rather more frank questioning of the sexual life of savages is also present. The largest section, however, remains that of 'Miscellaneous' and this is, in itself, indicative of the whole project; that despite the scientific pretensions, there is something 'miscellaneous' about his questions and their arrangement. The 1907 *Questions* represents an alteration in his attention to the material basis of savage life, but Frazer still fails to direct his informants toward a full apprehension of 'the simple folk' as his introduction terms them, as inhabiting a society with complex economic and political institutions.

Frazer was active in distributing his pamphlet of questions, in its various incarnations, over a thirty-year period. His method seems to have been to broadcast the document quite indiscriminately if his letter to Henry Jackson in 1888 is an indication. He lists the 'Geographical and Anthropological libraries' as places where 'any traveller who will take them' may obtain a copy; he sent them to missionary societies and the 'great trading companies', to colonial governments and to the Smithsonian Institution, but he also pressed friends to take up the cause and 'if you happen to know of any person likely to be able and willing to answer them from first hand knowledge of any set of savages, I should be much obliged if you could let me have his address'.[10]

Some fell on stony ground, of course. John Bourke, a Captain in the US Cavalry and author of a monograph on the ritual uses of urine, replied with a brief but polite refusal referring Frazer to his forthcoming book which might provide answers 'affirmative or negative, to many of your queries'.[11] James Wells of Beckenham, who introduced himself to Frazer as 'author of *Three Thousand Miles through Brazil*', regretted that he had not the time to devote to answering his questions, but in any case, despite a 'long and varied experience in that Empire', he had had very little actual contact with the natives. He offered, instead, a short reading list.[12]

Frazer's project soon ran into difficulties of a different kind, however. W. H. R. Rivers had raised objections to the use of questionnaires from their inception and when the *Journal of the Anthropological Institute* printed a supplement and began to record Frazer's informants' replies, the disagreement broke out into gentlemanly hostilities. Rivers' objections were to the unreliability of testimonies of all sorts, preferring instead the tangible evidence of physical culture, archaeology and anthropometrical analysis. Rivers' disagreement with Frazer was reproduced in the minutes recorded in the *Journal*. The dispute dragged on and Frazer became intensely annoyed when, on the publication of the revised *Questions* in 1907, Rivers wrongly reported one of Frazer's informants as holding the view that the whole exercise was without value. Frazer commiserated with his informant in a tone of barely suppressed rage:

> If my letter betrayed my annoyance, I hope you will understand and forgive it. You have suffered from Rivers too. He is a highly superior person, but you and I know that he is not infallible, and when he assumes the air of an oracle I am not inclined to put up with it. I did not need to learn from him that Questions may be abused. So may the Bible, so may anything.[13]

Rivers' dispute with Frazer was, perhaps, the consequence of professional rivalry. The *Questions* evoked a different response from among the amateur ethnographers Frazer aimed to enlist. Several notable anthropologists began their work as a direct result of receiving a copy of Frazer's booklet: Archer's work on the peoples of Lake Rudolph, Dundas on the Baringo and Hollis' and Hobley's researches in East Africa. P. A. Talbot, the author of *The Ekoi* and *Nigerian Perspectives*, wrote to Frazer in 1911 and again in 1913 paying tribute to the value of the *Questions*: 'Your vocabulary was followed for the Buduma Language and your list of questions was most useful all through'; 'Of course, all my information is put together on the basis of your questions . . .'[14]

In the Preface to the 1907 *Questions* Frazer commented on the revisions he had made to the original 1887 document:

> I have had the great advantage of conversing on the subject of the Questions with my friend the Rev. J. Roscoe of the Church Missionary Society, who has had long experience in the collection of ethnological information among the tribes of central Africa, particularly among the Baganda. The method of enquiry which I have recommended to collectors is the one which Roscoe has followed for years, and with the best results. Its practical success in his hands is a sufficient proof of the soundness of the principle.[15]

Roscoe was the friend Frazer wrote to from Loch Tay and the person Rivers misrepresented in his dispute with Frazer, and of all his informants Frazer came to regard Roscoe's 'testimony to the usefulness of my Questions as by far the most valuable and weighty I ever received'. The relationship between Frazer and Roscoe began in the 1890s and lasted until Roscoe died. They communicated regularly for almost forty years and Roscoe proudly declared himself a 'disciple of Sir James, to whose inspiration I owe my first love for this important branch of study'.[16] The relationship which was founded upon Frazer's *Questions* was extremely productive, since the books Roscoe went on to write owed their genesis and form to the 1887 booklet. The example of Roscoe and Frazer demonstrates the relationship between the anthropologist and his observing ethnographer and shows, in detail, the kind of anthropology which could be written out of the *Questions* project. With remarkable clarity, the relationship displays how Frazer's method accomplished his goal of scientific analysis.

At first sight, Roscoe and Frazer would seem to have little in common, since Roscoe was a missionary and traveller in East Africa and Frazer a sceptic and agnostic and largely tied to his study. Certainly Roscoe led a much more adventurous life than Frazer. In the 1890s Roscoe and his wife were captured by Arabs and condemned to death, the ransom to obtain their freedom arriving less than an hour before the planned execution. The relationship rapidly developed into a friendship. On his return to England, Roscoe catalogued Frazer's library for him, which must have been a monumental task on the one side and a signal confidence on the other.[17] Their letters, always signed 'Yours affectionately', are filled with touching gentilities.[18] They arranged to meet regularly for walks together when Roscoe was in Cambridge. Roscoe once proposed that they call each other by their first names, but Frazer gently declined: 'Nothing can alter our friendship, and as I grow older I become more and more averse to innovations of all kinds, even of names.'[19] When Ridgeway attacked *The Golden Bough* in 1915, over the disputed origins of Greek tragedy, it was to Roscoe that Lady Frazer turned for advice. Should she allow Sir James to see the offending work or should she hide it from him? Roscoe counsels against non-disclosure where 'the honour of *The Golden Bough*' is at stake. 'It will never be discarded because of the wonderful compilation of facts which make it an encyclopaedia for all time', he wrote.[20]

The letters cover a wide range of topics. The war oppressed Frazer's spirits and he wrote to Roscoe in 1914 that the prospect of war was 'terrible. The men who are responsible for it should be shot.'[21] But his fear was also for his research in that if things continued as they had during 1914, 'there may not be much of the British Empire left at the end of it'.[22] Ten years later, Frazer was worried by a different threat: 'What do you think are the prospects of the country under a Labour Government? I hear that they sent an Ambassador to make friends with the blood-stained bandits of Russia.'[23]

But theirs was hardly a relationship of equals, albeit one of friends. Frazer was Roscoe's superior, academically and socially, and Roscoe never forgot that Frazer was his mentor. In 1911, shortly after Roscoe's return to England from Uganda, he was appointed to the living of Ovington in Norfolk, an appointment in the gift of Cambridge University and due largely to his association with Frazer. Frazer's patronage of Roscoe dates from before the Ovington living. In 1907 Frazer wrote to Roscoe about 'a great scheme for promoting anthropological research from Liverpool as a centre', following his appointment as professor at Liverpool University. A fund would be established to study the 'savages in the British Empire', the first projects were to be to send Spencer and Gillen to Western Australia and 'to set you free for anthropological work in Central Africa'. But the project had a precondition in that Frazer wanted to know if Roscoe was willing 'to give yourself wholly to anthropology'. The Church Mission Society had not 'kept faith with you' and Roscoe could resign with honour.[24] The prospect of Frazer as God's rival was, luckily for Roscoe, never put to the test as Frazer disliked Liverpool and returned to Trinity and that particular scheme collapsed.

In 1912, however, Frazer revived Roscoe's projected Uganda expedition. Frazer initiated and strongly supported Roscoe's application to the Carnegie Trust of America, promising that the funds available would allow Roscoe to conduct his 'researches... on a large and liberal scale'.[25] The application failed, however, because Roscoe 'asked so little. But of course, the real obstacle has been the man's [Mr Woodward, the Carnegie administrator] own ignorance.' The whole episode confirmed, for Frazer, 'the very unfavourable opinion I have long held of American science, or, what professes to be such.'[26] The disappointment did not last, however, and Frazer went back to the Carnegie on Roscoe's behalf the following year.

Frazer then, at Rivers' suggestion, approached the Colonial Office, since he felt that the Carnegie would, in the end, baulk at funding an expedition to a British Protectorate: 'It is more natural that as an

Englishman you should work for the English Government than for the Yankees.'[27] In 1914 the answer from the Colonial Office arrived; they would help with the funds for an expedition, but Roscoe was to be excluded from working in Uganda where he had previously researched and was to be restricted to the East Africa Protectorate. Moreover, the salary was so meagre as to make the enterprise hardly viable.

Frazer felt that Roscoe needed to raise his academic profile beyond that of a returned missionary, if his projected researches were to come to fruition. In 1914, Frazer tried to get Roscoe a Fellowship at St John's, Christ's or Trinity Colleges, without success. He also proposed Roscoe for a series of lectures on anthropology at Oxford, in addition to the ones he had already given at Cambridge, Manchester, the Royal Institution and the CMS. With the coming of the war, however, it became clear that any expedition to Uganda would have to wait for the termination of hostilities. In 1918, Frazer was quick off the mark and this time with more success. The previous project of 1914 was revived in November 1918 and by April of the following year Frazer was intimately involved in the minutiae of planning the expedition and securing supplies of drugs, sugar, butter and jam.

Roscoe despatched all his notes and reports directly to Frazer from Uganda and Frazer ensured that what interest there was in the expedition was maintained in Britain. A brief preliminary report by Frazer was published in *The Times* and a fuller one in *Man* in April 1920, followed by another in November. But the expedition received more press coverage than Frazer had wanted. *Punch* printed a satirical article on Frazer's reports on the Bunyoro, and Frazer was further incensed by reports of the expedition in the 'low and vulgar' *Daily Mail* and the *Illustrated London News*.[28]

Roscoe's return from Uganda was greeted with a degree of public recognition of his achievements. The king instructed Winston Churchill, then the colonial secretary, to consult Roscoe about African affairs. Frazer was delighted for his friend: 'I always thought the King a sensible, as well as a good, man, and now I know it. Really, my dear Roscoe, you are making anthropology hum, as they say.'[29] Frazer was sincere in his admiration for his protégé. In September 1921 he wrote to Roscoe praising his work and confessing that 'it has been, as you know, one of the objects of my life for many years to enable you to carry out the work you have accomplished.'[30] In 1924, Frazer proposed yet another expedition to Roscoe, which

Roscoe, although sixty-four years of age, seemed ready to acquiesce to. He wrote to Frazer that his last expedition 'failed me in bringing results I had hoped. I do not wish to say much now, but try to realise what I believe to be in that region.'[31] Roscoe was unable to document the almost unknown peoples of the north-east, between Lake Rudolph and the southern border of Abyssinia. As it was, however, Roscoe was still able to publish three volumes of expedition reports.

All suggestions of a future expedition were brought to an end in 1928 when Roscoe suffered a thrombosis. When he died in 1932, Frazer wrote his obituary and paid him this tribute:

> As a field anthropologist, Roscoe had in his day few equals and probably no superior. He was a first-rate observer, with a keen sense of what is important and deserving of record; entirely free from theoretical bias ... Readers of Canon Roscoe's works have, therefore, the satisfaction of knowing that the stream of his discourse flows pure and clear from native sources, unsullied by passing through the too often turbid and weedy channel of an intermediary.[32]

Frazer's generous tribute to his friend as the pre-eminent 'field anthropologist' of his time was high praise indeed, but the second part of his tribute hardly rings true. Roscoe was deeply indebted to Frazer, and not only as his protégé. Frazer's pamphlets produced, shaped and structured Roscoe's 'field anthropology' so totally that far from flowing 'pure and clear from native sources', his discourse passed entirely through the 'channel' of an 'intermediary' – J. G. Frazer and Frazer's *Questions* of 1887 and 1907.

Roscoe's most important work as a 'field anthropologist' was done in the modern state of Uganda and the people he wrote most extensively about were the Baganda. The Baganda were not, however, an unknown people in Europe. On the contrary, Speke and Stanley had made Mutesa, the Kabaka of Buganda, a 'familiar person to the literate Englishman of 1885'.[33] Winston Churchill, probably at Roscoe's prompting, described the country of the Baganda as 'the pearl of Africa',[34] and the people were often favourably compared with both the Chinese and the Japanese. Victorian England concocted an image of the country and its people which also drew on some ancient mythologies. Grant describes a scene he witnessed in Mutesa's court when a man complained of the king's lack of generosity. The man was cut to pieces with reed knives, his limbs carried away openly.[35] The shade of the Timucuas reappears also in the reported practice of killing the first-born male child of a clan head out of fear that the birth was the signal for the death of the father.[36]

These early apprehensions of the people are filled with a terribly cruel humour. The high reputation of the Baganda was derived, it was claimed, from the fact that they, uniquely in the savage world, had invented the privy.[37] Or that when Speke presented Mutesa with a gun, he had a servant shot to test its accuracy. Or, Mutesa's reported offer to Mackay that he would divorce all his wives if Queen Victoria sent him one of her daughters.[38] But above all, the Victorian apprehension of the Baganda was accompanied by a sense of surprise at discovering in Africa that:

> [a]n authoritarian monarch, heading an aristocratic social struc-
> ture of governors, subgovernors, sub-subgovernors, and thou-
> sands of petty bureaucrats, ruled a million people ... A com-
> plete legal system, consisting of a hierarchy of courts to which
> one could appeal, was in place. Specialisation of labour had
> proceeded to the extent that many people no longer worked
> the land but made their living as tax collectors, army officers,
> bards, drummers, fishermen, house buliders, and executioners
> of the thousands sent each year to their death as human
> sacrifices.[39]

The term 'savage' in the *Questions* clearly had to be redefined to account for the Baganda. They were certainly savage in their cruel behaviour as reported by missionaries and travellers, but the term hardly seemed appropriate to such a sophisticated and centralised state.

Yet the Buganda which Roscoe entered as a missionary and field anthropologist was already in a state of terminal collapse. The first Europeans arrived in 1870 when Mutesa accepted help from Britain to maintain his position against the incursions of Arab traders. Stanley sent a telegram to England reporting Mutesa's request for missionaries to be sent. By 1877 the Protestants arrived and two years later the Catholics established their mission. Britain saw the useful-ness of establishing a bulwark in Buganda against the expansion of the German Empire in Tanganyika and as a consequence the British East Africa Company was given the reponsibility for the region. The growth of the Christian missions and the increase of British influence seriously threatened the traditional culture of the Baganda. Mutesa had himself embraced Islam, but in a rather fitful fashion, and when Gordon's army moved down the Nile, pushing Islamic fundamental-ists before him into Buganda, Mutesa felt threatened on every side: from the British and Christians within, from Gordon's plan of annexation of Buganda, and from the fundamentalists who agitated in the north. Mutesa was also crippled with gonorrhoea, another unwelcome import, and the final years of his reign saw him shifting violently between supporting and then denouncing both Christian and Muslim faiths.

In 1884, Mutesa's successor, Mwanga, inherited a state in turmoil as the different pressure groups struggled for control of the ancient kingdom. After the discovery of a plot to assassinate him was made known to Mwanga by a Catholic, he promoted the Christian star to the ascendant and attacked the Muslims, but then fearing *their* growing power, he massacred Christians the following year. By 1888 a coalition of Muslims, Protestants and Catholics rose in rebellion and exiled Mwanga, leaving the country open to a terrible civil war. The wars of religion saw the English and French Christians fighting each other and both fighting the Muslims. British soldiers were eventually brought in, to establish order and to establish the Uganda Protectorate in 1894. Meanwhile the kingdom had passed from Mwanga to his brother Kiwewa, to another brother Kalema, and finally back to Mwanga. He did not last long and in 1897 was deposed for the last time and his one-year-old son proclaimed king. In 1900 the English commissioner effectively dissolved the old order by a land settlement which gave all land over to private ownership. Certainly, the aristocracy benefited most from the land settlement, but the state which Mutesa ruled with such flamboyant cruelty was effectively dead.[40]

One would be hard put to discover any of this historical context from Roscoe's 'field anthropology'. Yet Roscoe was in Buganda for a large part of its terminal history.[41] His anthropological works see, not a people in the process of destruction, a culture fragmented and at war, but a people untouched by history. In seeing a primitive people, he failed to see a colonised people.[42]

What enabled Roscoe to dismiss history from his view was his adherence to Frazer's ethnographic project. The history Frazer's *Questions* evokes is not that of the British army mopping up another protectorate, but the 'history' of the evolution of mental processes. The objects of study became distanced, receding into the gloom of an evolutionary 'history' as Outina retreats in *The Golden Bough* illustration. The eighteenth-century stadial model of cultural evolution was retained by Frazer in many of its key aspects, but he emptied it of the dynamic and confrontational rhythm through which Scott had articulated the narrative of history, and diverted it towards a quest for evolutionary origins. It is not so much that the evolutionary question was not a legitimate question to ask, but that it obscured all other kinds of questions which the historical situation seemed to demand should also be addressed.

That is not to say that Bugandan politics do not exert their influence on Roscoe's work, albeit in a rather covert fashion. Roscoe's first publication was a paper delivered to the Anthropological Institute in 1901 and subsequently published in the *Journal*. 'Notes on the Manners and Customs of the Baganda' was delivered by an act of ventriloquism, not by Roscoe in person but by Frazer and announced as 'answers to the list of questions issued by Dr J. G. Frazer'.[43] In his introduction, Roscoe comments that he obtained his answers to the *Questions* from people assembled for him by the Katikiro, or Bugandan prime minister.[44] The Katikiro in 1901 was Apolo Kagwa and Roscoe's answers should be seen in the double contexts of, on the one hand, the shaping influence of Frazer's questions, and on the other the political intrigues of the Katikiro.

Kagwa was a great general of the Buganda, but he was also a Christian and a wily politician. He had led a party of Christian Bagandans against the other factions in the civil war and he had even wrestled the champions of neighbouring tribes for the right for his group to be received as exiles on their land. The information Roscoe offers, then, was gathered from individuals assembled by the main native political authority in the land, from one who had staunchly and successfully led his faction to victory in a bloody civil war and who ruled with the British over a subject people. Furthermore, the information was collected while the British Protectorate was busy demolishing the basis of native law and land tenure systems, the very bulwarks of Kagwa's own claim to traditional authority. It would be surprising, therefore, if an astute and courageous politician such as Kagwa did not attempt to influence the picture the British received of traditional Buganda, particularly as this was the very authority he was attempting to represent at the very moment when it was being – as Roscoe himself acknowledged – 'abolished'.[45] Kagwa had written his own book on the recent history of Uganda and his role in it. Roscoe's remarks that he could not get answers to all his questions because 'it is remarkable how soon they forget their old customs, and how little they know of the reasons for the things they do'[46] should be read, perhaps, in the context of an intense struggle for power between traditional and colonial governments which profoundly influenced the extent and the nature of the information and explanations he was likely to receive. Kagwa was the Katikiro for twenty-five years, an extraordinarily long period in such a hostile environment, and he would not have survived for so long without exploiting every opportunity which came his way, particularly a keen amateur 'field anthropologist'. Roscoe seemed untroubled by the source of his information. Indeed, in the book *The Baganda* which followed a decade later, he pays 'a debt of gratitude to my friend, Sir Apolo Kagwa, KCMG, Prime Minister and Regent of Uganda'[47] as if the role Kagwa played in the preparation of Roscoe's answers was a guarantee of their authenticity rather than a useful conduit for Kagwa's version of traditional Buganda.

But however great Kagwa's influence was on Roscoe, it was overshadowed by that of the *Questions*. The 1901 *Journal* paper faithfully replicates the structure of the *Questions*, in almost every respect, even to the point of reproducing the numerical scheme of Frazer's *Questions* in Roscoe's text.[48] It is not perhaps unusual to expect that Roscoe's paper *would* correspond so closely with the structure Frazer offers in the *Questions* since, after all, Roscoe did compose it that way and, anyway, Frazer wished to show to the Institute, and Rivers in particular, how useful his booklets could prove. But Roscoe's subsequent book, *The Baganda* (1911), described as 'one of the most important reports of a complex society we have',[49] was also deeply indebted to the *Questions* for its structure and for the kinds of information it presents.

Just as the 1901 *Journal* paper followed the model of the 1887/9 *Questions*, so *The Baganda* adheres to the reformulated 1907 *Questions*. After a 'General Survey of the Country' which was an innovation urged on Roscoe by Frazer in November 1910, the text settles down into a familiar pattern of reproducing the identical scheme recommended by Frazer's *Questions*: Birth Infancy and Puberty (chaper II), Marriage (chapter III), Sickness, Death and Burial (chapter IV), Relationship (chapter V), The Clans and their Totems (chapter VI), The King (chapter VII), Government (chapter VIII), Religion (chapter IX), Warfare (chapter X), Industries (chapter XI), The Keeping of Cows and Other Domestic Animals (chapter XII), Agriculture and Food (chapter XIII), Hunting (chapter XIV), Markets and Currency (chapter XV), Wells (chapter XVI), Folklore (chapter XVI). Chapters II–IV, in fact, reproduce much of the information contained in the *Journal* paper, written in Roscoe's characteristically flat style. The major innovation, but one which is reflected nonetheless in Frazer's revised 1907 *Questions*, is the inclusion of a lengthy chapter on Industries, and it is here, perhaps, that one can see the influence Roscoe had on Frazer when he reconstructed the *Questions*, shifting the emphasis more towards material production.

Frazer followed keenly the progress of his protégé's book. The letters are filled with Frazer's good advice as he warns Roscoe not to write about matters 'he had not had first hand experience of', advice Frazer hardly seemed to feel applied to himself.[50] Frazer read and re-read all of Roscoe's drafts and proofs, pursuing details with Roscoe: about the flaying of a particular individual whose skin protected the king from death; about beliefs concerning 'conception without cohabitation'; and offering advice on dealing with printers and chiding him for sloppy presentation. At one point, Frazer's letter shows how the text emerges directly from the *Questions* when he supplies and rearranges the chapter headings away from the model of the *Questions* which Roscoe had too slavishly followed.

Frazer's judgement of the completed work was glowing: 'I may now congratulate you on having produced a most valuable and perfectly original work, which should keep your name green.'[51] Frazer was rewarded with a handsome dedication for which he expressed his gratitude: 'It will always be a satisfaction to me as long as I live to think that I have in any way helped towards the producing of such a record of native African life.'[52] Later he commented that *The Baganda* had become a 'textbook' and he had every expectation Roscoe's other works would become 'anthropological classics' also.[53] 'Your work', he wrote, 'is likely to be much more permanent than mine; for facts remain when theories are obsolete and forgotten ... the interest in controversies is ephemeral and the interest in facts is perennial.'[54]

Histories of anthropology characterise Frazer's kind of anthropology as having been eclipsed by the functionalist school of British Social Anthropology, the hallmarks of which were the close engagement of a participant observer in a society and the production of a micro-sociological survey. Frazer's kind of 'armchair anthropology' was made redundant by a new breed of ethnographers, Malinowski most notably, and Frazer recognised his days were numbered in the Preface he wrote to *Argonauts of the Western Pacific* (1922) where he cedes authority to this new wave. But the collaboration between Frazer and Roscoe would seem to alter that received historical construction and point, instead, to Frazer and Roscoe setting the standard for future anthropological research some eleven years before *Argonauts*. Indeed, so struck was Frazer at the similarity between Malinowski's and the Roscoe–Frazer project that he wrote to Roscoe several times in 1920 about Malinowski: 'In time we may have a really first-rate man in B. Malinowski, who is quite willing to continue your work in Central Africa.'[55] Although Roscoe's text looks utterly unlike a Frazerian work in its emphasis upon one community, rather than a collation of significant facts, in its flattened factual style, rather than the grandeur of Frazerian prose, in its unwillingness to 'theorise' the information into significant tropes, it is, nonetheless, in its structure and genesis, utterly Frazerian. It is also an important landmark in the development of the discipline, and one which Frazer has never been credited with, even simply as a mentor and collaborator. Frazer was not – or at least should not have been – the kind of anthropologist the young turks wrote against, as is widely imagined, but a significant innovator of anthropological method.

The Baganda makes apparent the covert narrative structure of the method which is inherent in the *Questions*. Only the natives themselves are the objects of study: 'I have therefore made no reference to other books on the subject.'[56] Roscoe's Bagandan exists solely in the pristine world of his own text. The first chapter is remarkable for the unstructured mass of details which crowd into his 'General Survey of the Country'; some order has to be made to emerge from this undifferentiation. The order which emerges is a fictional biography of the native Everyman. The first five chapters follow an imaginary biographical narrative structure, from birth to puberty to marriage to maturity to death. The Bagandan persona is perceived as developing an imaginary selfhood and identity – not in the Le Moyne–Maussian sense of the persona as a *social* identity – but through the enactment of *ritualised* roles. That identity is securely defined, however, as 'traditional' and 'past': 'my aim has been to describe the social and religious life in the old days before their country, Uganda, came under the influence of Europe.' The creation of a biography for the savage out of the seeming undifferentiation which the text creates represents the construction of notional and fictional individuals with 'minds uninfluenced by foreign ideas'.[57] The effect, the *Frazerian* effect, is to present the Bagandan as historyless except for tradition (determined by Kagwa), without actuality except as he/she emerges from Roscoe's fictional biography (determined by Frazer's *Questions*).

The Baganda remain primal, ceremonial, superstitious, 'miscellaneous' people and few or no questions are aimed at discovering their history, their encounters with other peoples or with Europeans, their education, migration, their geographical or climatic situation. The Baganda, as shaped into a representable form by the *Questions*, have less presence as a people, than as a field of data exemplifying cultural phenomena. Throughout they remain a set of disconnected ideas and practices, conceptual shadows without social substance or a life in actuality.

Frazer's *Questions* subjects the rough field of information which the Baganda have become to symptomatic torsions whereby everything is geared towards the elaboration of a religious mentality. The questions seem to lead inexorably, obsessively, in one direction: to the contemplation of death – how it is achieved, how it is ritualised, how the dead return. Above all is the pressing assumption of the death of the objects of study, of the extinction of this resource. Yet Frazer's own method of eliciting data had already accomplished that death, snatching the Baganda from their lived existence to inhabit, instead, a ghostly world as scientific phenomena.

Frazer's ethnographic project had a consequence for the field anthropologist also. The *Questions* split the experiencing ethnographer from the accumulating anthropologist; 'eye-witnessing' is by remote control. Frazer 'sees' with someone else's eyes, subduing the viewer to a secondary role as one who cannot lend meaning to his vision. Like Simon Glover, the experiencing ethnographer can see only the fragments; only a Scott or a Frazer can see the whole scene. Hierarchy and authority are inscribed in that relationship as Frazer exerts his dominance over the information and its gathering. The *Questions* assume the world to be an inchoate mass of undifferentiated materials out of which some order, some hierarchy and authority can be made, some scientific distinctions can be pressed. Frazer is the intellect, the spirit behind the informant's vision, without whom the primitive scene is meaningless.

The positivist scientific impulse runs deep in Frazer in identifying a field of study, limiting its scope to Beliefs, Customs and Language, and employing field-workers with an extensive battery of instructions to elicit information.[58] The objective is the accumulation and cross-referencing of 'facts'. The whole is envisioned by Frazer as a network which spans the globe: from the geographically and culturally various locations the 'scientifically' collected data are collated by Frazer into a significant contribution to 'science'.

What Frazer meant by 'science' is rather like Marx's view of the truly socialist society, it is more inferred than declared. In his notebooks, Frazer thought of the various sciences arranged hierarchically on a ladder of ascending comprehensiveness. He wrote, 'Science will be complete, when the data of each special science are fully explained by the science next below it in complexity, so that the whole series of special sciences shall run into each other without any gaps.'[59] Frazer's notion of the goal of science envisages an end to inquiry in closure rather than an enabling of science to ask further questions. The seamless garment of science accomplishes its goal of finality by arranging its data-filled compartments in systems of domination, master disciplines aided by slave specialisms. Data derived from the field are submitted to the scrutiny of comparative anthropology with its 'higher complexity' and capacity for absorption. Information would pass from the natives (the Baganda) to the 'field anthroplogist' (Roscoe) to the theorist (Frazer): 'We start from a general idea consisting of a very few qualities and proceed downwards through genera, sub-genera, species, sub-species, etc., at every stop adding to the number of diverse qualities.'[60]

As an inversion of the inductive method, this would seem to be the opposite of scientific procedure. It approaches most closely what Johannes Fabian has called 'taxonomic rewriting': 'Taxonomic rewriting is never just a purely contemplative, aesthetic game of reducing messy data to elegant models ... the player is out to win. Winning the game consists of demonstrating synchronic relations of order beneath the flux and confusion of historical events and the expressions of personal experience.'[61]

To 'rewrite' cultural materials 'taxonomically' Frazer recasts primitive cultures into shapes and figures of difference, the purpose of which is to reorient the peoples of the world as spokes around the central hub of western knowledge and society. The cultures of others are thereby rendered as a spectacle surveyed and dominated by the viewing taxonomist. As a result, the world is radically simplified; simplified to the extent that its substance can be contained in a questionnaire. In the search for taxonomic truth, the exotic is reduced to the common, the mundane. The purpose of Frazer's 'completed science' seems to be surveillance, control and domination. 'Science' is power; scientific discourse gathers together, analyses, reflects upon and legislates for client 'special sciences'. The *Questions* were, for Frazer, the key to and the model for the accomplishment of a truly scientific hierarchy of knowledge.

The object, the goal of the science which constituted the real subject of his work was announced by Frazer in the introduction to the first edition of *The Golden Bough*: 'the primitive Aryan, in all that regards his mental fibre and texture is not extinct. He is amongst us to this day.'[62] Contemporary primitives (Bagandans especially) offered Frazer the opportunity to inquire into the nature of 'the primitive religion of the Aryans',[63] and to ask again some ancient questions.

The Aryans were, essentially, the construction of philologists, who posited an originating source for all Indo-European languages in a remote and barbaric past. The Aryans were an immensely potent source of speculation since to trace their presence in language, religion or 'manners' was to achieve a glimpse of the origin of humanity. For believers, the Aryans were to the nineteenth century what Plato's theory of forms was to the Renaissance – the *idea* from which everything descends and which everything imitates. For the cynical, as Mallory remarks, the Aryans rapidly assumed a ludicrous aspect as the 'phlogiston of prehistoric research'.[64]

Frazer's commitment and research in evolutionary theory, which shaped and determined his project, led him to engage also with theories of the origin of language. The question of Aryan language and the concern with 'the primitive religion of the Aryans' enabled Frazer to see into (what he considered to be) the well-springs of the evolution of human thought; issues which had their source in evolutionary science.

The Aryan controversy took two principal directions. The first and by far the most populated area of debate lay in the direction of trying to 'place' the Aryans. In attempting to 'discover' the homeland of the original Aryan peoples, it became a matter of national honour to lay claim to such a pedigree. As the claims of ownership became more extravagant, national pride gave way to racial preferences; skull measurements, perceived racial qualities, and the aesthetics of 'race' muddied the theory of the monogenesis and diffusion of languages. The biblical notion of the original tongue is, of course, a Hebraic myth adopted by the early Christian Fathers, then challenged in the eighteenth century. Once the Enlightenment had cut the restraints of fidelity to the biblical accounts and Hebraic supremacy, a deluge of competing claims to primacy, which J. P. Mallory has impressively catalogued, were generated over a 150-year period leading up to and beyond *The Golden Bough*.

In 1767 James Parson argued that Irish was the 'last remnant' of the ancient tongue, but he squared his account with the Bible by having Shem speak Hebrew and Japhet Magogian (Irish). William Jones in 1786 shifted the terms of the debate somewhat by supplying not only an original tongue, Sanskrit, but also an original homeland for the Aryans, in India. Theories of the original speech and homeland followed thick and fast. Schlegel agreed with Jones. In 1816 Bopp argued that Greek and Latin were not derived from Sanskrit but that all three were derived from one prior language. In 1813 Thomas Young introduced the term 'Indo-European' into the debate. Wilhelm Koppens in the mid-1830s argued for an Aryan homeland in west Turkistan. August Schleicher, in 1852, placed it by the Caspian Sea – indeed, in an excess of zeal he even composed a fable in reconstructed Indo-European. In 1859 Ernest Renan situated the homeland in Central Asia, on the Pamir Plateau, while in the following year Adolphe Pictet, using the term 'paleontologie linguistique', located it in Bactria, and even ventured a physical description of the 'beauty of Aryan bloodlines and the superiority of their intelligence'. Rask placed all European languages under the label 'Thracian' and plumped for a common homeland between Asia Minor and the Pannonian Plain. Albert Pike (1873) also expressed a belief in Aryan racial superiority and, basing his arguments on astronomical observations of the so-called 'Indic Asruns', situated the homeland in Sogdiana in 10,000 BC. Onwards and upwards: in 1886 Penka suggested that the Aryans were long-headed, blond Scandinavians; in 1889 Jubainville championed Asia, this time the Oxus river basin; the following year, T. H. Huxley pushed the homeland back to a 1,500-mile area from the Urals to the North Sea. At about the same time, Schrader's south-Russia theory became known in England, and Taylor was arguing that the Aryans were an improved race of Finns. By 1902 Kossinna had settled simply for a southward movement of northern cultures. But by far the most appealing theory is that of Tilak, an Indian scholar and friend of Gandhi's, who suggested the North Pole as the Aryan homeland following survivals in ancient Vedic and Iranian Cosmologies.[65] In view of all this speculation, it is hardly surprising that in 1911 the Linguistic Society of Paris reaffirmed its constitutional ban on papers dealing with the origin of language.[66]

If these manifold theories were not so deeply implicated in the formation of doctrines of racial superiority, the biologising of history and fascist myths of heredity, they would appear merely comic. It is to Frazer's credit that he refused to allow his researches to become embroiled in the heightening of European racial tensions fuelled by the Aryan debate, but few actually spoke out against it. Max Müller's opposition, in 1872, to the relating of linguistic and ethnological research is striking for its uniqueness: 'There are Aryan and Semitic languages, but it is against all rules of logic to speak, without an expressed or implied qualification, of an Aryan race, of Aryan blood, of Aryan skulls, and to attempt ethnological classification on purely linguistic grounds.'[67]

Müller's rather lonely voice seems like the cry of sanity in its pleading for the term Aryan to be viewed in its strictly linguistic sense and can be compared with both Pufendorf's distinction of 'Natural' and 'Adventitious' Men and Rousseau's noble savage, in that Müller similarly sees the term 'Aryan' as a useful but purely theoretical construction which has taken on an assumed life outside the rarified domain of speculation. The Aryan's existence is essential for discussion to be made possible, but in causing him to exist the Aryan distorts the very field of speculative inquiry he was created to illuminate.

Yet out of the philologists' speculative reconstructions of the Aryan language emerged a second branch of evolutionary conjectures about primitive religion, economy, manners, beliefs and customs. The value of the Aryan debate to Frazer lay not in its eventual findings but in the amount of information it generated and how it ordered that material. Those committed to the discovery of an Aryan homeland used, of course, linguistic evidence, but they also discussed the contemporary languages of those people inhabiting the region, together with an eclectic range of extra-linguistic evidence: myths, legends, folktales, material culture, geographical details, astronomical and astrological findings, research into ancient esoteric texts and much else. Although Frazer had little use for their ultimate conclusions, the accumulation over one and a half centuries of a vast repository of exotic 'facts' required just the kind of synthesising 'scientific' skills Frazer pre-eminently possessed. Implicit within the accumulation of all these data, however, were methodological innovations which Frazer could rightly regard as being consonant with Tylorian anthropological method: the identification of the salient cultural categories of myth, ritual, evolution. Taken as a body, the information represented a massive exercise in the comparative method essential to anthropological theorising as it was conceived in the late nineteenth century. Furthermore, the very nature of linguistic research in this area lay in the uncovering of 'traces' of the *Ursprache* and subsequent speculations about Aryan cultural practices detectable in contemporary societies. This search for 'traces' is reflected in the central element of Tylorian anthropology as 'survivals': the idea that 'ancient' or 'primitive' customs survive in the cultural practices of the contemporary peasantry and proletariat. The philologists could claim with justification to have practised a linguistic theory of survivals long before Tylor.

The philologists' assertion to have been at the forefront of innovation in evolutionary theory can be taken further than the matter of methodology. Indeed, Müller claimed in 1887 that he was 'a Darwinian long before Darwin': 'No student of the science of language can be anything but an evolutionist, for, wherever he looks, he sees nothing but evolution going on around him.'[68] There is justice in Müller's complaint that the historians and theoreticians of language deserved a place alongside the biologists, botanists and geologists regarded as Darwin's forebears. For his part, Frazer discovered in the philologists not only a storehouse of precious texts, nor simply confirmation of methodological correctness, but claims upon the original myth of origins: evolution itself.

The researches of philologists working in the area of the origin of language had a further significance for Frazer in confirming the abstract classification system he devised for his material. Frazer's classification of the evolutionary progress of mankind through the ages of magic, religion and science – the major theoretical innovation of the second edition of *The Golden Bough* – has been correctly assumed to have been derived from Comte's 'Law of the Three Stages', which were in their turn derived from a mixture of the stadial social theories of the Scottish and European Enlightenment. Frazer grafted his own evolutionary taxonomy of magic–religion–science onto Comte's trinity of theology, metaphysics and science. Similarly, Renan, to whom Frazer owes an acknowledged debt at least as great as that owed to Comte, offers a more ample but syllogistic set of permutations on the classical theme of the Ages of Iron, Brass and Gold, whereby the first age is religious but unscientific, the second is scientific but unreligious, and the third both scientific and religious.

Trinitarian schemes of development were an intellectual fashion throughout the nineteenth century, almost as if the evolutionists sought mythical solutions to the problem of myth. The evolutionists' allegories of time raise the question as to whether anyone can really believe a myth which does not have three parts. Father, Son and Holy Ghost? Paradise, Fall and Redemption? The trinity of thesis, antithesis and synthesis confers a mythical credence as the magical terms of these evolutionary schemes. The facts, details, theories, scholarship are simply and purely subservient drones working to enunciate this secret but ubiquitous code. Certainly a brief survey of philologists' trinitarian evolutionary schemes would yield rivals enough to Comte and Renan as influences on Frazer, but they were rarely unembellished metaphors of the tripartite evolution of language.

J. G. Herder, for example, developed his own trinitarian pattern for the development of language, linking it in turn to the metaphor of the human life-cycle of youth, maturity and old age. Each of these linguistic-cum-human ages corresponded respectively to the discourses of poetry, politics and science.[69] But the metaphors run riot as they spread their tentacular roots throughout human cultural history, for, just as languages and men grow to maturity, so nations, families, nature itself, grow from weakness to strength to excellence before withering and dying. In the face of such rampant natural power, the human agency is powerless to influence the burgeoning romantic metaphors. Language is a force of nature obeying its own laws of change; poor humanity is merely its agent.

For the German philologist Schleicher also, languages are 'organisms of nature' which evolve independently, diminishing the human role simply to that of observer of a natural phenomenon. In progressing from the sub-human to the human level, man moves from an evolutionary phase to a historical phase. It is at the point of entry into the historical phase that human language attains its highest level of perfection and can develop no further, but only undergo degeneration from this moment of perfection. Romantic metaphors of nature drive the discussion as language is seen to bud and blossom. Any specific social or cultural context is undercut by the radical historylessness of nature's cyclical time in a way which is reminiscent of Frazer's *Questions* and its implicit evocation of a human life-cycle. Frazer's separation of magic and science, upon which is loaded the wider division of primitive and civilised, is similarly suggestive of Schleicher's proposal that the more 'active' a 'people' has been in the historical era, the more the original language has been worn away. Thus English has been more involved in the process of history than Icelandic and has therefore preserved its original form less well; similarly for Hebrew as opposed to Arabic, Greek as opposed to Sanskrit, and so on. The whole pattern of binary oppositions is given a moral quality, for, the less eroded by history, the more integrity the language possesses. Consequently Lithuanian has the greatest integrity of all European languages. Languages are, therefore, composed on a graph which describes a partial sine curve: originating in sub-language, ascending to the evolution and rapid perfection of language, then degenerating with language's involvement with history.[70]

Of course, the relative integrity of languages contains a further subtext: that integrity is bought at the cost of political and economic backwardness. 'History' is unconsciously defined both in a very Frazerian way as participation in Victorian technological and imperial culture, and in a way which goes to the centre of Victorian anthropological assumptions. When Schleicher and other philologists write of the relative 'integrity' of languages untouched by history, or when Frazer makes a distinction between magic and science, they are acknowledging the primary role of anthropology to construct a discipline where there shall be, in Tylor's phrase, 'scarce a hand's breadth between an English ploughman and a negro of Central Africa'.[71] In defining the linguistic or anthropological subject they define 'otherness' as that which is 'mythical', 'magical', 'natural', 'historyless' or having 'integrity' in romantic metaphors which obscure their true meaning of 'colonised', 'proletarian', 'peasant', 'powerless' or 'foreign'.

Frazer's distinction between myth and history should be noted in this context, since myth, being a phase of man's evolution, is surpassed by history, which reflects man's self-conscious later phase. Similarly, magic is more primitive than religion, Frazer argues, because aborigines practise magic but not religion, because animals associate through contiguity and similarity, and because magical beliefs are still to be found among the European peasantry and proletariat.[72] All this goes to prove that myth, like magic, is one tremendous human error. 'Myths', he wrote in his translation of Apollodorus, 'are mistaken explanations of phenomena, whether of human life or of external nature.'[73] The eighteenth-century stadial theorists clearly lie behind Frazer's speculations on man's entry into history from primitive historylessness, with the important qualification that Frazer's criteria for that transformation are epistemological and 'mentalistic' rather than materialistic. In attempting to account for the evolution of man's intellect from the error of magic to the success of science, Frazer described what Foucault may have termed an 'epistemological threshold'.[74] Below that threshold, in the primitive world of non-scientific magic, knowledge is undifferentiated from 'experience' in a way which is not dissimilar to Aphra Behn's notable description of the savage state: 'All you can see, you see at once, and every moment see; and where there is no Novelty, there can be no Curiosity.' Beyond the epistemological threshold, after the fall from Behn's primitive grace and in the civilised world of Frazerian science, 'knowledge is not given but constructed'.[75] The world may, after the entry into history, be classified into the constructed orders, classes, genera of the scientific imagination.

But Frazer's euhemerism belies a further theme which runs throughout *The Golden Bough*: that myth, as a mistake made by all humanity, provides us with general truths. To find these one must dig beneath the surface of error. Behind myth lay magic for, as Frazer wrote in *Balder the Beautiful*, 'myth stood to magic in the relation of theory to practice'.[76] Magic was, for Frazer, the key epistemological factor which distinguished the primitive mind; it expressed the entire savage reality. Yet in Frazer's descriptions magic never possessed the wholly negative qualities of a dark psychology, but represented an honest, even gentlemanly attempt to deal fairly, if erroneously, with the world as the savage saw it. Indeed, the variety of magical practices could be construed as primitive man's creative response to the enigmas of his situation. Frazer edges towards, but never quite achieves, a view and an analysis of magic as a complex web of symbolic phenomena. Frazer never quite makes that leap into a study of the semiology of magic, although he came extraordinarily close, and remains within an essentially Enlightenment predilection for the formation of laws.[77]

But if myth is error it follows that so too is magic. Evans-Pritchard, for one, finds it hard to comprehend how Frazer could possibly conceive of a world founded on error: 'If primitive man really mistook an ideal connection for a real one and confused subjective with objective experience, his life would be chaos. He could not exist.'[78] Since primitive man does not live in chaos, Frazer must be wrong: magic is not error but difference. Beattie makes much the same point, although less tactfully: 'Nobody in their senses could possibly believe that all things that share some common quality, and all things that have once been in contact, are continually affecting one another: in a world so conceived almost everything would all the time be affecting almost everything else, and all would be chaos.'[79]

Beattie omits to mention that Frazer is careful to point to the necessity for human action, ritual, to bring about magical activity:

that the latent connectedness of the world (expressed in Frazer's notion of myth) lies inert until vitalised by human agency (Frazerian magic). But, even so, Frazer's critics seem to have a point. To paraphrase a frequent criticism, what is remarkable about Frazer's analysis of magic is not that he saw it as error, but that once mankind was in error anyone was ever capable of thinking their way out of it.

But Frazer's critics, justified though their objections may be, are asking of him questions which his work does not set out to answer. The trajectory of his thinking is inward, to origins – Aryan, Bagandan or otherwise – and not outwards, to a social life as it is really lived. A more serious charge can be levelled, however, at the very nature of the evolutionists' project which elided two distinct and separate questions: in attempting to answer the question of origins they substituted the 'how?' of influence for the 'why?' Evolutionists could be criticised for having, under the pretence of explaining *why* certain forms evolved, substituted an explanation of *how* they evolved. In various forms, the world begins in its Aryan roots, in poetry, but ascends to philosophy. Yet nowhere in Frazer's writings, or in the writings of the philologists, is the process of change attributed to anything other than the divine agency of evolution. What revolution or rite of passage brought humanity from one state of linguistic and cultural awareness to the next? Again, the question of 'essence', the essential driving force of evolution, is elided, and 'origins' are substituted for 'change'. In attempting to account for transformation, the evolutionists discovered only the stasis of origins.

Frazer is as culpable in this respect as any of his contemporaries but the tendency is particularly marked among the least adept philological evolutionists, as Hilary Henson has indicated in the case of Payne and Hyde Clark. Payne attempted to differentiate between European and primitive languages according to the absence or presence of the holophrase or portmanteau word: 'Holophrastic languages did not analyse and structure experience in the way that the European languages could: instead they merely gave general, undifferentiated impressions.' Hyde Clark, for his part, placed languages and cultures on a 'scale of progressive civilisation', in which Bushmen and Inuit ('Eskimo') were linked under the ludicrous heading of Polar–Pygmean. Both Sayce and Tylor rather patiently pointed out that 'society implies language, race does not'.[80] But Frazer is hardly free from such excesses. Given the easy commerce between anthropology and language studies, it is not a long way from Payne's distinction of holophrastic and European to Frazer's division of Magic and Science. Nor does Frazer escape from Hyde Clark's tendency to yoke culturally diverse peoples – the Timucua, the Baganda and South Russians, for example – often in the same sentence. In 1880, Sayce correctly diagnosed the condition when he wrote in his *Introduction to the Science of Language* that: 'The spirit of vanity has invaded the science of language itself. We have come to think that not only is the race to which we belong superior to all others, but that the languages we speak are equally superior.'[81]

All the evolutionists, Frazer included, seem to acknowledge that the evolution of language has involved a progressive growth of complexity – which is as much as to say that both philology and anthropology, being complex disciplines indicative of a higher level of cultural evolution, can only be written in 'advanced' languages. Languages and cultures which have not passed beyond a certain evolutionary level, an 'epistemological threshold', are not capable of the complexity required for reflection. Thus Schelling links each stage of human development with a parallel stage in the development of language, from the monosyllabic to the disyllabic and finally to polysyllabic complexity. Again the metaphor finds further applications in mankind's religious development from an original monotheism through successive stages of duotheism and polytheism to the absolute monotheism of revelation. Comte offers a refinement to this scheme by pinning states of language development to stages in evolution. Language originates in the theological stage, in myths, images and poetry. It then develops a capacity for abstraction during the metaphysical era, while in the present scientific phase its condition is, as yet, undetermined.[82] By such means the philological and anthropological projects created a discourse fundamentally marked by exclusivity. The commonwealth of letters, inhabited entirely by highly evolved Victorian gentlemen (itself divided into classes of 'field' ethnographers and 'theoretical' anthropologists) possessed of a 'polysyllabic' language, excluded the others not only on the grounds of 'race' and 'culture' but also on the grounds that the languages they spoke – or indeed, wrote in, if such an anomaly could be credited – were lower, lesser tongues incapable of the subtleties of civilised discourse.

Frazer should, of course, be viewed in this context, and his assumptions are neither more nor less outrageous than those of either his contemporaries or his predecesssors. All of them held an 'implicit assumption that linguistic distribution and interrelations exactly paralleled those of race and could be used as a proof for the latter where other evidence was lacking'.[83] Max Müller called this a 'method of making language itself tell the history of ancient times'. Although Frazer disagreed with many of the detailed findings of contemporary research, he nonetheless agreed with the general assumptions of the debate: the essentially eighteenth-century notion that the evolutionary progress of mankind is mirrored in the visible transformations of language. Language study is anthropology in miniature.

Marrett criticised *The Golden Bough*, with some justice, as 'a platonic myth'. Undoubtedly, the central themes of that myth, Frazer's unilinear scheme of development of human thought through stratified grades, represented an extreme reduction, but it should also be said that all unilinear evolutionary schemes posited an originary state. For Frazer the origin was to be found in a triangulation of animal mentality, aboriginal practice and proletarian custom.[84] Frazer shared the common contention that primitive peoples were subject to whimsy and incapable of making conscious distinctions between natural and supernatural phenomena. They were subject to unpredictable turns of events which they neither understood nor controlled. Their languages did not have the capacity for abstract generalisation, since they possessed neither the conceptual capacity nor the vocabulary for subtle distinctions and the perception of their 'error'. As Payne wrote in 1899, primitive language was 'slippery and unstable as a dream'.[85] Primitive languages were like subordinate sciences in the system of knowledge; they both required the discipline of superior discourses. Slippery instability was anathema to Frazer as much as it was to his contemporaries. It smacked too much of anarchy; at all costs, some form of order had to be wrung from the data.

The forms of order of science as demonstrated by Frazer's own work, however, offer an insight into the next historical phase of the fruitful relationship between linguistics and anthropology. *The Golden Bough* can be seen as a bridge between, on the one side, the Victorian world of the evolutionists and the attendant Aryan linguistic debate, and on the other, moving beyond speculations of 'origins' to twentieth-century anthropology and literary criticism, with their mutual indebtedness to structural linguistics.

Frazer would, of course, have been uncomprehending of any assertion that *The Golden Bough* in any of its editions was an extended exercise in structuralist method. He would, at a later date perhaps, have pointed to Lord Raglan's essay 'The Hero of Tradition' as a justification for his synthesising method. He would most certainly have cited the typological methods of medieval and Renaissance biblical scholars as a primary influence.[86] Typology was the process by which biblical scholars elucidated correspondences between the Old and New Testament. Their purpose was to prove that the New Testament retold stories prefigured in the Old. Correspondences were found by reducing the narratives of each text to their nuclei, nodal points of indispensable action or information without which the story could not be told. This form of literary criticism lies at the heart of much of Frazer's treatment of myth. For the purposes of comparison, diverse narratives are reduced to their nuclei and generalisations drawn from the correspondences so produced. The narrative of the priest of Diana at Nemi which frames *The Golden Bough* is just such a typological exercise exploded to encompass dozens of cultures, hundreds of myths and thousands of pages – a typological exercise lengthy even by the standards of biblical scholarship. The method is almost precisely that employed by later structuralist analysis, except that in terms of the sheer bulk of data so treated *The Golden Bough* makes Lévi-Strauss' efforts seem rather puny.

My contention is that structuralism in its method and procedures and in the scope of its ambition represents the master science, the completed science, which Frazer referred to and predicted in his notebooks: a way of knowing all the 'facts' of the world according to their shared narrative structures – which can be obtained through exercises such as the *Questions* project. Both Frazer's 'science' and structuralism use a typological method to control and process data, both are oriented around a central informing theory. In my view, the source of that theory is the same for both Frazer and structuralist linguistics and its progeny – structural anthropology and structuralist literary criticism – and it is this source which provides us with the 'why?' rather than the 'how?' of *The Golden Bough*'s evolutionary discourse.

It is in the chapter on sympathetic magic added to the second edition of *The Golden Bough* that Frazer identifies the truth that he believes the error of magic enshrines. Magic, the earliest phase in the development of human thought, functions through a law of sympathy divided into two constituents: the law of similarity (homoeopathic magic) and the law of contact (contagious magic).

> Thus far we have been considering chiefly that branch of sympathetic magic which may be called homeopathic or imita-

tive. Its leading principle, as we have seen, is that like produces like, or, in other words, that an effect resembles its cause. The other great branch of sympathetic magic, which I have called Contagious Magic, proceeds upon the notion that things which have once been conjoined must remain ever afterwards, even when quite dissevered from each other, in such a sympathetic relation that whatever is done to the one must similarly affect the other. [87]

These are the invariable laws not only of magical thought, but of all thought, science differing from magic only in its greater efficacy, its freedom from error. Fundamental to magic, therefore, is the need to know the secret nature of a thing if that thing is to be coerced. The nature of a thing, in true evolutionary style, is known by its origins, how it is caused to exist.

This further trinity of similarity, contact and causation is the element of truth contained in the error of magic. Frazer's identification of the principal cognitive structures of the human mind recalls the eighteenth century and the writings of David Hume: 'The qualities, from which this association arises, and by which the mind is after this manner conveyed from one idea to another, are three, viz., *resemblance, contiguity* in time or place, and *cause and effect*.'[88]

Frazer's discussion of the origins of human thought fit the terms of Hume's cognitive theory. Moreover, the whole of the narrative strategy of *The Golden Bough* can be seen as a reworking of the same Humean theories. The data of primitive peoples collected from the *Questions* are associated through resemblance and contiguity into significant patterns linked by an evolutionary chain of cause and effect. It is hardly surprising, then, that when Anatole France reviewed *Folklore in the Old Testament*, he wrote of Frazer's work as a whole that 'what Montesquieu was in his day Frazer is in ours and the difference in their works shows the progress of ideas', so apparent seemed the Enlightenment tendency of Frazer's intellect.[89]

But Frazer's casting of magic in the mould of Humean cognitive theory is suggestive not only of the eighteenth century but also of Frazer's great contemporary in structural linguistics, Ferdinand de Saussure. What the theory of magic was to Frazer, with his Humean distinctions of similarity and contiguity, the principles of linguistics were to Saussure, with syntagmatic and associative relations corresponding to Hume's. The comparison lies in the shared assumptions about the processes of mental association. The laws of similarity and contiguity are as apparent in Frazer's theories of myth as they are in Saussure's theories of language. For magic as for language the laws of association operate not simply to collect data (magical practices or words), but also to organise them in interrelated units forming families, systems, types (generic myths or magical actions; syntagmatic strings or paradigmatic relations). Similarly, language (for Saussure) and magic (for Frazer) contain comparable forms of structural order, whereby language and myths only become truly significant when the mythical or linguistic elements are composed within a system of myths or language. The true significance of a myth can only be seen in relation to other myths; words only signify in relation to other words. For Frazer, as for Saussure, it is the *system* which is significant, not the component parts. Frazer's primitive magician, like Saussure's practitioner of language, gives expression to a perpetually repeated message: the deep structures of the mental processes of association.

Critics of both Frazer and Saussure make remarkably similar complaints about their theoretical orientations. Both writers are said to lack the Humean notion of causation. Magic and language are derived from a social context as much as from mental processes, which both tend to ignore. Furthermore, critics complain that as magic and language are the effects of social causes, Frazer's and Saussure's excision of causation eradicates innovation and change, and thus an entire social context containing important ideological values which have formed both magic *and* language. Their literary styles and use of evidence make Frazer and Saussure read very differently, but they have a common ancestry in Enlightenment grand theory and a common concern to schematise the fundamental structures of human thought.

Koerner's biography of Saussure cites Pieter A. Verburg's widely adopted assertion that Saussure's contribution was 'an almost Copernican Revolution in the study of language' in that it moved inquiry away from historical development and towards a synchronic view of language as an arbitrary system of structural rules.[90] The danger with this is that, in promoting Saussure's reputation, it wrenches him out of his historical context and, by emphasising how much he differed from others, obscures how much he shared with his contemporaries, including Frazer. Koerner's biography shows, however, that Saussure was as concerned with 'origins' as his contemporaries were. On this basis, therefore, there seem worthwhile grounds for drawing further comparisons, perhaps even to the point of attempting to trace a Frazerian influence on Saussure.

Saussure was only three years younger than Frazer, but the first edition of *The Golden Bough* had been published some twenty-five years before his *Cours de linguistique générale* (given 1908–9, published 1915). A French translation of the important second edition of *The Golden Bough* followed almost immediately on the English original and, as a result, Frazer came to be held in high esteem in French-speaking countries, probably higher than in Britain. While Saussure was teaching his course in general linguistics he was also serving as a librarian of the Faculty of Letters and Social Sciences of the Sorbonne. As this was the period when Frazer's French reputation was growing, it seems inconceivable that Saussure was not at least aware of *The Golden Bough* and its central orientations. Critics favourable to Saussure have attempted to counter criticisms of his method by citing Saussure's reliance on sociological and anthropological authorities; his reiteration that language is not 'complete in the individual but exists perfectly only in the *masse*'. Joseph Vendreyes, a near-contemporary of Saussure's, claims that Saussurean linguistics is essentially sociological. Witold Doroszowski states that Saussure's ideas possessed an extra-linguistic provenance, while F. P. Dineen maintains that Saussure's information came from outside linguistics and that his concept of synchrony was evolved only after reading Durkheim. In short, Koerner's biography has Saussure absorbing ideas about the social nature of language from a wide range of sociological and anthropological contexts.

Moreover, the transition from a diachronic to a synchronic study of language was not the effect of an instant revelation, nor did he see the two as contradictory. In 1909, a year after his famous *Cours*, Saussure still held that a knowledge of historical linguistics was an indispensable prerequisite to a study of synchronic linguistics. Indeed his historical studies of language far outweigh, in quantity, his 'synchronic' works. His first important article was on Indo-European and he described Bopp as his 'master'. At Leipzig he took courses in Slavonic, Lithuanian, Celtic, Sanskrit and the history of the German language. At Geneva he taught courses not only on general linguistics, but on Sanskrit, Greek and Latin Phonology, the history of the Indo-European verb, Greek dialects and inscriptions, Homer, Gothic, Germanic dialects and the ancient and modern linguistic geography of Europe. In this biographical context, then, Saussure begins to look less like a Copernican revolutionary and much more like the product of his times, concerned with the same eclectic intellectual issues of Aryanism, evolution and origins. The case for Frazer being a significant part of his intellectual baggage is further strengthened by Saussure's own research into Germanic legends and a very Frazerian project on the classical myths of Theseus and Orion and other 'characters of antique mythology'.

The available biographical information on Saussure would indicate, therefore, that Saussure was turning over similar if not identical ideas to Frazer, and visiting the same authorities and planning similar projects. In searching for a controlling set of theoretical propositions, both writers discovered the same terminus in Hume. It is rather disheartening, then, to reverse the equation and to discover Frazer's virtual silence, in print, on the matter of language *per se*. Apart from the vocabulary and questions in the 1907 *Questions*, which he stated (in pride or mitigation) was 'drawn up by myself, without consultation with expert philologists', two essays – 'The Language of Animals' (a typically eclectic piece which isn't on the language of animals at all, but on folktales and myths of culture heroes who can speak with animals) and 'A Suggestion as to the Origin of Gender in Language' – plus numerous scattered references hardly amount to a total commitment to the subject.

Frazer's only extended exercise in comparative linguistics, and the only place where he enters into any kind of philological controversy, is the essay 'A Suggestion as to the Origin of Gender in Language'. Here he seems to be taking to task one of the assumptions generated by the Aryan debate, which was that the original Aryan tongue possessed grammatical gender.[91] This 'discovery' had been invested with aesthetic qualities and taken as further evidence for the superiority of the Aryan. In this essay, however, Frazer demonstrates that gender is evident in other savage languages, such as that of the Caribs of Surinam, Guiana and the Caribbean, who had exhibited few of the ascribed 'qualities' of Aryan superiority. There may well be a subtext to the essay whereby Frazer is using his data to undercut the racist fantasies of the Aryanists by an insistence on the facts of cultural diversity. So far so very good, but his conclusions go astray. Picking up on information received, in part, from answers to a question placed in the *Questions* he writes, '[g]rammatical gender may have been at first purely subjective, that is indicative only of the sex of the speaker, and not at all intended to imply, as it was afterwards understood to imply, any sex in the thing spoken of'. Frazer suggests that, in those languages which possess grammatical genders, two distinct dialects existed, one spoken by women, the other spoken by men. Men would say *terrus*, women would say *terra*, for example. This embodies a misconception which takes the notion of gender far too literally. Frazer commits the terrible blunder of taking gender to denote the sex of the speaker and not as indicating the conventions of linguistic analysis. Yet, even so, the essay, however mistaken, does attempt to relate language to the society from which it draws its evidence. Unusually for Frazer, it makes a halting attempt to read back from linguistic evidence to society.

So much for the published works; the unpublished writings hold a much more intriguing clue to Frazer's linguistic speculations. At the back of one of his notebooks, which is half-filled with notes taken from Sir Henry Maine's *Ancient Law*, is the following passage written in pencil. (Frazer's deletions are indicated by square brackets; parentheses indicate where I have completed or guessed a word):

> Language, spoken or written, is a species of signs. Signs are [means] [modes of conveying, by means] are modes of conveying [through impressions on the senses] thought between intelligent beings by means of sensible impressions. [Thence a solitary – perfectly solitary being could have no need of signs, including language.] Signs are of two kinds, representative & symbolical. [The former resemble the thing the notion of which they are either (?)] Representative signs convey notions of things by imitating the things the knowledge of which they are meant to impart; hence [they resemble] these signs *resemble* the things, [and since signs are] hence they are of the same kind of nature as the things; from which it follows that as signs are sensible impressions [the] representative signs can only convey [a know(ledge)] notions of sensible things. Symbolical signs, [do not] are not imitations of the things [which] the knowledge of which they convey, they do not resemble the things; the connection between such signs & the thing signified is hence conventional, and [is only] such signs are only significant to those who are aware of the 'convention', whereas the connection between [symb(olical)] representative and the thing signified is natural and rep(resentative) signs are usually intelligible to all who have sufficient intelligence to understand the things themselves. Examples of representative signs are paintings & statues: of symbolical signs . . .[92]

This passage almost certainly does not represent Frazer's own thoughts on the subject of language as a structure of signifying codes, but it is also clearly not copied, like the rest of the notes in the notebook, from an earlier text. The notes appear to be Frazer's attempts to piece together in his own mind the substance of someone else's argument.

Certainly the extract begins conservatively enough, with a reference to Lockean enculturation and the fundamentals of Enlightenment sensationalism. It also hints at Rousseau's 'Essay on the Origins of Language' in his evocation of the solitary savage without language. Rousseau and his controvertialists had outlined a paradox concerning the origins of language which seemed unbreakable. As James Stam describes it:

> The perfection of structure in language presupposes that it was designed by a reasonable being; man without the use of language is not a reasonable being; ergo, man was not the designer of language. The evolution of language by chance is excluded by the first premise; the invention of language by man is excluded by the above syllogism.

Herder put it more elegantly:

> No-one but God could invent language! However, no one but God could understand why no-one but God could invent it either! [93]

Frazer's briefest of brushes with this conundrum is significant in that his note momentarily contemplates the collapse of his evolutionist paradigm in the evocation of an *absolute* origin: 'a perfectly solitary being could have no need of signs'. The evolutionary model had determined that men and cultures evolved under the goad of their 'needs'; where 'need' does not exist, neither does evolution. Frazer's response is to turn, in a fog of ellipses, to the notion of 'conventional' structures; from evolutionary diachrony to structural synchrony.

It is a matter of conjecture whose thesis this note attempts to summarise, since it is too brief to identify the source with any accuracy. If Frazer had gone on to tackle the difficult matter of 'symbolical signs' in more detail, then the task would have been easier. But there are certain clues: first, the date, which probably belongs to the beginning of the 1880s; secondly, Frazer's use of the term 'conventional', which would suggest the note refers to the debate, which raged throughout the last third of the nineteenth century, over the 'conventionality' of language as opposed to its status as a natural order. In this area, linguistics moved very close to anthropology, possibly arousing Frazer's interest. Even Tylor, 'the father of anthropology', felt moved explicitly to refute the concept of language as an arbitrary system of signifying conventions:

> That the selection of words to express ideas was ever purely arbitrary, that is to say, such that it would have been consistent with its principles to exchange any two words as we may

exchange algebraic symbols, or to shake up a number of words in a bag and redistribute them at random among the ideas they represented, is a supposition opposed to such knowledge as we have of the formation of language.[94]

Frazer was, in his note at least, flirting with anthropological heresy. A more precise source may be offered by the notebook itself. Frazer was keen on making lists of books he had read or intended to read. In the same notebook in which this passage on language appears, he listed a number of works to 'read or finish reading': 'Hume's Treatise', as he calls it, is listed along with the Indo-Europeanist Max Müller's *The Science of Language* and *Chips from a German Workshop* and the early structuralists A. H. Sayce's *Introduction to the Science of Language* and W. D. Whitney's *The Science and Growth of Language*. Whitney must be a prime candidate given his pronouncement that:

> Every vocable was to us an arbitrary and conventional sign: arbitrary because any one of the thousand other vocables could have been just as easily learned by us and associated with the same idea; conventional, because the one we had acquired had its sole ground and sanction in the consenting usage of the community of which we formed a part.[95]

Whatever the provenance of Frazer's note, the presence of Hume, Müller, Sayce and Whitney in Frazer's list is more than simply fortuitous. For Frazer's note is representative of a nascent semiology – an awareness of our capacities to generate constellations of signifying structures from a few 'atomic' shaping principles – which finally came to fruition for Frazer in *The Golden Bough*. So too with the *Questions* project; an inchoate world of living actions is rendered into the 'factual' paradigms and structures of a questionnaire. The two dovetail into a Master Science.

To associate one of the revered founders of modern consciousness with a figure regarded as a 'verbose blimp of Victorian prejudice' who wrote his long books 'between a heavy tea and an even heavier dinner' is to raise several questions, not the least of which is the reason for Saussure's ubiquitous triumph as against Frazer's general eclipse. This cannot be wholly accounted for by the demise of Frazer's type of armchair anthropology; the twentieth century can outstrip the nineteenth in its roll-call of anthropological grand theorists. Nor is it simply a matter of functionalism replacing Frazer as a more workable model, since functionalism had an important antecedent in Frazer's own collaborations with Roscoe in the *Questions* project, and has been superseded by a symbolic anthropology and a view of societies as 'texts' rather than data – a view which is more in keeping with Frazer's position than Malinowski's. If Frazer's great compendium seems useful now only as ironic poetic decoration, the reason lies with Frazer's initial project of discovering the nature of the primitive religion of the Aryans. It is not just that the Aryans are no longer regarded as an important issue, but that the processes of myth and magic by which Frazer attempted to answer the question of origins do not seem sufficiently 'original'. From the structural paradigms of the *Questions* to the theoretical innovations of the second edition of *The Golden Bough*, Frazer's solution to the search for a primary cognitive fabric is simply not fundamental enough: language is prior to, more 'minimal' or 'fundamental' than magic. As a consequence, Lévi-Strauss sees culture shaped like a language and nowhere says that it is structured like magic; yet in many important respects his work is closer to a Frazerian project than he acknowledged.

Chapter 6

Causes célèbres in the myths of modernism: Melanesia and Brazil 1895–1970

> A culture wishing to free itself experiences a perpetual
> longing for the uncivilized.
>
> Huizinga[1]

My epigraph from Huizinga is intended to refer to the hidden motivations of a historically recurrent primitivism. It alludes to the primitive as a 'counterpoint' to controlling ideologies, whereby the representations of otherness can rupture those dominant codes and replenish the stock of cultural assets. In this formulation, primitivism has a distinct historical rhythm; lying dormant or latent in the cultures of the west until activated by the pressures of an irresistible subversion. At the moment of fracture, the primitive tears through the fissure, like some reborn *maenad*, butchering sacred cows and remaking our culture afresh. The primitive's historic role in western culture has been, in Scott's phrase, a 'matter of astonishment'.

The reinvented primitive has been used to oppose, successively, the hegemonic dogmas of the Renaissance, neo-classicism, romanticism ... In this version of the revolutionary history of primitivism, modernism is pre-eminently the latest and most complete act of primitive renewal of the west's cultural production. The modernist 'affinity' with or 'appropriation' of primitive materials[2] recapitulates those other moments of transformation. *Plus ça change.*

My purpose here is to discuss two *causes célèbres* in the 'affinity/ appropriation' of primitive materials: the Melanesians and the Bororo as they are represented in the writings of Malinowski, T. S. Eliot and Lévi-Strauss. This is hardly uncultivated ground; the general critical revision of these writers' works has become extensive, so extensive in fact that Huizinga's epigraph seems to find a new application. It is not only the primitive in modernism which signals modernism's desire 'to free itself' from the mastery of Victorian authority, but also the discovery of an 'appropriation' of the primitive in modernism which signals a postmodern desire to free itself from the hegemony of modernism. Contemporary critics and anthropologists 'free' themselves from modernist modes of writing by deconstructing modernist representations of the primitive. Primitivism is not dismissed from such writings but is reinvented as another challenging critical discourse.

My own writing is undeniably a part of that new primitivism in that it seeks to represent, not the primitive him/herself, but a representation of that representation.

Before this dissolves into utter solipsism, I should make my ambitions clear. I wish to look at the Bororo and the Melanesians not only through the writings of Malinowski, T. S. Eliot and Lévi-Strauss, but also through contemporary critical discourses. The Bororo and the Melanesians, initially *causes célèbres* in the invention of modernism, are also *causes célèbres* in the deconstruction of modernism. The Bororo and the Melanesians cannot be seen except through this double vision of a 'making' and 'unmaking' of their representations.

The deconstruction of modernist representations of the primitive seems to announce itself as the death of primitivism. The primitive appears to be 'unsayable', elusive, unrepresentable. This is not the case. Primitivism survives its deconstruction as a sceptically received set of discourses.

The critical analysis of modernist representations of the Bororo and the Melanesians emphasises the 'self-fashioning' of authorial personae. That identity is also deconstructed alongside the interrogation of modernist representations of the primitive to the point where self-fashioning is itself seen also to be an elusive and unrepresentable objective. Identity is, however, not abolished, but redefined – indeed made stronger and more pertinent – as a site of conflict and indeterminacy.

In writings about the Melanesians and the Bororo (and in writings *about writings* about the Melanesians and the Bororo), the making of a representation of the self is yoked to the making of a representation of the primitive to the extent that when one is 'unmade' or unravelled, so also is the other. The Melanesians and the Bororo depict the doubleness of cultural representations: a 'successful' cultural representation also accomplishes a triumph of self definition;

but the movement can be reversed into the dissolving of representations of culture and self. This chapter will attempt to chart this seemingly perpetual historical rhythm, in which selves, Bororo and Melanesians, are repeatedly made and unmade.

It is well known that Malinowski liked to compare himself to his fellow countryman Joseph Conrad and he is reported as once having said that 'Rivers is the Rider Haggard of anthropology: I shall be the Conrad.'[3] On the evidence of *Argonauts of the Western Pacific* the comparison is not well founded. Until, that is, one 'completes' *Argonauts* with another, supplementary text – the diary Malinowski kept during the period of fieldwork, unpublished until 1967.[4] As James Clifford, Clifford Geertz and many others have shown, the hidden authorial voice of *Argonauts* becomes abundantly and shockingly expressive in the diary.[5] Malinowski's texts also reflect back on Stedman's double text, *The Journal* and *A Narrative*. Written mostly in Polish 'with frequent use of English, words and phrases in German, French, Greek, Spanish, and Latin, and, of course, terms from the native languages'[6] the *Diary* is the *Argonauts* subtext as he fluctuates between different registers and voices, in different languages, lacerating himself with guilt for his sexual fantasies, his misfortune, his hatred for the Melanesians who were his hosts for two years.

In its early stages, the *Diary* records Malinowski's apprehension of the landscape recollected in tranquillity. The text begins in truly romantic fashion, reminiscent of Edward Waverley's sojourn by a Scottish loch and both Waverley and Malinowski picture themselves as the honest, objective, observer–hero overcome by the raptures of a negative capability which the scene induces:

> Marvellous sunset; it was cold and I was feeling rested. Felt not too distinctly or too strongly but surely that a bond was growing up between myself and this landscape. The calm bay was framed in the curving branches of a mangrove tree, which were also reflected in the mirror of the water and on the damp beach. The purple glow in the west penetrated the palm grove and covered the scorched grass with its blaze, slithering over the dark sapphire waters – everything was pervaded with the promise of fruitful work and unexpected success: it seemed a paradise compared with the monstrous hell I had expected.
>
> (*A Diary*, p. 10)

This description determines the anthropologist's apprehension of his subject; out of this complex come many of the work's obsessions, but whereas Scott used his landscape as a way of 'seeing' the conjectural history of mankind, Malinowski uses his landscape as a way of 'seeing' and dramatising the self. The loss of history from place is in direct proportion to the increase in the ego which predominates as it compels the landscape to reflect his mood. The pathetic fallacy bridges the sense of being alien by rendering the natural as a romantic text or painting 'framed' in representation. What can be represented can also be controlled, as the savage landscape is a mirror which reflects the familiar. But the picture begins to change midway through this description; the glow in the west is 'purple', it 'penetrates' the palm grove and 'covers' the 'scorched grass with its blaze', sunlight 'slithers' over 'dark sapphire waters'. The Fauvist contrasts record a radical instability in the scene, as 'unnatural' colour floods out of nature. Nature's painted gaudiness and the serpentine action of light infiltrate a post-lapsarian metaphor into the scene since the place *seems* a 'paradise' not a monstrous hell. The landscape is pitched into a textual arena which is consoling in its familiarity as Oceania is also a part of the fallen world. The sun, with its intimations of the fires of Hell, can be composed and neutralised, made familiar by recourse to edenic myth and European aesthetics.

Five days later, Malinowski quite literally braves these fires in a symbolic rite of passage by which he overcomes the landscape's demonic guardians.

> Fires had been kindled in a few places. Marvellous spectacle. Red, sometimes purple flames crawled up the hillside in narrow ribbons; through the dark blue of sapphire smoke, the hillside changes colour like a black opal under the glint of its polished surface. From the hillside in front of us the fire went on down into the valley, eating at tall strong grasses. Roaring like a hurricane of light and heat, it came straight toward us, the wind behind it whipping half-burned bits into the air. Birds and crickets fly past in clouds. I walked right into the flames. Marvellous – some completely mad catastrophe rushing straight on at me with furious speed. (*A Diary*, p. 11)

The anthropologist conquers the spirit of place by precisely the same rites of symbolic action as those whom he has ostensibly come to study. When the mythographer is mythologised, who then is the 'primitive'?

The initiated anthropologist may now plunder the landscape for its secret gems ('sapphire', 'opal') without fear of reprisal from the jealous gods. He enters a new state of being, a new familiarity with the landscape which enables him to strip it bare of its outward show of beauty:

The incomparably beautiful mangrove jungle is at close quarters an infernal, stinking, slippery swamp, where it is impossible to walk three steps through the thick tangle of roots and soft mud; where you cannot touch anything. The jungle is almost inaccessible, full of all kinds of filth and reptiles; sultry, damp, tiring – swarming with mosquitos and other loathsome insects, toads, etc. 'La beauté est la promesse de bonneheur' [*sic*]. (*A Diary*, p. 24)

Under the female moon the landscape tempts the anthropologist out of his rationality:

Marvellous. It was the first time I had seen this vegetation in the moonlight. Too strange and exotic. The exoticism breaks through lightly, through the veil of familiar things. Mood drawn from everydayness. An exoticism strong enough to spoil normal apperception, but too weak to create a new category of mood. Went into the bush. For a moment I was frightened. Had to compose myself. Tried to look into my own heart, 'What is my inner life?' No reason to be satisfied with myself. The work I am doing is a kind of opiate rather than a creative expression. I am not trying to link it to deeper sources. To organise it. Reading novels is simply disastrous. Went to bed and thought about other things in an impure way. (*A Diary*, p. 31)

Seduction, temptation, exoticism, fear, pollution, irrationality, the literary, masturbation: a mélange of associations forms around the landscape which is figured as a body, increasingly a female body, beautiful in aspect but odious to the touch.

Malinowski increasingly mingles seduction with a display of the 'secret filth' of a feminised landscape.

As I walked I threw enormous shadows in the palms and mimosas by the road; the smell of the jungle creates a characteristic mood – the subtle, exquisite fragrance of the green *keroro* flower, lewd swelling of the burgeoning, fertilised vegetation; frangipani – a smell as heavy as incense, with elegant, sharply drawn profile – a tree with an elegant silhouette, its green bouquet with blossoms carved in alabaster, smiling with golden pollen. Rotting trees occasionally smelling like dirty socks or menstruation, occasionally intoxicating like a barrel of wine 'in fermentation'. I am trying to sketch a synthesis . . . (*A Diary*, p. 85)

The synthesis will not form around the contrary sensory impressions of sight, with its recurrent adjectives of 'elegance', and smell which intoxicates and sickens. Fecundity is translated to rottenness and tied to the feminised negation of fertility in menstruation.

Menstruation as an index of female fertility is thus inverted as an index of the opposite, a mark of decay. Like the ancient romance conventions of recording the other green world, Malinowski's landscape exists in the same moral world as Spenser's Duessa in *The Faerie Queene*; her outward show of beauty is a snare to unwary men; under her clothes she hides her true bestial nature.

> ... that witch they disaraid.
> And robd of royall robes and purple pall,
> And ornaments that richly were displaid;
> Ne spared they to strip her naked all.
> Then when they had despoild her tire and call,
> Such as she was, their eyes might her behold,
> That her misshapen parts did them appall,
> A loathly, wrinckled hag, ill favoured, old,
> Whose secret filth good manners biddeth not be told.
>
> (Bk I, canto viii, stanza 46)

In dreams, the play of sexual difference is freed from its reliance upon the metaphor of the landscape:

> Today ... I had a strange dream; homosex., with my own double as partner. Strange autoerotic feelings; the impression that I'd like to have a mouth just like mine to kiss, a neck that curves just like mine, a forehead just like mine (seen from the side). I got up tired and collected myself slowly.
>
> (*A Diary*, pp. 12–13)

Malinowski writes the last sentence without any sense of irony, yet the dream and the diary is precisely an exercise in 'collecting himself'. In Melanesia, there is none with a mouth, neck or forehead 'just like' his. The physiognomic coordinates he emphasises are precisely those of anthropometric analysis. Broca and Camper measured skulls along the axes of the chin, forehead and lips to determine a racial hierarchy with the dolichocephalic European as paramount. The 'facial line' of late nineteenth-century anthropometry was measured, precisely, 'from the side'. The dream enunciates Malinowski's uniqueness in this place, his desire for an otherness 'just like mine', his sense of alienness which desires to transform the other into an autoerotic image of himself. Desire, bereft of an object, seeks itself, and only itself, as the only available – the only possible – representation. But the dream also enunciates his superiority in this place: his uniqueness is a sign of his ascendency.

Malinowski's struggle with the flesh and his sense of uniqueness is conveyed in other ways also. In the early stages of the diary, the reader is struck by the relative emptiness of the place; few people are described, those who are, are established as types arranged in orders of difference relative to Malinowski's uniqueness.

> Sketches: (a) Whites. 1. Hon. R. De Moleyns, nicknamed Dirty Dick – son of a Protestant Irish Lord. A thoroughbred, noble figure. Drunk as a sponge, so long as there is any whiskey to be had. After sobering up (I was present when he had his last bottle of whiskey) fairly reserved and cultured with strikingly good manners and very decent ... – 2. Alf[red] Greenaway 'Arupe' – from Ramsgate or Margate – working-class background – extremely decent and sympathetic boor; it's 'bloody' all the time, and he drops his h's and is married to a native woman and feels miserable in respectable company, particularly feminine. Has not the slightest wish to leave New Guinea. (b) Colored. Dimdim (Owani), modern Orestes – killed his mother when he ran amok. Nervous, impatient – quite intelligent – Life with De Moleyns completely uncivilised – unshaven, always wearing pyjamas, lives in extraordinary filth – in a house without walls – 3 verandas separated by screens – and he likes it. Much better than life at the Mission House. Better lubrication. Having a crowd of boys to serve you is very pleasant.
>
> (*A Diary*, pp. 39–40)

Malinowski is clearly fascinated by the racial and social types he observes, since their description engages a range of class and Stedman-like gradations of racial differences. But his writing also barely conceals his speculations about their sexuality. Malinowski feels that there is something rather 'gamey' about mixed marriages, drunkenness, men cohabiting, being 'served' by boys. This is a 'male' scene and one which seems antithetical to women since it comprises matricides; a male scene which counters the femininity of the tropical landscape. The apppeal to the Anglo-Irish aristocracy ('thoroughbred') and to Greek myth ('Orestes') merely intensifies the exotic danger of their transgressions of the femininity which is seen in the landscape ('in the beauty of the landscape I rediscover woman's beauty or I look for it' ... 'The pink body of the naked earth steeped in the dawn light').[7] Yet one would search *Argonauts* in vain for any mention of these people. They are clearly part of this place but censored from the 'official' anthropological text. The reason is twofold. The types he describes are colonial types, too close to the facts of the imperial project which Malinowski is himself ambivalently a part of. Hannah Arendt describes such individuals as being:

> Outside all social restraint and hypocrisy, against the backdrop of native life, the gentleman and the criminal felt not only the

closeness of men who shared the same colour of skin, but the impact of a world of infinite possibilities or crimes committed in the spirit of play, for the combination of horror and laughter, that is, for the full realisation of their own phantomlike existence. Native life lent these ghostlike events a seeming guarantee against all consequences ... The world of savages was a perfect setting for men who had escaped the reality of civilisation.[8]

'Life with De Moleyns [is] completely uncivilised'; these types approach too closely the reality of colonialism and the world of Malinowski's professed model, Conrad's *Heart of Darkness*. They are thus excised from the ethnography of this place because Malinowski is not concerned, as neither was Roscoe, with colonisation but with representing a myth of primitive life *before* colonisation. Ethnography is written as if the colonial encounter never took place; as if colonialists were not part of the landscape of savage life, indeed as if the anthropologist himself was not there.

Conrad and Malinowski share a similar ambivalence to narrative forms and the representation of the self. Marlow and Malinowski are trapped in inimical situations as participants *and* observers – Richardson's dilemma – which expose their assiduous identities attempting to shore up the rifts: to accommodate the exotic and hazard the uniqueness of their identities in these places or to disdain the alien and thus remain ignorant. Perversely, the crises of psychological alienation which both *Heart of Darkness* and the *Diary* record, far from blurring the grounds of identity, throw the observing selves into the sharpest relief as subjects searching for self-definition and thus, in Clifford's discussion, '*Heart of Darkness* offers ... a paradigm of ethnographic subjectivity'.[9]

Marlow's demeanour is that of a 'Bhudda' with which his unmannerly ascetic presence is compared. Malinowski also approaches the *acedia* of an ascetic, the condition which assails the saintly hermit exiled to the deserts in pursuit of enlightenment. Cassian, a fourth-century French monk from the Wadi Natrum, elaborates:

When accedie beseiges the unhappy mind, it begets aversion from the place, boredom, and scorn and contempt for one's brethren. Also, towards any work that may be done within the enclosure of one's lair, we become listless and inert. We lament that in all this while, living in the same spot, we have made no progress, we sigh and complain that bereft of sympathetic fellowship we have no spiritual fruit ... Finally we conclude that there is no health for us so long as we stay in this place short of betaking ourselves elsewhere as quickly as possible ...

One gazes anxiously here and there and sighs that no brother
of any description is to be seen approaching: one is forever in
and out of one's cell, gazing at the sun as though it were
tarrying to its setting: one's mind is an irrational confusion, and
no remedy it seems can be found.[10]

Malinowski's struggles to 'collect himself' or to 'sketch a synthesis'
resonate with the professions of the saints. The *Diary*, like the
ancient ascetic texts of St Anthony's hagiography or St Augustine's
Confessions, recalls *acedia* as the preparatory trial for the saint/anthro-
pologist in his struggle with the flesh and the demons of the wilderness. Malinowski's *Diary* constitutes a form of hagiography which
reduplicates the conditions of the ascetic rule in order to achieve a
text of canonical status. Out of seclusion and exile from the world of
the flesh (figured as a feminised landscape and 'uncivilised men')
come *acedia*, temptation and the struggle with demons, conversion
and finally, the written 'biography' of the struggle for enunciation of
this purified self. The process by which enunciation is achieved is to
endure a condition in which the saint/anthropologist becomes, in
Geoffrey Galt Harpham's description of the ascetic impulse: 'dead to
the world and recuperable only through textuality. At the same time
that one sought to become textual, however, one had to live in order
to have a biography: hence temptation'.[11]

Argonauts is Malinowski's achievement of 'complete narratability';
Clifford's 'ethnographic self-fashioning' or Geertz's 'I-Witnessing'.
The *Diary* and *Argonauts* record similar narrative movements to *The
Confessions*; 'from autobiography to philosophy to exegesis'. Malinowski gains enunciation in a quest, not only to offer an ethnography of Melanesia, but to make also an 'ethnography' of
himself, to become 'narratable'.[12]

But there are always demons. There must be demons if the *Diary* is
to be an ascetic narrative of transformation from confession to the
canonical exegesis of *Argonauts*, and *The Diary* is engaged in the
preliminary process of identifying and overcoming the 'demons' of
the landscape. The demons appear as unrepresentable phantoms
which gain access to narration through the narrative of the self in
turmoil. Malinowski begins to suppress that turmoil by designating
manichean boundaries in images and myths of purity and filth, of
male and female bodies and sexualities, and of transgressive rites of
passage. 'Seeming' beauty and feminine waste mark the place as a
gendered landscape occupied by Orestean matricides but through
which the figure of Malinowski strides casting 'enormous shadows'.

Malinowski's demons do not suffer the same fate as that recommended by Conrad's Kurtz; his solution is not to 'exterminate the brutes' but to 'write' them. Malinowski divides himself, as *homo duplex*, between the demonic chaos of the *Diary* and the primitive *dominium* of *Argonauts*, and Malinowski's demons are made to forfeit their demonic character by the exegesis of functionalism. Just as *Argonauts* writes out the presence of the colonists, so Malinowski writes in the natives as accommodated demons – accommodated to a functionalist model of harmony as their society is a balanced equation of basic needs and satisfactions provided for by an elaborate ecology of charters and institutions.

But it is not only the demonic Melanesians who are re-mythologised in this fashion. Malinowski also accomplishes his own mythologisation and his own hagiography, that of a young and intelligent man, a Pole possessing Austrian nationality but resident in England, who is visiting Australia when the First World War is declared. As an uncertain risk, due to his birth and subsequent wanderings, he cannot be allowed to roam free while the war rages. The Australian authorities detain him and then deposit him on a remote Pacific island where he lives for the duration of the war. He learns the local language and takes careful notes of everything he sees around him. At the end of the war he returns to England and from there travels to the Canaries where he writes up his observations as *Argonauts of the Western Pacific*. The book and the subsequent writings based on these experiences alter forever the way in which anthropologists write about their subject.

The myth of Malinowski's fieldwork makes a narrative out of the genesis of his heroic transformation of anthropology. In this aspect the 'demon' is the older form of anthropological discourse, the Frazerian evolutionary model, which must be exorcised from the text. Nor does it stop there: it is not only the Frazerian school which the text and its attendant myth exorcises, there is one further exorcism, that of the author himself. Whereas the 'I' predominates in the *Diary*, *Argonauts* subsumes the authorial presence into exegetical practice. What is registered as an anguished presence in the *Diary* is transformed into an absent presence in *Argonauts*.

In constructing the fiction that what we read is the Melanesians' untramelled social text, the anthropologist obscures the fact that what we really read is Malinowski's own written text. In many important respects *Argonauts* recalls most exactly the nineteenth-century novel of provincial manners. *Argonauts* is closer in spirit and in narrative strategy to those Victorian narrations which depict the webs of interrelated social networks, the presentation of a social microcosm, the omniscient 'absent presence' of an author, its size (huge), its sense of completeness (total), and above all its vision of a culture frozen in time, but about to be overwhelmed and destroyed by history.

For Clifford, Malinowski 'was not the Conrad of anthropology ... Anthropology is still waiting for its Conrad.'[13] Certainly if one reads from Malinowski to Conrad in that direct comparative fashion, then the comparison does not work, but if one reads Conrad and Malinowski within their different literary and anthropological domains then the analogy does begin to function. Malinowski comes closest to Conrad in the way in which the *Diary's* relationship to *Argonauts* is analogous to the relationship between *Heart of Darkness* and the classic realism of the nineteenth-century novel. It is only when one reconstructs a composite text which combines the ethnography of *Argonauts* with the subtexts contained in the *Diary* that Malinowski's comparison of his work with Conrad's begins to make sense. The various voices Malinowski actualises in that composite text accomplish some of the same effects as *Heart of Darkness*, which also shifts its vocal texture variously between Conrad, Marlow and Kurtz. Conrad's achievement is the collapsing of nineteenth-century realism, the detailed representation of the social world of *Middlemarch*, into the demonic abyss of colonial conquest. Malinowski's is found in the vertiginous descent to the plurivocal self-reflexivity of the *Diary*. Both Malinowski and Conrad, in their complex and fraught negotiations with the canonical texts of literature and anthropology, show how the ancient narratives of otherness no longer function; the seaman's or the explorer's tale can no longer carry the story from the Congo, nor can Frazer's anthropology contain Melanesia. The options which lay open to Conrad are remarkably similar to those which lay open to Malinowski, even if their solutions differ: to make narrations which acknowledge their implicit and inevitable failure but which show the inadequacies of old narrative forms for the modern colonial world; or to reconstruct the narration in a new self-image. Conrad chose the former in his novels which made an art form of awkwardness and miscomprehension; Malinowski chose the latter with *Argonauts'* omniscient monologue of primitive harmony.

Both Conrad and Malinowski brought their radical *acedia* to cultural representations. Their sceptical interrogations of the dissociated self and its narrations dislodged the other from its historical niche in representation and sent it spinning into new combinations of meaning and significance. Malinowski achieves his own hagiography in the face of the temptations of the savage demons, but the demons of the *Diary* also achieve an apotheosis of kinds in their transformation into 'argonauts'. What was seen as demonic and unnarratable in the *Diary*, has already begun to be remade in the title: *Argonauts of the Western Pacific*. The simile gestures towards a greater anomaly since Malinowski resituates the anthropological subject within the domain of myth yet simultaneously posits functionalist anthropology as the key to that mythology. The authority of the anthropologist is constructed out of the contradictory moment of simultaneously encoding and decoding, whereby the anthropologist is both the maker of the myth and its explicator.

The epic timbre is not unusual, of course, since European observers have tied preliterate peoples to ancient classical similes for over two hundred years and the metaphorical union of Melanesians with classical myth is accomplished with an ease sanctioned by previous mythical associations. But what is new in *this* ascription of the Melanesians as Argonauts is the Conradian undercurrent of the *Diary*. This is not the same as Ferguson's depiction of the Highlander as 'Spartan',[14] or Lafitau's classical Mohawks. Their similes functioned on the basis of a likeness founded upon identical stages of historical and cultural development. No such identity exists for Malinowski; his similes do not make the link between classical and savage peoples because it is informed by stadial theory – because their modes of subsistence or customs align – but because Malinowski shares the Conradian view that both the savage and the classical world express a definitive condition which is unchanged by historical or cultural progress. When Malinowski describes the matricidal 'Dimdim' as 'Orestes', he is employing the classical metaphor to gesture to an element in an unchanging universal psychology, primitive human urges, *hearts of darkness*, which are similarly distinguished by classical epithets (*eros* and *thanatos*, *Oedipus* and *Elektra*). The metaphor forges a new kind of nexus between the classical and the demonic savage, one in which the relativity of cultures, historical determinations and 'racial' differences are seen to be undercut by a universal psychology which remains essentially primitive.

In 1920, T. S. Eliot wrote a review of a performance of Gilbert Murray's translation of Euripides' *Medea* at the Holborn Empire.

Despite the necessity for Eliot to take the 'cheap seats' he proclaimed this to be an important theatrical occasion. The declaration is somewhat surprising since, with the exception of Sybil Thorndike who played the lead with 'legitimate success', Eliot seems not to have enjoyed the evening. Indeed he imagines 'that the actors of Athens, who had to speak clearly enough for 20,000 auditors to be able to criticise the versification, would have been pelted with figs and olives had they mumbled so unintelligibly as most of this troupe'. But this was not the usual hard review of the production, for there was no final-curtain dash to the telephone to record his impressions to a waiting editor. Eliot was not that kind of critic. In fact the production took place 'some years ago' and the performance had been brooding in Eliot's thoughts for a considerable time. Important matters were raised by a translation and production which received popular acclaim but, for Eliot, 'leaves Euripides quite dead'.[15]

More is at stake than Eliot's usual position of being out of step with the general opinion of what constitutes excellence. Eliot's review argued that the classics have lost their cultural supremacy, their position as the foundation of European literature, and the forming influences of the 'European mind' are threatened by translators who 'blur the Greek lyric to the fluid haze of Swinburne'. He declared that these are not 'faults of infinitesimal significance'.[16] The problem is twofold: a general decay in classical learning, which is part of tawdry modernity, and an importation into Hellenism of anthropological science. The review is worth quoting at length:

> As a poet Mr Murray is merely a very insignificant follower of the pre-Raphaelite movement. As a Hellenist, he is very much of the present day, and a very important figure in the day. This day began, in a sense, with Tylor and a few German anthropologists; since then we have acquired sociology and social psychology, we have watched the clinics of Ribot and Janet, we have read books from Vienna and heard a discourse of Bergson; a philosophy arose at Cambridge; social emancipation crawled abroad; our historical knowledge has of course increased; and we have a curious Freudian–social–mystical–rationalistic–higher-critical interpretation of the Classics and what used to be called the Scriptures. I do not deny the very great value of all work by scientists in their own departments, the great interest also of this work in detail and in its consequences. Few books are more fascinating than those of Miss Harrison, Mr Cornford and Mr Cooke, when they burrow in the origins of Greek myths and rites; M. Durkheim, with his social consciousness, and M. Lévy-Bruhl, with his Bororo Indians who convince themselves that they are parroquets, are

delightful writers. A number of sciences have sprung up in an almost tropical exuberance which undoubtedly excites our admiration, and the garden, not unaturally, has come to resemble a jungle. Such men as Tylor, and Robertson Smith, and William Wundt, who early fertilized the soil, would hardly recognise the resulting vegetation ... All these events are useful and important in their phase, and they have sensibly affected our attitude towards the Classics ...[17]

The attitudes expressed demonstrate a thorough immersion in the prevailing intellectual debates in England and France, which Eliot cultivated after his time spent in Cambridge and in Paris in 1909–11. Eliot's sceptical voice ranges over a wide continent where lives much that he sees to be of value consorting with his favourite *bêtes noirs*. In an argument which recalls Schleicher's theories of the rise and decay of languages, Eliot argues that the Greek and Latin languages, 'and *therefore* the English language', are 'passing through a critical period'.[18] This crisis is exemplified by the mawkish sentimentalism of the pre-Raphaelites, who lack rigour, which tokens a slackness of the social formation which allows 'emancipation' to 'crawl abroad'. But in his familiar critique of the contemporary modernity of emancipation, Eliot is infiltrating a new 'synthesis'. As a consequence of anthropological researches, new forms of knowledge are born and flow into each other in miscegenations of a quite promiscuous kind, breeding hybrids of hyphens and heady mixtures of intellectual fashions. The European Eden is taking on a Melanesian appearance which is not to be *entirely* deprecated; with a decent gardener we may yet be able to make a rosebed of this 'tropical exuberance'.

What began as a negative review of a Greek play becomes, in turn, an appraisal of the state of classical learning and its relevance to the modern world, a survey of anthropological and related science and finally a statement of intent to apply the anthropology better, a statement with profound implications for Eliot's poetics. The primitive is to play an essential role in this new synthesis of knowledge.

Eliot's review ties the primitive, obscured by the miasma of modern intellectual fashion which, for Eliot, was indistinguishable from chaos, to the classical text, itself mired by maudlin pre-Raphaelites. Extracted from this context, the savage may yet occupy a role in the 'tradition' of western cultural products which is analogous to the role played by the classical. Eliot exemplifies Hal Foster's discussion of the role of primitivism in modern art; modernists used the primitive in much the same way as the Renaissance used the classical, as a 'discovery' of the fundamental as a means to assault the modern

world and transform it. Both the savage and the classics offer a
ground of origins and a repository of models upon which a tradition
may be reformulated.[19]

Eliot briefly mentions the exemplary primitives in the *Medea*
review – the Bororo. The Bororo became an anthropological *cause
célèbre*; for a hundred years the Bororo have been held up to scrutiny
as each successive generation has challenged the previous one about
the significance of the Bororo, subtly altering the parameters of the
debate until the Bororo have emerged and re-emerged as 'new'
exemplars.

In 1894, Karl von den Steinen reported on the Bororo, a central
Brazilian tribe who believed themselves not to be human beings but
a species of parrots, and began a debate which has variously been
described as an 'ethnographic problem' and an 'enigma'. The shift
from problem to enigma is instructive of the way anthropology
makes its object. The substance of Steinen's report was that the
Bororo had told him that they were red macaws. The statement
engendered a minor controversy with major implications. After
Steinen's report, Lévy-Bruhl enlisted the Bororo as key data for his
notions of a distinctive primitive mentality. Eliot's review was
written in the midst of the Bororo debates which centred upon
Lévy-Bruhl. The significance of the Bororo resides in the fact that
they seemed to express a wholly different notion of 'identity'.

> What they [the Bororo] desire to express [...] is actual identity.
> That they can be both the human beings they are and the birds
> of scarlet plumage at the same time ...
> Primitive mentality sees no difficulty in the belief that such
> life and properties exist in the original and in its reproduction
> *at one and the same time*. By virtue of the mystic bond, a bond
> represented by the law of participation, the reproduction *is* the
> original, as the Bororo *are* the araras [macaws].[20]

The distinction which Lévy-Bruhl makes is between 'mentalities'.
'Civilised' mental operations are founded upon perceived differences in the way objects are apprehended; a 'primitive' mentality
relies upon the distinctions of the ideal qualities inherent in objects.
For the former, the latter is not 'logic' at all but an illogical and
aberrant 'error', as it was deemed in Frazer's designation. These
'observations' point to the centre of the representation of the anthropological subject. If the Bororo truly believe themselves to be parrots
then the circle of western rationality has reached its frontier. The
geographical remoteness of the dwellers of the emerald forest is

matched by the remoteness of the Bororo from western mental processes. The Bororo testify to the non-universality of western rationalism. In a very real sense, the Bororo represent an escape route from the oppressive circle of European hegemony. Inversely, however, the Bororo also affirm western rationalism; they are the inverted mirror image whereby the western self asserts its identity. In its inverted form the west discovers the proof of its existence; the self becomes aware of its existence in an encounter with its other.

Moreover, the Bororo's erroneous logic underlines the correctness of the west. The Bororo assist also in creating a *raison d'être* for anthropology; they are the Holy Grail of anthropology's quest, quintessential otherness, the justifying charter of absolute difference. Without the Bororo, anthropology would, quite literally, be 'unthinkable', there would not be any absolute term against which all other cultures could be measured. Like God, if the Bororo did not exist, they would have to be invented. At the poles of the world of culture differences, therefore, the Bororo and the European face each other from opposite ends of the mental spectrum. All other cultures are simulations, approximations of this panorama of cultural difference.

The Bororo are *the* originals discovered, and they occupy a place of authentic originality which is the equivalent for Eliot to the place of originality and authenticity which the rediscovered classics occupied in the Renaissance. What the myth of Marsyas was to Titian, the Bororo were to the modernists. Eliot returned repeatedly to the Bororo and their anthropological representations to clarify his position with regard to the significance of anthropological data and theory for modern literature. For example, in a review of 1916, Eliot discussed the significance of the Bororo:

> In his book on 'Les Fonctions mentales dans les sociétés inférieures' this author [Lévy-Bruhl] distinguishes sharply between a prelogical and logical mentality. The former is that of the Bororo of Brazil who has a parrot for his totem. Now according to M. Lévy-Bruhl, this is not merely the *adoption* of a parrot as an heraldic emblem, nor a merely mythological kinship or participation in qualities; nor is the savage *deluded* into thinking that he is a parrot. In practical life, the Bororo never confuses himself with a parrot, nor is he so sophisticated as to think that black is white. But he is capable of a state of mind into which we cannot put ourselves, in which he *is* a parrot, while being at the same time a man. In other words, the mystical mentality, though at a low level, plays a much greater part in the daily life of the savage than in that of the civilized man. M. Lévy-Bruhl

goes on to insist quite rightly upon a side of the primitive mind which has been neglected by older anthropologists, such as Frazer, and produces a theory which has much in common with the analysis of mythology recently made by the disciples of Freud.[21]

The final reference to Freud underscores his willingness to see the exemplary Bororo as a significant case within a much wider intellectual frame. Lévy-Bruhl's notions of the mental characteristics of primitive peoples with their distinctive capacities *'into which we cannot put ourselves'* for 'polysynthetic perception', 'collective representation' and 'mystical participation' offered Eliot the opportunity to engage the Bororo directly with the more ostensibly modernist concerns of poetic symbolism:

> Why, for all of us, out of all that we have heard, seen, felt, in a lifetime, do certain images recur, charged with emotion, rather than others? The song of one bird, the leap of one fish, at a particular time and place, the scent of one flower, an old woman on a German mountain path, six ruffians seen through an open window playing cards at night at a small French railway junction where there was a water-mill: such memories may have symbolic value, but of what we cannot tell, for they come to represent the depths of feeling into which we cannot peer.[22]

In the footnote to the above, Eliot refers to Caillet and Bade's article, 'Le symbolisme et l'âme primitive', as representing an approach which is 'interesting' to that proposed by I. A. Richards since, '[t]he authors ... apply the theories of Lévy-Bruhl: the prelogical mentality persists in civilized man, but becomes available *only to or through the poet* [my emphasis]'. Having made the conjunction between the savage and the classical, Eliot refines his connection by identifying the poet as the unique individual in modernity who still retains the primitive spirit of 'mystical mentality'. The capacity both savage and poet share is not simply that of making symbols or images but of *living in metaphor*. Robert Crawford comments:

> [t]his attitude may seem intensely romantic, but was acceptable to Eliot because sanctified through the anthropological eye. Highly charged personal reminiscence is bound up with the anthropological perspective which gives it an impersonal respectability ... These 'depths of feelings' ... look back to Eliot's ... 'canalisations of something again simple, terrible and unknown', but are linked directly to 'l'âme primitive'.[23]

The Bororo hold their fascination for Eliot not only as an emblem of prelogical mentality or savage cognition, or as a type of the ancient religious consciousness, but as an *alter ego* of the modern poet. The Bororo occupy a crucial role as exemplars in the development of Eliot's thinking about the relativity of observation and representation and the importance of language. The startling juxtaposition of human and parrot engages a correlative field of image associations which are significant without 'meaning' just as the 'images which recur, charged with emotion' affect the poet. Yet, finally, Eliot implies, the interrogation of these poetic and anthropological symbols will yield few tangible results, any attempt to theorise would be futile; their significance resides in the arrangement of these fragments.

The list Eliot inserted into the review of *Medea* is interesting also for what it omits: Frazer and Weston, central figures in the introduction of anthropology into classical scholarship and central also for *The Waste Land* are nowhere mentioned nor subjected to Eliot's scepticism. If Frazer's *magnum opus* had little lasting impact on the development of anthropology, *The Golden Bough*'s influence on literature and Eliot in particular, was immense. Eliot's omissions protect an important source of his poetics from the gaze of his own scepticism. Piers Gray has suggested that the reason why Eliot considered Frazer's 'achievement to be considerable' was because Frazer 'by concentrating on customs and rituals' enables us to 'reveal an underlying stability in the fluctuations of the historical process, and suggest the dimensions of the fields of human tradition'.[24] For Gray, Frazer's hold on Eliot derives precisely from the abstention from 'the attempt to explain' which *The Golden Bough* exemplifies.[25] What emerges is not therefore a theory nor merely a collection of data, but a 'vision' 'which gives him a growing influence over the contemporary mind'. Eliot admired Frazer's work for its potential to fracture what he perceived as the maudlin tendencies of romantic historicisation. But Frazer did 'theorise' about the mental state of primitives, indeed the entire work is cast wholly within that question and for Gray to be correct, Eliot would have had to have fundamentally misread or ignored a substantial part of *The Golden Bough* just as Frazer, when he had Downie read *The Waste Land* to him on Denis Saurat's recommendation, gave it up in bewilderment.[26] Frazer's failure to finish *The Waste Land* may be equalled by Eliot's dismissal of Frazer's central thesis in favour of another agenda which made an alternative reading of *The Golden Bough* possible for Eliot.

Wittgenstein compared the interest in ancient rites and customs largely fostered by *The Golden Bough* to the Victorian passion for building follies and ruins – the *frisson* of the archaic, glimpsed in the broken fragments of ancient cultural texts.[27] *The Golden Bough* has the substance of a Victorian dream. Its materials are, perforce, incomplete, since the project never will nor can be finished. Its narratives are violent, often sexy, given the sealing grace of the prehistoric distance of the uncivilised. The text's fragments of ethnography of contemporary savages (for there are no 'social wholes' in *The Golden Bough*) render all its subjects beyond the scope of history, and by discarding history promulgate the Victorian desire for the liberating agency of timelessness. *The Golden Bough* is that other of the Victorian imagination as it struggles to free itself from too much history by reconstructing its remote past in speculative reformulations of human evolution. Its unvoiced agenda is to make better versions of the narratives of the stadial theories of conjectural historians; this is evident in its insistence upon the undifferentiated nature of its cultural materials, almost as if what is known of the past is irrelevant to the text's procedures. Its landscape is an exotic medley of human cultural traces, follies and ruins.

It is perhaps in this way that Eliot read Frazer. By ignoring its central evolutionary thesis, the text takes on the appearance of a collection of fragments tied and retied together by compelling images and narratives which the reader assembles into shapes and patterns, a modernist book of the world. To read *The Golden Bough* as an articulation of an evolutionary theory is to produce a 'civilised' reading; to read it as a savage – as a Bororo might 'read' it – is to perceive the ideal qualities inherent in Frazer's mythical narratives. In the terminology of the contemporary nascent semiotics, Eliot promotes a (primitive) paradigmatic reading over a (civilised) syntagmatic reading of Frazer. The mental cast of the Bororo offers the key to understanding how the various juxtapositions of the book of fragments may be made to 'represent the depths of feeling into which we cannot peer'.

Yeats, who was as deeply influenced by Frazer as Eliot, also evoked the nature of the primitive mind to define what he meant by 'folk literature':

> I had been busy a very little while before I knew what we call 'popular poetry' never came from the people at all. Longfellow, and Campbell, and Mrs Hemans, and Macaulay in his *Lays*, and Scott in his longer poems are the poets of a predominant portion of the middle class, of people who have unlearned the

unwritten tradition which binds the unlettered, so long as they are masters of themselves, to the beginning of time and to the foundation of the world, and who have not learned the written tradition which has been established upon the unwritten.[28]

Implicit in this is an attack, not merely on extemporisations on folk material, but on the very basis of both romantic representation and rationalist analysis and categorisation, evident in the literary and antiquarian works of Scott. Class and literacy had irrevocably divorced Scott, and consequently the predominant model of representation of the primitive which he had initiated, from the subjects he wished to represent. Against this representation Yeats posits illiteracy and the existence of an oral tradition which preserves enshrined a state of mind unchanged since 'the beginning of time'.

But here the matter of origins which the evolutionists evoked is redefined; the *parousia* of an evolutionary initiation is invested with the qualities of *authenticity*. Yeats expressed a desire to render the authentic folk and to uncover this atavistic strain when he wrote: 'I have met with ancient myths in my dreams, brightly lit; and I think [folk tradition] allied to the wisdom or instinct that guides a migratory bird.'[29]

Yeats' evocation of primitive mentality as a construct of myths, dreams, wisdom, instinct, animal cognition, supplants Scott's nexus of romance, history, rationalism and morality, and fastens on Frazer's definitions of the primitive mind as being established upon a triangulation of 'animal mentality, aboriginal practice and proletarian custom', and he reverses the trajectory of Frazer's evolutionary pattern.

Frazer's purpose was to show how mankind had elevated itself from superstition, magic and religion, to attain the higher planes of rationalism. Frazer, like many other evolutionists, Tylor especially, was only partly successful in this endeavour, since by describing the 'irrational' practices of savages in such vivid detail he had also demonstrated the close proximity and persistence of savage and Western European civilised irrationality. The twin guiding spirits of Frazer's work were his scepticism of religious practices and his panegyric to modern culture; both scepticism and panegyric were anathema to both Yeats and Eliot. It is an 'inversion' of Frazer which Eliot adopts, just as he read *The Golden Bough* against its evolutionary grain. Eliot's championing of Frazer masks the processes by which Frazer's text was seen and reproduced as the inverted image of the author's 'scientific' intentions. 'Civilised behaviour', particularly the life in the cities, was but a veneer on an essentially savage psyche, and, as Lang had written, 'human nature remains potentially primitive!'[30]

Frazer's influence on Eliot and his fellow modernists does not derive from any ostensible statement of theory, not (as Gray would have it) because *The Golden Bough* did not contain any theory – but quite the reverse. Eliot's reading of *The Golden Bough* denied every significant component in Frazer's scientific project, and substituted for those a reconstructed pattern for the arrangement of the data in a form which is significant for the 'contemporary mind'. Eliot's thinking about the Bororo and related discourses is likewise profoundly sceptical of anthropological methods of research. The figure of the anthropologist, 'the participant observer', is shown by Eliot to be caught in the same crisis of objectivity which Scott had registered in his fiction and which anthropologists acknowledged some decades later. Compare this from *Notes Towards the Definition of Culture*:

> For to understand the culture is to understand the people, and this means an imaginative understanding. Such understanding can never be complete; either it is *lived*; and in so far as it is *lived*, the student will tend to identify himself so completely with the people whom he studies, that he will lose the point of view from which it was worth while and possible to study it.[31]

with this from Pierre Bourdieu's *Outline of a Theory of Practice*:

> The anthropologist's relation to the object of his study is filled with the makings of a theoretical distortion in as much as his situation as an observer, excluded from the real play of social activities by the fact that he has no place (except by choice or by way of a game) in the system observed, inclines him to a hermeneutic representation of practices, leading him to reduce all social relations to communicative relations and, more precisely, to decoding operations ... Exaltation of the virtues of distance secured by externality simply transmutes into an epistemological choice the anthropologist's objective situation, that of an 'impartial spectator' as Husserl puts it, condemned to see all practice as spectacle.[32]

The impossibility of the anthropological project of objective description means, to Eliot, that all knowledge of the other is subjected to a radical and sceptical relativity. But Frazer was also aware of the relativity of knowledge, when he wrote in a letter to Jackson that: 'There is no *absolute* way of looking at the world. The whole course of opinion (savage, philosophical, scientific) is only a perpetual approximation ever nearer and nearer to the [...] facts, but never by any possibility to reach them ...'[33] Frazer's 'cognitive relativism', to borrow a phrase from Dan Sperber, should be seen, perhaps, in relation to Eliot's own poetic practice.

> And so each venture
> Is a new beginning, a raid on the inarticulate
> With shabby equipment always deteriorating
> In the general mess of imprecision of feeling,
> Undisciplined squads of emotion.[34]

Both express the anxiety of non-arrival at their destinations, but there are of course important differences. Frazer's letter betrays a fear of the collapse of the goal of the master science and a surrender to the anarchy of relativistic knowledges; Eliot's poem is made out of the relativity Frazer fears, another 'step towards making the modern world possible for art'. This last quotation is from Eliot's essay on Joyce, in whose novel Eliot saw the most complete application of the primitivist model he had extracted from his counter-reading of Frazer:

> In using myth, in manipulating a continuous parallel between contemporaneity and antiquity, Mr Joyce is pursuing a method which others must pursue after him. They will not be imitators, any more than the scientist who uses the discoveries of an Einstein in pursuing his own, independent, further investigations. It is simply a way of controlling, of ordering, of giving a shape and a significance to the immense panorama of futility and anarchy which is contemporary history. It is a method already adumbrated by Mr Yeats, and of the need for which I believe Mr Yeats to have been the first contemporary to be conscious. It is a method for which the horoscope is auspicious. Psychology (such as it is, and whether our reaction is to be comic or serious), ethnology and *The Golden Bough* have concurred to make possible what was impossible even a few years ago. Instead of narrative method, we may now use the mythical method. It is, I seriously believe, a step towards making the modern world possible for art.[35]

Einstein remade physical science, as the classics remade the 'European mind', as Joyce remade Homeric myth, as Eliot remade Frazer's book and as the discovery of the primitive mentality of the Bororo remade our perception of the world. The modernist rearrangement of the materials of Frazerian anthropology – the making of a modernist narrative out of the unmaking of a Victorian evolutionary text – is also modelled upon an imitation of primitive mentality, discovered in the ideal of the Bororo. The Bororo are the very essence of modernism since it is their capacity to practise the relativity of 'the mythical method', the poet's art, which will make 'the modern world possible for art'.

Anthropology was not done with the Bororo. Lévi-Strauss was also their ethnographer, in his own inimitable fashion. But before his work on the 'Virtuous Savages' as he called them, could begin, it was necessary for him to clear the ground of some of the litter left by his opponents and rivals. He did this in a way which was worthy of his beloved Rousseau or Voltaire, with a precise, even delicate irony:

> At dawn, I got up to go out and visit the village; at the door I tripped over some pathetic-looking birds: these were the domesticated macaws which the Indians kept in the village so as to pluck them alive and thus obtain the feathers needed for head-dresses. Stripped of their plumage and unable to fly, the birds looked like chickens ready for the spit and afflicted with particularly enormous beaks, since plucking had reduced their body size by half. Other macaws, whose feathers had regrown, were solemnly perched on the roofs like heraldic emblems, enamelled gules and azure.[36]

Given the context of anthropological representations of the Bororo and their macaws, this can hardly be a neutral description. The birds seem to offer an ironic and pitiful commentary on the cognitive anthropology which had once championed them as offering a glimpse on another, greener world but which had only succeeded in leaving them thoroughly plucked. Lévi-Strauss' rejection of the debate reaches a peak of satirical virtuosity in the image of the naked birds staggering under the weight of their own beaks or in the final image of medieval heraldry – a European totem, outmoded and 'solemnly' ludicrous, with little or no significance here, among the 'virtuous savages'.

This ironic anatomising of the macaws and their attendant anthropological baggage is done for the purpose of disposing of one cognitive proposition only to replace it with another, his own. Having, almost literally, spurned the macaws with his heel, he can now reposition them in a more complex system of *bricolage*; but not before he has equally reinstated the Bororo in a fiction of the primitive *habitus*.

> It would not be quite accurate to say that, for the Bororo, there is no such thing as natural death: for them, a man is not an

individual but a person. He is part of a sociological universe: the village which has existed from the beginning of time, side by side with the physical universe, which is itself composed of other animate beings – celestial bodies and meteorological phenomena. Such is the belief, in spite of the temporary nature of the actual villages, which (because of the exhaustion of the land used for crop-growing) rarely remain in the same spot for more than thirty years. So what constitutes the village is neither the site nor the huts, but a certain structural pattern such as has been described above and which is reproduced in every village. It is therefore easy to understand why the missionaries, by interfering with the traditional layout of the villages, destroy everything.[37]

This passage is of considerable interest in a number of ways, not least because it asserts the Maussian contradiction of savage person-hood against civilised individuality. Implicit in this passage is the Maussian dictum that the 'story leads from a start in pure role without self to a finish in pure self without role'.[38] As in Le Moyne's depiction of Laudonnière and Outina, beginning and end stare at each other across the text; the Bororo who is all role but without self, Lévi-Strauss who is all self without role.

The key to the Bororo village plan is the degree to which it articulates 'a certain structural pattern' and in that emphasis Lévi-Strauss is not entirely free of Lévy-Bruhl's primitive mentalism since he replicates Lévy-Bruhl's division between space-oriented and time-oriented cultures which Lévy-Bruhl construed as the principal distinction between civilised and primitive man. Lévi-Strauss' con-templation of the 'virtuous savages' is also analogous to the Renais-sance contemplation of classical myth. Titian's *Flaying of Marsyas* depicts the structure of Apollonian differences founded upon the central theme of a distinction between the civilised and the wild; so too with Lévi-Strauss' making of a 'pattern' from the Bororo village architecture. In terms of a structuralist four-part homology, Titian: classical myth – Lévi-Strauss: the Bororo.

The older cognitive anthropology was spurned to reassemble this structural form of cognition, a world of sacred opposites, made by man, inhabited by man.

Animals, especially fish and birds, belong partly to the world of men, whereas certain terrestial animals belong to the physical universe. Thus the Bororo believe that their human form is a transitional state: between that of a fish (whose name they have taken as their own) and that of the macaw (in the guise of which they will finish their cycle of transmigrations).[39]

The Lévi-Straussian version of the Bororo macaw is an assemblage, a *bricolage* of all previous (and future) versions – and none of them. It is a form of primitive mentalism, in so far as it still persists from a previous age and is essential to all mankind but it is also a piece of hard-edged functionalism, since the transmigration of the soul is the mythical form of the economic necessity felt by the Bororo to change their habitation, either in marriage or to find better agricultural land. Yet, it is none of these completely, since the Bororo macaw is a site, a terminal proposition, like other terms, in a system which is greater than any single explanation. It is a myth in a system of mythology, except that the system is greater than the mythology. The system is open-ended and can embrace all and every term. It is the system of the human mind at work in regular and orderly fashion and applies just as much to savages as to ethnographers; indeed, within the system (and nothing is outside the system, not even refutations of the system), no true distinction is made between anthropologists and savages.

The Bororo way of thinking is governed by a fundamental opposition between nature and culture; just as Eliot envisioned his Bororo as modernist poets because their mentality seemed to encapsulate the poet's striving for a metaphorical apprehension of the world, so too, Lévi-Strauss' Bororo are the very models of the structural anthropologist, being, as he describes them, 'even more sociologically minded than Durkheim and Comte'. Bororo-ness and structural anthropology is the master science, the quintessence of the structure of human thought.

Titian's image contained the sceptical presence of Midas and in Lévi-Strauss' text there is the sceptical presence of the grammatical double negative: 'It would not be quite accurate to say...there is no such thing as'. The double negative serves a more complex purpose than the simple algebra of grammar may recommend; the double negative carries implications of the statement which is negated into the affirmation; a grammatical strategy which makes affirmation contingent upon its negative forms. The contingent nature of framing the Bororo within the double negative has a further effect. The making of the 'structural pattern' in Lévi-Strauss' Bororo village is simultaneously unmade and the 'true nature' of the Bororo is therefore shaded from full gaze by the nature of its enunciation; a concurrent entry and removal from discourse whereby the anthropological object is both enunciated and hidden from view.

A more extravagant manifestation of simultaneous unmasking/

masking of the native is disclosed when Lévi-Strauss writes of his motivations in undertaking an extensive journey through the Amazon in 1938 which 'seemed to take [him] back to the time when there was as yet no division among God's creatures':

> I had wanted to reach the extreme limits of the savage; it might be thought that my wish had been granted, now that I found myself among these charming Indians whom no other white man had ever seen before and who might never be seen again. After an enchanting trip up-river, I had certainly found my savages. Alas! they were only too savage. Since their existence had only been revealed to me at the last moment, I was unable to devote to them the time that would have been essential to get to know them. The limited resources at my disposal, the state of physical exhaustion in which my companions and I now found ourselves – and which was to be made still worse by the fevers of the rainy season – allowed me no more than a short busman's holiday instead of months of study. There they were, all ready to teach me their customs and beliefs, and I did not know their language. They were as close to me as a reflection in a mirror; I could touch them, but I could not understand them. I had been given, at one and the same time, my reward and my punishment. Was it not my mistake, and the mistake of my profession, to believe that men are not always men? that some are more deserving of interest and attention because they astonish us by the colour of their skin and their customs? I had only to succeed in guessing what they were like for them to be deprived of their strangeness: in which case, I might as well have stayed in my village. Or if, as was the case here, they retained their strangeness, I could make no use of it, since I was incapable of even grasping what it consisted of. Between these two extremes, what ambiguous instances provide us with the excuses by which we live? Who, in the last resort, is the real dupe of the confusion created in the reader's mind by observations which are carried just far enough to be intelligible and then are stopped in mid-career, because they cause surprise in human beings similar to those who take such customs as a matter of course? Is it the reader who believes in us, or we ourselves who have no right to be satisfied until we have succeeded in dissipating a residue which serves as a pretext for our vanity?[40]

The language runs the gamut of the anthropologist's self-fashioning emotions of elation and despair as Lévi-Strauss 'out-rousseaus' Rousseau. The dream of limits is realised – not realised but 'revealed' – in the ultimate savage who is also 'charming'. But 'alas!', there is the plangency. Lévi-Strauss has no time, a busy schedule, he is tired, ill. The ultimate savage is so close; he is like a mirror's reflection. But perhaps this is for the best since to describe is to ruin; it is better to keep the astonishment of the colour of their skin; better to keep them in the forest gloom. They are so 'deserving'; we are so 'ambiguous'.

Lévi-Strauss' work has attracted numerous literary epithets: romantic, symbolist, an 'ideal–typical Russian/Czech formalist' poet.[41] To add one further may not materially advance the cause, but his writings seem a constant reminder of a modernist hypothesis. He makes a structure, arbitrary but complete and derived wholly from language and then proceeds to challenge it with examples of the anomalous. The vision of the virtuous savages has a certain beauty derived from the alterity of Bororo life; where we are individuals they are personas. They live in a sociological universe close to the land, we live in the waste lands of great cities in isolation, in a universe of crushing powers. Their sense of continuity survives in spite of, because of their transitory nature; we do not move but are lost to our past. His depiction of the Bororo is polemical; break the structural pattern, as the missionaries break the village plan, and the whole comes tumbling down. The vision is all the more poignant because it too is fading, destroyed by our representatives who do not understand these harmonies and in our ignorance we defile. It is this aspect of Utopian moralising which led Octavio Paz to dub ethnography 'the critique of progress':

> A descendant of Montaigne and Rousseau, of Sahaguin and Las Casas, Lévi-Strauss's answer is a good one: respect other societies and change one's own. This criticism culminates in the critique of the central idea which inspires our society: progress. Ethnography was born at almost the same time as the idea of history was conceived as uninterrupted progress: it is not strange that it should be, simultaneously, the consequence of progress and the critique of progress. Naturally, Lévi-Strauss does not deny this: he situates progress in its historical context, the world of the modern West, and points out that it is not a universal historical law nor a standard of value applicable to all societies.[42]

Lévi-Strauss' vision coincides with Eliot's in important respects. Both saw, in their re-reading and reconstruction of the Bororo material, the opportunity to evolve new systems of understanding of the primitive and their relationship to modernity. That recuperation of the Bororo was achieved by a radical reappropriation of prior representations. Ultimately for Lévi-Strauss and for Eliot, the Bororo contributed to a critique of the contemporary and their oppositional example liberated the poet within, allowing another 'ecology of mind' to be voiced.

The modernist affinity with, or appropriation of, anthropological materials effectively dispersed the panopticon disciplinary gaze of the Frazerian notion of science. Ethnographic data were dislodged from their role in the evolutionary catalogue of human error and redirected towards other goals – the construction of the self, art in the 'modern' world, and the fundamental structures of cognition. The modernists envisioned a new kind of dialogue with their primitive subjects where other – hitherto silent – voices held a dialogue with a centrally located tradition of literary and critical materials. Undoubtedly, modernists reappropriated anthropological material for the new order; an appropriation as extensive as the borrowing of classical form had been for the Renaissance. Of course, the dialogue was never equal, and the messages were misheard and misrepresented. But modernism in anthropology and poetry cut the bands of imperial grand theory, allowing the accumulated data of savage life and the *acedia* of the alienated identity to spill out of the strictures of evolutionary models.

Yet the Bororo 'enigma' persisted beyond their frequent rewritings as modernist myths and redefinitions as definitive primitive mentalists, modernists and structural anthropologists. Christopher Crocker revisited the Bororo; Sperber summarises his findings:

> It turns out that (1) only men say 'we are red macaws'; (2) red macaws are owned as pets by Bororo women; (3) because of matrilineal descent and uxorilocal residence, men are in important ways dependent on women; (4) both men and macaws are thought to reach beyond the women's sphere through their contacts with spirits.
>
> In metaphorically identifying themselves with red macaws, then, the Bororo ... seek ... to express the irony of their masculine condition.[43]

Does it come down to this, then, after a century of debate and speculation about the nature of the primitive mind: an error in translation, a metaphor, a salvo in a Brazilian sex war, the Amazonian equivalent of a vaudeville joke about the mother-in-law?

Or does it? There is after all clause (4), the sanity clause; as Sperber writes 'the red macaws metaphor is itself based on a belief in real contacts with spirits'.[44] The Bororo may not be the birdmen they were thought to be, nor modernists either; they are not structuralist anthropologists ... yet. The threshold to the primitive mind which the Bororo represented is still open, the door has closed somewhat but anthropologists have left it slightly ajar. The avian Bororo are too significant a guarantee of anthropology to be relinquished entirely.

18 Matisse, *Riffian Standing*, 1912

Chapter 7

Third eye/evil eye

Pause there, Morocco,
And weigh thy value with an even hand.
If thou beest rated by thy estimation,
Thou dost deserve enough, and yet enough
May not extend so far as to the lady;
And yet to be afeard of my deserving
Were but a weak disabling of myself.
As much as I deserve? Why, that's the lady!
I do in birth deserve her, and in fortunes,
In graces, and in qualities of breeding;
But more than these, in love I do deserve.
What if I stray'd no farther, but chose here?

The Merchant of Venice[1]

Gustave Moreau is said to have remarked of Matisse that he was 'destined to simplify painting'[2] and his portrait of *Riffian Standing* (figure 18) could be said to go some way to accomplishing that 'destiny'. Matisse spent several months in Morocco in the winters of 1911–12 and 1912–13 and painted a number of Moroccan subjects, among them this portrait of a Riff tribesman, if, indeed, a portrait it can be called since a 'simplification' of kinds is going on here, but it is not of painting, as Moreau would have it, but of representation.

The 'painting' is extraordinarily complex; this painting is about colour, and the relationship of tones to each other. The figure exists between two juxtaposed planes of green and blue and his outline is barely distinguishable from these – his representation contains nothing but paint. Matisse is seemingly reinventing the portrait, not as a representation of an individual as in West's image of Guy Johnson, but as a representation of the qualities of light. In that

219

sense, the Riff tribesman also endures an overshadowing as deep as that of Karonghyontye, except that here it is not an overtly imperialist–romantic ascription which determines his representation, but an obsession with the nature of paint as a medium. The figure's presence is of interest solely as the bearer of colour; an exotic vessel reflecting light. Other than as a problem of or as an opportunity for painting, he is irrelevant. His 'Riffian-ness' is bleached out of this painting just as his 'colour' predominates. The Riffian steps into the full blaze of colour only to be overshadowed by his own brilliance.

Matisse's deconstruction of the romantic penumbra of the exotic was to empty it of its ideological contents and recapitulate it as a purely formal matter. For Matisse, painting is about paint. Men and women, particularly other men and women, if they have anything to do with painting at all, are there as the convenient demarcations of colour fields.

The image promises a rich visual experience, but to see the Riffian, we must arrest all other faculties so that 'simplified' sight may flood the apprehension of the image. The 'presence' of the Riffian must be dematerialised in order for his essential colour to be released in an intensified and purified form. The Riffian's body gives out its colour like a flower gives out its smell, as the quintessence of himself. The colour is barely enclosed in form, indeed, its power resides in its capacity to escape from the object, the body, which would hope to contain it. In this liberation of sight, the Riffian's bodily 'presence' is transformed into his disembodied 'essence' in a dense mist of coloured vapour.[3]

His colour is his revelation. But in order to see him in this way, it is necessary to suspend an exegetical or analytical frame of mind – scepticism won't do it, nor will questions about his mode of subsistence or his kinship taxonomies. The picture is dissociated from analysis and cannot be 'validated' or 'invalidated'. The Riffian is never quite *there*; he is an abstraction of himself, drawn out of his world as the colour escapes his body. His dematerialised essence marks the place where his world is to be discovered in its purified form. He becomes an ineffable presence, an angelic presence, a ghost, a presence of visual extravagance; he is impenetrable and incomprehensible by any means other than as a spectacle which overwhelms sight.

An ethnographic counterpart of Matisse's image is contained in this extract, where Clifford Geertz and his collaborators present an ethnographic 'description' of a Moroccan bazaar:

> To the foreign eye, a mid-Eastern bazaar, Sefrou like any other,
> is a tumbling chaos: hundreds of men, this one in rags, that one
> in silken robes, the next in some outlandish mountain costume,
> jammed into alleyways, squatting in cubicles, milling in plazas,
> shouting in each others' faces, whispering in each others' ears,
> smothering each other in cascades of gestures, grimaces, glares
> – the whole enveloped in a smell of donkeys, a clatter of carts,
> and an accumulation of material objects God himself could not
> inventory, and some of which He could probably not even
> identify . . . sensory confusion brought to a majestic pitch. To an
> indigenous eye, it looks much the same; but with one essential
> difference. Embodied in all this high commotion, and in fact
> actualized by it, is, Revelation (maybe) aside, the most powerful
> organizing force in social life: *mbadla*.[4]

The text foregrounds the tropes of sensory experience. Auditory,
olfactory and, most of all, visual sense contribute to the illusion of
primary experience and immediacy. Geertz et al. accomplish the
same sense of visual extravagance as Matisse; the bazaar is a sight
which overwhelms sight. But the description splits sight between the
reader's sensory capabilities and the primary experiencing senses of
the viewer; these are themselves further split between the 'foreign
eye' and the 'indigenous eye'. The 'foreign eye' is subject to 'sensory
confusion brought to a majestic pitch'; the senses are evoked merely
to be confounded by what they sense as an orgasmic overcharge of
the senses. To the 'foreign eye', the *suq* at Sefrou dissolves into
'tumbling chaos'. The text accomplishes its primary narrative
strategy to create a problem which the text itself will then solve.[5]

Many of the strategies of ethnographic narrative are in evidence
here. First and foremost, the description is a 'synecdochic evocation
of a social whole through the representation of its parts',[6] a familiar
trope for representing otherness by describing a single cultural
aspect which appears immensely significant as a key to the whole
culture but which is nonetheless a riddle or seemingly inexplicable
event to the reader. The anthropologist spins a cultural description
out of the entrails of an apparent conundrum.

The usual triadic relationship of reader–text–author has, in the
ethnographic text, to be redrawn, to encompass a further compli-
cation. In Geertz's description, there are four perspectives: the
reader's (the foreign eye), the native's (the indigenous eye), the
author's (the third eye) and the 'social reality'. 'Social reality' is
rendered a site of impossible confusions, an obscure, obscured and
problematic text. A range of powerful vocabularies frame its difficulty as the discourse borrows the language of warfare, of drama

(costume not clothing), and of the Bible. In whose land do gestures 'smother'? In Pandemonium? Certainly God cannot inventory the *suq*'s infinite variety. Is God, too, a foreigner in Sefrou? There is a sense in which this social reality can never be described; but it must *always* be represented: as war, as sensory confusion, as drama, as biblical revelation.

Yet having made the object of its gaze dissolve into 'tumbling chaos' the text applies the first of its *speculae*: the 'indigenous eye' sees, smells, hears much the same but it has a key to crack its code. That key, however, is further locked inside the casket of language, *mbadla*. *Mbadla* is 'the most powerful organizing force in social life' yet neither the 'foreign eye' nor the 'indigenous eye' can communicate its meaning. The indigenous eye knows everything and, therefore, 'sees' nothing, whereas the foreign eye sees everything but knows nothing. This is Belmont in reverse: Morocco teases Venice with the promise of hidden treasures to test its 'deserving' and we need the occult skills of Portia's father or the special talents of an ardent suitor to win this prize.

How 'we' see is just as complex yet wonderfully easy. Sight seems totally uninhibited; we simply look, but the 'foreign eye', the reader's eye, is placed in direct opposition to the 'indigenous eye' in a system of 'seeing' which is also a system of power. The text creates the fiction that the 'indigenous eye' sees more, farther than 'us' but this is only true in the Morocco of the opaque social reality; whereas in the territory of the text, who is 'foreign'? Who is 'indigenous'? In the text, the 'foreign eye' is the indigenous eye, here the Moroccan is both 'foreign' and blind. We, the readers, alternatively foreign and indigenous – written as foreign, but truly natives of the text – we see farther than the Moroccans and they are what we see, while to them we are invisible. However much 'we' as readers may wish to approach the native on equal terms, the textual operations by which 'we' come to know their difference renders 'us' as indelibly dominant.

That dominance is variously constructed around an evocation of notions of 'difference' central to which is the relative possession or dispossession of 'consciousness'. The 'foreign eye' has the potential, as yet uninformed and latent but about to be informed and made explicit by the text it is reading, to conceive of other kinds of existence, to embrace other lives. The foreign eye can represent to itself its own consciousness in its capacity to conceive of other ways of living. The 'indigenous eye', blinded by the miasma of its social reality and its inability to read the text of which it is the subject, has no capacity to be aware of 'others' and is excluded from self-consciousness. The indigenous eye sees only itself in social inter-action, but it is unaware of itself as an *actor*; the foreign eye is an absent presence, a ghost who slips by unnoticed in the *suq*. The native lacks that self-consciousness which the foreigner has in abundance, the ability to be, in Geertz's phrase, 'put in touch with the lives of strangers'[7] and to conceive of a world different from its own. Without consciousness, the Sefrouis are bereft of the possi-bility to represent themselves to themselves, or to others. Without self-representation or interpretation, they can neither speak of what is significant in their lives nor change their existence. Like the Riffian, they have no history, they do not change, their only time is the present. So caught up are they in the game of their lives they cannot communicate or interpret the rules by which they are playing. They need an anthropologist. Which leaves the third eye, unannounced yet omnipresent, that sees everything, knows how to look and is both author and hero of this text, father and suitor. Geertz himself opens the casket and solves the riddle he has caused to exist.

Where is this omniscient narrator situated? Where is the third eye? This eye is clearly neither 'foreign' nor 'indigenous, it can range the mid-eastern generality to discover the unexceptionally specific in Sefrou. From all of this geographic, cultural material it can clinch the typical, the representative, the 'synecdochic'. It can also construe order from tumbling chaos and reveal that revelation beyond Revelation by translating *mbadla*.

Geertz et al. translate *mbadla* as 'exchange'. Not surprising, really, for a text about a market, but it trails behind it the sobriquet of being 'the most powerful organising force in social life'. The extent to which market forces are a greater advance in anthropological think-ing upon previous 'most powerful organising forces' is an open question. Geertz appears to say little more, unremarkably and tautologically, than that markets are the places where exchange is carried on.

Only the anthropologist is able to see both with a foreign and an indigenous eye and come close to the Foucauldian panopticon, a mode of surveillance which maintains an imperial view and which renders culture as spectacle.[8] Talal Asad remarks that this is a 'char-acteristic form of theological exercise ... to attribute meanings to an alien practice'[9] and thus to discover the immanent order (*mbadla*) of human chaos. Whereas God cannot inventory the chaos of Sefrou, the anthropologist can.

Geertz et al. elaborate further upon the significance of their method:

> The need is for 1) a qualitative formulation of the information situation in the suq as the Moroccans themselves conceive it, followed by 2) an analysis of the relation of that situation thus conceived to the process of exchange as it actually takes place ... in the ordered muddle of the bazaar encounter.[10]

Mbadla as economic exchange is now retranslated as communication exchange and culture here is reduced to communicative relations, but again of two different kinds: firstly, qualitative, that is, subjective statements made by Moroccans themselves, an 'information situation' temporary and unformed; secondly, 'the process of exchange' as it 'actually takes place', objective, permanent and observed by the spectator–ethnographer. The anthropologist establishes the contrasting modes of communication exchange as corresponding to either side of the oxymoron 'ordered muddle': order is (western) observation and actuality, muddle is (Moroccan) speech and absent consciousness.

In Geertz's discussion, the part (*mbadla*) comes to stand for the whole (*suq*, Sefrou, the Middle East). Ironically, the discourse adopts the strategies of primitive magic, as magic is defined by anthropologists themselves. Magic, for Leach and many others, is essentially an error of cognition involving the mistaken reading of metaphor as metonymy.[11] Yet the anthropologist who believes that the part stands for the whole would appear to believe in the magic of synecdoche as firmly as the primitive magician who obtains the nail parings or hair clippings of his client/victim with which to perform his magical acts. For Frazer, magic was science in error; a belief that the world could be coerced by a force of will and (mistaken) experimental procedures. The world of others must be beckoned to us to be brought within our 'power'. Representation is a magical act described as science.

Geertz argues that the 'cogency of our explications' must be measured 'against the power of the scientific imagination to bring us into touch with the lives of strangers'[12] and it is on these terms that he beckons to the Sefrouis. But again there is a disequilibrium between the terms of the equation which Geertz et al. evoke. On the one hand is 'cogency', 'explication', 'power', and science; on the other hand is 'the lives of strangers'. In between is 'touching'. How do these 'foreign' and 'indigenous' 'hands' touch? Geertz et al. are the go-betweens bringing together the foreign and the indigenous, the reader and 'the read'. It is not, of course, expected that the 'lives of strangers' contain such things as 'power', 'explication', 'cogency', science; it is almost hoped that they do not since they would be 'us' not 'them' if they did. The touching cannot be mutual or equal since it is between an organism, the living body of the native, and a faculty of human sciences. But what softens, or attempts to soften, this bear-hug into an embrace is the inclusion of the word 'imagination' which smooths out the hard and angular shape of 'science' with its evocation of a sympathetic subjectivity, Geertz himself, interposed between the institution of knowledge and the real world of the flesh of living beings. Geertz's own humanity, or at least his capacity for 'imaginative' thought, acts as guarantor that the encounter will do no harm, will be subtly and sympathetically conducted. But 'imagination' is not just any old abstract noun, so indelibly inscribed is 'imagination' on the picturesque and romantic text; its presence deflects the scientific trajectory by joining it with the equally powerful, though (for Geertz) less loaded, discourse of the literary.

At a fundamental level, the third eye constructs its narrative upon the foundations of a romantic paradox which states that others are a complete enigma and are transparent to us[13] and that metaphors can be rededicated as metonymies to accomplish the magical acts of science. There would seem to be no clearer indication of the fictional nature of anthropological discourse than the hidden assumptions that the world is an enigma which can be known but which remains an enigma none the less, and that all associations are true, if not for all time then for the duration of the text's hold upon its reader. What literary critics used to call the 'suspension of disbelief' appears to be as necessary a part of entering this anthropological discourse as entering the literary. In 1977 in his inaugural lecture as Professor of Anthropology at Oxford University, Rodney Needham fought an already belated rear-guard action against what he conceived of as the squatters who had moved into his 'subject'.[14] In his lecture, the literary and the anthropological appear to occupy opposite ends of an imaginary intellectual spectrum. The literary text is an imaginative construction of a reality which may or may not exist; the point about the literary text is that it is not meant to be real, it may even be simply not meant. Its companion, literary criticism is, in contrast to the anthropological text, a site of controversy and debate, unfinished and inconclusive where competing inscriptions cross and recross its boundaries often obscuring or departing from the literary text which is its ostensible subject matter. Anthropology, on the other hand, aspires to a kind of transparency, where the writing evaporates as the culture which is its subject gains ascendancy.[15] Only bad anthropology draws attention to itself as writing; literature is nothing but writing.

Needham's defence of his discipline was only partly directed against those outside the subject, a more worrying (for him) development was the enemy within, since anthropologists increasingly recognised that anthropological writing is also 'writing' and that:

> The tricks through which ethnography claims truth are no less complex than those through which the novel claims fiction.[16]

> Anthropological writings are themselves interpretations, and second and third order ones to boot. They are, thus, fictions; fictions in the sense that they are 'something made', 'something fashioned' – the original meaning of *fictio*.[17]

As anthropology has found each of its inventions to be unworkable or unacceptable it has abandoned its claims to science and relocated itself within the refuge of the arts. If it is no longer possible to write 'science', it is still possible to write 'texts'.

Clifford Geertz has embraced this newly found sense of 'textuality'; his own enthusiasm extends to a willingness to compare a Berber sheep raid to *Madame Bovary*.[18] Geertz's achievement has been to write immensely readable ethnography while at the same time challenging, along with others, the assumption that ethnographic description is an essentially neutral or 'transparent' discourse. His own work embodies both a sceptical apprehension of the discipline and an act of faith in its inherent virtue. For Geertz, anthropology's 'source is not social reality but scholarly artifice'[19] and, further, the specific shape of that artifice is to be discovered in the realm of the literary, which has always been anthropology's shadow and *vice versa*, in their often competing and sometimes complementary claims of cultural representation.

Steven Tyler's review of Paul Friedrich's poetry emphasises the textual status of anthropology when he writes that the Structuralist analogy of language and culture goes beyond the discovery of meaningful patterns to an apprehension of something else which is also a part of anthropology: 'Culture as well as language is a structure in process involving meanings and contexts, and many of its symbols are analogous in part to poetic figures ... Culture is, to a significant degree, a work of art.'[20]

If culture is to anthropology what literature is to criticism – a work of art – then according to Webster, 'narrative theory can make clearer to us the dialogue implicit in both fieldwork and ethnography, and help overcome the dogma which obscure the dialectic of fiction and truth inherent in both.'[21] 'Ethnography is fiction (not falsehood!)' proclaims Bob Scholte[22] echoing Geertz, 'something made or something fashioned.' Or, as Webster writes: 'All are "stories" in the sense of narrative, whether truth or fiction, whose meaning has become free from the original conditions of their production and remains open to new social contexts and an indefinite series of possible "readers".'[23] If culture 'is an ensemble of texts, themselves ensembles'[24] then anthropology is 'text cubed', or fiction; but what kind of 'fiction' is anthropology?

'The ethnographic discourse tradition within or against which discontent has arisen is defined ... as the holistic and lifelike representation of a social world through several writing conventions [extrapolated] from the nineteenth-century fictional [sic] genre of realism.'[25] The linking of anthropology to nineteenth-century realism has much to recommend it if it is overlooked that 'realism' is at least as varied – as 'cubed' – in its manifestations as 'anthropology'. Nonetheless, the analysis of narration, first, third or ominiscient, would appear to have some valid applications for both discourses as would the shared endeavour to produce a 'holistic and lifelike representation of a social world'. Both anthropology and realism rely upon synecdoche as a means to present the 'typical' or 'representative' social situation. 'The standard literary discriminations ... of plot, point of view, characterisation, content and style'[26] would appear to make some sense when relocated in the ethnographic text. In these respects, *Middlemarch* may well be a forerunner to other later ethnographic descriptions and something at least would be gained from a discussion of *Middlemarch* as ethnography and *vice versa*. But there is something inadequate in the comparison; an essential feature of the realist text, indeed the principal reason for it being designated 'realist', is its attitude to mimesis. As Abrams defines it, realism is a form of 'fiction which will give the illusion that it reflects life and the social world as it seems to the common reader' and 'the subject is represented, or 'rendered', in such a way as to give the reader the illusion of actual and ordinary experience'.[27] Of course, the production of such 'illusions' is a consequence of highly artificial literary codes and registers, but the application of the literary conventions of realism to anthropology founders upon the fact that classic realist novels confidently assert that there is nothing within the text which is 'different' from anything outside the text. One seamless garment, a continuous stream of consciousness of the 'real' unites the textual social world with the lived social world of the reader. Anthropology assumes the exact opposite, that the social world described is, above all else, *different*. Anthropology is anthropology and not realism because what is in the text is predicated upon the fact of its difference.

Indeed even more might be gained by reversing the equation and viewing anthropology as an inverted mirror of the realist novel. Steven Webster makes a rather different point about anthropology's difference from realism when he defines 'ethnographic realism' as 'a reifying and critically impotent naturalism' which has 'paralleled literary realism rather as an inversion or negation of it'.[28] But this is also to misunderstand the nature both of realism and, more tellingly, of naturalism. Naturalism need not be either critically impotent nor 'reifying'. Quite the contrary, naturalism takes hold of realism's categories – of the material nature of social existence, of the wholeness of selfhood, of the continuity of time and events – and overloads them to the point where the complacent apprehension of the 'real' implodes under the pressure of a world of described 'things'. This is a role for which anthropology is particularly suited with its injection of the exotic otherness of the world into the 'real', and in many instances it is precisely this role which anthropology has performed within the literary domain.

Webster elaborates upon the nature of anthropology's parallel but inverse relation to literary realism as being, firstly, an encouragement to suspend doubt in the literary which is inverted in ethnography where doubt is discouraged. In the literary 'another order of temporality is evoked' while ethnography 'suspends the temporality of the order' it evokes. Literary realism 'recreates the particular characters and things of reality, ethnographic realism objectifies abstractions which transcend these particulars in another reality'[29] which also recalls Geertz's axiom that anthropologists 'don't study villages, they study in villages'.[30] But again, is not encouraging the suspension of doubt not very nearly the same thing as discouraging doubt? Is not suspending temporality simply evoking another temporality? And recreating 'the particular characters and things of reality' does indeed involve the objectification of 'abstractions'; to believe otherwise is to demonstrate little understanding of the process of signification going on in the symbolic codes of the language – in image, symbol, metaphor – the very stuff of the literary.

Discussion of anthropology as realism, or as an inversion of realism, or as naturalism, hits again upon the oxymoron that anthropological writing paradoxically attempts to render the *habitus* realistically while simultaneously describing its unavailability to realism's treatments: 'ordered muddle'. Whereas realism makes a narrative out of an assumed agreement about the continuity of the 'real', anthropology makes a narrative out of an assumed discontinuity of the 'real'.

For Stephen Tyler, the literary discourse closest to anthropological text is not realism nor naturalism, but fantasy. Like fantasy, anthropology must also use the devices of realism to trap the unsuspecting.

> An ethnography is a fantasy, but it is not a fiction, for the idea of fiction entails a locus of judgment outside the fiction, whereas an ethnography weaves a locus of judgment within itself, and that locus, that evocation of reality, is also a fantasy ... [I]t is realism, the evocation of a possible world of reality *already known* to us in fantasy [my italics].[31]

Tyler captures well the circularity and hermeticism of a discourse which identifies 'whole societies from the sovereign codes of cultural organisation'[32] but as a workable definition of 'fantasy' this will not do either. Tyler seems to be adopting a rather secluded and formalist view of the 'other green world'. The world inhabited by the savage subject is seen as being separate, out-there, not-here, them-not-us, a pastoral interlude only. This is fantasy, fit for 'lunatics and poets', as Theseus similarly remarks at the end of *A Midsummer Night's Dream*.

Yet there is a much more troubling and troublesome notion of 'fantasy' than that which Tyler allows, which speaks of transfiguring and doubt. Fantasy can be reread against the grain of Theseus and Tyler as a strategy of uncertainty, indeed for the novelist Wilson Harris, realism and fantasy have the potential for a much more fruitful rapprochement in that he perceives 'realism and fantasy as a threshold into evolution and alchemy. That threshold is a component of the mental bridge within and across cultures.'[33] In this version the 'fantasy' is always incomplete, and in its incompleteness lies the possibility of transformation under the pressure of remaining questions.

What is revealing is Tyler's insistence upon the familiarity of this foreign identity. That which is 'already known' about a world which is unknown is its textual structure; this has particular piquancy since these worlds do not have texts. What the anthropologist brings to these worlds is not the social reality he/she claims to discover there, but text; for anthropology, 'they' do not even exist until they exist as text. A text, moreover, which is 'already known'.

The production and consumption of texts is one of the key indices in anthropology's scientific programme of classification of the world's cultures.[34] Literacy has taken its place alongside 'savagery', 'barbarism', 'pastoralism' as a marker of a profound mental gulf separating preliterate from literate peoples. Literacy has provided a further sign of difference between 'writing' subjects and 'written' subjects; the real difference between the foreign and indigenous eyes. The primitive appears in textual form, not as a writing but as a speaking subject, transcribed. The primitive speaking subject transcribed is seen as a solution to the problem of authenticity and his/her spoken testimony gives a seal of approval, the ring of truth, to the written textualisation of the subject by appealing to an oral communication which exists independently, as it were, of writing. Anthropology is writing; nothing but writing. But it is an ancient belief that writing cannot be trusted, so writing disguised as speech acts as guarantor to writing which aspires to truth.

Since Rousseau's *Essay on the Origin of Languages*, language has been used as an 'index of the degree to which nature is corrupted by the false sophistication of culture'. Speech is its primal form – the 'healthiest and most natural condition of language' – whereas writing is a 'debilitating mode of expression'.[35] The western myth of origins is deeply concerned with condemning writing 'as a destruction of presence and a disease of speech'. For Derrida, the 'ethic of speech is the delusion of presence mastered', 'the image of a community present to itself, without difference. Writing is ... a condition of social inauthenticity.'[36]

Speech seems to offer anthropology the opportunity to validate its textualisation of primitive culture. In a sense, speech acts as realism's 'locus of judgment' outside the 'fantasy' of anthropology's 'evocation of a possible world of reality'. Similarly, the *parole* of the primitive speaking subject authenticates the *langue* of the anthropologist's written textualisation; of course, this is a delusion since both *parole* and *langue* exist nonetheless as text.

The delusion deepens with the assumption that the speaking subject is 'free' to say what he/she likes. The speaking subject's freedom of speech is a part of the validation since free speech is implicit in the ideology of western democracy which gave rise to the myth of origins as a primitive utopia of speech without tyranny. In this way authority is approved by the subject's authentic voice of acquiescence. The anthropologist seeks and obtains a mandate for his/her textualisation from the authentic voice of written speech. Yet it is the very idea of the freedom of speech of the speaking subject which undermines and invalidates the use of written testimonies as a means of achieving an authentic picture of primitive societies. It is not so much that the speaking subject tends to speak in rather typical, if not stereotypical ways, which smacks of inauthenticity, it is that it accomplishes an effect opposite to that intended. Speech is valued not as evidence, but as accent. The timbre of authenticity produces the effect of snatching this voice from its body, from its world, from the very context the anthropologist's representation of which it is there to underwrite. The primitive speaking subject inhabits, not the world of living beings, but the world of the text; a disembodied voice 'free' to speak, but 'free' also from social existence, 'the death of man as a social being'.[37]

Another paradox is therefore present in anthropological representation, that of, in Derrida's words, 'an ethnocentrism *thinking* itself as anti-ethnocentrism, an ethnocentrism in the consciousness of a liberating progressivism.' For Derrida, this 'violence of the letter' 'of difference, of classification and of the system of appellations' is the 'anthropological war' consonant with and analogous to 'colonial or military oppression'.[38]

Contemporary anthropology is a radically split epistemology as displayed in its rhetorical and narrative strategies, its relationship with other kinds of texts, in its field of representations and in its attitudes to language and speech. In its textual relationship to a 'social reality' (us/them, repetition, tautology, oxymoron, self-fashioning) and its textual relationship to other texts (realism, naturalism, fantasy, romance) it expresses itself in complex metaphors and multiple analogies. This split is further evidenced in the fact that its own metaphors have given a shape, order and a context to the other which if they could be said to have assisted colonialism, have also provided the principal basis for the attack upon colonialism.

The manicheism of anthropology is written into every oxymoronic, narrative and ideological construction as the *sine qua non* of its representations. Onto the narrative strategies of phenomenological and objectivist description, the pastoral forms of town and country, the economic discourses of high and low class, the nostalgic ideologies of ancient and modern, the materialist philosophies of primitive and civilised, are mapped the historical forms of coloniser and colonised. The dualism of cultural representation is also the textual structure anthropology has given to our understanding of the process of time, either as projections back to a lost world or as a marker of progress.[39] Stanley Diamond captures these splits well when he writes that 'anthropology, abstractly conceived as the study of man, is actually the study of men in crisis by men in crisis'.[40]

Geertz's evocation of *Revelations* is ironic in this context. Anthropological representations of *colonised or post-colonial people* transfigured as a *primitive people*, are the ethnographies of a post-apocalyptic era *as if it were genesis*. The primitive world, thus constructed, is filled with symbolic power for a western readership, where political, economic and imperialist power is legitimated, transfigured and misrecognised; 'euphemised' (in Bourdieu's usage) to 'make it possible to transfigure relations of force by getting the violence they ... contain misrecognised'.[41]

Geertz and his collaborators capture the 'oxymoronic' nature of the anthropological project.

> The authors of this book caught a particular society in a particular place at a particular time. From that encounter, as unique to us as to those we confronted, we have tried to construct a picture – or, more accurately, a related set of pictures – of what that society is like, how it got to be that way, and, so far as we can figure it out, why. To this last question – unanswerable, unavoidable, and the one by which such enterprises as this are justified – our response has been to conceive of social order as meaningful form and to conceive of meaningful form as embedded in the life, from one angle deeply singular, from another deeply familiar, the Sefrouis live.[42]

Geertz is disarmingly honest in all his writings, careful to specify the particular nature of the text his reader reads. The text will obey the Aristotelian unities in its synchronic 'slice' through Moroccan society. His language is that of entrapment and 'confrontation'; of astonishment at the shock of the other, a slight Gothic *frisson*. The 'last question' remains 'unanswerable' but is nonetheless the 'justification' for the whole 'enterprise'. '*Why?*' In prejudging the 'why' of it as 'unanswerable' anthropology's justifying charter, its reason why, is hidden from view. Anthropology hides its object while ostensibly seeming to describe it in realistic detail. In this way

anthropology perpetuates itself and justifies its acts of representation as an open question never to be resolved.[43]

Having broached the question, it is quickly but firmly elided into
firstly a tautology and then an oxymoron. The answer, which is an
'unanswer', to 'why' is that social order is 'meaning*ful* form' which is
rather meaning*less* except that it tautologically repeats the term:
social order is 'social order'. Meaningful form is 'embedded' in the
'life ... the Sefrouis live'; 'social order is social order is social order'. It
is surprising how many anthropological texts come to sound like a
poem by Gertrude Stein.

'Embedded' in that final sentence about form being embedded in
'life' is the crucial 'oxymoron'. The life the Sefrouis live is 'deeply
singular/deeply familiar'. 'Singular familiarity' describes, not a
people, nor a culture, nor even a 'most powerful organising force',
but a dilemma as surely as does Petrarch's lover's 'cold fire'. But this
can only be experienced by those who see 'deeply' – the 'scientific
imagination' again but which seems here to be less a statement about
professional abilities than about the anthropologist's ardour.

The oxymoron is a rhetorical trope much used by anthropologists
and petrarchan lovers. The petrarchan lover is often, like the anthropologist, the 'third eye', the outsider who pines for his beloved who
is promised elsewhere. The paradoxical oxymoron perfectly circums-
cribes an impossible sexual desire. There is something of the petrarchan lover about the anthropologist in his passion for a subject
which cannot or will not satisfy his desire but leaves his questions
unanswered, and in the voyeuristic nature of a discipline which
construes culture as 'an ensemble of texts ... which the anthropologist strains to read over the shoulders of those to whom they
properly belong'.[44] The oxymoron is, for anthropologist and petrarchan lover, the perfectly evocative linguistic construction for a discipline or for a poetics of desire which appears to represent what it
cannot – will not – make apparent.

Clifford Geertz's relocation of anthropology within the literary
and the subsequent debate in the 1980s among American 'culture
critics' which it inspired turns on a contradictory – an oxymoronic –
response to anthropology's subjects. Geertz, and after him, Scholte,
Marcus, Tyler, Clifford and others, are surely right to indicate the
textual and, more specifically, literary nature of anthropological
writings, but each of the literary genres, forms or categories they tie
into the anthropological text by way of allusion or comparison is
inadequate to the task. Anthropological writing conceived of as

narration reveals a complex arrangement of narratorial representations. Ethnography's use of metaphor and imagery repeatedly
slips into the poetics of paradox and desire in the shapes of tautology
and the enigmatic oxymoron. The narrative forms of realism,
naturalism and fantasy fail to grasp the unique narrative moment of
anthropology. What emerges instead is a sense of discursive crisis
from which the anthropologist's own subjectivity emerges as a guarantor of the truth of his text and the nobility of his intentions but
which, in negotiating the pitfalls of representation, effaces the
subject of discourse. The apprehension of the anthropologist's crisis
of representation is substituted for the apprehension of his/her
subject.

Geertz's style is often a key to his argument, as the shape of his
sentences mirrors the shape of his thought, to the point that it is
often difficult to distinguish between the self-reflexive style and the
subject-matter. He is a master of the subordinate clause and the dash.
As all good stylists know (and Geertz is a very good stylist), the really
important work is done in the subordinate clause, in parentheses, as
it were; the shape of the sentence carries its meaning. The rhetoric of
repetition, tautology and oxymoron relocates in textual form the
visual language of doubling. Having posed the initial doubleness of
the encounter with 'otherness' (us and them/'indigenous and
foreign') the subject is ramified into multiple splits which increase
arithmetically. The Moroccan *suq* appears as an anamorphic image of
an inchoate social life requiring the anthropological perspective to
render it clearly in representation. Yet it is not Sefrou's *suq* which
appears as 'chaos', but the textual strategy of chaos Geertz adopts
which spreads instantaneously through his representation.

But chaos too has a structure, the organic or atomic structure of
splitting, branching, splitting again. Each splitting of the discourse is
caused by, but also annulled by, repetition, tautology or the oxymoron. Tautologies proclaim their difference by repeating their same-
ness; oxymorons insist upon the similarity of difference. These
strategies appear to heal the breach in understanding 'other cultures', but yet, conversely, cause that breach to exist. In this context,
anthropology offers 'solutions' to 'problems' it has made, but those
'solutions' are themselves 'problems'. The oxymoron is the 'solution'
to the 'problem' of tautology. *'Mbadla'* is to 'Exchange' what 'muddle'
is to 'order'. Power descends from such equations since it offers a
'solution' to the 'problematic' other by cancelling both problem and
solution in the mystery of paradoxical homologies. Except, of course,

that for anthropology to be possible, the cancelling must never be complete and the *'why?'* is never stated.

Geertz returns again to one of anthropology's sacred texts, to the slightly open door of the Bororo, about whom he writes:

> [I]t is unsatisfactory to say either that the Bororo thinks he is literally a parakeet ... that his statement is false or nonsense ... or yet again that it is false scientifically but true mythically ... More coherently it would seem to be necessary to see the sentence ['I am a parakeet'] as having a different sense in the context of the 'finite province of meaning' which makes up the religious perspective and of that which makes up the common-sensical. In the religious, our Bororo is 'really' a 'parakeet', and given the proper ritual context might well 'mate' with other 'parakeets' – with metaphysical ones like himself, not common-place ones such as those which fly bodily about in ordinary trees.[45]

In this passage, cultural representation begins its progress through anamorphic chaos, splitting again between order and muddle, science and myth. The passage seems to reject the reductionism of those textual forms which embody objectivity, meaning, order, and which approximate science, but achieve their goal of cohesion by misrecognition, denial and eradication. Geertz appeals to his reader 'to see the sentence as having a different sense in the context of the "finite province of meaning" which makes up the religious perspective and of that which makes up the common-sensical'. Science and myth are, in Geertz's text, simply reinscribed and rededicated to an alternative polarity respectively of 'common sense' and 'religion'. What appears as a rejection of the hated dialectic is merely a renegotiation of the polarised universes of science and myth in favour of an appeal to 'coherence'.

The Bororo, *our* Bororo in Geertz's characteristic embrace of the native, are too precious a commodity to surrender to the collapse of interpretation without some effort to rescue them. But as Geertz applies more scepticism to their birdlike difference and to the metafictions which have accumulated around them, the more they emerge as exotic others. As the anthropological subject is encroached upon by the commonplace – the common-sensical – so it must be removed from the full gaze and concealed within the territory of the quotation marks. The commentary on the Bororo undergoes a certain recirculating and purging of the loaded terms – science, myth, savage mind, primitive mentality – in order to project an image of the honest anthropologist struggling with discourse. Parakeet translates to a parenthetical 'parakeet'; Primitive Mentality transmutes to 'primitive mentality'; fictio to 'fictio'. To protect his imaginary from the real or commonplace, Geertz must reposition his Bororo deep within the fortress of the conditional parentheses where words can exist as simulations of what they seem to be. Far from bringing the Bororo to a truer light, they are further hidden from view, and the more the Bororo are sceptically interrogated and demystified, the more they are reinscribed as a 'problem' or an 'enigma'. Parenthetical words uttered by a parenthetical people.

The Bororo, when recapitulated as the 'Bororo', are still, though, an exemplary people. Their exemplary nature is due to their ability to inhabit, to *become* the discourse they choose. Their 'coherence' can be apprehended by a shifting of terms to accommodate them to our appreciation and understanding of 'the finite province[s] of meaning'. They live, not now in a world of spirit-trees and spirit-parrots, but in the world of discourses, hopping from code to code, perching on their narrative branch for as long as it suits, discursively 'mating' with other discursive simulations and then moving on in an argument which recapitulates Lévy-Bruhl's original assertion that 'life and properties exist in the original and in its reproduction *at one and the same time* ... The reproduction is the original'.[46] The Bororo *were* the exemplars of a primitive mentality; of modernist art, of a 'structural pattern'; the 'Bororo' *are* now exemplary discourse-shifting postmodernists. Just like Geertz. Just like us. We are all 'Bororo' now.[47]

Geertz's renegotiation of the 'Bororo' as an assemblage of discursive strategies descends from a bundle of uncertainties: uncertainty about the 'science' of anthropology, about representation, about writing, but above all about the *writer*. In the past, matters might have been less politically correct but life was easier, as Paul Rabinow writes:

> Postmodernism moves beyond the (what now seems to be an almost comforting) estrangement of historicism, which looked, from a distance, at other cultures as wholes. The dialectic of self and other may have produced an alienated relationship, but it was one with definable norms, identities and relations. Today, beyond estrangement and relativism, lies pastiche.[48]

Geertz's writing practices are a response to the postmodern condition of estrangement from those 'definable norms, identities and relations'. 'Anthropology' is itself in quotation marks, 'a way of speaking' like the 'Bororo' when they are being 'parrots'. These words can now exist only in quotation marks or in parentheses to acknowledge their simulated and constructed natures.

Geertz inserts his descriptions within the parentheses of a sceptical questioning, but he nonetheless makes a representation. Geertz's description of the *suq*, with all the oxymoronic 'ordered muddle' of a narrative of chaos, throws out from itself the Riffian-like colour of its presence if not its tangible apprehension. The alternative to Geertz's narrative and stylistic strategies of sceptical parentheses, subordinate clauses, tautologies and oxymorons is to seek refuge in 'pastiche' or to acknowledge that the discipline is dying. Geertz and the Culture Critics are writing in an interregnum between dominant discourses but with no immediate prospect of a new discourse for anthropology on the horizon, except for the literary and its associated critical discourses – which are themselves in a similar state of dispersal. The empire of stories has fallen. Older forms are constantly recirculated, revivified, simplified, complicated, deconstructed, parodied in the interregnum. The death of the discipline seems imminent. No-one quite believes their own words; no-one quite believes their own fictions: self-consciousness is a priority; self-consciousness is a problem.

The history of 'alienated relationships', of a colonised people misrecognised as a primitive people has brought the anthropological project to a terminal state. The subjects of anthropology are no longer mute, or speaking subjects only, but writing presences making their own representations independently from or in defiance of their anthropological representations. 'Anthropological subjects' are, now, beyond the capacities of anthropology to represent them. There is now a new manicheism, not that of the Apollonian signification of wild and civilised which lies behind Rabinow's identification of a previous age of 'definable norms, identities and relations'. The new manicheism is an unmaking of the manicheism of cultural representations; its material is not to distinguish kinds of beings but to distinguish kinds of representation.

Homi Bhabha insists that 'the question of identity can never be seen beyond representation'[49] and thus he reverses the dialectic of self and other in that it is representation which constructs identity, not the other way round. Bhabha defines the historical construction of identity in a familiar dualistic fashion as 'two ... traditions in the discourse of identity': 'the philosophical tradition of identity as the process of self-reflection in the mirror of (human) nature: and the anthropological view of the difference of human identity as located in the division of Nature/Culture.'[50]

Bhabha's extremely broad distinctions raise the question of whether the two movements in the strategies for the representation of identity are analogous, complementary or contradictory. However, all three adjectives seem to fit Geertz's writings as the subject emerges out of an anthropological discourse deeply embedded in the situating of identity in the structural matrix of social roles. Geertz's achievement is to attempt to evoke a conjunction of both 'traditions' of the representation of identity; to add to 'anthropological' identity a sense of a personable embrace. But that joining of the traditions is only possible if the Bororo are seen as the 'Bororo', more to the point, as *'our Bororo'*. Or while the *suq* remains in representation as 'ordered muddle'. Remove that transfiguration, that embrace, and the primitive subject becomes a 'depersonalised, dislocated ... subject': 'an incalculable object, quite literally difficult to place. The demands of authority cannot unify its message nor simply identify its subjects.'[51]

Anthropology's third eye meets the gaze of 'the evil eye, that seeks to outstare linear history and turn its progressive dream into nightmarish chaos'[52]; the gaze of those denied a presence except in the *mis*representations of their identities; the gaze of Marsyas, Outina, Joanna, Roza's Brazilian slave child, the Riffian.

Bhabha deconstructs the philosophical tradition in the discourse of identity and in so doing issues a complete denial also of the anthropological construction of the primitive identity as a 'persona'. Bhabha's rereading of Fanon attempts to replace the 'anthropological' notion of native identity as a plenitudinous – though 'muddled' – subject with an 'incalculable', an 'unrepresentable' subject which 'returns as a persistent questioning of the frame, the space of representation, where the image – missing person, invisible eye, oriental stereotype – is confronted with its difference, its Other'.[53] Geertz's postmodern anthropological subject is countered by Bhabha's postmodern postcolonial subject; whereas Geertz's Moroccans flood the eye with Matisse's colour, Bhabha's 'postcolonials' are invisible to representation. Geertz attempts a rapprochement between the philosophical sense of selfhood and the anthropological notion of the person to make an ethnographic representation; Bhabha sees identification, subjectivity and representation as the markers of imperialism's designation of its subject peoples. In many respects, Bhabha would seem the absolute antipathy of anthropology, particularly Geertz's anthropology (ironically, given Geertz's literary and critical aspirations). For Bhabha, for the other to be truly other the strategies of representation must be utterly denied, systematically subverted, cancelled or erased from representation; their fabrication must be marked by the hide and seek of erasure. Only by denying representation – both 'philosophical' and 'anthropological' – can the native be truly represented. This postmodern/postcolonial self is a field of negative definitions cancelling the doubleness of identity by inhabiting the double negative of 'not being not there'. In this situation the subject becomes opaque, 'incalculable', emptied of 'content', but recognised because 'empty'. The postcolonial subject emerges as a shadow figure, 'tethered' to the more substantial presence of an erroneous western subjectivity.[54]

The ascetic stricture which the 'empty' subject connotes contrasts with the libidinal discharge which flows from the 'full' subject, but it is a false dichotomy which replicates the very essentialism and manicheism which Bhabha would seem to wish to subvert. Geertz's 'full' and Bhabha's 'empty' subjects are *both*, in their different ways, improvisations on the same themes of the manichean economy of the self: alternating states of limitation and excess, celibacy and promiscuity, by which the individual or social organism regulates its health. Bhabha's reconstruction of Fanon's psychology of colonialism depicts the postmodern/postcolonial self as a product of the historical intervention of imperialism's denial of the enabling features of humanity: language, law, civil society, culture. The urge for conquest is a desire for the subjugation of otherness to bring it within the surveillance of the imperial self. The coloniser substitutes an image of dominance and imperial power for the colonised sense of other; the colonised self looks at the world and sees a reflection of imperial power which has replaced an enabling sense of otherness. The colonial condition prevents, therefore, the formation of workable forms of social and cultural life by creating psychological dependence on substituted colonial domination. Bhabha insists upon a recognition of the historical fact of colonisation as the determining feature of native cultures; to see, not anthropological 'genesis' but Fanon's 'apocalypse'. But Bhaba's preliminary insistence upon a Fanonesque view of history rapidly gives way to an admitted sense of 'historylessness' in Bhaba's writings on the postcolonial world of the incalculable subject.[55] It is not so much that history is another strategy of hegemonic representation, nor that the historical achievement of independence from the empire removes the colonialists' distorting mirror to return the subjected peoples to their rightful sense of identity, but that the colonial rupture has made, in Bhaba's adoption of Fanon's phrase, 'a constellation of delirium' which enacts and re-enacts a tragic cycle from which no recuperation is possible and which renders the colonial subject silent, invisible and unformed, since language, law, civil society, culture consist of the replicated divisions of colonial identity. '[If the [colonial] subject of desire is never simply a Myself, then the Other is never simply an *It-self*, a font of identity, truth or mis-recognition . . . [M]an *as* his alienated image, not Self and Other but the "Otherness" of the Self inscribed in the perverse palimpsest of colonial identity.'[56]

Bhabha inserts the misrepresented, forgotten or omitted historical presence which reminds us that we read not 'genesis' but 'apocalypse', not 'primitive' but 'colonised'. Paradoxically, this is done by denying the possibility of representation and of history. What seems to begin, therefore, as the insistence upon the historical situation of the native subject reinscribed as a postcolonial subject, finds its terminus in the erasure of that history except as a denial of its enunciation. To deconstruct the problem as one of a textual conflict between unrepresentable 'real' and untenable 'written' identities and to counter the nightmare of history with an evasion or denial of history is not to attempt to deal with the *effects* of that history. What is gained in the creation of 'the secret art of invisibleness'[57] is an awareness of those who lie outside representation; what is lost is the perception of the anthropological 'persona': an identity of social roles, obligations, connections, contexts and histories.

For anthropology even to begin its work it must predicate the existence of a subject rooted in a matrix of social and cultural formations. In addition, those culturally specific formations must share some common elements with formations from other cultures for anthropological representations to assume a common ground of signification and meaning. In his deconstruction of the tropes of identity, Bhabha displaces the anthropological subject with the image of a dislocated postcolonial subject who is invisible and appears 'contentless' to anthropology. Such a subject is compelled to represent him/herself paradoxically as an 'absent presence' in representation, an ellipsis. Bhabha denies Geertz's anthropological masses, Geertz is blind to Bhabha's postcolonial subject. Bhabha counters anthropology's insistence upon a rooted plenitudinous subject of analysis with a dislocated 'invisible' or representationally 'empty' identity.

The key term is dislocation. Geertz's literary metaphor of the *suq* insists, above all, on the evocation of a locale. Moroccans are indistinguishable from the place, *their* place; they grow out of and exist only in Morocco, 'jammed into alleyways, squatting in cubicles, milling in plazas'. They are overwhelmingly *there*, and their 'reality' is enforced by their massed presence as an undeniable, incontrovertible fact. The postcolonial subject's radical challenge to cultural representation begins fundamentally in the denial of a sense of place. The panopticon vision withers if there is not a landscape to survey, if there is no 'there' to be in, no 'there' to see. A sense of place is the first denial in the writings of dislocated postcolonial writers.

Homi Bhabha's theoretical formulation of the postcolonial subject is radically antithetical to the spirit of anthropological representations. But it is more than just anthropology which stands to lose from these acts of denial:

> Without anthropology neither modern poetry nor modern art would be what it is today, for anthropology has given modern artists the mood of distance and estrangement from their own familiar traditions, and, by enriching and relativizing the storehouse of knowledge, symbols, and odd and diverse facts out of which poets or artists fashion their work, has enabled their exploitation of the archaic, the exotic, the primitive, the primordial, the universality of myth and symbols, and the relativity of language and thought.[58]

The denial of a sense of place to the dislocated begins to unwind the sense of identity – 'philosophical' or 'anthropological' – which was constructed upon the foundation of cultural misrepresentation and concludes with a questioning of the 'art forms' within which that was articulated. The postcolonial, in Bhabha's formulation, expresses identity by repudiating identity, represents by renouncing representation, makes art by disclaiming art. What may this 'secret art of invisibleness' look like?

Alone in his study, Raj, the narrator of Neil Bissoondath's *A Casual Brutality*, contemplates the maps of India, Casaquemada (a fictional Caribbean island) and Canada which cover the walls of the room. The maps are a representation of codes of meaning which possess locutionary force, special signs which will be found to be increasingly unfathomable. As emblems of space and time the maps tell stories, narratives which correspond to Raj's (and Bissoondath's) past, present and future. But the maps are an index, not of the situation of an identity located in time and space, but of an opposite tendency. The map is a symbol of the consequences of a history of splitting, division and dislocation:

> My eyes travelled east across Africa, through the Middle East, past the Arabian Sea to the cone of the Indian Subcontinent. Then, searching, the way back by sea: south through the Indian Ocean past Madagascar, around the cape of Good Hope into the South Atlantic: north – cutting a path between South America and the west coast of Africa – up to the Caribbean, past Trinidad up the chain to the wobbly red circle that marked Casaquemada.[59]

The many locations of the maps are rendered into a few key sites as Raj's visual journey mimics the historical voyages of his ancestors, the indentured labourers of the subcontinent. Raj continues but does not complete the migration of his ancestors to the North Atlantic and Canada. The map is a representation of the world ripe for domination, or destruction. But Raj holds no such dominion. In Raj's reading of the map, space is ungraspable and contradictory, too large, too small: 'I am, by birth, Casaquemadan: by necessity disguised as choice, Canadian. There was Canada, there was Casaquemada, the one unseizably massive, the other unseizably minute.'[60]

Spatial representations evoke a crisis of identity in the relocated narrator who cannot bring the maps to signify his situation. Bissoondath's own narrative identity is similarly modelled on the contingent fictional identities he evokes. In a short story Bissoondath writes that 'a person moved, was driven by a spasm beyond human control like a piece of meat moving through intestine', and 'it is a version, more tragic, of continental drift'.[61] Raj's distinction raises the question of authorial situation: into what context can these texts be inserted? In which of the maps' topographies would these writings constitute a significant landmark? India, the Caribbean, Canada?

As it is with space, so it is with time – the history of the dislocated will not take significant shape. Bissoondath's list of characters is a rollcall of those dispossessed of their history: their origins conspire to frame their destruction or compel their flight: 'I lost myself on the roads, rivers and names of the maps the way one can lose oneself – the past, the present, the future, one's very being – in the slow, steady mesmerizing movements of fish in an aquarium.'[62]

The stories repeat the failed attempts of characters to fix the 'fluid holding pattern' of time and to make coherent historical narratives of maps which do not dissolve into absurdity, negation and violence. Bissoondath's characters live with a past which has 'formed but does not inform'.[63] Even the inherited images of India acquire the contours of a dark myth which is distant and unavailable. In 'Digging up the Mountains', Hari Beharry holds Biswasian hopes for his new home where time and place may chime: 'It was in this house that Hari planned to entertain his grandchildren and their children, to this house that he would welcome future Beharry hordes, from this house that he would be buried. The house spoke of generations.'[64] The continuity of the Indian patriarchy in the New World, a version of the past stretching into and structuring the future, life on a minor epic scale, 'now', as Bissoondath comments, 'seemed absurd'.[65]

Almost as an admission that the postcolonial cannot know history, only 'time', Bissoondath writes: 'Time kaleidoscopes. The past is refracted back and forth, becomes the present, is highlightened by it, is illuminated by it, is replaced by it. In this rush of sparkle and eclipse, only the future is obscured, predictability shattered. Yesterday becomes today, today steps back from itself, and tomorrow might never be.'[66] When time is substituted for history, Bissoondath's characters are subject to the unpredictability of the endless present tense when even 'today steps back from itself'.

The coordinates of time and space fail to give the world its sense of density and substance, a sense of origins which lends authority to acts of naming. The fictional Caribbean island of *A Casual Brutality* is located by a myth of origins and naming in an immediately post-Columbus era:

> [A] malcontent aboard a Spanish ship was marooned on the little, uninhabited island. The Spanish captain, a man not totally devoid of compassion, ordered that a hut be constructed of tree branches for the malcontent, a man of disputatious character named Lopez...
>
> Three months later, the captain once more put in at the island to see whether the malcontent had learnt his lesson. He found that Lopez had set fire to the hut around himself, his blackened skeleton propped up, as if lounging in comfort, against a scorched beam in the centre of the ashen ruins. In his log, the captain had penned a brief entry: 'Casa quemada.' House burnt. 'Lopez muerto.' Lopez dead. And so, from these simple words, brutal in their brevity yet inconsequential among the thousands he had scribbled in his impatient script, the island got its name and its embryonic myth.[67]

Lopez, expelled from human society, initiates history as suicide in a reiteration of the Hobbesian paradigm: 'simple', 'brutal', 'brief', 'inconsequential'. For the Spanish captain the tale seems hardly worth the telling. The island's myth of origins evokes biblical genesis but acts as a perverse denial of locutionary authority. In the short story, 'There are Lots of Ways to Die', a failed historian of Casaquemada recounts his reason for failure: it is not because of a lack of ability but 'because our history doesn't lead anywhere. It's just a big black hole. Nobody's interested in a book about a hole.'[68]

Incapable of history and the satisfactions of an edenic myth, the island is doomed to repeat *ad infinitum* the conditions of its origins. Any modern Lopez, noisy and intractable, is a problem to be solved by a method imported from South American dictatorships, but perfectly recalling the island's myth of origins. Troublemakers are taken to the remote forests and a small house of logs and twigs, big enough to hold a man, is built next to a tree. A chain is attached at one end to the tree, at the other end it is secured around the man's genitals. A razor is provided. The house is set on fire. The options are simple, brutal, brief and inconsequential – cut or burn.[69]

To date Bissoondath's writings have been explorations of these themes: incoherent space, the disintegration of an already fractured past, voices speaking in a void, a drift towards violence, the flight to security in Canada and the life of an emasculated immigrant. All his narratives deal, in varying shades, with people caught between cutting or burning and Bissoondath's narrative world is charted between those two polar regions. Redemption comes in the shape of those who return to Casaquemada from exile in Toronto; they have messianic fervour but compromised ministries. Kayso, the civil rights lawyer who campaigned against police brutality, meets his Calvary electrocuted by a 'life-size electric sex-doll'.[70]

Yet this is not to suggest that the triangulation of space, time and myth does not produce narratives which make a sense of the past cohere into a realised historical vision. At the climax of the novel *A Casual Brutality*, Casaquemada jerks into an even more extensive spasm of random violence and police massacres. While Raj attends to his dying grandfather, the police raid his home and kill his Canadian wife and three-year-old son. Raj, in a state of anguished bewilderment, finds himself in the hills above Lopez City, at the old colonial fort which surveys the island below:

> And I felt that, somehow, those men who had sweated and strained here, making their little play at fortification only, just

over a century and a half later, to cut their losses and run in a well-orchestrated theatre of brassbands and flag-raising, were in no small measure responsible for the fact that my wife and my son were dead, that my home was a shambles, that Madera [a policeman], gun in hand, was down there somehow satisfying his bloodlust. Those men who had sweated and strained had had other, more valuable lessons to teach, but they had paid only lip-service to their voiced ideals, had offered in the end but the evils of their actions, had propagated but the baser instincts, which took root and flourished so effortlessly in this world they called, with a kind of black humour, *new*.[71]

If these two sentences are meant to account for the lacuna in the history of the dislocated, and if this is Raj's portion of truth – that Casaquemada is a failed experiment in nationhood, one of many, grasping at all the vices of colonial pedagogy, ignoring all its virtues, the place the colonialists 'overlooked' (in both senses of the word) – then it is, however true, ultimately painfully banal. Its locutionary force derives from a naive, even simplistic realism: a strict linearity of historical mechanics connecting chains of events from cause to ultimate effects, from Lopez to murdered wife and child, as if the apocalypse of Casaquemada was present in and sprung from its genesis. But behind Bissoondath's evocations of space, time and myth lie the further, more problematic dimensions of representation, tradition and identity, which counter and overwhelm the texts' fundamentalist realism.

Raj's myth of the fall of Casaquemada is only the threshold from which it is possible to begin to elaborate a counterpoint to dominant ideological categories. To the dislocated, representation is a lie. Art, Bissoondath seems to feel, has the potential to be the most pernicious of lies since it is willed self-delusion. Victoria Jackson, the expatriate teacher of 'An Arrangement of Shadows', contemplates the landscape of the Caribbean island shortly before she commits suicide – islands and suicide forming a terrible objective correlative in Bissoondath's work as the 'not being' of suicide comes to correspond to the 'no place' of the island:

> The landscape – how foreign a word it now seemed, since she had come to think of it with the local phrase as simply 'The Hills' – this landscape, once viewed as a possible watercolour, failed to revive her, depressed her a little more even.
> She had lost her sense of the picturesque. Despite herself, she had learnt quickly that the picturesque existed not by itself but in a quiet self-delusion, in that warping of observation which

convinced the mind that in poverty was beauty, in atrophy quaintness, the hovel a hut.[72]

For the dislocated, mimetic forms – the 'hills' and their associated representations of landscape, watercolour, the picturesque – are not merely inauthentic representations, misrecognitions, but 'writings' in a different script, alien languages forgotten or unlearned. This self is not discovered in, nor recognised by this art. It is only in the radical subversion of art, art subjected to violence, clinically violated or riotously delimbed, that the misrecognised image can be turned to gesture at the site of enunciation: 'Through the door ahead of her the hills, their ugliness bared that morning by brilliance like disease by a scalpel'.[73]

Bissoondath's islanders and Toronto immigrants are constantly reminded that they are bounded by mimesis, inhabiting representations or metaphors of the self as the reflected vehicles of constructed models. The fiction of time and place, of myths of origin, is a form of mimicry, for 'to accept this life was to accept second place. A man who had tasted first could accept second only with delusion.'[74] The 'second place' of island life itself acquires the status of art as something made, a fiction or a 'delusion' of misrepresentation. Joseph the businessman returned to his island in the story 'Insecurity' only to discover that 'You couldn't claim the island: it claimed you': 'The island of his birth, on which he had grown up and where he had made his fortune, was transformed by a process of mind into a kind of temporary home. Its history ceased to be important, its present turned into a fluid holding pattern which would eventually give way.'[75]

Hari Beharry muses on attempting to fix 'the fluid holding pattern' in acts of naming: 'He started thinking about giving [his house] a name, like a ranch: Middlemarch, Rancho Rico, Golden Bough.'[76] Bissoondath's irony subverts these mimetic rites, gently as in Hari's case, more acerbically in the case of the acronyms invented by Trinidadian revolutionaries: 'You ever hear about the Popular Insurrection Service Squad? Or the Caribbean Region Association of Patriots?'[77] The comic subversions of fantasies of belonging and grotesque political action transform the 'local colour' of the exotic mimic into absurdity and negation as in Raj's grandfather's story of the island dance contest won by a one-legged man with a crutch? His prize was a brand new bicycle. Or his Uncle Grappler's more sombre version of Casaquemadan history as the achievement of independence and, hence, 'the right to do nothing'. Increasingly, the fictions turn to the vision of madman Sunil, the human race talks 'about freedom and light but ... in its fear, in a queer perversion of its vision, welcomed slavery and darkness'.[78]

Bissoondath's strength comes from his illuminations of a postcolonial subjectivity which is permitted only restricted areas of representation within the binary codes of colonialism's manichean mimesis: white, black/possessor, dispossessed. In Toronto, Raj sees abundant examples of the ways in which the dislocated subject contrives to manipulate his own representation:

> I had not come to Toronto to find Casaquemada, or to play the role of ethnic, deracinated and costumed, drawing around himself the defensive postures of the land left behind. And this display of the rakish, this attempt at third world exoticism, seemed to me a trap, a way of sealing the personality, of rendering it harmless to all but the individual.[79]

The 'I' which speaks here is both intriguing and instructive since it speaks by what it disavows. Its locutionary force derives from a denial of a voice. The alternative to the mimicry of 'playing the role of the ethnic', substituting self with representation, cannot be said to exist except as a negation of that representation. The dislocated subject carries with him to Toronto the Casaquemadan solution – cut or burn – trim the self into a shaped misrepresentation ('deracinated and costumed') or seek consuming negation. But just as Raj refuses 'to play the role of ethnic', and wear an off-the-peg representation so Bissoondath is faced with the same dilemma. How can narrative escape representation without fleeing towards negation? Is Bissoondath's work an exercise in negation which comprehends its own inability to enunciate an unrepresentable identity or which presents us, alternatively, with a manipulated representation? Does Bissoondath cut or burn? Or is it possible for fiction to emanate from a place which is always 'not'? A voice which makes, but is not 'in' its narrative?

His narratives will not cohere into unities which lend identity to their subjects. His language constantly reaches for the negative form. Not what is, but what is not: denial, negation, the mirror's reflection. In so doing, Bissoondath uses words, as Raj says, not as tools of inquiry, but in their most dangerous capacity, as agents of concealment. Bissoondath's writing perpetually attempts to uncover the nature of the postcolonial while at the same time acknowledging that writing always ultimately effaces the postcolonial self.

Bissoondath's writings assume a large degree of detachment: a problematic strategy of obliqueness both to the subject and form of the fiction. Fiction which attempts to lend a voice to those who are voiceless in accents which are necessarily someone else's ('picturesque' or 'rakish') must be circumspect. In *Digging up the Mountains*, Bissoondath writes of this sense of necessity, in producing fictions which are always incomplete, unresolved: 'all in passing ... visions fraught with the insubstantial, footnotes forming of themselves no whole, offering but image and sensation as recompense for endless motion.'[80]

One such offering of image and sensation is delivered in the story 'There are Lots of Ways to Die', where the friend of a friend is found dead 'in the washroom of a Cinema. A girl was with him. Naked. She wasn't dead. She's in a madhouse now.'[81] Another footnote to an irrecoverable story.

The place these postcolonial subjects occupy becomes an ellipsis, a figure of omission, between two statements: an implied but unrealised presence. Recalling the failed historian, Bissoondath writes 'books about a hole': a black hole from which a voice emanates. He elevates the syntactical figure of ellipsis to a rhetorical trope for, by evoking lives disrupted by the random events of 'kaleidoscopic time', the unpredictable and disruptive are the very means by which his writing reveals, not the subject him/herself, but the acts of concealment effacing that identity. This subject can only be evoked by the negative values of language. Bissoondath's characters exist in the interstices, the 'gaps' between narratives of origin, places of residence, representations of the self. Bissoondath thus cuts through the banality of Raj's historical construction to offer a vision of colonial identity which is anything but banal.

For Bissoondath colonial intervention, migration, dislocation and neglect have wrought a perpetuating sense of fracture. Bissoondath's dislocated identities show themselves in fragments, just as the texts themselves are disjunctive, abridged, mutilated in their repetitions, reversals, the journeyings between Casaquemada and Toronto, the framings of image and action. Little is ever offered or taken whole, things perpetually recede into opacity or are scattered and redistributed through the novel and stories. Framed, truncated images disrupt the strident linear narrative with a different counter rhythm causing it to stumble over obstacles laid in its path.

The unelaborated sense of self is disclosed by omission as the dispossessed views him/herself as an object discoursing on its strangeness: 'I notice that I notice', or on the blankness of its social constructions: 'I do not lead. I never have. I have only practised avoidance.' The world of the postcolonial subject is a subjunctive state, viewed obliquely, tilted at an angle: 'Everything seems to have rounded corners, everything seems somehow soft.' 'Life swimming in delusion, life shimmering in fantasy.'[82] The constant replication of division which marks the postcolonial identity is most powerfully conveyed by the refugee who waits for his wife at the airport, twenty years after the unnamed war which pulled them apart: 'It was like viewing, in rapid succession, the positive and negative of the same photograph: the vision was tricked, the substantial lost, so that even the angular concrete of the airport car park across the way was emptied, became unreal.'[83]

Fictional acts of displacement become for Bissoondath the appropriate – the decorous – medium for the expression of a postcolonial vision, but what political or historical vision descends from Bissoondath's elliptical voices? Bissoondath's voices are always alone, inspected, threatened, lost. The self is an ellipsis where difference is estrangement and the anthropological view of human identity is met with constant denial. Thus isolated from his/her social role, his/her class and his/her community, the individual can neither control the representations language throws up nor embrace its history. But the very unavailability of communal myths, languages and historical narratives in his writings is the process by which the postcolonial subject is 'known' or 'recognised'. Bissoondath's postcolonials cannot break the ellipsis out of its confining parentheses to uncover its presence. Yet, paradoxically, this evocation of a state of dislocated historylessness is accomplished by calling forth a great deal of history of locations: Lopez's house must be constructed for it to be burned and Raj offers a naive historical construction which perpetuates the colonial dualism of the marginalised postcolonial engaged in dialogue with the imperial centre. Into these constructions, Bissoondath introduces a third figure, the hungry ghost at the feast, known by what it lacks.

Marlene Nourbese Philip shares an at least comparable history of dislocations with Neil Bissoondath. Her 'migrations' lead from Africa to the Caribbean to Toronto. In *Looking for Livingstone: An Odyssey of Silence*, Philip has extended and resituated her poetic analysis of language, which she began in *She Tries her Tongue* (where she drew heavily on nineteenth-century philological discourse), more overtly in the adjacent domain of exploration and colonisation. As an inversion of the genre of the male quest narrative the text replicates and subverts many of the themes of the chivalric romance as the text's narrator searches in Africa for the 'blatant beast' of colonial darkness.

The object of her search is David Livingstone, the missionary, explorer, ethnographer and (for Philip's narrator) the archetypal figure of sexual and cultural oppression. But Livingstone is also the missionary of the heresy of the Word; of language as an agent of oppression. He appears, unbidden, in the narrator's dreams as the explicit phallogocentric demon of linguistic, sexual and racial difference:

> HE – LIVINGSTONE – AND I COPULATE LIKE TWO BEASTS – HE RIDES ME – HIS WORD SLIPPING IN AND OUT OF THE WET MOIST SPACES OF MY SILENCE – I TAKE HIS WORD – STRONG AND THRUSTING – THAT WILL NOT REST, WILL NOT BE DENIED IN ITS SEARCH TO FILL EVERY CREVICE OF MY SILENCE[84]

From this subconscious encounter with the demon descend the myriad examples of a reality of catastrophic suffering. Rapacious white words underpin a history of witch-burnings, colonial conquests and the 'transplanting' and dislocation of peoples, which destroyed cultural possessions. The litany would seem endlessly predatory upon those who have no power, no history, no memory, no language. What remains is the empty husk of a humanity ravaged by imperial words, a theme which Philip broached also in *She Tries her Tongue, her Silence Softly Breaks*:

> This
> disfigurement   this
>   dis
> memberment
>   this
>   verbal crippling
>   this
> absence of voice
>   that
> wouldnotcould   not
> sing[85]

In the dream, Philip assigns to Livingstone the status of a 'succubus', which, in demonology is invariably female, and by this simple act of inversion the victim redirects the language of the demonised female against its inventor, while simultaneously pronouncing her 'absence of voice'. Philip's complaint against 'language' is filled with such moments of articulating a presence through the representation of absence.

Philip assigns a linguistic provenance to a myth of the origins of unequal differences and fractured black female identities. In the beginning, Philip writes:

> God first created silence: whole, indivisible, complete. All creatures – man, woman, beast, insect, bird and fish – lived happily together within this silence, until one day man and woman lay down together and between them created the first word. This displeased God deeply and in anger she shook out her bag of words over the world, sprinkling and showering her creation with them. Her word store rained down upon all creatures, shattering forever the whole that once was silence. God cursed the world with words and forever after it would be a struggle for man and woman to return to the original silence. They were condemned to words while knowing the superior quality of silence.[86]

Philip's exploration of the relationships between language, 'race' and femininity rededicates the myth of Genesis to reflect a paradise lost through sexual–linguistic 'first sin'. In the beginning was, not the 'male' word, but the silence of a female deity, a prelinguistic Eden. But sexual difference, having engendered a gendered language, rapidly devolves to a system of racial difference as 'mounted armies of words ... colonise the many and various silences of the peoples round about, spreading and infecting with word where before there was silence'.[87]

'Remove a thing – a person – from its source,' Philip writes, 'from where it belongs naturally and it will lose meaning – our silence has lost its meaning.'[88] The text's narrator is therefore engaged in a double quest, for Livingstone but also for the essential quality of Africa, its 'silence', as a counter to a language indelibly tainted by imperial phallogocentrism. The narrator encounters in her Swiftian travels a number of peoples each bearing a name which is an anagram of silence – the Ecnelis, Lenseci and so on – who have perfected various ways of dealing with language and silence.

What is being enunciated in this articulation of a presence through the representation of absence is a state of *lack* of enunciation. This seemingly paradoxical sentence is only paradoxical if silence is seen as the antithesis of speech. The demonic Livingstone's main error, his heresy given the scriptural qualities of Philip's text, is to assume that identity can *only* be ascribed to the speaking subject; that only language makes presence and that that which cannot be said is, in the manichean economy of identity, an index of the 'empty subject'. The 'empty subject' for Livingstone is black and female, to be 'filled', sexually and verbally, by the plenitudinous white male. But for Philip, speech is *contiguous* to silence since what is said only indicates what is unsaid; language proves the existence of silence. Silence is 'latent' in enunciation, proclaiming the potential for a 'future biblical with anticipation', as if colonialism's erasing of identities creates (inadvertently) the latent potential for the construction of new identities in the present and future.

Claire Harris writes that 'the only effective creative responses, faced with the abomination [of black history], are surrealism and fact'.[89] For Harris, black women's exclusion from presence, their lack of status as enunciating subjects, would seem to compel them to embrace the Geertzian oxymoron in that conjunction of 'surrealism and fact'. Language and narrative are reformed – deformed – into strange combinations; a kind of baroque narrative architecture as language is made to sprout magic realist cupolas, contradictions of styles which gesture to contradictory states of identity.

Philip pursues an alternative course when she writes about 'a new house of language' in the essay 'Making the House our Own, Colonized Language and the Civil War of Words'.[90] She combines architectural and medical imagery and she speaks of, as Harris describes it, 'detoxifying the English Language'. She proposes that black women writers work upon the structure/body of language until the 'equation between the image and the word [is] balanced again'. In *Looking for Livingstone*: 'The word does not belong to you – it was owned and whored by others long, long, before you set out'; 'My words were not really mine – bought, sold, owned and stolen as they were by others.' Language is untrustworthy, predicated as it is upon the Livingstonian premise that language inscribes the 'unspeakable' nature of the black woman.[91]

Philip's 'cure' is radical. She desires to recuperate the literary by a millenarian purging, an emptying out and a scrubbing clean of the language. Central to this ambition is a challenging of metaphor:

> Tongue-tied rests
> in the 'is like' of simile
> defies the is[92]

Such writings have a simple ambition to demystify or confront the racist encodings of the 'white words' by reconstructing the 'bridge between speech and magic' and achieving the 'is', in a perfectly expressive minimalist poetics.

In *Looking for Livingstone* the narrator is placed in a verbal sweat house where she 'sweats' words. Ultimately, she has only three words left, 'root words', which refuse to be shed, 'Birth', 'Death' and 'Silence'. Philip's interest in root words, the essential qualities of purged language, lies in the opposite direction from Harris' surrealism and factuality and from the 'anthropological' construction of identity. Philip's alternative to metaphor is a colourless and abstract representation more consonant with the refined 'silence' of prelapsarian existence, a pristine language that passively and virtuously lies beyond pollution. Paradoxically, language is only tolerable when it approaches the condition of silence.

The prospect of 'unspeaking' language, Philip's narrator's purification of language, acts as an anchor for a dislocated identity as the linguistic/'racial' paradigm – the body of language – is sweated down to its essentials. It is as St Augustine described heaven, where 'we will be able to see our thoughts'.[93] But in *distilling* language there is a danger that language may also be *stilled* to a language without etymology, a language denied the defining characteristics *of* language: no accent, no dialect, no syntax, no grammar. This would be language as atomic particles, without system or difference. It is also a language without rhetoric or currency, conceived of as a purified nomenclature. Philip's 'root words', a poetics purged of structure, are valued as *objects*; abstract monoliths between which blow the winds of silence. The main function of such a language is to gesture to that which separates words: silence. She writes:

> There *were* two separate strands or threads – word *and* silence – each as important as the other. To weave anything I first had to make the separation...[94]

>   Word
> and Silence
>   balance in contradiction
> Silence and Word
>   harmony of opposites
> double planets
>   condemned
> to together[95]

> It is the coarsest of currencies, you know – the word – crass and clumsy as a way of communication; a second cousin, and a poor one at that, of silence.[96]

Lyotard (and Harpham after Lyotard) describes a tendency in modern art in which 'the image is both fetishized and discredited in the name of the unrepresentable'.[97] Philip takes this manichean tension between the unrepresentable 'true' subject which language cannot utter and the actual but 'false' representation which language makes available, to its extreme and radical conclusion. The word is objectified, 'fetishized and discredited' by Philip in the name of the unrepresentable silence. Increasingly, in *Looking for Livingstone*, Philip turns away from language towards the purer form of silence:

>   Silence
>   Trappist
>   Celibate
>   seeking
>   The absolute
>   in Virgin
>   Whole[98]

This is an enigma which extends much further even than Bissoondath's elliptical identities seeking enunciation in the 'exotic' or 'picturesque': wordless words, the pure form of the formless, an identity which speaks without speech, an articulate silence. Silence for Philip is 'the off-limits of the imagination',[99] which means that nothing the reader reads is *it*; the subject of this text lies outside the limits of textuality, outside discourse.

In her state of dislocation and exile from the Africa of her origins, beset by the Livingstonian demon, plagued by the swarms of rapacious white words, and set upon the ascetic's task of purification and enunciation, Philip's narrator experiences an acedia as extreme as either St Anthony or Malinowski. But here it is inverted; it occurs neither in the Wadi Natrum nor in exotic Melanesia, but in the place of *her* migration, the cities of North America, the new heart of darkness. Yet the text brings the reader back repeatedly to, as Philip puts it, 'the true discovery' which is 'just me, me and more me'.[100] The insistent egocentrism of *this* hagiography raises an interesting prospect: as silence, the subject of the text, becomes increasingly situated in an extra-textual off-limits, the 'real' subject, identity, takes its place. The poem documents an identity trying to achieve enunciation through that which cannot be made a substantial textual presence.

The structuring form of *Looking for Livingstone* is the epic journey or quest for the source of silence, but as the source cannot be represented the familiar identity tropes of the epic quest fill that void with the language of self-discovery. 'Every cell within me released its ancient and collective wisdom. No longer was body separate from mind and spirit.'[101]

The narrator seems to repossess herself, expelling the demonic presence of Livingstone, but only by the same kind of purification, objectification and 'fetishizing' of the self as that to which language was subjected. The narrator turns herself – as a displaced subject experiencing the world – into an object of display to herself – as an observing subject immune to experience.[102] The 'real' subject becomes articulate, that much is true since she is now able to crush Livingstone with a series of devastating arguments. But that articulate being only comes about by secluding itself to become an object like language, the self as a 'root word'.[103] Philip's narrator achieves the substantial, irreducible status of a noun in its distilled/stilled form, purged of its differences, purged of its currency in a world of social exchanges.

The two objects of the quest are finally discovered simultaneously: the narrator confronts Livingstone and, after a lengthy exchange, she 'surrenders to the silence within'. The surrender seems like a simulacrum of death in that the speaking subject embraces eremitic silence, not the world of speaking/living beings:

> The traveller seeks
>   contentment
> in silence
>   containment
> of press of circle upon circle
> that cleanses
>   the pollute
>   the profane in word
> to confine within small
>   large[104]

The metamorphosis from speech to silence is not accomplished without a considerable sense of loss since the price of self-fashioning is to come to resolution through the relinquishing of desire. The double quest, then, of the epic motif, can be seen to have two destinations, one metaphysical, the other ascetic. The destination of Philip's metaphysics is to evoke the wondrous ellipsis of silence; her asceticism purifies the language of enunciation to its minimal, emaciated limit.[105]

The poem's meaning, undiscoverable in what it says (but only discoverable in what it says) is communicated directly to its reader through, but in spite of, language. The goal is unmediated communication. 'Might I,' Philip asks in *She Tries her Tongue*, 'Like Philomela ... sing/ continue/ over/ into pure utterance?' (p. 98).

Not without cost. The 'unspeakable' self is necessarily diminished in its metaphysical 'vitality' by being transformed into discourse. Furthermore, language cannot be 'distilled' to the ascetic values of Philip's root words. It remains, as Bakhtin writes, 'populated – overpopulated with the intentions of others'.[106] Much the same can be said for the self since it too is 'overpopulated with the intentions of others' and does not achieve the status of a 'root word' without some diminution, the loss of a social presence or 'persona'. One consequence of this reformulated identity is the re-presentation of an essentialist version of a 'silent' Africa.[107] To prove the existence of the chauvinist intentions of language, a prelinguisitic Africanité must be assumed to act as foil and victim. Can other African voices become audible in this poem? Or must they be drowned out by the silence so that Philomela can sing?

Philip may claim that her quest has led to the union of body and mind to produce a healed identity, but it is achieved only by erecting a different opposition in its place. The text ends with a 'surrender to the silence within' as the 'body' of a written identity contains a 'soul' of silence. Philip reconstructs the *homo duplex*, not as Le Moyne's colonist, the dislocated Calvinist white man, but as a dislocated ascetic black woman. In attempting to remake a vision of a unified and holistic identity in which the outer world of social intercourse is relinquished in favour of an inner world of spiritual purity, Philip reinvents the *double régime* afresh but nonetheless as a recapitulation of the ancient anatomical tropes of spiritual and bodily interiors.

Philip's and Bissoondath's ambitions lie in different directions. Philip is driven by an evangelical sense of empowerment of the voice of black women; Bissoondath catalogues the impotence of the (usually male) postcolonial subject. Yet in an important sense their 'secret arts of invisibleness' accomplish similar effects in that both radically deconstruct the modes of representation and in so doing their works evoke a sense of the absence of postcolonial identities in representation. Their art is to make a literature of loss – Philip's 'silence' or Bissoondath's historian's claim that 'it's just a big black hole', document a postcolonial world without 'ethnography', without access to representation, without a social text. Philip attempts to recuperate from that loss a paradoxical voice founded on silence. Her fictional Africans (the Lenseci and others) exist *as fictions* without actuality, as polemical and linguistic ciphers, and without the host of practices which constitute the fabric of social experience. There is, of course, no obligation on Philip or Bissoondath to elaborate an ethnography for their creations; indeed, there is every reason why they should not in the postmodern, postcolonial world after anthropology, since it is the misrepresentations of history which they hold responsible for their narrators' condition of lacking 'an objectifying confrontation with otherness'.[108] For Philip cultural representation carries with it the taint of Livingstonian language and power; for Bissoondath it would simply be an absurd project. Bissoondath's and Philip's different responses avoid the procession of historicism, estrangement and relativism, not through pastiche, but through a radical resistance and denial; postmodernist play has turned to postcolonial pain.

Yet can any text be entirely purged of the compulsion which inheres in 'the anthropological view of the difference of human identity'?

Chapter 8

Different masks

People are more powerful when they die.   *Yoruba proverb*

For Bhabha, Bissoondath and Philip, dislocated postcolonial identities cannot be constructed outside representation, except as absence.
The space outside representation is an ellipsis, 'silence'. The space
inside is filled with the rejected discourses of 'the philosophical
tradition of identity' and 'the anthropological view of the difference
of human identity'. Hence in my reading, postcolonial writers' and
critics' dissensions from the Apollonian designation of difference are
involved in a further manicheism, an oppositional but still manichean strategy founded upon negation and 'silence'. Plenitude is
answered by an inverse but corresponding absence; language by its
manichean double, silence; 'inside' by 'outside'. These texts are
themselves written inside the recurrent configurations of absolute
difference – inevitably so given their 'dislocated' situations. In their
journey from misrepresentation they travel further into the maze of
representation's making.

My purpose in this chapter is to speculate on an alternative to this
remade manicheism in the work of contemporary Nigerian writers.
Their writings engage with the political and historical issues of the
postcolonial condition and with the philosophical and the anthropological constructions of identity but from a context of writing within
a located cultural context. What emerges as a consequence of their
situation within cultural traditions is neither a reconstruction of
anthropological manicheism nor a 'secret art of invisibleness', but a
series of texts which radically break with those manicheisms of
Apollonian differences and present instead a renegotiated, rede-

fined representation which offers different masks rather than masks of difference.

The first one-and-a-half pages of Chinua Achebe's *Anthills of the Savannah* contain over twenty references to time. It would be surprising indeed if a novel by Achebe did not concern itself with the past and the movement of time and its effects; all his previous novels have blended and reworked the often contradictory forms of classical realism and historical romance into an African context to the extent that he has largely set the agenda for the subsequent development of the African novel. An early critic of Achebe's, the Canadian novelist Margaret Laurence, recognised the importance of his achievement and its determining effects upon African writing when she wrote that he sees 'history in terms of people with names and conflicts and places of belonging. His sense of social injustice is like a white-hot sword wielded through his powerful irony.'[1] His novels have a constant point of reference in the historical formation of the Igbo people before and after their colonisation and their status in the postcolonial nation state of Nigeria.

But time is different from history – more elusive, challenging. Bissoondath writes of the postcolonial experience of time as being 'kaleidoscopic', the 'rush of sparkle and eclipse'. Achebe's novel similarly explores the fragmentation of temporal structures and a postcolonial condition is also articulated through the novel's representation of time. For Bissoondath 'kaleidoscopic time' becomes the index of a wider dislocation; Achebe's investigation of time is the signal of a different kind of enunciation.

The keywords in Laurence's assessment of Achebe's achievement rest on his attitude to the fundamental forms of a particular kind of fictional realism: 'people', 'names', 'places', 'conflict'. Such minimal definitions of realist narrative are supplemented in Achebe's fictions by the equally minimal and fundamental narrative strategy of cause and effect or the sequential nature of events in time. Achebe's foregrounding of time in *Anthills of the Savannah* marks a new inquiry into the nature of narrative as a way of apprehending and controlling fictional worlds through the temporal sequence of events. Achebe's text offers a glimpse into fiction's 'atomic structure', as it were, and takes as its principal subject the nature of narrative in an age of oppression.

Christopher Oriki's witnessing of time is destabilised in the presence of His Excellency. The first words of the novel refer to time being 'wasted' or repeated. 'How many times, for God's sake, am I expected to repeat it?', 'I would never have said it again that second time.' Minutes grow to 'fullness', silence is a matter of duration, not quiet, which 'grows rapidly into its own kind of contest'. Recorded time, 'the crazy logbook of this our ship of state', falsifies the past making it impossible 'to point to a specific and decisive event and say: it was at such and such a point that everything went wrong'. Sequence is distorted, for the 'present was there from .the very beginning' and 'now' is the past, and 'long ago' – 'a year ago?', 'two years?' – becomes 'the end'. A day is not time but a quality, since 'days are good or bad for us now according to how His Excellency gets out of bed in the morning'.[2]

It is not merely the State which the dead hand of His Excellency rests upon, for his dark and ludicrous dominion spreads to encompass the perception of time itself. The novel begins by asking how, in these dark days, narrative can be made when time itself is usurped. How can the novelist repossess time, which has been stolen, and return it to narrative to order events into stories? Repossessing time becomes imperative for the artist who lives under tyranny, for the control of time is an unendurable despotism, more terrible than the control of history. Under despotism, history, however distorted, can still be written: art can take a kind of revenge. But without time narrative is impossible. The insistence upon a regard for temporality makes *Anthills of the Savannah* a radical text because it views the production of narrative as profoundly political in the context of a struggle against oppression for the right and means to order experience into coherence. Time, as a main constituent of narrative, becomes the first and last line of defence against tyranny.

In Achebe's novel time is not the 'kaleidoscopic' endurance of loss and fragmentation. Time proceeds 'relativistically'; its dimensions are not single and unilinear, but multiple and interrelated. The narrations are framed within 'temporalisations' of an intricate and diagnostic kind. In Chris' narration, for example, tenses are used to indicate unfolding dimensions of time and tyranny. The narration foregrounds the present tense and thereby conveys a characteristic perspective on its subject. The present tense normally indicates a sense of 'shared time' or 'coevalness' but Achebe's use of the present tense has the opposite effect. Achebe asserts coevalness only to depict the way in which the regime denies participation in the present. His Excellency promulgates the notion that time and the state are shared, common property, but simultaneously the dictator is in sole possession of both the state and the present: 'His Excellency speaks ...' 'I say nothing ...'[3] The present implies a closeness of contact – face to face, even intimate. Yet in Achebe's usage it affirms the opposite – difference and distance. Through the use of the present tense, Chris and His Excellency appear to share the same place at the same time, yet conversely, the text demonstrates the opposite, that the dictator has taken possession of this discourse.[4]

But His Excellency is not entirely successful. Whenever the present tense is used, it is used as a signal for the narrator to present a commentary on the event just witnessed. In this quotation, the present opens upon an alternative and subversive commentary in an alternative and subversive 'present':

> But His Excellency speaks instead. And not even to him the latest offender but still to me. And he is almost friendly and conciliatory, the amazing man. In that instant the day changes. The fiery sun retires temporarily behind a cloud; we are reprieved and immediately celebrating. I can hear in advance the many compliments we will pay him as soon as his back is turned: that the trouble with His Excellency is that he can never hurt a man and go to sleep over it. (p. 3)

The text creates a double present tense whereby event and commentary share the same temporal dimension. Irony is achieved by the evocation of events which are happening, and a commentary which is provided simultaneously, in an alternative 'now'. The dictator is outside this dialogue between narrator and reader. Only the narrator and the reader possess human texture since they share jokes, allusions and stories which render their 'now' more substantial, more 'real' than that other 'now'. The dictator's present is denied such textured actuality and emerges as the negative reflection of the substantial presence of narrator and reader who are engaged in secret dialogue. His Excellency may lay claim to the present but his claim is undercut by a narrative which seeks an alternative dimension in the present. The narrator, again and again in this novel, achieves his or her status as narrator by transcending the dictator's present and attaining a level where he or she can negotiate a dialogue with the reader. The narration passes beyond the dictator's present tense to reconstruct other times, other conspiracies.

A similar kind of narrative strategy is employed in the relationship of time to language. In this case the double present tense of narration aligns exactly with the two languages of despotism and dissent. Chris is tuned to the subtle nuances of spoken and unspoken dialects. He can 'read in the silence of their minds' the states of despair afflicting his colleagues (p. 2). Chris' own subtlety is contrasted with His Excellency's logocentric simplicity and directness: 'Soldiers are plain and blunt' (p. 4). Again, as with time, the struggle for the control of words establishes the workings of tyranny as appearing to share a language of clarity and directness from which one is, in reality, excluded: 'I was excluded from what he was now saying; his words were too precious to waste on professional dissidents' (p. 4). Yet again, the act of exclusion from language makes language the site for an ironic confrontation. The denial of dialogue within the hierarchy of power enables dialogue outside that hierarchy between narrator and reader: 'I liked the look of terror on my colleagues' faces when I used the word *dissociate* and the relaxation that followed when they realised that I was not saying what they feared I was saying' (p. 5). The reader needs to be tuned in to Chris' playful language to follow its twists and turns. The word 'dissociation', with which Chris has so much fun at the expense of his colleagues, captures Chris' kind of irony which requires one not to say what one is saying. This capacity to generate other kinds of lightfooted speech multiplies as the novel progresses.

Chris Oriki, the 'Commissioner for Words', gives way to Beatrice with her first-class degree in English, a degree won with the help of ancestors who hacked 'away in the archetypal jungle' and 'subverted the very sounds and legends of daybreak to make straight [her] way' (p. 109). There is a paradoxical quality about this metaphor, as if to 'make [language] straight' it has to be bent by subversion. In the face of His Excellency's 'plainness and bluntness', one must use a language of shaded and intricate textures. Elaborate metaphors become, by their very complex nature, subversive of the official language of brutality:

> I knew then that if its own mother was at that moment held up by her legs and torn down the middle like a piece of old rag that crowd would have yelled with eye-watering laughter. (p. 42)

This disturbing image of violation perfectly expresses the 'blunt' world of mass violence where dictatorships thrive. To counter this kind of language, its alternative must become twisted into fantastic shapes of elaborate metaphors to envisage a possible world of speech coeval with the world of 'bluntness' and brutality.

> The birds that sang the morning in had melted away even before the last butterfly fell roasted to the ground. And when

songbirds disappeared, morning herself went into the seclusion of a widow's penance in soot and ashes, her ornaments
and fineries taken from her – velvets of soft elusive light and
necklaces of pure sound lying coil upon coil down to her
resplendent breasts: corals and blue chalcedonies, jaspers and
agates veined like rainbows. So the songbirds left no void, no
empty hour when they fled because the hour itself had died
before them. Morning no longer existed.   (p. 31)

Ikem's hymn to the sun is one of many experiments with language
contained in the novel as each narrator attempts to discover a
language freed from the taint of oppression and expressive of a
personal and communal autonomy. This piece of lapidary expendi-
ture with its personifications, dialectics and use of special terms such
as 'void' seems resonant of the style of Soyinka at its most exotic and
undisciplined. The whole is done with a degree of irony at Ikem's
expense as the lyricism gradually digs itself into a hole of mock-epic
hyperbole. Ultimately, this kind of language offers no viable alternative to His Excellency in the politics of language which the novel
establishes. Although its power is acknowledged, it leads nowhere
and in its excess it turns in on itself and constitutes its own self-
parody.

For Beatrice, the liberating agency of language is contained in the
mixture of a child's game and 'her friendship with strange words':

> World inside a world inside a world, without end. *Uwa t'uwa* in
> our language. As a child how I thrilled to that strange sound
> with its capacity for infinite replication till it becomes the moan
> of the rain in the ear as it opened and closed, opened and
> closed. Uwa t'uwa t'uwa t'uwa; Uwa t'uwa.
>   *Uwa t'uwa* was a building block of my many solitary games. I
> could make and mould all kinds of thoughts with it. I could
> even rock it from side to side like my wooden baby with the
> clipped ear.   (p. 85)

The beautiful authenticity of this quirky and familiar remembrance goes, as in the case of the matter of time, to the foundations of
narrative. Beatrice imaginatively reconstructs an area of cultural
autonomy and personal privacy out of the formative stage of
language. 'All kinds of thoughts' are reconstructed out of these
'building blocks' in a way which is reminiscent of Marlene Nourbese
Philip's reducing of language to its 'root words' or T. S. Eliot's
inquiry into the unaccountable and irreducible 'mystical mentality'.
The significant difference from Eliot's and Philip's essentialisms,
however, is that their evocations end in 'silence' or 'the depths of

feeling into which we cannot peer'. Beatrice's epiphanies of the fundamentals of language elaborate alternative cultural contexts which are felt throughout Achebe's novel as emblems of a certainty of an Igbo 'world inside a world' which His Excellency cannot control. Time and language are made to enunciate, not an elliptical or 'secret art of invisibleness', nor the 'faded poor souvenirs of passionate moments', but an Igbo matrix out of which the 'infinitely replicated' narratives pour (p. 85).

Beatrice's 'friendship with strange words' embodies a spirit of optimism not previously present in Achebe's fiction, but it is a pretty close-run thing. After all, the apparent facts of life under His Excellency do not look auspicious. The nation is deracinated and silenced by a postcolonial regime which elevates these conditions to a 'fact of life'. More than once, the novel questions whether its narrators are doomed 'travellers whose journeys from start to finish had been carefully programmed in advance by an alienated history?' The text asks almost despairingly, 'what must a people do to appease an embittered history?' (p. 220).

Yet the spiral of decline begins to unwind itself in the novel, firstly through a type of ironic self-referential humour. Beatrice at one point responds to Ikem's statement that 'a novelist must listen to his characters who after all are created to wear the shoes and point the writer to where it pinches'. With the words, 'Now hold it! Are you suggesting I am a character in your novel?' Beatrice points to the fabricated nature of the text she inhabits, just as Dante's guide pointed to the main sights in her tour of the created universe. She ushers in a torrent of referential devices enclosed within her text like 'worlds within worlds' or words within words. She gestures towards Achebe's own writing: 'Girls at war! thought Beatrice with a private smile.' 'As a matter of fact I do sometimes feel like Chielo in the novel, the priestess and prophetess of the Hills and the Caves.' But the referential nature of the text spills out beyond Achebe's own fictions to Aristotle, for example, when Ikem says, 'As the saying goes, the unexamined life is not worth having.' Or to Christopher Okigbo with the strategically placed references to Mother Idoto (pp. 97, 115, 114, 101). *Anthills of the Savannah* is, in part, an essentially optimistic manifesto of the power of 'the literary' in all its variety and humanistic potential to offer an alternative epistemology to that of the state, another constellation of meaning to articulate postcolonial identities and to nurture outlawed political ideologies.

Achebe's text is founded upon the notion of the contrary and the contradictory nature of appearances. Art is defined in terms of an 'ultimate enmity between art and orthodoxy'. Art's role is to contradict and as such it moves in ways which are themselves contradictory. Art fails in its task of capturing the grandeur of divinity, so it 'ritualises incongruity' and by 'invoking the mystery of metaphor', art captures the 'unattainable glory' by its opposite – 'mundane starkness'. For Achebe, this oppositional character of art does not signify the chaotic and unstable nature of human experience nor the elliptical nature of identity; on the contrary, by its paradoxical nature art affirms the irreducible and unchangeable stability of the human personality. 'We can only hope to rearrange some details in the periphery ... Even a one-day-old baby does not make itself available to your root-and-branch psychological engineering, for it comes trailing clouds of immortality' (pp. 100, 103, 100). The movement from the peripheral nature of understanding to the central core of Wordsworthian 'clouds of immortality' is, perhaps, too easy a transition for anyone but a believer in the leap of faith which art can accomplish. If, paradoxically, the diffuse and apparent chaos of the postcolonial social world Achebe depicts is but the artistic form of representation of deeper, permanent and implicit meanings, where are these to be sought and found in his own artistic practice?

One possible source lies in the Igbo myth of Idemili which Achebe recounts in *Anthills of the Savannah*. Idemili was sent to temper masculine power by ritualising access to titles in traditional society. A man only knows if his supplications to the goddess have been successful if he remains alive three years after the rituals have been performed. His Excellency does not observe the proper forms of the ritual and ignores their results. Reading from ritual practice to the practice of political power, His Excellency has, metaphorically, broken one of the fingers of chalk, the key test in Idemili's rituals of supplication. Idemili claims what is rightly hers and the rejected despot is dead within three years. 'Such is Idemili's contempt for man's unquenchable thirst to sit in authority on his fellows' (p. 104).

This theological interpretation renders the narrative pattern visible as mythological history. Time and language are remade and repossessed by Igbo myth and made to enunciate a historical destiny. Reading is revelatory and involves a typological reading from one mythical narrative to the variety of social and political narratives the novel contains. The Frazerian typologies of myth are invested with historical and political significances which anthropology had rendered irrelevant to its procedures. Similarly, paradox is not rendered as a Geertzian oxymoron of the narrative of a 'tumbling chaos' but as a site of Igbo cultural representation.

Ultimately such reading is celebratory and optimistic since myth enables disorder to be 'theologically' rendered. In *A Man of the People*, Chief Nanga is not only unpunished but rewarded for his crimes because, as the novel puts it, there is no owner to reclaim what is rightfully his.[5] *Anthills of the Savannah* marks the 'return of the owner' in a myth of righteous retribution which acknowledges the strategic importance of variety but finally insists upon the efficacy of the mythical narrative to order experience and to enable fiction. Myth, as archetypal story, is not only the means by which we read the signs of cultural beliefs; it is the means by which social justice is enacted. Human society is a work of art to Achebe, inasmuch as it 'ritualises incongruity' into the ultimate order of mythology.

Achebe's mythological principle is also, of course, a historiographic principle since it condenses the historically various into the mythological narrative. But this is a two-way street; myth is not the terminus of history and the process can be reversed. Myth becomes significant when it is vitalised – not as Frazer would have had it, by ritual behaviour – but by history. Without the historically specific, mythology is a reference without referent. At best, mythology without history is simply exotic decoration and at worst, it creates alienated elliptical postcolonial identities. Without myth, history is an alienated journey of the embittered:

> 'It is the story ... that saves our progeny from blundering like blind beggars into the spikes of the cactus fence. The story is our escort; without it, we are blind. Does the blind man own his escort? No, neither do we the story; rather it is the story that owns and directs us.'[6]

There is a danger, however, that such theological readings compose too comforting a unity for this demanding novel. The novel's final challenge concerns Chris' legacy which is, typically, a problem of language. The process of deciphering his last words again foregrounds the act of interpretation with which Chris began the novel. Emmanuel and Beatrice both interpret his words differently, both weave them into webs of significance. The final device of the novel replicates its narrative strategy as the multiple narrators construct a triangulation around a 'centre which cannot hold' – it is unknown, misunderstood, misheard or variously interpreted. The condition is familiar in Achebe's first novel, *Things Fall Apart*, where the British colonialists misunderstand and misinterpret the novel the reader has just read as a colonialist anthropological text, *The Pacification of the Primitive Tribes of the Lower Niger*.[7] It is a repeated pattern in Achebe's work that misinterpretation symbolically crystallises the crisis of colonial intervention. *Anthills of the Savannah* marks a departure from that cycle of misinterpretation, that 'constellation of delirium'. Communication, in this novel, is partial and fragmentary; interpretation is plural and productive. Both Emmanuel and Beatrice construe the words differently, but both find the solace of meaning. The 'centre cannot hold', in the sense of offering an absolute specificity, but in this novel only His Excellency's 'blunt and plain' language demands the absolutely specific; the Commissioner for Words offers a enunciation which is more contingent, but also more various.

Elesin Oba, the central figure of *Death and the King's Horseman*, is the kind of articulate amorist and ritual quester familiar in the plays of Wole Soyinka. His is an eloquence which is charted through successive plays: the Bale of Baroka, Jero, Professor, Kongi, the Madmen.[8] Each character's facility with language is combined with a growing sense of danger as they talk themselves, and others, into the transgression of boundaries and the fracturing of taboo.

Elesin's social position as the King's Horseman defines his role in the rituals which follow the death of the Alafin, the king or *oba* of Oyo. The Horseman will commit suicide in order to follow the dead Alafin into the world of the ancestors. His unique duties and obligations made the best freely available to him: 'The juiciest fruit on every tree was mine.' The rules and protocol of the rites of passage made a refusal of his every whim impossible, yet there is more to Elesin than the grasping appetite of a spoilt aristocrat:

> Split an iroko tree
> In two, hide a woman's beauty in its heartwood
> And seal it up again – Elesin, journeying by,
> Would make his camp beside that tree
> Of all the shades in the forest.[9]

The appeal of Elesin's fast-flowing, humorous imagery transforms acts of ritual piety into lovingly-performed devotions. Elesin may have the dangerous appetite of a decadent, but his language testifies to a zest and vitality which captivates those of whom he demands favours.

Elesin recasts the folktale of the 'Not-I' bird; a spirit bird whose song announces the death of those who hear it.[10] Elesin's poetry moves rapidly through a series of dramatic vignettes of individuals' encounters with the death-bird. As each persona makes their *entrée* into the tale, Elesin builds a vivid description of the traditional Yoruba *polis*. A world of farmers, priests, courtesans, hunters, gods and animals is created as Elesin's tongue calls into presence a kind of *Alarinjo* masquerade,[11] a Menippean procession of Yoruba social types which, true to its satirical intent, creates an image of social cohesion and completeness while simultaneously subjecting that social text to a withering sarcasm.

> Death came calling
> Who does not know his rasp of reeds?
> A twilight whisper in the leaves before
> The great araba falls?
> ...
> He snaps
> His fingers round his head, abandons
> A hard-won harvest and begins
> A rapid dialogue with his legs.   (pp. 11–12)

The social, natural and metaphysical world of the Yoruba is contained in Elesin's poem, all controlled by and under the dominion of death.

> There was fear in the forest too.
> Not-I was lately heard even in the lair
> Of beasts.   (p. 13)

Even the gods are tied to the world of nature and the society of man by their fear of death:

> Ah! companions of this living world
> What a thing this is, that even those
> We call immortal
> Should fear to die.   (p. 13)

In the plenum of his tale, all but Elesin are the subjects of death; his egocentricity soars, putting him beyond the natural world, beyond the world of men, beyond even the gods.

> My rein is loosened.
> I am master of my Fate. When the hour comes
> Watch me dance along the narrow path
> Glazed by the soles of my great precursors.
> My soul is eager. I shall not turn aside.   (p. 14)

Elesin is unique in all the world since only he is the sole master of his fate. Elesin is the essential Yoruba man: 'The town, the very land was yours.'

The Horseman's ritual role and the pivotal focus of Soyinka's drama is the transition of Elesin from the world of the living to that of the ancestors. This is expressed dramatically in the scene and dialogue between Elesin and the Praise-singer which is a prelude to Elesin's dance into the world of the ancestors. Elesin intends to dance himself into a death-trance in the midst of the market women. He starts to dance and Elesin and the Praise-singer commence their poetic dialogue:

> Praise-singer: Elesin Alafin, can you hear my voice?
> Elesin: Faintly, my friend, faintly.
> Praise-singer: Elesin Alafin, can you hear my call?
> Elesin: Faintly, my king, faintly.   (p. 41)

Elesin is no longer *Oba* but *Alafin*, a promotion in rank, but also an acknowledgement of the new relationship which exists between the spirit of the dead Alafin and the spirit of Elesin, as if the two were now in union. The Praise-singer begins the exchange as himself ('Faintly, my friend, faintly') but is rapidly transformed into the voice of the departed Alafin ('Faintly, my king, faintly'). For the rest of the dialogue Elesin talks to the dead king. The dialogue of spirits detaches the voice from the characters; in the rituals of the dead the word escapes from human identities as language becomes the possession of the ancestors. The mask of the *Ara Orun* speaks in Soyinka's dramatic recreation of the *egungun* rites.

Social persona becomes equally fluid. The hierarchical ranks and domains of the 'Not-I' *entrée* of the body politic (Alafin, Oba, Praise-singer) lose their static ordering powers and slip from voice to voice. The *egungun* is dissolving and reformulating the identification and fixing of the individual and social selves. The ritual dialogue ends when Elesin declares that 'strange voices guide my feet'. Elesin sinks into a deeper trance, the voice of the Praise-singer regains its body. The Praise-singer returns to prose; he speaks directly at first as he grapples with the difficulty of relating what he has seen, but faced with the impossibility of description, his language begins to flex and grow with proverbial forms.

> No arrow flies back to the string, the child does not return through the same passage that gave it birth. Elesin Oba, can you hear me at all?   (p. 44)

Language and the Praise-singer are both being stretched to the limits of endurance. The Praise-singer 'appears to break down', so too does language as the stage directions take over:

Elesin dances on, completely in a trance. The dirge wells up louder and louder. Elesin's dance does not lose its elasticity but his gestures become if possible even more weighty. Lights fade slowly on the scene.(p. 44)

The Praise-singer attempts to express the experience prosaically, then by circumlocution and oblique linguistic strategies, until language is finally lost in music, an illustration of Soyinka's belief that: 'Tragic music is an echo from that void ... All understand and respond for it is the language of the world.'[12]

Elesin's pageant of the Yoruba *polis* is dissolved by the gaze of the mask in a way which holds a metaphysical significance for Soyinka. In his dramatic reconstruction of Yoruba ritual, Soyinka is drawing upon two principal sources, the indigenous practices of Nigerian peoples and the kind of anthropological interpretation of rites of passage offered by Arnold Van Gennep in which social life is seen as a series of transitional passages from one status to another, from one occupation to the next, from group to group, institution to institution. Within this process important changes (birth, social puberty, marriage, parenthood, advancement to a higher class, occupational specialisation and death) have an attendant ritual to allow the individual to pass from one persona to another. These rites of passage, different in their phenomena are nonetheless similar in their structures and consist of three distinct phases: separation, transition (*marge*), and incorporation (*agregation*). The similarity of the structures of otherwise different rituals makes social life resemble a natural regularity and rhythm which is 'governed by a periodicity which has repercussions on human life, with stages and transitions, movements forward, and periods of relative inactivity'.[13] Rites of passage impart a 'rhythm' to the social order which appears to reflect a universal regenerative process for nature and for man.

> The phenomenon of a transition may be noted in many other human activities, and it recurs also in biological activity in general, in the applications of physical energy and in cosmic rhythms. It is necessary that two movements in opposite directions be separated by a point of inertia, which in mechanics is reduced to a minimum by an eccentric and exists only potentially in circular motion. But, although a body can move through space in a circle at a constant speed, the same is not true of biological or social activities. Their energies become exhausted, and they have to be regenerated at more or less close intervals. The rites of passage ultimately correspond to this fundamental necessity, sometimes so closely that they take the form of rites of death and rebirth.[14]

Soyinka's drama of 'transition' brings presence to this indefinite anthropological narrative. Where Van Gennep alludes to the 'mechanical' character of rites of passage, Soyinka's drama crackles with proverbs and the dramatic manifestation of the *egungun*. Soyinka writes both within and against the anthropological construction of his own cultural identity. 'Transition', in Soyinka's reworking of the term, is the tempo of social life as it imitates the dynamic force of nature. The Yoruba *egungun* dramas act as a gate between the living and the dead and it is in these most important of rituals that traditional society poses its social questions, formulates its moralities and sees its order reflected in the mirror of the masquerade.

The performers of *egungun* are always men, hidden under layers of clothing, sometimes carrying whips, and speaking in disguised voices since they are *Ara Orun*, messengers from heaven. The performers are the spirits of the dead ancestors reincarnated in the form of the masqueraders. In social crises they are called on to carry away ills, execute criminals, and expel dangerous individuals. In less turbulent times they entertain the village. The two traditions of the *egungun* cult, the religious rite and the masquerade entertainment, form a rich context of contemporary practice and cultural history for Soyinka's drama: the 'Not-I' sequence recalls an *alarinjo* masquerade, the drama of transition embodies the ritual of the *Ara Orun*.[15]

The sacred dramas depict the transition of the spirit from the realm of the living to *egbe*, the domain of the dead, and they act as the transitional phase or 'gate' between the two worlds. Similarly, the masquerades have a social function as satire and as the preserver of traditional Yoruba culture. It is this context of African cultural possessions which enables Soyinka to instil a Yoruba presence into the aridity of the anthropological construction of rites of passage. The *egungun* rituals assert social orders but also dissolve them in the drama of transition from one state to another; the liminal rituals both make and unmake the world. For Soyinka, the participant immersed in the ritual is 'enabled to transmit its essence to the choric participants of the rites'.[16] Ritual drama is a communal experience undertaken by the individual on behalf of the community as it reflects 'powerful natural' or 'cosmic influences' which are 'internalized' and the 'titanic scale of their passions' transforms the stage into the 'affective, rational and intuitive milieu of the total communal experience, historic, race formative, cosmogonic'.[17] Soyinka's language is reminiscent of Ikem's 'hymn to the sun', but also of Mircea Eliade:

'Initiation is the reenacting of the world and the tribe. On this occasion, the whole society is resubmerged in the mythological time of the creation, and returns from it regenerated.'[18] The ritual pushes the conceptual and linguistic tools which shape selves and societies to the point of collapse but the *egungun* also affirms the stability of the natural and social order; it represents the capacity for a society to see itself differently and affirm or re-evaluate its own contents.

Traditional Yoruba society sees Elesin's ritual suicide as a socially necessary and aesthetically pleasing spectacle. The ritual suicide is an embodiment of a paradoxical liminality where the mask can gain utterance in the social world and thereby divest language and hierarchy of fixed statuses: 'The moon was my messenger and guide. When it reached a certain gateway in the sky, it touched that moment for which my whole life has been spent in blessings.'[19] Such a juncture of time and place constitutes the moment of miraculous intervention of this world in the other, and Elesin Oba is the point of that miraculous interface. Yet the worlds of the living and of the dead are opposites, and the point of their intersection is a paradox.

Soyinka redefines traditional Yoruba belief as paradox. As with Achebe, Soyinka draws together the different strands of myth and liturgy in a way which indicates the paradoxical nature of the gods. A central example for Soyinka is the myth of creation which places Ogun, the god of 'war, iron, metallurgy, explorer, artisan, hunter, and guardian of the road', at the centre of creativity. In the beginning there was a single omnipotent deity, Orisa-nla (a praise-name of Olodumare's indicating an earlier phase of his existence), a creator-god who was assisted in his creative acts by a slave, Atunda. In an attack upon the godhead, Atunda rolled a boulder on the god smashing him into myriad fragments, each of which became an *orisa*, divine embodiments of powers and attributes. Ogun was that fragment which contained the original deity's creative essence. At first the *orisas* were isolated from mankind by an impenetrable forest barrier, which the principal *orisas* each failed to cross. Ogun harnessed the elements of fire and stone and forged a sword with which he cut a path to man. (Elesin Oba is an Ogun-type since the drama of transition re-enacts Ogun's original forging of a passage between the different worlds of the Yoruba cosmology.) In recognition of his feat, the *orisas* offered Ogun supremacy over gods and men, which he refused, but he accepted instead the crown of Ire. With Ogun at their head the armies of Ire embarked on an imperial campaign, viciously suppressing her neighbours and growing in military strength. At the height of the battle, however, Ogun became drunk with palm wine and gripped by a battle-frenzy slaughtered his own men. Later, when he realised his mistake, he fled from direct involvement in the affairs of men.

Soyinka's retellings of the myths of creation and the destruction of the men of Ire have an inverted paradoxical binary structure. The first tells of the epiphany of the god, the second of his retreat from men; the first of his creative use of the elemental forces for the benefit of man, the second of his use of the same forces for his destruction. Ogun is thus a paradoxical deity, his creativity laying the foundations for eventual destruction.[20] Ogun represents for Soyinka the 'maverick' and unpredictable: a rebellious and revolutionary figure who disrupts the status quo of social and cosmic order. His capacity as a dramatic and poetic symbol is to unfix, interrogate or destroy the complacencies of political and cultural representation. Yoruba myth contains a far-reaching political philosophy: 'This [Yoruba] society manifests the familiar Hegelian tension – that much is conveniently apposite. There is the apparent stasis ... contradicted and acted upon when events demand by the revolutionary agent, *Ogun*.'[21]

The Hegelian 'moment' is symbolised in Soyinka's version of Yoruba metaphysics in the figure of Ogun. His paradoxical presence as both creator and destroyer brings the chaos and reformation of revolution and he thus represents the catalytic 'moment' or interface of opposites in Hegelian dialectic.

> Ogun is the embodiment of Will, and the Will is the paradoxical truth of destructiveness and creativeness in acting man.[22]

> Yoruba myth is a recurrent exercise in the experience of disintegration, and this is significant for the seeming distancing of will among a people whose mores, culture, and metaphysics are based on apparent resignation and acceptance but which are, experienced in depth, a statement of man's penetrating insight into the final resolution of things and the constant evidence of harmony.[23]

Soyinka's Elesin is informed by Soyinka's particular borrowings from and reconstructions of Yoruba belief. As a participant in the rituals of the *ogboni* cult, and as an Ogun-type and culture hero, his ritual persona stands precisely poised in the transitional spaces between worlds: the human and the divine, the living and the ancestors, the past and the future. Yet true to the narrative of the myth of Ogun, his creative role as a figure of transition also involves acts of destruction.

Ruin begins with the very gift of eloquence which enabled Elesin to triumph as the essential Yoruba man. Elesin's smooth-tongued conquest of the market-women procures the acquiescence necessary for him to marry a young woman on the eve of his ritual suicide. Elesin artificially embroils sexual desire in the wider metaphysical and social processes of transition from the world of the living to the world of the ancestors. To procure his young bride he argues that his spirit should not be burdened by the weight of unused and henceforth unuseful seed which would be better 'planted in the earth of his own choice', and that the ensuing offspring, conceived at a critical time, would be a special gift to the living he leaves behind because it would be a child of transition, neither of this world nor of the next. Yet what he proposes is a dubious gift since it is an *abiku*, a half-child, a miraculous monstrosity, a destroyer of mothers and a symbol of cultural and political deformity in the nation.

The *abiku* is a lesser chthonic power in the Yoruba pantheon, a child born with a desire for death. It returns again and again to its mother always dying in infancy until its mother also dies from the exhaustion of childbirth. Ulli Beier explains Soyinka's fascination with *abiku* as a symbol of man's obsession with 'causing extinction in his own image',[24] and Soyinka's poem, 'Abiku' expresses this theme:

> Night, and Abiku sucks the oil
> From lamps. Mothers! I'll be the
> Suppliant snake coiled on the doorstep
> Yours the killing cry.

> The ripest fruit was saddest
> Where I crept, the warmth was cloying.
> In the silence of webs, Abiku moans, shaping
> Mounds from the yolk.[25]

Iyaloja, disturbed by Elesin's proposed marriage, accuses him of purely lustful intent. Elesin protests:

> Who speaks of pleasure? O women, listen!
> Pleasure palls. Our acts should have meaning.[26]

It is delightfully disingenuous in its truth-twisting, but Elesin's powerful gift augurs the potential for dangerous corruption. Iyaloja, and the market-women, captivated but also alarmed by the manipulative power of Elesin's rhetoric, express a growing sense of tension:

'This language is the language of our elders, we do not fully grasp it'. 'The voice I hear is already touched by the waiting fingers of our departed. I dare not refuse.'

The dominant poetic form of Elesin Oba's and the Praise-singer's language is the aphoristic wisdom of the proverb. Yoruba idiom is itself highly elaborated with proverbial speech involving puns and metaphors which can only be elucidated by reference to the common currency of proverbs. Soyinka's adoption and transliteration of proverbial form mirrors naturalistic Yoruba speech. Soyinka's borrowings from traditional Yoruba proverbs are extensive; there is hardly a dramatic moment in the dialogue between Yoruba characters which is not expressed by a proverb taken from Yoruba idiom. The Praise-singer scolds Elesin:

> Because the man approaches a brand-new bride he forgets the long faithful mother of his children.
> (*Aríyàwó-ko-ìyálé.*)[27]

Elesin uses proverbs to bolster his authority and for self-aggrandisement:

> Where the storm pleases, and when, it directs
> The giants of the forest.
> (*Ibi ti o wu èfùfù lèlè ní í darí ìgbé sí, ibi ti o wu olówó eni ni ran ni lo.*)

> What elder takes his tongue to his plate,
> Licks it clean of every crumb? He will encounter
> Silence when he calls on children to fulfil
> The smallest errand!
> (*Àgbà t'ó je àje-ì-wèhìn ni y io ru igbá rè dé' lé.*)[28]

Iyaloja uses proverbs as a warning to Elesin to curb his appetites:

> Eating the awusa nut is not so difficult as drinking water afterwards.
> (*Ati je àsálá (Awusa) kò tó ati mu omi sí i.*)[29]

Elesin expresses his readiness to join the ancestors through proverbs:

> The kite makes for wide spaces and the wind creeps up behind its tail; can the kite say less than – thank you, the quicker the better?
> (*Àwòdì to'o nre Ìbarà, èfùfù ta á n'ídi pá o ni' Isé kúku yá.*)

> The elephant
> Trails no tethering-rope; that king
> Is not yet crowned who will peg an elephant.
> (*Ajanaku ko l'ẽkàn, oba ti yio mu erin so koi je.*)

The elephant deserves
Better than that we say 'I have caught
A glimpse of something'. If we see the tamer
Of the forest let us say plainly, we have seen an elephant.
(*Àjànàkú kuro ninn 'mo ri nkan fìrí', bi a ba ri erin ki a ni a ri erin.*)

The river is never so high that the eyes
Of a fish are covered.
(*Odo ki ikun bo eja l'oju.*)[30]

When Elesin fails in his suicide and he is imprisoned by the colonial authorities, Iyaloja and the Praise-singer condemn him with the cruel irony of proverbs.

We said you were the hunter returning home in triumph, a slain buffalo pressing down on his neck; you said wait, I first must turn up this cricket hole with my toes.
(*A kì í ru eran erin l'órì ki a máa f'ese wa ìrè n'ile.*)

What we have no intention of eating should not be held to the nose.
(*Ohun ti a kì í je a kì ífí run imú.*)

The river which fills up before our eyes does not sweep us away in its flood.
(*Odo ti o t'oju eni kun ki igbe 'ni lo.*)

The bush-rat fled his rightful cause, reached the market and set up a lamentation. 'Please save me!' – are these fitting words to hear from an ancestral mask? 'There's a wild beast at my heels' is not becoming language from a hunter.
(*Okete fi ija sehin o de oja o wa kawo l'eri, and E jowo, e gba mi o, ko ye egungun; eran ni o nle mi bo, ko ye ode.*)

If there is a dearth of bats, the pigeon must serve us for the offering.
(*Bi a kò bá rí àdán à fi òòdè sebo.*)[31]

The English-language medium of the play is greatly enlarged in its range of metaphorical references by the constant insertion of a Yoruba idiom. In all but one instance it is the Yoruba characters who speak in proverbs. The single example of the District Officer's proverb is delivered as a justification for his action in 'saving' Elesin from death:

I thought, are these not the same people who say: the elder grimly approaches heaven and you ask him to bear your greetings yonder; do you really think he makes the journey willingly?
(*Àgbàlagbà nfi ìrójú lo sòrun a ni ki o kílé kí ó k'ónà; ojú rere l'o finlo?*)[32]

Pilkings' misapplication of the proverb in this case only displays his lack of comprehension of the culture he pretends to rule; just as his wearing of a masquerader's costume to the viceroy's ball commits a blasphemy against the *egungun*. His incomprehension of the significance of Elesin's ritual role in his culture further emphasises the richness of the Yoruba language compared to that of its oppressors. The proverb in the mouth of the District Officer exposes an ostentatious misrepresentation and incomprehension of Yoruba culture; elsewhere the confrontation with the historical situation of colonialism is achieved by a manipulation of the traditional idiom. The proverb '*Orule bo àjá mole, aso bo ese idi, awo fẹ̀re bo inu ko je ki a ri iku aseni*' is rendered into English by Delano as, 'the roof covers the ceiling, the clothes cover the bad parts of the body, the thin skin which conceals the heart prevents us seeing the death planned by the secret plotter', which Soyinka transforms into:

> We know the roof covers the rafters, the cloth covers the blemishes; who would have known that *the white skin covered our future*, preventing us from seeing the death our enemies had prepared for us.[33]

However, there is more to Soyinka's use of the proverb than either a desire for authentic linguistic colour or anti-imperialist sentiment; the syntax of the proverb form enables Soyinka to enunciate his wider philosophical and social theories. Iyaloja's intricately proverbial speech in praise of Elesin is again a translation and transformation of the Yoruba:

> It is the death of war that kills the valiant,
> Death of water is how the swimmer goes
> It is the death of markets that kills the trader,
> And death of indecision takes the idle away
> The trade of the cutlass blunts its edge
> And the beautiful die the death of beauty.
> It takes an Elesin to die the death of death ...
> (*Ikú ogun ní i pa akíkanjú, iku odò ní ípa òmùwè, ikú ara rire ni ipa arewa, màjàmàsá ni ipa onitiju; òwò ti ada ba mo ni ika ada l'ehin*.)[34]

Soyinka's translation of the Yoruba proverbs also recalls a biblical parallel in its use of the Hebrew superlative. But these gnomic pronouncements are profoundly ambiguous. The first implied sense is that social roles determine identity and that 'specialists' die sympathetic deaths according to the inclinations of their natures and skills. Yet it also implies that it is the end of the medium of their lives which destroys people; thus the end of war marks the end of valour, and so on. The Yoruba syllogisms twist their way through paradox and contradiction to attain the conclusion that 'the death of death' envisages the possibility of eternal life and the social continuity which Elesin's death ensures. But the key to Iyaloja's proverbial speech is not only to be found in her transcendent conclusion, but also in the 'torsions' the language undergoes in the process of utterance. The speech focuses on the shifting of meanings within words in different contexts, as in 'It takes an Elesin *to die the death of death.*' An internal tension is evoked as the semantic field of the word is subjected to the proverb's paradoxical convulsions. Her speech spirals through opposing conditions from consolation, to the beneficent refinement of spiritual expertise within a sympathetic universe which acknowledges individual predilections, to a nihilistic finality and closure, to the collapse of a social order and the loss of the transcendent capacity of ritual.

Proverbs have formal and cognitive similarities to Soyinka's philosophical and metaphysical notions of the transition from the world of the living to the world of the dead, making them especially suited to his ritual drama. The ritual state is a state of paradox and the proverb is the vehicle for the expression of paradox. A transposition or commutation occurs between the ritual of transition and the proverb which enables the ritual to be present in the rich verbal texture of the play. Proverbs approach most closely the poetic expression of creative paradox which is the dominant metaphysic of Soyinka's construction of the Yoruba social order.

Yet these proverbs have a perfectly clear meaning because they are used rhetorically and dramatically and not just figuratively and metaphorically. As Albert Cook has written:

> The metaphoric framing of the proverb draws on the subsidiary differences between the items compared ... only for rhetorical force: the hearer's effort to spell out the analogy and the likeness exhausts this force, whereas in poetic metaphors the differences between the items of likeness induce the hearer to dwell on the myth-suggestive, changed ground that the differences and the likenesses taken together activate.[35]

The rhetorical force of the proverbs in Soyinka's play, while evoking the metaphysical paradox, directs the reader back again to the social matrix from which the proverb originated. The 'trajectory', as it were, of Soyinka's play is always towards the social, and not out from the social towards the misty paradoxes of eternity, although he uses these areas to charge his poetry with a sense of the numinous.

The proverb has a practical application in the society of the play, for Soyinka maintains, at the local syntactical level as at the grand and metaphysical, a dialectical dialogue between the numinous ideal and the social.

In his introduction to *Death and the King's Horseman*, Soyinka writes:

> The confrontation in the play is largely metaphysical, contained in the human vehicle which is Elesin and the universe of the Yoruba mind – the world of the living, the dead and the unborn, and the numinous passage which links all three: transition. *Death and the King's Horseman* can be fully realised only through an evocation of music from the abyss of transition.

He points to the play's 'threnodic essence', a song of lamentation which is the play's quintessential expression of a sense of loss. Plangency is evoked in Elesin's failure and his transformation from a role of sacred honour to impious dishonour which is paralleled by an equal shift in the type and quality of his language.

> My powers deserted me. My charms, my spells, even my voice lacked strength when I made to summon the powers that would lead me over the last measure of earth into the land of the fleshless.
>
> . . .
>
> It is when the alien hand pollutes the source of will, when a stranger force of violence shatters the mind's calm resolution, this is when man is made to commit the awful treachery of relief, commit in his thought the unspeakable blasphemy of seeing the hand of the gods in this alien rupture of his world.[36]

This is articulate enough, but wholly different from his earlier eloquence: poetic metaphor, quick-tongued allusiveness, dramatic and linguistic tensions have all dissipated; he has lost the world he once held in his linguistic grasp in the 'Not-I' *entrée* to the world of the play. Instead of proverbs he now speaks in abstractions: 'the source of will', 'the force of violence', 'mind's calm resolution', 'awful treachery of relief', 'alien rupture'. Elesin no longer controls his world through proverbial language, since he has lost the capacity to give a voice to 'the Yoruba mind' which proverbs express. Instead he grapples desperately with a devalued language where there was once a profound and confident image of a world held in equilibrium by the creative ego of Elesin. The play replicates the binary structure of the myth of Ogun; having made the world by his creative ritual acts, Elesin, like Ogun at Ire, unmakes it in an act of destructive failure.

It is at this point that the orality of the play becomes evident by its absence. A disjuncture is felt between this speech and Elesin's earlier proverbial extravagance because, when heard, this speech is virtually unintelligible, dramatically it is 'inaudible'. The play has already dramatised several kinds of language, proverbial, numinous and colonial dialogues, which have established the antithesis of poetic and anti-poetic speech. Elesin in his disgrace introduces a further dimension – a language which is an imitation of philosophical discourse lacking both the numinous rhapsody and the social expressiveness of the proverb. Elesin's new speech jars on the ear and wrenches the carefully established rhythm of proverbial speech out of its metre into language without Yoruba decorum. By cruel contrast, Iyaloja answers this speech with apt proverbs, revealing the world and the language which Elesin has lost.

The use of discordant speech as an indication of wider social disorder is familiar in Soyinka's works, but it is particularly the case in *Death and the King's Horseman* where the proverbial commonplace, heightened to the level of enunciating a social and religious cohesiveness and harmony, is counterpointed with cacophony. Soyinka's play documents the loss of a distinctive 'Yoruba world', with its powerful religious nucleus and rules formulated by a rich and productive proverbial speech, but Soyinka warns producers of his play not to transform his metaphysical drama into a 'facile' clash of cultures.[37] His evocation of 'the universe of the Yoruba mind' shows that world 'alongside' other worlds, notably the British imperialists'; a vision of cultures resonant in each other.

The play documents the historical process of 'closure' and 'enclosure' of traditional Yoruba culture which is caused by the failure of its language and its ritual to perpetuate and regenerate its social forms. The play represents Yoruba culture within a tragic view of history. Indeed, that tragic process is begun by Elesin himself in the ' Not-I' sequence with his procession of Yoruba social types. The Yoruba world of natural, social and metaphysical orders is made to cohere into a unity, but a unity which is also an enigmatic paradox: a social life made coherent by ritualised death. *Death and the King's Horseman* reconstructs a society as a myth. Elesin is the 'I' which resolves the enigma of 'Not-I', the perfectly expressive mythical voice of the Yoruba world of the play and which, when he fails, sends 'Our World ... tumbling in the void of strangers.'

Death and the King's Horseman ends with the dubious promise of an *abiku* child as the symbol of the new state born of the collapse of the traditional world which Elesin both represented and destroyed. *The Road* depicts the postcolonial *abiku* state 'tumbling in the void'. The play is set in a Nigerian scrap yard on a stage littered with the detritus of the modern automobile industry. The 'Aksident Store' is home to a group of drivers, lorry-park touts and petty gangsters, ruled over by the Professor, a demented preacher engaged in a strange linguistic quest. Just as the touts search the roadside sites of accidents for automobile spares, the Professor accumulates the scripts and signs of the modern world searching for 'the Word' – the language of the *Ara Orun* gained and lost by Elesin Oba which will bring both an apoclaypse of confusion and a new genesis of order.

But another, more ancient 'plot' converges with and underlies this scenario. Kotonu, a driver who refuses to drive his truck, has been involved in an accident. His lorry ploughed into a masquerade taking place on the road. The festival was dedicated to Ogun, the god of the road, and the accident victim was the masked dancer, Murano, the Professor's personal servant. Murano, a mute and terribly disfigured presence on stage, is in a state of *Agemo* which Soyinka glosses as 'the passage of transition from the human to the divine essence'.[38] For much of the play, Murano is in a state which signifies the 'visual suspension of death' until he rediscovers the *egungun* mask he had been wearing at the time of the accident. The play ends with the liberation of Murano through the agency of the mask and the god which possesses him takes his revenge upon the Professor who 'held a god captive'.

The play's exploration of the postcolonial condition evokes the concerns of both Bissoondath and Philip: individuals are lost in political and social orders which will not function in a language which will not enunciate. Although the play covers much of the same ground as both Bissoondath's and Philip's texts in its presentation of a deracinated or dislocated postcoloniality, that world is made to converge with the masked traditions of the Yoruba *egungun*. Soyinka offers a different strategy of resistance from that proposed either by Bissoondath or Philip, one which does not culminate in 'a secret art of invisibleness' nor the denial of cultural representation. The fragmented and dislocated postcolonial world of *The Road* is neither 'silent' nor 'elliptical' but it remodels Yoruba materials into new modes of enunciation. The presence of the crippled *agemo*-figure comes to be expressive of another, *Yoruba* dimension – Ogun, the *egungun* mask, the cults of the dead – reinvested with contemporary significance. Murano's mutilated body is an index of a dislocated consciousness, of ascetic rejection, and also of a cultural 'presence' which goes beyond both denial and pastiche. Soyinka reveals the landscape of the postcolonial world of the Yoruba and the play's combination of a stark realism and fantastical myth is, in Wilson Harris' phrase, a 'mental bridge within and across cultures'.[39]

Soyinka's writings explore the mythical structures of human action in a daily routine of acts of destruction and creation: constantly reiterated narratives of the myth of Ogun, the Yoruba creator/destroyer. However terrible the stories, *the* story which underlies them is profoundly optimistic in its message. The story gives access to a world of meaning secured by a myth of origins. For both Soyinka and Achebe, western constructions of their cultures are *also* a part of the mythical panoply, to be subverted and redefined from within. Both Achebe's and Soyinka's works are situated in apparent incongruities: Idemili as the tamer of dictatorial regimes or the Yoruba pantheon prefigured as members of the Nigerian middle class (*The Interpreters*). Their metaphors are startling in their effects, yet there is never a sense in which the very basis of metaphor is shaken. The variety of metaphorical associations only proves the illimitable extent to which the mythical structures apply.

Soyinka's mythical metaphors populate the world with significance. In *The Road* that significance finds its focus in Murano's masked presence. Like Idemili in Achebe's novel, Murano symbolises an ancient cultural tradition which demands presence, acknowledgement and retribution in the contemporary postcolonial state. But Murano embodies other significances also; the crippled mask is an eloquent dramatic incarnation of the damaged and violated postcolonial subject. Murano as the crippled presence of a traditional culture will not stay buried in the detritus of contemporary society, but returns to exact a divine vengeance on those who would dismiss him. Murano's 'muteness' in the play – which is the opposite of Philip's silence – speaks eloquently as a social context is articulated through Murano's body.

Repeatedly postcolonial writers return to the body's representation to restate an objectifying confrontation with a world of misrecognitions. Nadine Gordimer's novel *The Conservationist* has a central figure who is eventually lost in a delirious miasma of events which erase his identity while, back on his farm, the body of a murdered black man, buried at the beginning of the novel, is gradually washed from its secret location to emerge to our view, a relentless symbol of colonial guilt bodily manifested. In Ayi Kwei Armah's *The Beautyful*

Ones are Not Yet Born the body is heavily laden with political significance as he locates his critique of political corruption in Ghana literally within the body's frame, in its intestines and bile ducts as the unnamed characters drown in the excrement and phlegm of political corruption. At the end of the novel, Armah parodically re-enacts the body's entrance into the world, as a corrupt politician is reborn through the birth canal of a stinking latrine. Wole Soyinka's protagonists enter the house of death to learn new messages from the body of the dead to frame a social world for the living. The image of the violated body reveals a history of violence and misrepresentation; the bodies surface in all their nightmarish actuality.

But the bodies in postcolonial representations should not be read as all accomplishing the same goals. Bissoondath's story 'Veins Visible', as the title might suggest, evokes an alarming image of the body of the dislocated postcolonial. Vernon, the central character of the story, has a dream which conjures the terrible Marsyan image of the *corps morcelé*; the self envisioned as a mutilated, truncated torso[40]:

> Then as if it was the most natural thing in the world, he found himself lying on the sidewalk looking up at the sky, ink blue with curls of diaphanous white cloud. That something was not right he was fully aware, but only when he tried to get up did he realise that his torso had been severed diagonally from just under his ribcage to the small of his back. His hips and legs lay two feet away, beyond reach, like the discarded lower half of a mannequin.
> Curious, he examined his lower half. The cut had been clean. There was no blood. The wound appeared to have been coated in clear plastic and he could see the ends of veins pulsing red against the transparent skin.
> There was, he knew, no danger.[41]

The *corps morcelé* recurs throughout Bissoondath's writings, as people are framed in windows, caught in photographs, rendered in portraits reduced to 'footnotes forming of themselves no whole'.[42] (This is perhaps too solemn, there is a joke hidden in this body: the lower half is *two feet* from the torso.) The image seems strangely unmotivated; the body's realisation is simply enunciated in terrible stasis. The Marsyan body is never restored to its wholeness, the wound is never sutured as Bissoondath insists on fingering the cut to inflammation. In the dream of the body, Vernon, helpless on the pavement, seeks help from a friend. 'It was Hari. Then it was Peter. Then Hari again. Then it was no one again. Just a man. The man had no arms. Despair.'[43]

The social context – the social text – which the body reveals is contingent, elliptical, *morcelé*; the postcolonial subjunctive is never rendered an indicative.

Ben Okri's writings also conjure the image of the body in his embrace of a grotesque anti-aesthetic, as in the story 'A Hidden History' where an unnamed narrator, an 'earthbound, black angel', records the destruction of an unnamed street in an unnamed city. The residents are evicted, and the street becomes a rubbish dump for the other citizens. A figure wanders into the view of the angel and the residents of a tower block:

> he was of the devil, cursed in the Bible; that his sperm was black, he was a descendant of an ape; remembering that he was one of those who tainted, took their jobs and their fathers' jobs, took their women; and that he had a member big enough to shame the human race.
>
> they held their breath as they watched him going up and down, circling inevitably towards the rubbish bin lining. He got to the lining and opened it and dipped his hand in. His eye twitched. He brought out a bloodied leg: its toes were big and blue-black with a strange rot of the feet. He brought out a hand that was gnarled and withered like a twig ... Then He brought out the head of a black woman, roughly hacked, the eyes still open and bloated, the nose cut like a harelip that had repeated itself. He brought them out, smelling, listening, thorough in his investigation. He was drawn by the temptation to list.[44]

Okri, like Bissoondath, compels us to gaze upon what we would wish to discard – the postcolonial body which has been dismissed from representation or misrepresented as primitive or exotic. Okri, like Bissoondath, turns to the mutilated social body of the postcolonial to force a confrontation with a world of misrepresentations, but Okri fits the image of the body to express, not his elliptical identity, but the nature of English racism.

Ben Okri visits many of the same dark places of the postcolonial *habitus* as Bissoondath, but his writings have an underlying commitment to the explicability of human affairs, in metaphor, narrative structure or tragic–ritual shape. The story 'Laughter Beneath the Bridge' takes the Biafran war as its theme but the narrator is a non-combatant, a potential victim of the conflict. A young man remembers his wartime childhood when, abandoned by his teachers who have fled from the approaching troops, he is rescued from the shattered remains of his boarding school by his mother. Unwillingly he leaves his school friends to an uncertain fate and encounters the terrors of military roadblocks and the random violence of a vicious soldiery. But this is no ordinary narrator, as he fills his narration with bizarre 'tilted' observations:

> I remember it as a beautiful time: I don't know how. Sirens and fire engines made it seem like there was an insane feast going on somewhere in the country....
> The taste of madness like the water of potent springs, the laughter of war: that is perhaps why I remember it as a beautiful time.[45]

They return to find their home town occupied by troops and the river blocked by bodies. He renews his friendship with Monica, an adolescent girl 'of the rebel tribe' whose brother had been killed and family driven into the forest by the rampaging townsfolk. The story ends with the men from the town attempting to clear the river of corpses while Monica, dressed as an *egungun* masquerade spirit dances through the town. The masqueraders are confronted by the soldiers who tear off Monica's mask and demand that she 'speak her language'. She replies in the rebel tongue and is dragged off by the soldiers never to be seen again. At that moment the river is cleared of bodies.

The story appears to assume Soyinkan mythic proportions. At one level, it is a reworking of the scapegoat myth in which Monica, dressed in the garb of an ancestral spirit, is the sacrificial victim required by the community to rid itself of the putrefying consequences of war. She is the innocent 'sin-eater' who must carry away the accumulated evil of the war so that social equilibrium can be reinstated.[46] Yet having established this familiar trope the story proceeds to interrogate it, displaying its insufficiencies. The centre from which this questioning radiates is again the use the story makes of the *egungun*. The entry of the *egungun* into the community was a time of disruptive reappraisal and ritual cleansing. The *egungun* played a role in traditional society which was revered and regulatory; the *egungun* was the receiver of sacrifice not the sacrifice. The story therefore evokes the tradition but enacts a travesty of the tradition, the destruction of the ancestral links with the world of the dead.

As in Soyinka's *The Road*, the story hinges upon a reading of the mask and its enigmatic presence. The fracturing of ties with the rituals of the past is figured by the soldier who unmasks the *egungun*, which is an act of sacrilege punishable by death; further destruction, not an end of war, will ensue when the community sacrifices its identity by making a scapegoat of its ancestral past. Thereafter, the community has lost its ability to grasp its meaning, a fact which is underlined by the linguistic dissonance of the four languages (the English the story is written in, the indigenous language of the town, Monica's 'rebel' language and the 'spirit-tongue' of the *egungun*) which permeate the story. But most poignant of all is Okri's description of the *egungun*. Nothing is 'traditionally' correct here: the *egungun* is a thing for adults not children; it is a Yoruba not a rebel tradition; the mask should be worn by a man not a young girl.

> ...they were building a mighty *egungun* – one that would dwarf even the one with which ja-ja johnny walked over the River Niger, long ago before the world came to be like this. I asked who would ride the *egungun* and the others still wouldn't say. On Saturday afternoon I was just strong enough to go and see the masquerade for myself. The town stank. It was true: the boys had built this wonderful *egungun* with a grotesque laughing mask. The mask had been broken – they say Monica's temper was responsible – but it was gummed back together.[47]

Okri's text goes beyond denial, ellipsis and pastiche while nonetheless evoking all those elements. It evokes Soyinka's images of a traditional culture around which the story is constructed, yet it nonetheless depicts Monica's mask as fractured. Modern post-war, postcolonial Nigeria cannot, for Okri, be figured in Murano's remembered role as the avatar of Ogun – Monica can challenge no-one – but neither is it figured in *morcelé* silence and pastiche. The story belongs wholly within the body of an African 'tradition' as an affirmation and evocation of Yoruba culture, but it also enacts a travesty of that culture. The story can only be read in terms of this new mask: 'an insane laughing mask split in the middle of the face'.

One final and perhaps most eloquent example. In *The Famished Road*, Azaro the *abiku* narrator of the novel, is shown some photographs taken by his friend, the enigmatic itinerant photographer:

> [H]e opened the case of his camera and brought out a bundle of fine smelling pictures. He looked through them and gave them to me. They were pictures of a fishing festival, of people on the Day of Masquerades. The *egungun*s were bizarre, fantastic and big; some were very ugly; others were beautiful like those maidens of the sea who wear an eternal smile of riddles; in some of the pictures the men had whips and were lashing at one another. There were images of a great riot. Students and wild men and angry women were throwing stones at vans. There were others of market women running, of white people sitting on an expanse of luxurious beaches, under big

umbrellas, with black men serving them drinks; pictures of a child on a crying mother's back; of a house burning; of a funeral; of a party, with people dancing, women's skirts lifted, baring lovely thighs. And then I came upon the strangest photograph of them all, which the photographer said he got from another planet. It was of a man hanging by his neck from a tree.[48]

The images range over the terrain of postcolonial Nigeria where the traditional jostles with new formations: the ancient icons of the masked festivals, *Mami Wata* and the *egungun* are juxtaposed with those of tourism, sex, riot, political dissension and lynchings. These images are the new collective indices of African identity, the new masks. Azaro marvels at this collection of multiple fragments; none wholly fit together, none can be made into a whole. For Azaro the photographs *are* his history in all its multiplying fragments. His identity is born out of these ancient and new worlds laid before him by the photographer, who tells Azaro that 'When I look at the pictures of dead people something sings in my head. Like mad birds.'[49]

Chapter 9

Masks of difference

When narrated identity is unbearable.   *Julia Kristeva*[1]

This book began with the analysis of a counterfeit emblem: an anamorphic image as a metaphor of cultural representations. Beck's image represents its subject through a double distortion: by the technology of anamorphism and by the stylisation of its subject. To gain sight of *its* subject is to lose sight of *the* subject; Africa and America are sealed behind the mask of 'Africa' and 'America'. For Beck, to distort is to represent – his skill is measured by the degree of his distortions. The greater the anamorphism, the greater his renown; the more obscure his image, the more clearly he appears to represent his subject in his distorting/elucidating mirror. Sight is distracted and sent spinning into other configurations of meaning. The simulacra of cultural representations are founded upon this movement into another way of seeing, another mode of apprehension. To cross the threshold into the simulation and to gain this vision of the enigmatic presence of other people does not come without some cost. We cannot see as Behn's natives could see: 'All you can see, you see at once, and every moment see.' Our sight is veiled; our thoughts are masked. The 'constellation of delirium' afflicts not only the 'viewed' but also the viewer, where more or less elaborate versions of 'teratology' – the pseudo-science of monsters – is the master discourse.

'Teratology' begins in separation, in the Apollonian act of distinction. Division initiates a proliferation which ramifies into the manicheism of soft and hard primitives, of a spectrum of beings, of anthropometrically distinguished types. The quantity of types

288

embodies qualitative discriminations: savage personas constructed solely of social roles, contentless peoples or 'full subjects' from which an exotic plentitude issues, classical archetypes, noble savages, violent natural men, historical remnants, colonised peoples rewritten as primitive peoples. Either their social orders embody a fixity sealed against time and the progress of history, or they are the spirit of a turbulent historical vortex, expended by history and passing into a penumbra of mystery. The constellation of delirium throws out its identifications in a seemingly unstoppable productiveness: racial classes, colour types, models of evolutionary originals, erroneous magicians, pre-literate communities, demonic spirits, connoisseurs of death, structural exemplars, mutilated bodies, sexual presences and, in a return to Beck's blurred anamorphism, the 'ordered muddle' of another life.

All these masks of difference are determined by narrative demarcations which structure representations. At every stage, narration substantiates representation, endowing the unknown and incalculable other with a known and familiar code or discourse. Ovidian myth offers the decorum of a classical frame for the other to become the subject of a narrative of differences and the royal *entrée* incorporates that difference within the semiotics of regal power. From these images of power and formality descend a lineage of related narratives which embody the representation of other peoples: the Vitruvian satyric scene, the moral debates on music, romance, allegory, picaresque, colonial histories, conjectural histories, *acedia*, evolutionary narratives, modernist novels, naturalism, realism, fantasy, landscape descriptions, self-portraits of the observer.

The representation of other cultures invariably entails the presentation of self-portraits, in that those people who are observed are overshadowed or eclipsed by the observer. As a consequence the substantial presences of others are ignored or lost from view in the drama of the self seen in the imbroglio of contact. The masks of difference are codes which disguise, hide, misrepresent or circumscribe, but never describe, those other peoples of the world. The others are always 'masked' by the narratives, structures, images which the observer makes. What is fashioned and refashioned is a euphemisation of power in that materials which ostensibly purport to describe other people are effectively concerned with European self-representation and identity.

This makes for a very simplified account of the texts and images I have tried to discuss in this book. The history of cultural representations in anthropology, literature and art becomes essentially the same message endlessly repeated in different forms. The story begins as it ends in misrepresentations through which power is legitimated, transfigured and misrecognised.[2]

It is, of course, true that these images and writings *do* represent the 'euphemisation of power', but it is not the whole truth. If cultural representations were *only* about power disguised, then the notion of the power so disguised is thin, founded as it so often is upon the subjectivity of the anthropologist, writer or artist who made the representation. It is also the case that that subjectivity is never whole, nor completed, nor successfully constructed out of more diverse or 'exotic' notions of selfhood which are on display in the savage world. On the contrary, these texts show how extremely partial, temporary, fragmentary and fragile is that 'self fashioning'.

More importantly, to see cultural representations in anthropology, literature and art simply as euphemised power is to ignore a recurrent and insistent note of dissent from that 'power'. The case of anthropology is a case in point, since anthropology has been subjected to the most withering critique as a discipline of 'euphemised power'. Much of this critique has been justified, but anthropology has also exhibited a remarkable capacity to be constantly on the point of transforming itself. Its central informing tenets have changed with extraordinary frequency as it shifts the whole ground of its interpretations: from the study of laws, to the influence of climate, to 'race', to evolution, functionalism, structural functionalism, structuralism, networks, ethnomethodology . . . Anthropology's character resides not only in its chameleon historical development but also in the ways it has subjected itself to a perpetual critique of its own discourses, exposing its inner workings to scrutiny, enabling us to peer into its self-reflection. Anthropology has made and unmade its narratives in ways which have sceptically interrogated and subverted its own structures. The other – however that otherness is constructed – is subjected both to a sublime form of structuring, where the narratives of a known world are forced on to the representations of an unknown savage world, and to another 'destructuring' which, radically displaces what went before as the embrace of the anomalous materials of otherness has to encompass also the dislocation of the preconceived modes of representation.

In that context of a constant instability of representations, Carlo Ginzburg's declaration that the 'essence' of the 'anthropological attitude' rests on a 'dialogic disposition' is helpful[3] – except that one could read this at least two ways, that is, dialogically. The 'anthropo-logical attitude' could be construed as that representation of the world as a manichean dialogue of 'euphemised power' which renders the world divided.[4]

An alternative reading avoids this barren scenario. 'Dialogic' as a literary term in current use has accumulated properties quite differ-ent from those of 'dialogue'. What, in *Rites de Passage*, Van Gennep distinguished as the rites of separation, *marge* and incorporation, which Turner developed into his more sophisticated notions of 'liminality' and 'symbolic inversion', correspond to Bakhtin's 'dialo-gism' of 'classical' and 'Carnival' texts, in 'topsy-turveydom' and the 'world-upside-down', in the Green World or Second World and in festive comedy. Anthropologists, art historians and literary critics have turned over the same kinds of ideas in their attempts to theorise the nature of 'otherness', albeit that that 'otherness' presents itself as the festive Green World of 'the forest outside Athens' or as a 'salvage' ritual.[5]

The 'anthropological attitude' in this dialogical reading expresses a double movement: images of arrest, of closure, of euphemised power are simultaneously presented with images which remain open, unnarratable and uncertain. In the process of appropriating myths, kinship systems, cultural artifacts (or whatever) for represen-tation, cultural representation constantly 'refashions' its own mater-ials and significations to the point that proliferating modifications often overwhelm the original or subvert its dominant discourse. Indeed, the dominant discourse may be so eclipsed by its unruly progeny that it is stifled or remains unvoiced or unspeakable. Ulti-mately, the worlds of others cannot be completely masked and other languages and narratives transgress the systems of difference. In this context, the western representation of other peoples is a metaphor for representation itself envisaged as a struggle for mimesis[6] since there is always something 'incalculable', anomalous or dissident *within* these texts and images which offers a recalcitrant challenge to the acts of representation and narration. To see these images and texts simply as euphemised power is to ignore that which is repudi-atingly present at the very moment in which the strategies and structures of difference are assembled: Midas is beside Apollo; 'Des-perate Jack' stands behind Captain Stedman; *Argonauts* is paralleled by the *Diary*.

This dialogical reading of the 'anthropological attitude' returns us also to the *other* counter-image to the anamorphic representation:

19 Picasso, *Les Demoiselles d'Avignon*, 1907

the mask of the *Ara Orun*. Against Beck's simulation is placed the 'authentic artifact'. It is still a representation, still a mask which covers the identity of those who wear it, but it is a mask made and worn by Africans to represent themselves to themselves.

It is also the case, however, that masks such as this have had a seminal influence on modern western art. Picasso's *Les Demoiselles d'Avignon* (figure 19) has been exhaustively analysed as the moment of a radical departure for modernism when the African mask renews European painting.[7] Picasso employed an extremely limited range of representational skills to depict the women; they are pink globes and lines which show their role, not as individuals but as bodies. The same is true of the masks in the painting. The masks lack any kind of specificity, history or cultural location. Their purpose is not to represent but to hide, to mask, to cover up the faces of the prostitutes. Their African-ness is nearly an irrelevance since they act not to disclose, but to conceal. Picasso employs a self-consciously limited 'vocabulary' which is part, also, of the painting's considerable power. In that respect, the painting is an appropriation of African cultural forms wrenched from their social and cultural significance and rededicated to an agenda alien and antithetical to the mask's own meanings.[8]

Yet Picasso spoke to Malraux of the African masks he had seen at the Trocadero (which became the masks of *Les Demoiselles*) in a way which does not entirely fit the charge of a reconstructed modernist imperialism: 'For me the masks were not just sculptures. They were magical objects ... intercessors ... against everything – against unknown, threatening spirits ... They were weapons – to keep people from being ruled by spirits, to help free themselves. *If we give a form to these spirits, we become free.*'[9] Picasso acknowledges the independent nature of the African artifact. The masks in *Les Demoiselles d'Avignon* announce their presence as incalculable, dissident 'difference', as 'free', escaping even the mode of modernist representation through their incongruity.

It is also a possibility, available in Picasso's own terms, that Picasso saw himself and the mask's new hegemonic modernist environment as one of the 'spirits' the African mask was made to avoid. He seems to acknowledge that at the moment of its inscription *into* modernism, the mask proclaimed its 'freedom' – not only from 'spirits', but also *from* modernism.

A similar moment of inscription and 'avoidance' is available also in the related anthropological domain, as Malinowski observed: 'The African is becoming an anthropologist who turns our own weapons against us. He is studying European aims and pretences, and all the real and imaginary acts of injustice.'[10] Resistance transforms the African into an anthropologist, able to turn 'our own weapons against us'. Malinowski's observation on the reversal of anthropology's gaze shows the radical and subversive potential of cultural representations, when used by anthropology's erstwhile subjects as a powerful means of opposition and self-definition. Africans gain access through the medium of 'anthropology' to a radical critique of colonisation.

It is in – *against* – these contexts of 'euphemised power' that postcolonial writers elaborate their denials.

In their different ways, the writings of Bhabha, Philip and Bissoon-dath are determined by their locations – the diasporas of the 'dislocated' subjects of an imperial history. Here the panopticon gaze of cultural representations is met by the contingent *morcelé* visions of people without a place; evolutionary and historical schemes are thrown awry by the effects of a 'kaleidoscopic' time, language is countered by silence, presence by ellipsis. Colonial intervention, migration, dislocation, cultural representations have wrought a perpetuating sense of fracture, a tragic cycle from which no recuperation is possible and which renders the subject silent, invisible, unformed, since representation consists of the replicated divisions of colonial identities. The dispossessed live an alienated image of man, where the 'otherness of the self' gains enunciation through fragmentation, misrecognition, isolation, silence.

Homi Bhabha also returns to the mask as a trope of an unrepresentable identity and resistance:

> What I have called mimicry is not the familiar exercise of dependent colonial relations through narcissistic identification so that, as Fanon has observed, the black man stops being an actional person for only the white man can represent his self-esteem. Mimicry conceals no presence or identity behind its mask: it is not what Césaire describes as 'colonization–thingification' behind which there stands the essence of the *présence africaine*. The menace of mimicry is its double vision which in disclosing the ambivalence of colonial discourse also disrupts its authority.[11]

The image of the mask is, in his terms, a sign of 'no presence'. Yet Bhabha seems to reproduce the very quest for identity which he condemns in both the 'philosophical' and the 'anthropological' 'traditions in the discourse of identity'. He peers behind the mask, seeing the mask as a supplement to the (unrepresentable) identity of the subject. In reality, he *does* discover the identity of the actor, not the anthropological *'présence africaine'* certainly, but an identity of 'no presence'; the mask is a postmodern/postcolonial ellipsis.

Soyinka, Achebe and Okri adopt attitudes to the 'embittered history' of postcolonial cultures similar to Bhabha, but their possession of cultural histories allows them to move in precisely the opposite direction, elaborating identities with which to (in Picasso's term) 'free themselves' and to turn (in Malinowski's term) 'our own weapons against us'. Their responses to the challenges of cultural representation are not to narrow the vocabulary to Picasso's limited expressiveness, nor to confine it within the limits of a *'présence africaine'* – to fetishise the mask and the language – but to recast English within the linguistic structures of the Yoruba proverb or Igbo myth. Okri, Soyinka and Achebe make extensive use of their ethnographies in ways which acknowledge the radical potential of cultural representations, turning the 'weapons' of cultural description 'against European aims and pretences' and so reinvest the mask with new roles.

This book will end where it began, with the mask of the *Ara Orun*.

The *egungun* acted on the Alafin's behalf as an agent of social control and political manipulation of the populace since the cult executive, the *Oje*, were the means by which the Alafin made his presence felt throughout his empire as his rule gradually expanded during the seventeenth and eighteenth centuries to encompass much of Yorubaland.[12] The mask's role was to represent those powers by which the Alafin ruled his empire and it is, therefore, an instrument of central authority, a representation of 'euphemised power'. But it is also a simulacrum of other powers which need not always be identified with those of the Alafin. The *egungun* could turn its gaze against the Alafin – as it turned against Elesin Oba and the Professor – just as it could be made to enforce his will. The mask, in an important sense, is not a royal portrait. It bears the marks of a lineage, not of an individual. No individual identity is represented; it is not concerned with the expression or survival of a self, royal or commoner. The mask has its own 'incalculable', anomalous or dissident identity.

A mask has an aura of ambivalence and ambiguity about it. It is a disguise, it hides what we most need to know, the substantial presence of the wearer who is rendered a spiritual presence by the donning of a mask. Ethnography, history, the history of art, particularly that branch which deals with the 'primitive', cracks and redistributes the codes the mask 'masks'. These discourses are already in place in my description: what and how I choose to write about it, what and how I am *able* to write about it, is formed by this history of discourses and representations.

This mask and this viewer occupy different cultures, different histories, different times and this mask's presence announces itself as 'difference' instantly I begin to attempt a description. In that description the mask must, at all costs, be made to signify something more than just itself, something different, something 'other'. Yet the feeling lingers also that a more private apprehension of this object is possible beyond the codes of ethnographic or historical discourses; that at an intimate or inner level, the 'level of art' perhaps, I share something with this mask and with the human beings who made it and wore it. That it 'speaks' to me as 'art', beyond all this chatter of 'cultural differences'. The mask seems to ask me to possess and yet dispose of knowledge of its presence; truly to 'know' it I must pass beyond or relinquish knowledge. Far from being a mask of difference, it is the discourses of differences which 'mask' our similarities, our mutual identity. What comes between the mask and my recognition of its mutuality is the discourse by which I gain knowledge of it. The apprehension of the mask is determined from without by an exegetical compulsion which maintains as its central tenet that for every text there is an exegesis, a critic for every artwork, an ethnographer for every village. The compulsion clings to a belief that there is communication between the mask and the viewer who sees through it to the world it 'masks'.

Yet for the Yoruba, the actor behind the mask ceases to exist as an identifiable being once he has entered the masquerade, and any individual in the community who identified the actor rather than the *Ara Orun* he impersonated was liable to pay an extreme penalty for committing the blasphemy of turning a mask in the service of the ancestors into a portrait. For the ancient Greeks also, the mask's 'being is exhausted in its features', as John Jones writes:

> To think of the mask as an appendage to the human actor is to destroy the basis of the ancient masking convention by inviting the audience to peer behind the mask and demand of the actor that he shall cease merely to support the action, and shall begin instead to exploit the action in the service of inwardness.[13]

Apprehensions of the mask, as artistic or historical or cultural product, may be constructed out of just such a single desire to put everything to 'the service of inwardness' as if the prospect of a mask *without* an inside were anathema, like the thought of a body without a soul. The true challenge and enigma of the mask may be that 'its being *is* exhausted in its features', that the mask abrogates empathy to the pressing need to show eidetic reality.[14]

The reality it shows may not offer much comfort.

In Nigeria in 1980, I commissioned an *egungun* troupe to perform; I had arrived too late in the year to see their usual public performances and so had to pay them to put on a special one for me. The action took place in the central open space of Erin Osun, a small Yoruba town in the south-west. At first, I was the only audience,

seated on a rickety bench under a tree, but as the excellent masqueraders hit their stride the space rapidly filled with good-humoured
spectators. The group was rightly famous as the most accomplished
alarinjo performers in the district. The acrobats somersaulted and
gyrated their way through a series of masquerades of animals and
men – a complete *entrée* of Yoruba social types which culminated in
the masked representations of the *oba* and his wife, complete with
suckling children. The performance was coming to a close and the
elderly leader of the group began his final song. Everyone gathered
in close as the singer gave an impressive peroration. Then, a dis-
orderly giggle, which had started at the back of the crowd, gradually
became universal laughter and threatened to put the good man off
his praise for my generosity and his group's talents. The crowd
parted and the final mask walked through, saluted and held out its
hand for me to shake. I had to bend over because this was a little one.
A child in pith helmet, khaki shorts and shirt, woollen socks and
white gloves. This mask was different; it was painted white and a
very sunburnt pink.

This was my mask? Me? *The Real Me?*

297

Notes

Introduction

1 Ernest Renan, 'De l'Origine du Langage' (Paris, 1859), cited in Jacques Derrida, *Of Grammatology* (1967), translated by Gayatri Spivak (London, 1976), p. 123.

2 See Brian Street, *The Savage in Literature* (London, 1975), D. C. R. Goonetilleke, *Developing Countries in British Fiction* (London, 1977).

3 See Talal Asad (ed.), *Anthropology and the Colonial Encounter* (London, 1973), p. 79.

4 William Fagg, John Pemberton III and Bryce Holcombe, *Yoruba: Sculpture of West Africa* (London, 1982), p. 76.

1 The satyr anatomised: Venice 1570

1 In the Autumn of 1948, M. O'C. Drury and Wittgenstein were walking in Phoenix Park, Dublin. Drury asked Wittgenstein if he thought Hegel a 'deep thinker'. Wittgenstein replied that he did not think he would get on with Hegel. '[He] seems to me to be always wanting to say that things which look different are really the same. Whereas my interest is in showing that things which look the same are really different. I was thinking of using a motto for my book, a quotation from *King Lear*; 'I'll teach you differences!' [Then laughing] 'The remark "You'd be surprised!" wouldn't be a bad motto either.' Cited in Rush Rhees (ed.), *Recollections of Wittgenstein* (Oxford, 1984), p. 157.

2 A. Gentili, *Da Tiziano a Tiziano. Mito e allegoria nella cultura veneziana del Cinquecento* (Milan, 1980) and Susanna Biadene (assisted by Mary Yakush) (eds.), *Titian* (Venice 1990), p. 372.

3 F. Hartt, *Giulio Romano* (New Haven, 1958) and Biadene, *Titian*, p. 370.

4 Ovid, *Metamorphoses*, translated with an introduction by Mary M. Innes (Harmondsworth, 1955), p. 144–5.

5 J. Neumann, *Le Titian Marsyas écorché vif* (Prague, 1962).

6 P. Fehl, 'Realism and Classicism in the Representation of a Painful Scene: Titian's *The Flaying of Marsyas* in the Archiepiscopal Palace at Kromeriz', *Czechoslovakia Past and Present: Essays on the Arts and Sciences*, ed. Miroslav Rechsigl, 2 vols. (Hague, 1968), vol. II (Olympus); J. Rapp, 'Tizians Marsyas in Kremsier', *Pantheon*, 45, 1987 (Orpheus); cited in Biadene, *Titian*, p. 370.

7 Neumann, *Le Titian Marsyas écorché vif*.

8 E. Panofsky, *Problems in Titian: Mostly Iconographic* (London, 1969).

9 Neumann, *Le Titian Marsyas écorché vif*, and Biadene, *Titian*, p. 370.

10 Jean-Louis Scheffer, 'Thanatography, Skiagraphy' (from *Espèce de chose mélancholie*), translated with an afterword by Paul Smith, *Word and Image*, 1, 1985, 191–6 (p. 195).

11 For bibliography see Biadene, *Titian*, p. 347 especially E. Panofsky and F. Saxl, 'A Late Antique Religious Symbol in Works by Holbein and Titian', *The Burlington Magazine*, 49, 1926, and Panofsky, *Problems in Titian*.

12 Jurgis Baltrusaitis, *Aberrations* (Paris, 1983), pp. 16–17.

13 For a general discussion of the semiotics of torture and abjection see Elaine Scarry, *The Body in Pain: The Making and Unmaking of the World* (Oxford, 1985), pp. 20, 182 and Julia Kristeva, *Powers of Horror: An Essay on Abjection* (*Pouvoirs de l'horreur*, 1980) (New York, 1982).

14 Scarry, *The Body in Pain*, pp. 28, 37, 19.

15 Lionello Puppi, *Torment in Art: Pain, Violence and Martyrdom* (New York, 1991), p. 51.

16 Cf. Pieter Spierenburg, *The Spectacle of Suffering: Executions and the Evolution of Repression: From a Pre-industrial Metropolis to the European Experience* (Cambridge, 1984) and Puppi, *Torment in Art*.

17 Puppi, *Torment in Art*, p. 120.

18 Spierenburg, *The Spectacle of Suffering*.

19 Ibid., p. 54.

20 For a discussion of the status of executioners and skinners see Spierenburg, *The Spectacle of Suffering*, pp. 16–39.

21 Puppi, *Torment in Art*, Preface.

22 Lynn Frier Kaufmann, *The Noble Savage: Satyr and Satyr Families in Renaissance Art* (Michigan, 1984), pp. 20–1.

23 Quoted in Robert Ralston Cawley, *The Voyagers and Elizabethan Drama* (London, 1938), p. 369.

24 William Browne, *Poems*, 2 vols. (London, 1894), vol. II, 31 quoted in Cawley, *The Voyagers and Elizabethan Drama*, p. 369.

25 H. W. Janson and Anthony Janson, *History of Art* (London, 1973), 3rd edition, 1988, p. 202.

26 Kaufmann, *The Noble Savage: Satyr and Satyr Families in Renaissance Art*, pp. xx, 29, 43.

27 Ibid., pp. 6, 10, 26, 29–30.

28 Richard Bernheimer, *The Wildman in the Middle Ages* (Cambridge, Mass., 1952), p. 112 also cited in Stephen Horigan, *Nature and Culture in Western Discourses* (London, 1988), p. 60.

29 Hayden White, 'The Forms of Wildness', in E. Dudley and M. Novak

(eds.), *The Wild Man Within: An Image in Western Thought from the Renaissance to Romanticism* (Pittsburgh, 1972), p. 16 and Renan, 'De l'Origine du Langage'.

30 Kaufmann, *The Noble Savage: Satyr and Satyr Families in Renaissance Art*, pp. 35–6.

31 Anthony Pagden, 'Dispossessing the Barbarian', in Pagden (ed.), *The Languages of Political Theory in Early Modern Europe* (Cambridge, 1987), p. 80.

32 Hayden White, 'The Forms of Wildness', p. 18.

33 Kaufmann, *The Noble Savage: Satyr and Satyr Families in Renaissance Art*, p. 35.

34 Horigan, *Nature and Culture in Western Discourses*, p. 52

35 Rudolf Wittkower, *Allegory and the Migration of Symbols* (London, 1977), p. 65.

36 Cawley, *The Voyagers and Elizabethan Drama*, p. 292.

37 Wittkower, *Allegory and the Migration of Symbols*, p. 56.

38 Ibid., p. 64.

39 John Berger, *The Guardian*, 14 April 1993, 2, 4:1.

40 J. Sawday, 'The Fate of Marsyas: Dissecting the Renaissance Body', in Lucy Gent and Nigel Llewellyn (eds.), *Renaissance Bodies: The Human Figure in English Culture c. 1540–1660* (London, 1990), p. 110ff.

41 Palma il Giovane cited in Francesco Valcanover, 'An Introduction to Titian', in Biadene, *Titian*, pp. 3–28 (pp. 23–4).

2 Identity and its others: Florida 1564–91

1 C. Jung, 'An Initial Dream', *Psychology and Alchemy* (1953), *Collected Works*, translated by R. F. C. Hull, 20 vols. (London), vol. XII (1989), p. 89.

2 Roy Strong, *Art and Power* (Woodbridge, 1984), p. 47; see also Steven Mullaney, 'Strange Things, Gross Terms, Curious Customs: The Rehearsal of Cultures in the Late Renaissance', *Representations*, 3, 1983, 40–67 (p. 45).

3 See Bernheimer, *The Wildman in the Middle Ages*.

4 Strong, *Art and Power*, pp. 75, 86, 106, 51.

5 Ibid., pp. 71–3.

6 Wittkower, *Allegory and the Migration of Symbols*, p. 14.

7 Marc Bouyer et Jean-Paul Duviols, 'La Florida illustrée' in *Mémoire D'une Amérique*, Musée du Nouveau Monde (La Rochelle, 1980) and P. Hulton, *The Work of Jacques Le Moyne de Morgues*, 2 vols. (London, 1977).

8 Jacques Le Moyne de Morgues, *Brevis Narratio eorum quae in Florida Americae provincia Gallis acciderunt, secunda in illam Navigatione, duce Renato de Laudonnière classis Praefecto* (1591) in Hulton, *The Work of Jacques Le Moyne de Morgues*, p. 121.

9 Hulton, *Jacques Le Moyne de Morgues*, p. 117 (my emphasis).

10 Le Moyne, *Brevis Narratio*, in Hulton, *Jacques Le Moyne de Morgues*, p. 120.

11 Quoted in Strong, *Art and Power*, p. 33.

12 Anthony Pagden, 'Dispossessing the Barbarian' in Pagden (ed.), *The Languages of Political Theory*, p. 80.
13 Le Moyne described Laudonnière as 'a friend of the [royal] family' in Le Moyne, *Brevis Narratio* in Hulton, *Jacques Le Moyne de Morgues*, p. 119.
14 Marcel Mauss, 'A Category of the Human Mind: the Notion of Person; the Notion of Self' (translated by W. D. Halls), in Martin Carrithers, Steven Collins and Steven Lukes (eds.), *The Category of the Person: Anthropology, Philosophy, History* (Cambridge, 1985), pp. 1–25.
15 Ibid., p. 17.
16 Ibid., p. 20. See also A. Momigliano, 'The Quest for the person ...' in ibid., p. 84.
17 Quentin Skinner, 'Sir Thomas More's Utopia', in Pagden (ed.), *The Languages of Political Theory*, p. 134.
18 Ibid., p. 134.
19 Thomas Browne, *Religio Medici*, p. 152, cited also in M. Roston, *Renaissance Perspective in Literature and the Visual Arts* (Princeton, 1987), p. 62.
20 S. Collins, 'Categories, Concepts or Predicaments', in Carrithers, et al. (eds.), *The Category of the Person*, p. 62.
21 John Calvin, *Institution de la Religion Chrestienne* (1536), also cited in Nicolai Rubinstein, 'The History of the Word *Politicus*' in Pagden (ed.), *The Languages of Political Theory*, p. 55 see also Alastair Duke, Gillian Lewis and Andrew Pettegree (trans. and eds.), *Calvinism in Europe 1540–1610: A Collection of Documents* (Manchester, 1992).
22 For a general discussion see L. Dumont, 'Christian Beginnings of Modern Individualism,' in Carrithers et al. (eds.), *The Category of the Person*, p. 100.
23 Ibid., p. 113.
24 Le Moyne, *Brevis Narratio*, in Hulton, *Jacques Le Moyne de Morgues*, p. 119.
25 Cf. Mauss, 'A Category of the Human Mind'.
26 J. S. La Fontane, 'Person and Individual in Anthropology', and Michael Carrithers, 'An Alternative Social History of the Self', in Carrithers et al. (eds.), *The Category of the Person*, pp. 136 and 234.
27 Comenius quoted in Russell Fraser, *The Language of Adam: On the Limits and Systems of Discourse* (Columbia, 1977), p. 15.
28 R. S. Loomis, *The Development of Arthurian Romance* (London, 1963); W. P. Ker, *Epic and Romance* (New York, 1897); L. A. Hibbard, *Medieval Romance in England* (Oxford, 1961); M. H. Abrams, *A Glossary of Literary Terms* (London, 1981); Barbara Babcock (ed.), *The Reversible World* (Ithaca, 1978).
29 Edmund Spenser, *The Faerie Queene* (1590), edited by A. C. Hamilton, (Harlow, 1977), Book VI, canto viii, stanzas 45–6.
30 Edmund Spenser, *The Faerie Queene*, Book VI, canto x, stanzas 6, 8.
31 Ibid., stanzas 11, 12.
32 Jean de Léry, *Histoire d'un voyage faict en la terre de Brésil* (1578), André Thevet, *Les singularitez de la France antartique* (1558).
33 Babcock, *The Reversible World*, pp. 14–32.

34 Thomas Nashe, *The Unfortunate Traveller* (1594) (Harmondsworth, 1972), p. 254.
35 Babcock, *The Reversible World*, pp. 14–32.
36 Spenser, *The Faerie Queene*, Appendix 1: 'A Letter of the Authors', p. 737.
37 Koestler quoted in Michael Seidel, *Satiric Inheritance: Rabelais to Sterne* (Princeton, 1979).
38 Thomas Nashe, *The Unfortunate Traveller*, p. 369.
39 Ibid.
40 Le Moyne, *Brevis Narratio*, in Hulton, *Jacques Le Moyne de Morgues*, p. 144.
41 Hulton, *Jacques Le Moyne de Morgues*, p. 20, Bouyer and Duviols ('La Florida illustrée') offer a slightly different account.
42 Jean Ribault, *La complète et véridique découverte de la Terra Florida* (London, 1563); Nicholas Le Challeux, *Discours de l'histoire de la Floride contenant le crualté des Espagnols* (1566); Jacques Le Moyne de Morgues, *Brevis Narratio* (1591).
43 Le Moyne, *Brevis Narratio*, in Hulton, *Jacques Le Moyne de Morgues*, p. 135. This extract from Le Moyne's text should also be read in relation to engraving number 32 (Hulton, *Jacques Le Moyne de Morgues*) which depicts a native American execution in the same manner.

3 The lovers of Paramaribo: Surinam 1663–1777

1 John Wilmot, Earl of Rochester, 'A Satire against Reason and Mankind', line 225, *Selected Poems*, edited with an introduction and notes by Paul Hammond (Bristol, 1982), p. 66.
2 R. A. J. Van Lier, 'Introduction', in Captain John Stedman, *A Narrative of a five years expedition against the revolted negroes, in Surinam, Guiana ...* (1796), facsimile reprint with an introduction by R. A. J. Van Lier (Barre, 1971), p. v. For Stedman's full title see p. 87.
3 Aphra Behn, *'Oroonoko' and Other Prose Narratives*, edited by Montague Summers (New York, 1967).
4 For a general discussion of 'participant observers' and 'self-fashioning' see Clifford Geertz, *Works and Lives: The Anthropologist as Author* (Cambridge, 1988), chapter 1.
5 John Locke, *Essay Concerning Human Understanding*, 1689, cited in J. Fabian, *Time and the Other: How Anthropology Makes Its Object* (New York, 1983), p. 108.
6 Behn, *Oroonoko*, p. 184.
7 For a discussion of travellers' clothing being searched by natives see Mary-Louise Pratt, 'Fieldwork in Common Places', in Clifford and Marcus (eds.), *Writing Culture: The Poetics and Politics of Ethnography* (London, 1986), p. 37.
8 Behn, *Oroonoko*, p. 131.
9 Laura Brown, 'The Romance of Empire: *Oroonoko* and the Trade in Slaves', in Felicity Nussbaum and Laura Brown (eds.), *The New Eighteenth Century* (London, 1987), p. 51.

10 Behn, *Oroonoko*, p. 131.
11 Pufendorf quoted by Istvan Hont, 'The Language of Sociability and Commerce', in Pagden (ed.), *The Languages of Political Theory*, p. 263.
12 Behn, *Oroonoko*, p. 132.
13 R. L. Meek, *Social Science and the Ignoble Savage* (Cambridge, 1976), pp. 24–7.
14 John Locke, *Two Treatises of Government* (1690), edited by Peter Laslett (Cambridge, 1960), pp. 319, 357.
15 Thomas Blackwell, *An Inquiry into the Life and Writings of Homer* (London, 1735), pp. 12, 40.
16 Jacques Derrida, *Of Grammatology* (1967), translated by Gayatri Spivak (London, 1976), p. 115.
17 Behn, *Oroonoko*, p. 188.
18 Ibid., p. 171.
19 P. Hulton, *The Work of Jacques Le Moyne de Morgues*, 2 vols. (London, 1977), p. 164.
20 Behn, *Oroonoko*, p. 201.
21 Cited in Gary B. Miles, 'Roman and Modern Imperialism: A Reassessment', *Comparative Studies in Society and History*, 32:4, October 1990, 629–59 (p. 642).
22 Behn, *Oroonoko*, p. 200.
23 Cf. Brown, 'The Romance of Empire', p. 51 and Carole Fabricant, 'The Literature of Domestic Tourism and the Public Consumption of Private Property' in Felicity Nussbaum and Laura Brown (eds.), *The New Eighteenth Century* (London, 1987), p. 261.
24 Brown, 'The Romance of Empire', p. 49ff.
25 Some sense of that 'new situation' can be gathered from the nature and volume of the trade in African slaves. According to Patrick Manning (*Slavery and African Life* (Cambridge, 1990)) the volume of slave exports remained fairly level throughout the sixteenth century at about 16,000–19,000 individuals per annum. The end of the sixteenth century saw, however, a marked increase in the numbers annually subjected to the middle passage: by the early decades of the seventeenth century, the figure had reached 25,000; by the time Behn wrote *Oroonoko*, in 1688, 40,000 individuals were enslaved every year. Thereafter, the figure climbed sharply to between 80,000 and 120,000 annually for most of the eighteenth and a large part of the nineteenth centuries. These figures should also be considered against those which reflect voluntary migrations; Kingsley Davis (cited in Martin Green, *Dreams of Adventure, Deeds of Empire* (New York, 1979)) estimates that between 1720 and 1830, 52 million people changed their land of residence and that in ten generations from the Elizabethan period, the world population of people of British descent increased from 7 million to 140 million.
26 Shaftesbury, *Characteristics of Men, Manners, Opinions and Times*, vol. 1, pp. 221–2 also cited in Richard Ashcraft, 'Leviathan Triumphant', in E. Dudley and M. Novak (eds.), *The Wild Man Within: An Image in Western Thought from the Renaissance to Romanticism* (Pittsburgh, 1972), p. 166.

27 Landeg White, 'For Captain Stedman', *For Captain Stedman* (Liskeard, 1983).
28 Captain John Stedman, *The Journal of John Gabriel Stedman 1744–1797: Soldier and Author*, edited by Stanhope Thompson (Mitre Press, 1962), p. 8.
29 Ibid., p. 251.
30 Ibid., p. 12.
31 Since writing this chapter, Mary-Louise Pratt has published a short study of John Stedman in *Imperial Eyes* (London, 1992), pp. 90–102. Although Pratt's discussion is concerned only with Stedman's *A Narrative*, her work confirms some of my arguments.
32 Stedman, *A Narrative*, p. 54.
33 Stedman, *The Journal*, p. xxiii.
34 Ibid., p. 53.
35 Ibid., p. vi.
36 Ibid., p. 67.
37 Ibid., p. 55.
38 Ibid., p. 61.
39 R. A. J. Van Lier, 'Introduction', Stedman, *A Narrative*, p. vii.
40 Ibid., pp. vii–xi.
41 Stedman, *A Narrative*, p. 15.
42 Stedman, *The Journal*, p. 119.
43 Stedman, *A Narrative*, p. 19.
44 M. M. Goldsmith, 'Liberty, Luxury and the Pursuit of Happiness', in Pagden (ed.), *The Languages of Political Theory*, p. 249.
45 Stedman, *A Narrative*, p. 255.
46 Ibid., p. 181.
47 Stedman, *The Journal*, p. 137; *A Narrative*, p. 281.
48 Stedman, *The Journal*, p. 130.
49 Stedman, *A Narrative*, p. 283.
50 Stedman, *The Journal*, p. 140.
51 Stedman, *A Narrative*, pp. 63, 100.
52 Deuteronomy, 28: 54–7.
53 Stedman, *A Narrative*, p. 324.
54 Ibid., p. 219.
55 Ibid., p. 217.
56 Ibid., p. 216.
57 Ibid., p. 215.
58 Ibid., p. 208.
59 Ibid., p. 213.
60 Ibid., p. 213.
61 Spenser, *The Faerie Queene*, Book II, canto xii, stanza 66.
62 Stedman, *A Narrative*, p. 17.
63 Ibid., p. 18.
64 Stedman, *The Journal*, p. 120.
65 Stedman, *A Narrative*, pp. x, 53, 182; *The Journal*, p. 145.
66 Stedman, *A Narrative*, p. 62.
67 Stedman, *The Journal*, p. 125.
68 Ibid., p. 143.

69 Ibid., p. 143.
70 Stedman, *A Narrative*, p. xv.
71 Stedman, *The Journal*, p. viii.
72 Ibid., p. ix.
73 Ibid., p. 312.
74 Ibid., p. 369.
75 Ibid., p. 352.
76 Ibid., p. 269.
77 Stedman, *A Narrative*, p. 64.
78 Ibid., p. 113.
79 Ibid., p. xviii.
80 Stedman, *The Journal*, p. 339.
81 Stedman, *A Narrative*, p. 236.
82 Ibid., p. 379.

4 Making history: Scotland 1814

1 Jean Baudrillard, *Simulations* (New York, 1980), p. 13.
2 Notes on 'Mascarade Nuptiale' by José Conrado Roza, Musée du Nouveau Monde, La Rochelle, France.
3 John Hemming, *Amazon Frontier: The Defeat of the Brazilian Indians* (London, 1987), pp. 124–5.
4 Margaret Syvret and Joan Stevens, *Ballière's History of Jersey* (Chichester, 1981), chapter 25.
5 Jules David Prown, *John Singleton Copley*, 2 vols. (Cambridge, Mass., 1966), vol. II, p. 306.
6 Prown, *John Singleton Copley*, pp. 302–5.
7 *Spectator*, 6 July 1712, cited in Robin Simon, *The Portrait in Britain and America: 1660–1940* (Oxford, 1987), p. 19.
8 Simon, *The Portrait*, pp. 56, 68.
9 J. G. Lockhart, *Memoirs of the Life of Sir Walter Scott, Bart.*, 7 vols. (Edinburgh, 1837–8), vol. I, pp. 139–43.
10 Sir Walter Scott, *The Fair Maid of Perth* (1826), pp. 17–18. All references to Scott's novels are to *The Centenary Edition of the Waverley Novels* (Edinburgh, 1879–81) except *Waverley* (1814), edited by Claire Lamont (Oxford, 1981).
11 Lockhart, *Memoirs of Sir Walter Scott*, pp. 142–3.
12 Quoted in Gen. David Stewart of Garth, *Sketches of the Character, Manners and Present State of the Highlanders of Scotland*, 2 vols. (Edinburgh, 1822), vol. I, p. 60.
13 J. Adams, *Curious Thoughts on the History of Man* (London, 1789), p. 47.
14 William Robertson, *The Situation of the World at the Time of Christ's Appearance* (Edinburgh, 1759), p. 34.
15 Dr Samuel Johnson, *A Journey to the Western Islands of Scotland*, edited by R. W. Chapman (Oxford, 1970), p. 39.
16 Ibid., p. 24.
17 Ibid., p. 79.
18 Sir Walter Scott, 'The Culloden Papers', *Prose Works*, 28 vols. (London, 1835), vol. xx, article ix pp. 1–93 (p. 2).

19 Mrs A. Grant of Laggan, *Essays on the Superstitions of the Highlanders*, 2 vols. (London, 1811), vol. I, pp. 1–2.

20 Ibid., pp. 4, 63.

21 Quoted by Sir Walter Scott, 'Ancient History of Scotland', *Prose Works*, vol. xx, article xii (London, 1835), pp. 302–76 (p. 321).

22 R. Redfield, *The Primitive World and its Transformations* (Cornell, 1953), p. 45; Arthur J. Toynbee, *A Study of History* (London, 1961).

23 Scott, 'Ancient History of Scotland ', p. 363.

24 H. Baudet, *Paradise on Earth: Some Thoughts on Images of non-European Man*, translated by Elizabeth Wenholt (London, 1965), p. 50.

25 Scott, 'The Culloden Papers', p. 10.

26 See Meek, *Social Science and the Ignoble Savage*; R. L. Meek, *Turgot on Progress* (Cambridge, 1973); R. L. Meek, 'The Scottish Contribution to Marxist Sociology', in J. Saville (ed.), *Democracy and the Labour Movement* (London, 1954), pp. 84–102; M. Harris, *The Rise of Anthropological Theory* (London, 1968), pp. 14–15; Adam Smith, *Essays on Philosophical Subjects*, edited by Dugald Stewart (Dublin, 1795).

27 For a general discussion of the representation of time in anthropological writings, see James Boon, *From Symbolism to Structuralism* (Oxford, 1972); Fabian, *Time and the other*.

28 Scott, 'The Culloden Papers', p. 13.

29 Ibid., pp. 10, 15.

30 P. Anderson, 'Components of the National Culture', *New Left Review*, 50, 1968, 3–57 (p. 47).

31 For general discussion of the antiquarian field, see M. Dorson, *The British Folklorists: A History* (London, 1968), pp. 107–118.

32 For general discussion of these distinctions, see Harris, *The Rise of Anthropological Theory* and Clifford Geertz, *The Interpretation of Cultures* (New York, 1973), chapter 3.

33 For a discussion of Panlus and the myth and history debate, see James H. Stam, *Inquiries into the Origin of Language: The Fate of a Question* (New York, 1976), p. 71.

34 Robert Southey, *History of Brazil*, 3 vols. (London, 1810), quoted in Hemming, *Amazon Frontier*, p. 48.

35 Sir Walter Scott, *Letters*, edited by H. J. C. Grierson, 12 vols. (London, 1932–7), vol. v (1818), p. 115.

36 Sir Walter Scott, 'The General Preface to the Waverley Novels', in *The Centenary Edition*, pp. 5–19 (p. 8).

37 Scott, *Rob Roy* (1817), Introduction, pp. 38, 3, 18.

38 Ibid., pp. 52, 227, 249.

39 Scott, *Waverley*, chapter 24.

40 Scott, *Legend of Montrose*, chapter 3.

41 Scott, *The Chronicles of the Cannongate*, pp. 407–8.

42 Scott, *Waverley*, p. 96.

43 Scott, *The Heart of Midlothian*, p. 505.

44 Ibid., pp. 532–3.

45 For a general discussion of the crisis of anthropological objectivity, see P. Bourdieu, *Outline of a Theory of Practice* (Cambridge, 1977); Geertz, *Works and Lives*; Fabian, *Time and the Other*.

46 Scott, *The Fair Maid of Perth*, p. 452.
47 Ibid., p. 458.
48 Ibid., p. 339.
49 Fabian, *Time and the Other*, pp. 86–7.
50 Scott, *Waverley*, p. 73.
51 Ibid., p. 74.
52 Ibid., p. 76.
53 Ibid.
54 John Milton, *Paradise Lost*, Book II, lines 594–6.
55 Scott, *Waverley*, p. 76.
56 Dante Alighieri, *The Divine Comedy*, translated by H. Boyd (London, 1802), pp. 189–90.
57 Scott, *Waverley*, p. 78.
58 Scott, 'The General Preface to the Waverley Novels', p. 17.
59 Major John Richardson, *Wacousta!* (1832) (Toronto, 1924), p. 193.
60 Ibid., chapters 29–30.

5 'Do they eat their enemies or their friends?': Cambridge and Buganda 1887–1932

1 L. Wittgenstein, *Remarks on Frazer's 'The Golden Bough'*, edited by Rush Rhees, translated by A. C. Miles (Retford, 1979).
2 J. G. Frazer, *The Golden Bough* (1890; Avenil reprint, New York, 1981), pp. 236–7. A reprint of the first edition with added illustrations.
3 *The Golden Bough*, Avenil reprint of the first edition.
4 Unpublished letter to Rev. J. Roscoe, 18 July 1915, J. G. Frazer, unpublished notebooks and correspondence, the Frazer Collection, Wren Library, Trinity College, Cambridge. All unpublished letters quoted are from the Frazer Collection.
5 Mary-Louise Pratt, 'Scratches on the Face of the Country', in H. L. Gates (Jnr), *'Race', Writing and Difference* (London, 1986), pp. 138–62, (p. 145).
6 In 1887, Frazer's categories of questions were: Tribes; Birth, Descent, Adoption; Puberty; Marriage; Disease and Death; Murder; Property and Inheritance; Fire; Food; Hunting and Fishing; Agriculture; War; Government; Oaths and Ordeals; Salutations; Arithmetic; Writing; Measurement of Time; Games, Dances; Magic and Divination; Religious and Political Associations; Men as Women, Women as Men; Sleep Forbidden; Ceremonial Uncleanness; Doctrine of Souls; Demons and Spirits; Scapegoats; Guardian Spirits; Resurrection; Heavenly Bodies etc.; Sacrifice; Miscellaneous Superstitions.
7 J. G. Frazer *Questions on the Customs, Beliefs and Languages of Savages* (Cambridge, 1907, reissued 1910 and 1916), Preface, p. 5.
8 Ibid., Preface, pp. 6–7.
9 Ibid., Preface, p. 7.
10 Unpublished letter to Henry Jackson, 31 May 1888.
11 Unpublished letter to Frazer from John Bourke, 26 December 1888.
12 Unpublished letter to Frazer from James Wells, 8 August 1889
13 Unpublished letter to the Rev. J. Roscoe, 12 May 1907.

14 Letters to Frazer from P. A. Talbot, 25 May 1911, and 7 February 1913.
15 Frazer, *Questions* (1907), Preface, p. 10.
16 Rev. J. Roscoe, *Immigrants and their Influence in the Lake Region of Central Africa*, Frazer Lecture II (Cambridge, 1923).
17 Robert Ackerman, *J. G. Frazer: His Life and Work* (Cambridge, 1987), p. 210.
18 A term which Ackerman claims Frazer used with no other correspondent, see *J. G. Frazer*, p. 260.
19 Unpublished letter to Roscoe, 4 March 1914.
20 Unpublished letter to Lady Frazer from Roscoe, 20 November 1915.
21 Unpublished letter to Roscoe, 30 July 1914.
22 Unpublished letter to Roscoe, 25 August 1914.
23 Unpublished letter to Roscoe, 27 January 1924.
24 Unpublished letter to Roscoe, 15 December 1907.
25 Unpublished letter to Roscoe, 6 November 1912.
26 Unpublished letter to Roscoe, 27 March 1913.
27 Unpublished letter to Roscoe, 27 November 1913.
28 Unpublished letter to Roscoe, 23 November 1920.
29 Unpublished letter to Roscoe, 31 January 1921.
30 Unpublished letter to Roscoe, 9 September 1921.
31 Unpublished letter from Roscoe to Frazer, 19 January 1925.
32 J. G. Frazer, 'Obituary of Canon Roscoe', *Nature*, 17, December 1932.
33 Eli Sagan, *At the Dawn of Tyranny* (London, 1986), p. 5.
34 Ibid., p. 7.
35 Ibid., p. 163.
36 Ibid., p. 200.
37 Ibid., p. 11.
38 Ibid., p. 24.
39 Ibid., p. xv.
40 For an account of the history of the Baganda, see Sagan, *At the Dawn of Tyranny*, pp. 4–55, and *African Encyclopedia* (Oxford, 1974) from which this sketch is derived.
41 His memoirs do speak about it, but there are regarded by Roscoe as a wholly different kind of writing, more personal, less important, less 'scientific'.
42 In this general context, see David Goddard, 'Limits of British Anthropology', *New Left Review*, 58, 1969, pp. 79–89.
43 Rev. J. Roscoe, 'Notes on the Manners and Customs of the Baganda', *Journal of the Anthropological Institute*, 31, 1901, 117–30, and Rev. J. Roscoe, 'Further Notes on the Manners and Customs of the Baganda', *Journal of the Anthropological Institute*, 32, 1901, 25–80.
44 Roscoe, 'Further Notes on the Manners and Customs of the Baganda', p. 26.
45 Roscoe, 'Notes on the Manners and Customs of the Baganda', p. 117.
46 Ibid., p. 118.
47 Rev. J. Roscoe, *The Baganda* (London, 1911), p. x.
48 The text begins with 'Tribes and Clans', as in Frazer, then 'Birth Descent Adoption' followed by 'Baptism' (a new section but following closely Frazer's *Questions* starting at question 10). The text continues

with: 'Skin Markings' as in Frazer's question 18, 'Women' picks up Frazer at question 23 on 'girls in puberty' and 'marriage', 'Disease and Death', 'Totems and Clans' (an extension of the first section of Frazer's scheme) 'Birth' (an excursus on Frazer's second section), 'Adoption', 'The Birth of Twins' (an answer to a 'Miscellaneous Superstitions' question); back to 'Marriage', 'Disease and Death', 'Bones' (an answer to question 57), 'Murder', 'Property and Inheritance', 'Fire', 'Food', 'Hunting', 'Fishing', 'Agriculture', 'War', 'Journeying' (a new section), 'Government', 'Oaths and Ordeals', 'Salutations', 'Arithmetic and Money' (a conflation of two of Frazer's sections), 'Measurement of Time', 'Games', 'Magic and Divination', 'Doctrine of Souls', 'Heavenly Bodies', 'Miscellaneous'. Only at the end, when he has run the whole gamut of Frazer's questions does he feel able to append a few answers to his own questions: 'Men's Duties', 'Dress and Decoration', 'Cattle Herding' (actually an answer to Frazer's supplementary question) 'Market Places' and 'Sympathy between Human Beings and Plantain Trees' (a very Frazerian topic).

49 Sagan, *At the Dawn of Tyranny*, p. 5; the work is also praised by Ackerman, *J. G. Frazer*.
50 Unpublished letter to Roscoe 3 July 1907.
51 Unpublished letter to Roscoe, 1 March 1911.
52 Unpublished letter to Roscoe, 26 March 1911.
53 Unpublished letter to Roscoe, 27 November 1911.
54 Unpublished letter to Roscoe, 15 November 1911.
55 Unpublished letter to Roscoe, 12 October 1920.
56 Roscoe, *The Baganda*, Preface, p. x.
57 Ibid.
58 Frazer was not the first; Lewis Henry Morgan had used questionnaires before, distributed through the Smithsonian Institution, to contribute to *Systems of Consanguinity*.
59 Quoted in Ackerman, *J. G. Frazer*, p. 51.
60 Ibid., p. 48.
61 Fabian, *Time and the Other*, pp. 98–9.
62 Frazer, *The Golden Bough* (1890 first edition), Preface, p. x.
63 Ibid., p. x. and Ackerman, *J. G. Frazer*, p. 81.
64 J. P. Mallory, 'A History of the Indo-European Problem', *Journal of Indo-European Studies*, 1:1, 1973, 21–65 (p. 60).
65 Mallory, 'A History of the Indo-European Problem', 21–65.
66 R. W. Wescott, 'The Evolution of Language: Reopening a Closed Subject', *Studies in Language*, 19:1/4, 1967, 67–81 (p. 67).
67 Müller (1872) quoted in Hilary Henson, *British Social Anthropology and Language: A History of Separate Development* (Oxford, 1974), p. 120.
68 Müller (1887) quoted in E. F. K. Koerner, *Toward a Historiography of Linguistics: Selected Essays* (Amsterdam, 1978), p. 31.
69 For a description of the evolutionary schemes of Comte, Renan and Herder, see Stam, *Inquiries into the Origin of Language*.
70 August Schleicher, 'The Darwinian Theory and the Science of Language' (1863), translated by Alexander V. W. Bikkers, and 'On the Significance of Language for the Natural History of Man' (1865),

translated by J. Peter Maher, in E. F. K. Koerner (ed.), *Linguistics and Evolutionary Theory* (Amsterdam, 1983), pp. 1–82. For a description of the evolutionary schemes of Schleicher, see Koerner, *Toward a Historiography of Linguistics* and J. P. Maher, 'More on the history of the Comparative Method: the Tradition of Darwinism in August Schleicher's work', *Anthropological Linguistics*, 8:3:2, 1966, 1–12, and Stam, *Inquiries into the Origin of Language.*

71 E. B. Tylor, *Primitive Culture* (London, 1871), p. 7.
72 E. E. Evans-Pritchard, *A History of Anthropological Thought* (London, 1981), p. 187.
73 Frazer quoted in Ackerman, *J. G. Frazer*, p. 282.
74 Michel Foucault, 'Cuvier's position in the History of Biology', *Critique of Anthropology*, 13 and 14, Summer 1979, 125–30 (p.126).
75 Foucault, 'Cuvier's position in the History of Biology', p. 127.
76 J. G. Frazer, *The Golden Bough*, third edition, 12 vols. (London, 1906–15), vol. XI, p. 88.
77 See John Skorupski, *Symbol and Theory: A Philosophical Study of Theories of Religion in Social Anthropology* (Cambridge, 1976), p. 178.
78 Evans-Pritchard, *A History of Anthropological Thought*, p. 150.
79 J. Beattie, *Other Cultures: Aims, Methods and Achievements in Social Anthropology* (London, 1964) also quoted in Skorupski, *Symbol and Theory*, p. 138.
80 Henson, *British Social Anthropology and Language*, pp. 15, 56.
81 A. H. Sayce, *Introduction to the Science of Language*, 2 vols. (London, 1850), vol. I, p. 75.
82 For a discussion of Schelling's system of the parallel evolution of myth and language and Comte's system of the parallel evolution of language and belief, see Stam, *Inquiries into the Origin of Language*, p. 210ff.
83 Henson, *British Social Anthropology and Language*, p. 5.
84 Evans-Pritchard, *A History of Anthropological Thought*, p. 187.
85 Quoted in Henson, *British Social Anthropology and Language*, p. 10.
86 See Peter Munz, *When the Golden Bough Breaks: Structuralism or Typology?* (London, 1973).
87 J. G. Frazer, *The Golden Bough*, abridged edition (London, 1922), p. 49.
88 David Hume, *A Treatise of Human Nature* (1739), edited by D. G. C. McNab (London, 1962), pp. 54–5.
89 Quoted in R. A. Downie, *Frazer and The Golden Bough* (London, 1970), p. 59.
90 E. F. K. Koerner, *Ferdinand de Saussure* (Braunschweig, 1973), pp. 9ff.
91 Henson, *British Social Anthropology and Language*, p. 9.
92 J. G. Frazer, unpublished notebooks, The Frazer Collection, Cambridge.
93 Stam, *Inquiries into the Origin of Language*, p. 102; Herder, *Treatise on the Origin of Language*, quoted in Stam, p. 127.
94 Tylor cited in Henson, *British Social Anthropology and Language*, p. 16.
95 William Dwight Witney, 'Language and the Study of Language' (1867), in *Whitney on Language: Selected Writings of William Dwight Witney*, edited by Michael Silverstein (Cambridge, Mass., 1971), p. 10.

6 *Causes célèbres* in the myths of modernism: Melanesia and Brazil, 1895–1970

1 Huizinga quoted in Baudet, *Paradise on Earth*, pp. 38–9.
2 The two attitudes to modernists' use of primitive artifacts are represented, respectively, by W. Rubin (ed.), *'Primitivism' in Twentieth-Century Art*, Museum of Modern Art, 2 vols. (New York, 1984) and Hal Foster, *Recodings: Art, Spectacle, Cultural Politics* (Washington, 1985).
3 Malinowski to B. Z. Seligman, quoted in R. Firth (ed.), *Man and Culture* (London, 1957), p. 6; Anderson, 'Components of the National Culture', p. 47; James Clifford, *The Predicament of Culture: Twentieth Century Ethnography, Literature and Art* (Harvard, 1988), p. 96.
4 B. Malinowski, *Argonauts of the Western Pacific* (London, 1922) and *A Diary in the Strict Sense of the Term* (New York, 1967). Page references in the text are to this edition.
5 See Geertz, *Works and Lives*, pp. 73–101; Clifford, 'On Ethnographic Self-Fashioning: Conrad and Malinowski', in T. C. Heller et al. (eds.), *Reconstructing Individualism* (Stanford, 1986) reprinted in Clifford, *The Predicament of Culture*; G. Stocking, 'Empathy and Antipathy in *Heart of Darkness*', in *Readings in the History of Anthropology*, edited by Regna Darnell (New York, 1974), pp. 85–98; H. Payne, 'Malinowski's style', *Proceedings of the American Philosophical Society*, 125, 1981, 416–40.
6 Malinowski, *A Diary*, p. 299.
7 Malinowski, *A Diary*, pp. 83, 95.
8 H. Arendt, *Imperialism* (New York, 1968), quoted also in Patrick Brantlinger, *Rule of Darkness: British Literature and Imperialism 1830–1914* (London, 1988), p. 268.
9 Clifford, *The Predicament of Culture*, p. 100.
10 Cassian quoted in Geoffrey Galt Harpham, *The Ascetic Imperative in Culture and Criticism* (Chicago, 1987), p. 73.
11 Harpham, *The Ascetic Imperative in Culture and Criticism*, p. 73.
12 See ibid., pp. 73–91.
13 Clifford, *The Predicament of Culture*, p. 96.
14 Adam Ferguson, *An Essay on the History of Civil Society*, 1767, edited by Duncan Forbes (Edinburgh, 1966).
15 T. S. Eliot, 'Euripides and Professor Murray', *Selected Essays* (London, 1966), pp. 60, 64.
16 Ibid., p. 61.
17 Ibid., pp. 62–3.
18 Ibid.
19 See Foster, *Recodings*, pp. 184–5.
20 L. Lévy-Bruhl, *How Natives Think* (*Les Fonctions mentales dans les sociétés inférieures*, 1910) (Princeton, 1985), pp. 77, 84.
21 T. S. Eliot, Review of *Group Theories of Religion and the Religion of the Individual, International Journal of Ethics*, October 1916, p. 116, quoted in Piers Gray, *T. S. Eliot's Intellectual and Poetic Development 1909–1922* (Brighton, 1982), p. 138, see also, pp. 138–9, 177–80, 249–50, and Robert Crawford, *The Savage and the City* (Oxford, 1987), pp. 92, 98.

22 T. S. Eliot, 'The Use of Poetry and the Use of Criticism', in *Selected Prose of T. S. Eliot*, edited by Frank Kermode (London, 1974).

23 Crawford, *The Savage and the City*, pp. 198–9, see also p. 107.

24 Gray, *T. S. Eliot's Intellectual and Poetic Development*, pp. 129–30.

25 Gray, *T. S. Eliot's Intellectual and Poetic Development*, pp. 131.

26 Downie, *Frazer and The Golden Bough*, p. 21.

27 Wittgenstein, 'Remarks on Frazer's *The Golden Bough*', pp. 18–41.

28 W. B. Yeats, 'What is popular poetry?', *Ideas of Good and Evil* (London, 1903), p. 16.

29 W. B. Yeats, *Essays and Introductions* (London, 1961), p. viii.

30 Andrew Lang, *Social Origins* (London, 1903), p. 23.

31 T. S. Eliot, *Notes Toward a Definition of Culture* (London, 1962), p. 41; cf. Gray, *T. S. Eliot's Intellectual and Poetic Development*, p. 140.

32 Bourdieu, *Outline of a Theory of Practice*, p. 1.

33 Quoted in Ackerman, *J. G. Frazer*, p. 88.

34 T. S. Eliot, 'Four Quartets', *Collected Poems 1909–1962* (London, 1963), p. 203.

35 T. S. Eliot, 'Ulysses, Order and Myth', in *Selected Prose of T. S. Eliot*, edited by Frank Kermode (London, 1974), pp.177–8.

36 Claude Lévi-Strauss, *Tristes Tropiques* (1955), translated by John and Doreen Weightman (Harmondsworth, 1973), pp. 284–5.

37 Ibid., p. 304.

38 Mauss, 'A Category of the Human Mind'; cf. M. Hollis, 'Of Masks and Men', in Martin Carrithers et al. (eds.), *The Category of the Person*, p. 220.

39 Lévi-Strauss, *Tristes Tropiques*, p. 304.

40 Ibid., pp. 436–7.

41 See Boon, *From Symbolism to Structuralism*; Geertz, *Works and Lives*, p. 33.

42 Octavio Paz, *Claude Lévi-Strauss: An Introduction*, 1967, trans. by J. S. Bernstein and Maxine Bernstein (London, 1971), pp. 97–8.

43 J. Christopher Crocker, 'My Brother the Parrot' in *The Social Use of Metaphor*, edited by J. David Sapir and J. Christopher Crocker (Pennsylvania, 1977), pp. 164–92, p. 192, summarised in Dan Sperber, *On Anthropological Knowledge* [*Le Savoir des Anthropologues*, 1982] (Cambridge, 1985), p. 37.

44 Sperber, *On Anthropological Knowledge*, p. 38.

7 Third eye/evil eye

1 William Shakespeare, *The Merchant of Venice*, Act 2, Scene 7, lines 24–35.

2 D. Mannering, *The Paintings of Matisse* (London, 1989), p. 70.

3 This reading of Matisse's painting was suggested by an anthropological essay on a wholly different subject, Papuan pig-hunting ritual; see A. Gell, 'Magic, Perfume, Dream . . .' in I. M. Lewis (ed.), *Symbols and Sentiments* (London, 1977).

4 Clifford Geertz, H. Geertz and L. Rosen, *Meaning and Order in Moroccan Society* (Cambridge, 1979), p. 197.

5 See G. Marcus, and D. Cushman, 'Ethnographies as Texts', *Annual Review of Anthropology*, 11, 1982, 25–69 (p. 41).

6 See Steven Webster, 'Realism and reification in the Ethnographic Genre', *Critique of Anthropology*, 6:1, Spring 1986, 39–62 (p. 41).

7 See Geertz, *The Interpretation of Cultures*, p. 16.

8 See Bourdieu, *Outline of a Theory of Practice*, p. 1 and Renato Rosaldo, 'From the Door of his Tent', in James Clifford and George E. Marcus, *Writing Culture: The Poetics and Politics of Ethnography* (London, 1986), p. 92.

9 Talal Asad, 'The Concept of Cultural Translation', in Clifford and Marcus (eds.), *Writing Culture*, p. 161 and Talal Asad (ed.), *Anthropology and the Colonial Encounter* (London, 1973).

10 Geertz et al., *Meaning and Order in Moroccan Society*, p. 198.

11 Edmund Leach, *Culture and Communication* (Cambridge, 1976), pp. 29–32.

12 Geertz, *The Interpretation of Cultures*, p. 16.

13 Wittgenstein quoted in Geertz, *The Interpretation of Cultures*, p. 13.

14 R. Needham, *Essential Perplexities, an Inaugural Lecture Delivered Before the University of Oxford*, 12 May 1977 (Oxford, 1978).

15 A point of view which Geertz describes: 'Good anthropological texts are plain texts, unpretending. They neither invite literary–critical close reading nor reward it.' Geertz, *Works and Lives*, p. 2. See also on the 'transparency' of anthropological writings, Clifford and Marcus (eds.), *Writing Culture*, p. 2.

16 Steven Webster, 'Dialogue and Fiction in Ethnography', *Dialectical Anthropology*, 7, 1982, 99–114 (pp. 102–3).

17 Geertz, *The Interpretation of Cultures*, p. 15.

18 Ibid., p. 15.

19 Ibid., p. 16.

20 S. A. Tyler, 'The Poetic Turn in Postmodern Anthropology: The Poetry of Paul Friedrich', *American Anthropologist*, 86:2, 1984, 328–336 (p. 328).

21 Webster, 'Dialogue and Fiction in Ethnography', p. 105.

22 Bob Scholte, 'The Charmed Circle of Geertz's Hermeneutics', *Critique of Anthropology*, 6:1, Spring 1986, 5–15 (p. 8).

23 Webster, 'Dialogue and Fiction in Ethnography', p. 103.

24 Geertz quoted in Scholte, 'The Charmed Circle of Geertz's Hermeneutics', p. 6.

25 Webster, 'Realism and Reification in the Ethnographic Genre', p. 41.

26 Ibid., p. 51.

27 M. H. Abrams, *A Glossary of Literary Terms* (London, 1981), pp. 152–3.

28 Webster, 'Realism and Reification in the Ethnographic Genre', p. 39.

29 Ibid., p. 53.

30 Geertz, *The Interpretation of Cultures*, p. 22.

31 Steven A. Tyler, 'Postmodern Ethnography', in Clifford and Marcus, *Writing Culture*, p. 139.

32 Stephen Slemon, 'Monuments of Empire: Allegory/Counter Discourse/Post-Colonial Writing', in *Kunapipi*, 9:3, 1987, p. 14.

33 Wilson Harris quoted in Stephen Slemon, 'Magic Realism as Post-Colonial Discourse', *Canadian Literature*, 116, Spring 1988, p. 21.
34 Asad (ed.), *Anthropology and the Colonial Encounter*, p. 79.
35 Christopher Norris, *Deconstruction: Theory and Practice* (London, 1982), p. 33.
36 Derrida, *Of Grammatology*, pp. 142, 139, 136.
37 See A. Shelton, 'Volosinov on the Ideology of Inversion', *Journal of the Anthropological Society of Oxford*, 9:3, 1978, 191–6 (p. 196).
38 Derrida, *Of Grammatology*, p. 120 and discussed in David Spurr, 'Colonialist Journalism: Stanley to Didion', *Raritan*, 2, Fall 1985, pp. 35, 48.
39 See Fabian, *Time and the Other*.
40 Stanley Diamond, *The Search for the Primitive* (New York, 1979), p. 93.
41 P. Bourdieu, 'Symbolic Power', *Critique of Anthropology*, 13 and 14, Summer 1979, 77–85 (p. 83).
42 Geertz et al., *Meaning and Order in Moroccan Society*, p. 16.
43 See Jean Baudrillard, *Simulations* (New York, 1980), pp. 13–14.
44 Geertz quoted in Scholte, 'The Charmed Circle of Geertz's Hermeneutics', p. 6.
45 Geertz, *The Interpretation of Cultures*, p. 121.
46 Lévy-Bruhl, *How Natives Think*, p. 80.
47 See Clifford, *The Predicament of Culture*, p. 173.
48 Paul Rabinow, 'Representations are Social Facts', in Clifford and Marcus, *Writing Culture*, p. 249.
49 Homi K. Bhabha, 'Interrogating Identity', *ICA Documents*, 6, 1987, p. 6.
50 Ibid., p. 5.
51 Homi K. Bhabha, 'Foreword: Remembering Fanon', Frantz Fanon, *Black Skin, White Masks*, *(Peau Noire, Masques Blancs*, 1952), translated by Charles Lam Markmann with a Foreword by Homi K. Bhabha (London, 1986), p. xxii.
52 Bhabha, 'Interrogating Identity', p. 8.
53 Ibid., p. 5.
54 Bhabha, Foreword to Fanon, *Black Skin, White Masks*, p. xiv.
55 The term 'historylessness' is Bhabha's own, see 'Interrogating Identity', p. 9.
56 Bhabha, Foreword to Fanon, *Black Skin, White Masks*, pp. xviii, xiv–xv.
57 Bhabha, 'Interrogating Identity', p. 7.
58 Tyler, 'The Poetic Turn in Postmodern Anthropology: The Poetry of Paul Friedrich', p. 329.
59 Neil Bissoondath, *A Casual Brutality* (Bloomsbury, 1988), p. 312.
60 Ibid., p. 34, 312.
61 Neil Bissoondath, 'Man as Plaything, Life as Mockery', 'Continental Drift', *Digging up the Mountains* (Harmondsworth, 1987), pp. 178, 145.
62 Bissoondath, *A Casual Brutality*, pp. 34–5.
63 Ibid., p. 377.
64 Bissoondath, 'Digging up the Mountains', *Digging up the Mountains*, p. 14.
65 'Digging up the Mountains', p. 15.
66 Bissoondath, *A Casual Brutality*, p. 18.
67 Ibid., p. 37.

68 Bissoondath, 'There are Lots of Ways to Die', *Digging up the Mountains*, p. 92.
69 *A Casual Brutality*, p. 211.
70 Ibid., p. 343.
71 Ibid., pp. 366–7.
72 'An Arrangement of Shadows', *Digging up the Mountains*, p. 112.
73 Ibid., p. 116.
74 'There are Lots of Ways to Die', *Digging up the Mountains*, p. 81.
75 'Insecurity', *Digging up the Mountains*, p. 72.
76 'Digging up the Mountains', p. 5.
77 'The Revolutionary', *Digging up the Mountains*, p. 26.
78 *A Casual Brutality*, p. 178.
79 Ibid., p. 221.
80 'Continental Drift', *Digging up the Mountains*, p. 146.
81 'There are Lots of Ways to Die', *Digging up the Mountains*, p. 90.
82 'In the Kingdom of the Golden Dust', p. 98, 'The Cage', pp. 67, 57, both in *Digging up the Mountains*; *A Casual Brutality*, p. 372.
83 Bissoondath, 'Man as Plaything, Life as Mockery', p. 173.
84 Marlene Nourbese Philip, *Looking for Livingstone: An Odyssey of Silence* (Ontario, 1991), p.25.
85 *She Tries Her Tongue: Her Silence Softly Breaks* (Charlottetown, 1989), p. 94.
86 *Looking for Livingstone*, p. 11.
87 Ibid., p. 12.
88 Ibid., p. 58.
89 Claire Harris, 'Poets in Limbo', *A Mazing Space: Writing Canadian Women Writing*, edited by Smaro Kamboureli and Shirley Neumann (Edmonton, 1986), p. 124.
90 'Making the House our Own: Colonized Language and the Civil War of Words', *Fuse*, 8:6, Spring 1985.
91 *Looking for Livingstone*, pp. 43, 52, 43.
92 Ibid., p. 22.
93 St Augustine cited in Harpham, *The Ascetic Imperative in Culture and Criticism*, p. 25.
94 *Looking for Livingstone*, p. 54.
95 Ibid., p. 34.
96 Ibid., p. 72.
97 Harpham, *The Ascetic Imperative in Culture and Criticism*, p. 191.
98 *Looking for Livingstone*, p. 56.
99 Ibid., p. 22.
100 Ibid., p. 62.
101 Ibid., p. 42.
102 Harpham describes the moment of 'conversion' when the ascetic accomplishes a division in which 'the knowing self splits off from the being self, and observes it from a position magically free from being known, free from representation ... far from uniting the self (conversio) inculcates a sense of the otherness of the self.' Harpham, *The Ascetic Imperative in Culture and Criticism*, p. 98.
103 *She Tries her Tongue*, p. 86.

104 *Looking for Livingstone*, p. 39.
105 'Metaphysics culminates in a state of wordless knowledge ... Asceticism, by contrast, culminates not in the knowledge of essences but in self-transformation, accomplished through the agency of writing.' Harpham, *The Ascetic Imperative in Culture and Criticism*, p. 92.
106 M. Bakhtin, *The Dialogic Imagination*, translated by C. Emerson and M. Holquist (Austin, 1981), p. 294, also cited by Harpham, *The Ascetic Imperative in Culture and Criticism*, p. 11.
107 Philip, *Looking for Livingstone*, p. 70.
108 Bhabha, Foreword to Fanon, *Black Skin, White Masks*, p. xviii.

8 Different masks

1 Margaret Laurence, 'Ivory Tower or Grassroots?: The Novelist as Socio-Political Being', in *A Political Art: Essays in Honour of George Woodcock*, edited by W. H. New (Vancouver, 1978), p. 23.
2 Chinua Achebe, *Anthills of the Savannah* (London, 1988), pp. 1–2.
3 Ibid., p. 3.
4 For a parallel discussion of the presentation of time scales and the use of the present tense in anthropology, see Fabian, *Time and the Other*.
5 Chinua Achebe, *A Man Of the People* (London, 1966).
6 Achebe, *Anthills of the Savannah*, p. 124.
7 Chinua Achebe, *Things Fall Apart* (London, 1958).
8 *The Lion and the Jewel* (1963), *The Jero Plays* (1964, 1973), *The Road* (1965), *Kongi's Harvest* (1967), *Madmen and Specialists* (1971) in Wole Soyinka, *Collected Plays*, 2 vols. (Oxford, 1973–4).
9 Wole Soyinka, *Death and the King's Horseman* (London, 1975), pp. 18–9.
10 A possible source for Soyinka's death-bird could be the Yoruba proverb, 'The witch-bird was heard to screech yesterday, and a child dies today, who does not know that the death of the child was caused by the bird.' (Aje ke lana omo ku loni; tani ko mo pe aje ana l'o pa omo je.) Oloye J. O. Ajibola, *Owe Yoruba* (Ibadan, 1971), p. 4.
11 *Alarinjo*, literally in Yoruba, 'he who dances while he walks', but referring to the popular dramatic aspect of *egungun* rather than the rituals of the *Ara Orun*.
12 Wole Soyinka, *Myth, Literature and the African World* (Cambridge, 1978), p. 145.
13 Arnold van Gennep, *The Rites of Passage* (1908), trans. by Marika B. Vizedom and Gabrielle L. Caffee, introduction by Solon T. Kimball (London, 1960), p. 3.
14 Ibid., p. 194.
15 There are many forms of Yoruba masked rituals which inform Soyinka's dramaturgy, the most significant being *egungun* in all its forms. It is so popular and widespread that it has developed its own poetic convention, *iwi*. Two kinds of performers chant *iwi*: *oje* and *eleesa*. *Oje*, 'he who wears the *ago*', refers to performers who are distinguished by the voluminous costumes of the *egungun* cult, whereas *eleesa*, 'he who does not', is included in the performance purely on the basis of his individual talents as a performer. Although *iwi* contains praises to

individual gods its main concern is with the praise of men, both living and dead. There are several main characters: *Alabebe*, 'the one with the fan', *Pararaka*, 'the one who goes about', both of whom dance, *Alagbo*, 'medical concoctions', who prays for people. *Alarinjo*, 'dances while he walks', *Ajebegijo*, 'dances with wooden masks', and *Onidan*, 'the dramatist', whose roles are to perform dances, poems and plays. *Onidan* metamorphoses into animal and human characters: the ape, royal python, crocodile, tapa, prostitute, policeman. An *egungun* group will perform most of the year, travelling the countryside, owing allegiance to the *Alagba*, the titled head of the cult who maintains the traditions of *egungun*. *Egungun* has a long and illustrious history. Hugh Clapperton described a 'masque' at Oyo in 1829, and an eighteenth-century *Onidan* performer, Esa Ogbin, was presented with the mantle of Ologbojo, the founder of the mosque at Oyo, by the Alafin Abiodun. See J. A. Adedeji, 'The Place of Drama in Yoruba Religious Observance', *Odu*, 3:1 (1966); Beier, Ulli, 'The *egungun* Cult among the Yorubas', *Présence Africaine*, 18, 1958; J. P. Clarke, 'Aspects of Nigerian Drama', *Nigeria*, 89, 1966; J. C. de Graft, 'Roots in African Drama and Theatre', in M. Banham and Clive Wake, *African Literature Today*: 8 (London, 1976); Ruth Finnegan, *Oral Literature in Africa* (Oxford, 1970); K. C. Murray, 'Dances and Plays', *Nigeria*, 19, 1939; Oyin Ogunba, 'Theatre in Nigeria', *Présence Africaine*, 58, 1966; O. Olajubu, 'Iwi Egungun Chants – an Introduction', *Research in African Literature*, 5:1, 1974; Robert Plant Armstrong, *The Affecting Presence* (Illinois, 1971); Ola Rotimi, 'Traditional Nigerian Drama', in Bruce King (ed.), *Introduction to Nigerian Literature* (Lagos, 1971); P. A. Talbot, *Life in Southern Nigeria* (London, 1923).
16 Soyinka, *Myth, Literature and the African World*, p. 33.
17 Ibid., p. 43.
18 *Initiations, rites, sociétés secrètes*, p. 273, cited in Marc Auge, 'Towards a Rejection of the Meaning–Function Alternative', *Critique of Anthropology*, 13 and 14, Summer 1979, pp. 61–75.
19 Soyinka, *Death and the King's Horseman*, p. 62.
20 Soyinka, *Myth, Literature and the African World*, pp. 27–30.
21 Wole Soyinka, 'Who's Afraid of Elesin Oba?' (unpublished conference paper delivered at University of Ibadan, 23 November 1977).
22 Soyinka, *Myth, Literature and the African World*, p. 150.
23 Ibid., p. 151.
24 Ulli Beier, 'A Dance of the Forests', *Black Orpheus*, 8, 1960, p. 57.
25 Wole Soyinka, *Idanre and Other Poems* (London, 1967), p. 30.
26 Soyinka, *Death and the King's Horseman*, p. 20.
27 See Ajibola, *Owe Yoruba*, p. 54.
28 Soyinka, *Death and the King's Horseman*, p. 14; Ajibola, *Owe Yoruba*, p. 78; Isaac O. Delano, *Owe L'Esin Oro* (Ibadan, 1966), p. 74; hereafter Soyinka, Ajibola, Delano.
29 Soyinka, p. 22 (Ajibola, p. 56; Delano, p. 54).
30 Soyinka, p. 41 (Ajibola, p. 57; Delano, p. 55); Soyinka, p. 42 (Delano, p. 44); Soyinka, p. 43 (Ajibola, p. 45; Delano, p. 45); Soyinka, p. 43 (Delano, p. 119).

31 Soyinka, pp. 68, 75 (Ajibola, p. 49; Delano, p. 2); Soyinka, p. 68 (Ajibola, p. 89; Delano, p. 146); Soyinka, p. 69 (Delano, p. 145); Soyinka, p. 69 (Delano, p. 116); Soyinka, p. 75 (Ajibola, p. 59).

32 Soyinka, p. 64 (Ajibola, p. 80; Delano, p. 141).

33 Soyinka, p. 63 (Ajibola, p. 57; Delano, p. 149).

34 Soyinka, p. 43 (Ajibola, p. 80; Delano, p. 141).

35 A. S. Cook, *Language and Myth* (Bloomington, 1980), p. 219.

36 Soyinka, *Death and the King's Horseman*, pp. 68, 69.

37 Ibid., Preface.

38 Soyinka, *Collected Plays*, vol. I, p. 149.

39 *The Womb of Space* (Westport, Conn. 1983), pp. 69–70, quoted in Stephen Slemon, 'Magic Realism as Post-Colonial Discourse', *Canadian Literature*, 116, Spring 1988, p. 21.

40 See J. Lacan, 'Le Stade du Mirroir', *Ecrits* (Paris, 1966), see also C. Brooke-Rose, *A Rhetoric of the Unreal* (Cambridge, 1981).

41 Bissoondath, 'Veins Visible', *Digging Up The Mountains*, p. 221.

42 Bissoondath, 'Continental Drift', *Digging Up The Mountains*, p. 145.

43 Bissoondath, 'Veins Visible', p. 221.

44 Ben Okri, 'Hidden History', *Incidents at the Shrine* (London, 1986), pp. 88–9.

45 Okri, 'Laughter Beneath the Bridge', *Incidents at the Shrine*, pp. 3, 9.

46 See for example, Soyinka's *The Strong Breed*.

47 'Laughter Beneath the Bridge', pp. 18–19.

48 Ben Okri, *The Famished Road* (London, 1991), p. 263. I am grateful to Prema Cutrona for drawing my attention to this passage.

49 Ibid., p. 264.

9 Masks of difference

1 Kristeva, *Powers of Horror*, p. 141.

2 See Bourdieu, 'Symbolic Power'.

3 Carlo Ginzburg, *Clues, Myths and the Historical Method* (1986), translated by John and Anne C. Tedeschi (London, 1989), p. 159.

4 See Clifford, *The Predicament of Culture*, pp. 21–54, 'Experiential, interpretive, dialogical, and polyphonic processes are at work, discordantly, in any ethnography, but coherent presentation presupposes a controlling mode of authority' (p. 54).

5 See K. Dwyer, 'On the Dialogic of Fieldwork', *Dialectical Anthropology*, 2:2, 1977, 143–51; Clifford, *The Predicament of Culture*, pp. 21–54.

6 The point is made analogously by Marcia Pointon when she depicts the representation of the female body in art as 'the site of the struggle for mastery over the process of mimesis'; *Naked Authority* (Cambridge, 1990), p. 83.

7 Rubin (ed.), *'Primitivism' in Twentieth-Century Art*; Foster, *Recodings*, pp. 181–2.

8 See Robert Hughes, *The Shock of the New* (London, 1991), p. 24.

9 Picasso quoted in William Rubin, 'Picasso', in Rubin (ed.), *'Primitivism' in Twentieth-Century Art*, p. 255.

10 B. Malinowski, *The Dynamics of Culture Change*, p. 58, quoted in Asad (ed.), *Anthropology and the Colonial Encounter.*
11 Homi K. Bhabha, 'Of Mimicry and Men: the Ambivalence of Colonial Discourse', *October*, 28, 1984, p. 321.
12 Fagg et al., *Yoruba: Sculpture of West Africa*, p. 76.
13 J. Jones, *On Aristotle and Greek Tragedy* (London, 1971), pp. 44–5 cited also in A. David Napier, *Masks, Transformation, and Paradox* (Berkeley, 1986), p. 9.
14 See Napier, *Masks, Transformation, and Paradox*, chapter 1.

Select bibliography

Abalogu, Uchegbulam N., Garba Ashiwaju and Regina Amadi-Tsiwala (eds.), *Oral Poetry in Nigeria* (Lagos, 1981).

Abimbola, Wande, 'Iwapele: the Concept of Good Character in Ifa Literary Corpus', in Wande Abimbola (ed.), *Yoruba Oral Tradition*.

  'The form of Ese Ifa', *Lagos Notes*, 3:1 (1971).

Abimbola, Wande (ed.), *Yoruba Oral Tradition*, Ife African Languages and Literatures series, 1 (Ibadan, 1975).

Abrahamsson, H., *The Origin of Death*, Studia Ethnographica Uppsaliensia, vol. III (Uppsala, 1951).

Abrams, M. H., *A Glossary of Literary Terms* (London, 1981).

Achebe, Chinua, *A Man of the People* (London, 1966).

  Anthills of the Savannah (London, 1988).

  Things Fall Apart (London, 1958).

  'The Black Writer's Burden', *Présence Africaine*, 59 (1966).

Ackerman, Robert, *J. G. Frazer: His Life and Work* (Cambridge, 1987).

Adams, J., *Curious Thoughts on the History of Man* (London, 1789).

Adedeji, J. A., 'A Yoruba Pantomime', *Ibadan*, 29 (1971).

  'The Place of Drama in Yoruba Religious Observance', *Odu*, 3:1 (1966).

Ajibola, Oloye J. O., *Owe Yoruba* (Ibadan, 1971).

Akanji, Sangodare, 'The Lion and the Jewel and the Swamp Dwellers', *Black Orpheus*, 6 (1959).

Amin, Samir, *Eurocentrism* (London, 1989).

Anderson, P., 'Components of the National Culture', *New Left Review*, 50 (1968), 3–57.

Andrzejewski, B. W., and G. Innes, 'Reflections on African Oral Literature', *African Languages*, 1 (1975).

Anonymous, 'National Dramatist', *West Africa*, 19 December 1964.

Appiah, Kwame Anthony, *In My Father's House* (London, 1992).

Arendt, H., *Imperialism* (New York, 1968).

Aries, P., 'At the Point of Origin', *Yale French Studies*, 43, 15–23.

Armstrong, Robert Plant, *The Affecting Presence* (Illinois, 1971).

  'Tragedy – Greek and Yoruba', *Research in African Literatures*, 7:1 (1976).

Asad, Talal (ed.), *Anthropology and the Colonial Encounter* (London, 1973).

Ashley, Kathleen M., *Victor Turner and the Construction of Cultural Criticism: Between Literature and Anthropology* (Indiana, 1990).

Atkinson, Paul, *The Ethnographic Imagination: Textual Constructions of Reality* (London, 1990).

Auge, Marc, 'Towards a Rejection of the Meaning–Function Alternative', *Critique of Anthropology*, 13 and 14 (Summer 1979), 61–75.

Awe, B., 'Praise Poems as Historical Data', *Africa*, 44 (October, 1974).

Awobuluyi, Oladele, 'Stylistic Repetition in Yoruba Poetry', *Ibadan*, 29 (1971).

Babalola, S. A., *Ijala – The Poetry of Yoruba Hunters* (Oxford, 1967).
  The Content and Form of Yoruba Ijala (Oxford, 1966).
  'The Characteristic Features of the Outer Form of Yoruba Ijala', *Odu*, 1:1 (1964).
  'The Delights of Ijala', in Wande Abimola (ed.), *Yoruba Oral Tradition*.

Babcock, Barbara (ed.), *The Reversible World: Symbolic Inversion in Art and Society* (Ithaca, 1978).

Bachofen, J. J., *Myth, Religion and Mother Right: Selected Writings of J. J. Bachofen*, translated by Ralph Manheim, preface by George Boas, introduction by Joseph Campbell (London, 1967).

Baker, J. R., *Race* (Oxford, 1974).

Bakhtin, M., *The Dialogic Imagination*, translated by C. Emerson and M. Holquist (Austin, 1981).

Balandier, G., *The Sociology of Black Africa*, translated by D. Garman (London, 1970).

Baltrusaitis, Jurgis, *Aberrations* (Paris, 1983).
  Anamorphoses (Paris, 1984).

Bamgbose, Ayo, 'Fagunwa and the Yoruba Folktale Tradition', in Wande Abimbola (ed.), *Yoruba Oral Tradition*.

Banham, M. and Clive Wake, *African Literature Today* (London, 1976).

Banton, M., *West African City* (Oxford, 1967).

Barker, Francis, et al. (eds.), *The Politics of Theory* (Colchester, 1983).

Barker, Francis, et al. (eds.), *Europe and its Others*, 2 vols. (Colchester, 1984).

Barrett, D. B., *Schism and Renewal in Africa* (Oxford, 1968).

Barth, F., 'On the Study of Social Change', *American Anthropologist*, 69 (1967).

Bascom, William, *Ifa Divination* (Bloomington, 1969).
  'Creativity and Style in African Art', in D. Biebuyck (ed.), *Tradition and Creativity in African Art*.
  'Four Functions of Folklore', in A. Dundes (ed.), *The Study of Folklore*.

Bastide, Roger, 'Variations sur la négritude', *Présence Africaine*, 36 (1961).

Baudet, H., *Paradise on Earth: Some Thoughts on Images of Non-European Man*, translated by Elizabeth Wenholt (London, 1965).

Baudrillard, Jean, *Simulations* (New York, 1980).

Béart, C., 'A propos du théâtre africain', *Traits-d'Union*, 15 (1957).

Beattie, J., *Other Cultures: Aims, Methods and Achievements in Social Anthropology* (London, 1964).

Behn, Aphra, *Oroonoko and Other Prose Narratives*, edited by Montague Summers (New York, 1967).

Beier, Ulli, 'Ibo and Yoruba Art', *Black Orpheus*, 8 (1960).
'A Dance of the Forests', *Black Orpheus*, 8 (1960).
'The Egungun Cult among the Yorubas', *Présence Africaine*, 18 (1958).
'Les Masques Guélède', *Etudes dahoméenes* (Porto Novo, 1966).
'Yoruba Folk Operas', *African Music*, 1:1 (1954).
Beier, Ulli, and G. Gbadamosi, *Yoruba Poetry* (Ibadan, 1959).
Ben-Amos, D., 'Folklore in African Society', *Research in African Literatures*, 6:2 (1975).
Berger, Harry, Jr, *Second World and Green World* (Oxford, 1988).
Berger, John, *The Guardian*, 14 April 1993, 2, 4:1.
Bernheimer, Richard, *The Wildman in the Middle Ages* (Cambridge, Mass., 1952).
Berry, J., *Spoken Art in West Africa* (London, 1961).
Besterman, T., *A Bibliography of Sir J. G. Frazer* (1934).
Bhabha, Homi K. (ed.), *Nation and Narration* (London, 1990).
Bhabha, Homi K., 'Difference, Discrimination and the Discourse of Colonialism', in F. Barker (ed.), *The Politics of Theory* (Colchester, 1983).
'Foreword: Remembering Fanon', in Frantz Fanon, *Black Skin, White Masks* (*Peau Noire, Masques Blancs*, 1952), translated by Charles Lam Markmann with a foreword by Homi K. Bhabha (London, 1986).
'The Other Question: Difference Discrimination and the Discourse of Colonialism', in *Literature, Politics and Theory*, edited by Francis Barker et al. (London, 1986).
'Representation and the Colonial Text: A Critical Exploration of Some Forms of Mimeticism', in Frank Gloversmith (ed.), *The Theory of Reading* (Brighton, 1984).
'Interrogating Identity', *ICA Documents*, 6 (1987).
'Of Mimicry and Men: the Ambivalence of Colonial Discourse', *October*, 28 (1984).
Biadene, Susanna (assisted by Mary Yakush) (eds.), *Titian* (Venice 1990).
Bidney, D., *Theoretical Anthropology* (New York, 1967).
Biebuyck, D. (ed.), *Tradition and and Creativity in African Art* (London, 1969).
Bird, C., 'Heroic Songs of the Mande Hunters', in Richard Dorson (ed.), *African Folklore*.
Bissoondath, Neil, *A Casual Brutality* (Bloomsbury, 1988).
Digging up the Mountains (Harmondsworth, 1987).
Blackwell, Thomas, *An Inquiry into the Life and Writings of Homer* (London, 1735).
Boisserain, J., and J. C. Mitchell (eds.), *Network Analysis: Studies in Human Interaction* (The Hague, 1973).
Bolt, Christine, *Victorian Ideas of Race* (London, 1977).
Boon, James, *From Symbolism to Structuralism* (Oxford, 1972).
Other Tribes, Other Scribes (Cambridge, 1982).
Boston, J. S., 'Some Northern Ibo Masquerades', *Journal of the Royal Anthropological Institute*, 90 (1960).
Bourdieu, P., *Outline of a Theory of Practice* (Cambridge, 1977).

'Symbolic Power', *Critique of Anthropology*, 13 and 14 (Summer 1979), 77–85.

Bradley, P., 'An Index of the Supernatural, Witchcraft and Allied Subjects in the Works of Sir Walter Scott', 2 vols. (unpublished thesis for Fellowship of the Library Association, 1966).

Brantlinger, Patrick, *Rule of Darkness: British Literature and Imperialism 1830–1914* (London, 1988).

Brill, E. V. K., 'The correspondence between Jacob Grimm and Walter Scott', *Hessiche Blatter fur Volkskunde*, 54 (1963).

Brooke-Rose, C., *A Rhetoric of the Unreal* (Cambridge, 1981).

Brown, D., *Walter Scott and the Historical Imagination* (London, 1979).

Bryson, Norman, *Calligram: Essays in New Art History from France* (Cambridge, 1988).

Carrithers, Martin, Steven Collins and Steven Lukes (eds.), *The Category of the Person: Anthropology, Philosophy, History* (Cambridge, 1985).

Cawley, Robert Ralston, *The Voyagers and Elizabethan Drama* (London, 1938).

Chambers, Robert, *Illustrations of the Author of Waverley* (1822), (Edinburgh, 1825).

Chapman, M., *The Gaelic Vision in Scottish Culture* (London, 1978).

Chinweizu, and Onwuchewka Jemie and Ichechukwu Madubuike, *Towards the Decolonization of African Literature* (Enugu, 1980).

'Towards the Decolonization of African Literature', *Transition*, 48 (1974).

Clarke, J. D., 'Ifa Divination', *Journal of the Royal Anthropological Institute*, 69 (1939).

Clarke, J. P., 'Aspects of Nigerian Drama', *Nigeria*, 89 (1966).

Clifford, James, *The Predicament of Culture: Twentieth Century Ethnography, Literature and Art* (Harvard, 1988).

'On Ethnographic Self-Fashioning: Conrad and Malinowski,' in T. C. Heller et al. (eds.), *Reconstructing Individualism* (Stanford, 1986).

Clifford, James, and George E. Marcus, *Writing Culture: The Poetics and Politics of Ethnography* (London, 1986).

Cochrane, J. G., *Catalogue of the Library of Sir Walter Scott at Abbotsford* (Edinburgh, 1838).

Cohen, Abner, *Custom and Politics in Urban Africa* (London, 1969).

Two Dimensional Man (London, 1979).

Collings, Rex, 'A propos', *African Arts*, 2:3 (1969).

Cook, A. S., *Language and Myth* (Bloomington, 1980).

Cook, David, *African Literature* (London, 1973).

'Of *The Strong Breed*', *Transition*, 13 (1964).

Crane, R. S., 'Anglican Apologetics and the Idea of Progress', *Modern Philology*, 31 (February and May 1934).

Crawford, Robert, *The Savage and the City* (Oxford, 1987).

Crawford, Thomas, *Scott, Writers and Critics* (Edinburgh, 1965).

Cregeen, E. R., 'The Changing Role of the House of Argyll in the Scottish Highlands', in I. M. Lewis (ed.), *History and Social Anthropology*, Association of Social Anthropologists Monograph 7 (London, 1968).

Cusac, M. H., *Narrative Structure in the Novels of Sir Walter Scott* (The Hague, 1969).

Darwin, Charles, *The Descent of Man and Selection in Relation to Sex*, 2 vols. (London, 1870–1).
On the Origin of Species by Means of Natural Selection (London, 1859).
Davis, N. Z., 'The Reasons of Misrule: Youth Groups and Charivaris in Sixteenth-Century France', *Past and Present*, 50 (1971).
De Graft, J. C., 'Roots in African Drama and Theatre', in M. Banham and Clive Wake, *African Literature Today*: 8 (London, 1976).
De Lery, Jean, *Histoire d'un voyage faict en la terre de Bresil* (1578).
Delano, Isaac O., *Owe L'Esin Oro* (Ibadan, 1966).
Dennett, R. E., *Nigerian Studies or The Religious System of the Yoruba* (1910), (London, 1968).
Derrida, Jacques, *Of Grammatology* (1967), translated by Gayatri Spivak (London, 1976).
Detienne, M., *Les Jardins d'Adonis* (Paris, 1972).
Devlin, D. D., *Author of Waverley* (London, 1971).
Diamond, Stanley, *The Search for the Primitive* (New York, 1979).
Dobrizhoffer, Martin, *Account of the Abipones: An Equestrian People of Paraguay*, 3 vols. (London, 1822).
Donald, James, and Ali Rattansi, *'Race', Culture and Discrimination* (London, 1992).
Dorson, M. (ed.), *African Folklore* (New York, 1972).
Dorson, M., *The British Folklorists: A History* (London, 1968).
'Current Folklore Theories', *Current Anthropology*, 4:1 (1963).
Douglas, Mary, *Natural Symbols*, 1970 (Harmondsworth, 1973).
Downie, R. A., *Frazer and 'The Golden Bough'* (London, 1970).
Dudley, E., and M. Novak (eds.), *The Wild Man Within: An Image in Western Thought from the Renaissance to Romanticism* (Pittsburgh, 1972).
Duerden, Denis, *African Art* (London, 1974).
Duerden, Denis and C. Pieterse, *African Writers Talking* (London, 1972).
Duke, Alastair, Gillian Lewis and Andrew Pettegree (trans. and eds.), *Calvinism in Europe 1540–1610: A Collection of Documents* (Manchester, 1992).
Dundes, A. (ed.), *The Study of Folklore* (New Jersey, 1965).
Durbin, M. A., 'Linguistic Models in Anthropology', *Annual Review of Anthropology*, 1 (1972), 383–410.
Durkheim, Emile, *Selected Writings*, edited and translated by Anthony Giddens (Cambridge, 1972).
The Elementary Forms of the Religious Life (1915), translated by J. W. Swain (London, 1976).
Dwyer, K., 'On the Dialogic of Fieldwork', *Dialectical Anthropology*, 2:2 (1977), 143–51.
Eliot, T. S., *Collected Poems 1909–1962* (London, 1963).
Notes Toward a Definition of Culture (London, 1962).
Selected Essays (London, 1966).
Selected Prose of T. S. Eliot, edited by Frank Kermode (London, 1974).
Review of *Group Theories of Religion and the Religion of the Individual*, *International Journal of Ethics* (October 1916), 116.
Ellison, R. E., 'A Bornu Puppet Show', *Nigerian Field*, 4 (1935).

Elphinstone, H. Mountstuart, *An Account of the Kingdom of Caubal and its Dependents in Persia, Tartary and India* (London, 1815).

Euba, Akin, 'The Interrelationship of Music and Poetry in Yoruba Tradition', in Wande Abimbola (ed.), *Yoruba Oral Tradition.*

Evans, Edward Payson, *The Criminal Prosecution and Capital Punishment of Animals* (London, 1906).

Evans-Pritchard, E. E., *A History of Anthropological Thought* (London, 1981).

Fabian, J., *Time and the Other: How Anthropology Makes its Object* (New York, 1983).

   'Language, History and Anthropology', *Philosophy of the Social Sciences*, 9(1):1.26 (1979).

Fagg, William, John Pemberton III and Bryce Holcombe, *Yoruba: Sculpture of West Africa* (London, 1982).

Fagg, W., 'The African Artist', in D. Biebuyck (ed.), *Tradition and Creativity in African Art.*

Fanon, Frantz, *A Dying Colonialism* (Harmondsworth, 1970).

   Black Skin, White Masks (Peau Noire, Masques Blancs, 1952), translated by Charles Lam Markmann with a foreword by Homi K. Bhabha (London, 1986).

   The Wretched of the Earth (New York, 1968).

   Toward the African Revolution (Harmondsworth, 1970).

Favret-Saada, Jeanne, *Deadly Words* (Cambridge, 1981).

Fehl, P., 'Realism and Classicism in the Representation of a Painful Scene: Titian's *The Flaying of Marsyas* in the Archiepiscopal Palace at Kromeriz', *Czechoslovakia Past and Present: Essays on the Arts and Sciences*, 2 vols. (The Hague, 1968), vol. II.

Feldman, B., and R. D. Richardson, *The Rise of Modern Mythology* (Bloomington, 1972).

Ferguson, Adam, *An Essay on the History of Civil Society*, 1767, edited by Duncan Forbes (Edinburgh, 1966).

Fernandez, J. W. (ed.), *Beyond Metaphor: The Theory of Tropes in Anthropology* (Stanford, Calif., 1991).

   'Folklore as an Agent of Nationalism', *African Studies Bulletin*, 5:2 (1962).

Finnegan, Ruth, *Oral Literature in Africa* (Oxford, 1970).

   Oral Poetry (Cambridge, 1977).

Firth, R., *Symbols: Public and Private* (London, 1973).

Firth, R. (ed.), *Man and Culture* (London, 1957).

Fiske, C. F., *Epic Suggestion in the Imagery of the Waverley Novels* (Yale, 1940).

Fodeba, K., 'La Danse Africaine et la Scéne', *Présence Africaine*, 27 (1958).

Forbes of Culloden, Lord President, *Works*, 2 vols. (Edinburgh, 1747).

Forbes, Duncan, 'The Rationalism of Sir Walter Scott', *Cambridge Journal*, 8:1 (1953).

Forde, C. Daryll, *African Worlds* (London, 1954).

   The Yoruba-speaking Peoples of South-West Nigeria, Ethnographic Survey of Africa – Western Africa 4 (London, 1951).

Forge, A. (ed.), *Primitive Art and Society* (London, 1973).

Fortes, Meyer, *Oedipus and Job in West African Religion* (Cambridge, 1959).

Foster, Hal, *Postmodern Culture* (London, 1985).
  Recodings: Art, Spectacle, Cultural Politics (Washington, 1985).
Foucault, Michel, 'Cuvier's Position in the History of Biology', *Critique of Anthropology*, 13 and 14 (Summer 1979), 125–30.
  'Truth and Power: An Interview with Michel Foucault', *Critique of Anthropology*, 13 and 14 (Summer 1979), 131–7.
Fox, Richard G. (ed.), *Recapturing Anthropology: Working in the Present* (Santa Fé, 1991).
Fraser, D., 'The Symbols of Ashanti Kingship' in D. Fraser and Cole, (eds.), *African Art and Leadership* (London, 1972).
Fraser, Robert (ed.), *Sir James Frazer and the Literary Imagination* (London, 1990).
Fraser, Russell, *The Language of Adam: on the Limits and Systems of Discourse* (Columbia, 1977).
Frazer, J. G., *Questions on the Customs, Beliefs and Languages of Savages* (Cambridge, 1907, reissued 1910 and 1916).
  Questions on the Manners, Customs, Religion, Superstitions, etc. of Uncivilized or Semi-Civilized Peoples (Cambridge, 1887).
  The Golden Bough (1890 first edition) (New York, 1981).
  The Golden Bough (1922 abridged edition) (London, 1974).
  The Golden Bough (third edition), 12 vols. (London, 1906–15).
  'Supplement to *Questions on the Manners, Customs, Religion, Superstitions, etc. of Uncivilized or Semi-Civilized Peoples*', *The Journal of the Anthropological Institute*, 18 (May, 1889), 431–9.
  Unpublished notebooks and correspondence, The Frazer Collection, Wren Library, Trinity College, Cambridge.
Frazer, Sir James, *Totemism and Exogamy: A Treatise on Certain Early Forms of Superstition and Society* (London, 1910).
  'A Suggestion as to the Origin of Gender in Language', *The Fortnightly Review*, n.s. 68 (January 1900), 79–90.
  'The Language of Animals', *The Archaeological Review*, 1 (April – May 1888), 81–91, 161–81.
Friedman, J. Block, *The Monstrous Races in Medieval Art and Thought* (London, 1981).
Frobenius, Leo, *The Childhood of Man*, translated by A. H. Keane (London, 1909).
  Leo Frobenius 1873–1973, Eine Anthologie mit einine Vorwart von Leopold Sedar Senghor, Studien Kulturkunde 32 (Wiesbaden, 1973).
Frobenius, Leo, and Douglas C. Fox, *African Genesis* (London, 1938).
Galton, Francis, *Hereditary Genius* (London, 1869).
Gates, H. L., *Figures in Black: Words, Signs and the 'Racial' Self* (Oxford, 1987).
  'Race', Writing and Difference (London, 1986).
  Black Literature and Literary Theory (New York, 1990).
Gayle, A., *The Black Aesthetics* (New York, 1972).
Geertz, Clifford, *The Interpretation of Cultures* (New York, 1973).
  Works and Lives: The Anthropologist as Author (Cambridge, 1988)
Geertz, Clifford, H. Geertz and L. Rosen, *Meaning and Order in Moroccan Society* (Cambridge, 1979).

Gent, Lucy and Nigel Llewellyn (eds.), *Renaissance Bodies: The Human Figure in English Culture c. 1540–1660* (London, 1990).

Gentili, A., *Da Tiziano a Tiziano. Mito e allegoria nella cultura veneziana del Cinquecento* (Milan, 1980)

Gerard, A., 'Preservation of Tradition in African Creative Writing', *Research in African Literatures*, 1:1 (1970).

Gessell, Arnold, *Wolf Child and Human Child* (London, 1941).

Gimbutas, Marija, 'Old Europe c. 7000–3500 BC: The Earliest European Civilisation before the Infiltration of Indo-European Peoples', *Journal of Indo-European Studies*, 1:1 (1973), 1–20.

Ginzburg, Carlo, *Clues, Myths and the Historical Method* (1986), translated by John and Anne C. Tedeschi (London, 1989).

Gleason, J., *A Recitation of Ifa – Oracle of the Yoruba* (New York, 1973).

Gloversmith, Frank (ed.), *The Theory of Reading* (Brighton, 1984).

Gluckman, Max (ed.), *Essays on the Ritual of Social Relations* (Manchester, 1962).

Gobineau, Joseph Arthur, Comte de, *Selected Political Writings*, edited by M. D. Biddis (London, 1970).

Goddard, David, 'Limits of British Anthropology', *New Left Review*, 58 (1969), 79–89.

Godfrey, R. C., 'Late Medieval Linguistic Meta-theory and Chomsky's Syntactic Structures', *Word*, 21:2 (1965), 251–6.

Goffman, Erving, *Strategic Intervention* (Oxford, 1970).
  The Presentation of Self in Everyday Life (New York, 1959).

Goody, Jack, *Death, Property and the Ancestors* (London, 1962).
  The Domestication of the Savage Mind (Cambridge 1977).

Goonetilleke, D. C. R., *Developing Countries in British Fiction* (London, 1977).

Grant of Laggan, Mrs A., *Essays on the superstitions of the Highlanders*, 2 vols. (London, 1811).

Grant, Stewart W., *The Popular Superstitions of the Highlanders* (Edinburgh, 1823).

Gray, Piers, *T. S. Eliot's Intellectual and Poetic Development 1909–1922* (Brighton, 1982).

Green, Martin, *Dreams of Adventure, Deeds of Empire* (New York, 1979).

Grierson, H. J. C. (ed.), *Sir Walter Scott Today* (London, 1932).

Griffiths, Gareth, Helen Tiffin and Bill Ashcroft, *The Empire Writes Back*, London, 1989.

Haddon, A. C., *History of Anthropology* (London, 1934).

Hailes, Lord, *Annals of Scotland* (Edinburgh, 1776).

Hainard, Jacques, and Roland Kaeht (eds.), *Naître, Vivre et Mourir* (Neuchatel, 1981).

Harley, G. W., 'Notes on the Poro in Liberia', *Papers of the Peabody Museum*, 19 (1941).

Harpham, Geoffrey Galt, *The Ascetic Imperative in Culture and Criticism* (Chicago, 1987).

Harris, M., *The Rise of Anthropological Theory* (London, 1968).

Hartt, F., *Giulio Romano* (New Haven, 1958).

Heller, P., *Dialects and Nihilism* (Cambridge, Mass., 1966).

Hemming, John, *Amazon Frontier: The Defeat of the Brazilian Indians* (London, 1987).

Henn, Tom R., *The Lonely Tower* (London, 1958).

Henson, Hilary, *British Social Anthropology and Language: A History of Separate Development* (Oxford, 1974).

Hesse, Mary, The Stanton Lectures 1980, 1–81 (unpublished lecture notes deposited in the History and Philosophy of Science Library, Cambridge).

Hibbard, L. A., *Medieval Romance in England* (Oxford, 1961).

Hillier, Susan, *The Myth of Primitivism: Perspectives on Art* (London, 1991).

Hodgen, M. T., *Early Anthropology in the Sixteenth and Seventeenth Centuries* (Philadelphia, 1964).

Hoffman, D., *Barbarous Knowledge* (Oxford, 1967).

Holloway, John, *Widening Horizons in English Verse* (London 1969).

Hooker, J. R., 'The Anthropological Frontier: The Last Phase of African Exploitation', *Journal of Modern African Studies* (1963), 449–55.

Hopkins, N. S., 'The Modern Theatre in Mali', *Présence Africaine*, 53 (1965).

Horigan, Stephen, *Nature and Culture in Western Discourses* (London, 1988).

Horton, Robin, 'Igbo – An Ordeal for Aristocrats', *Nigeria*, 90 (1966).
  'Ikuki – The Tortoise Masquerade', *Nigeria*, 94 (1967).
  'New Year in the Delta', *Nigeria Magazine*, 67.
  'The Kalabari Ekine Society: A Borderland of Religion and Art', *Africa*, 33 (1963).

Horton, Robin, and Ruth Finnegan (eds.), *Modes of Thought* (London, 1973).

Huet, Marie-Hélène, 'Living Images: Monstrosity and Representation', *Representations*, 4 (Fall 1983), 73–87.

Hughes, Robert, *The Shock of the New* (London, 1991).

Hulton, P., *The Work of Jacques Le Moyne de Morgues*, 2 vols. (London, 1977).

Hume, David, *A Treatise of Human Nature* (1739), edited by D. G. C. McNab (London, 1962).

Hymes, D., *Reinventing Anthropology* (New York, 1969).

Idowu, E. Bolaji, *Olodumare – God in Yoruba Belief* (London, 1962).

Irele, Abiola, 'A Defence of Negritude', *Transition*, 13 (1964).
  'Tradition and the Yoruba Writer', *Odu* (n.s.) 1:1 (1975).

Jahn, J., *A History of Neo-African Literature* (London, 1968).
  Muntu: An Outline of Neo-African Culture (London, 1961).

Jakobson, R., 'La première lettre de Ferdinand de Saussure à Antoine Meillet sur les anagrammes', *Homme*, 11.2 (1971), 15–24.

Jameson, Fredric, 'Third World Literature in an Era of Multinational Capitalism', *Social Text* (Fall 1986).

JanMohamed, Abdul R., *A Manichean Aesthetics: The Politics of Literature in Colonial Africa* (Amherst, 1983).

Janson, H. W., and Anthony Janson, *History of Art* (London, 1973), third edition, 1988.

Johnson, Dr Samuel, *A Journey to the Western Islands of Scotland*, edited by R. W. Chapman (Oxford, 1970).

Johnson, Edgar, *Sir Walter Scott: The Great Unknown* (London, 1970).

Johnson, Rev. S., *The History of the Yorubas* (1921), (Lagos, 1976).

Jones, E. D., *African Literature Today 11* (London, 1980).

The Writing of Wole Soyinka (London, 1973).

Jones, G. I., 'Masked Plays of South-Eastern Nigeria', *Geographical Magazine*, 18:5 (1945).

'Okorosia', *Nigerian Field*, 3 (1934).

Josipovici, Gabriel, *Writing and the Body* (Brighton, 1982).

Jung, C., *Psychology and Alchemy* (1953), *Collected Works*, translated by R. F. C. Hull, 20 vols. (London), vol. xii (1989).

Jung, C. G. and C. Kerenyi, *Introduction to a Science of Mythology*, trans. by R. F. C. Hull (London, 1951).

Kamboureli, Smaro, and Shirley Neumann (eds.), *A Mazing Space: Writing Canadian Women Writing* (Edmonton, 1986).

Kames, Lord (H. Homes), *Sketches of the History of Man*, 2 vols. (Edinburgh, 1774).

Kane, Mohamadou, 'The African Writer and his Public', *Présence Africaine*, 58 (1966).

Kaufmann, Lynn Frier, *The Noble Savage: Satyr and Satyr Families in Renaissance Art* (Michigan, 1984).

Ker, W. P., *Epic and Romance* (New York, 1897).

Kermode, Frank, *Romantic Image* (London, 1957).

Kieckhefer, Richard, *Magic in the Middle Ages* (Cambridge, 1989).

Koerner, E. F. K., *Ferdinand de Saussure* (Braunschweig, 1973).

Toward a Historiography of Linguistics: Selected Essays (Amsterdam, 1978).

Koerner, E. F. K. (ed.), *Linguistics and Evolutionary Theory* (Amsterdam, 1983).

Koerner, E. F. K., '1876 as a Turning Point in the History of Linguistics', *Journal of Indo-European Studies*, 4:4 (1976), 333–53.

'Toward a Historiography of Linguistics: Nineteenth and Twentieth Century Paradigms', *Anthropological Linguistics*, 14:7 (1972), 255–80.

Kristeva, Julia, *Powers of Horror: An Essay on Abjection* (*Pouvoirs de l'horreur*, 1980) (New York, 1982).

Kroeber, A. L., *The Nature of Culture* (Chicago, 1952).

Kroetsch, Robert, 'Disunity as Unity: A Canadian Strategy', in Colin Nicholson and Peter Easingwood (eds.), *Canadian History and Story* (Edinburgh, 1986).

Kunapipi, Special issue in Celebration of Chinua Achebe, 12:2 (1990).

Lacan, J., *Le Séminaire I* (Paris, 1975).

'Le Stade du Miroir', *Ecrits* (Paris, 1966).

Lafitau, J. F., *Customs of the American Indians Compared with Customs of Primitive Times* (*Mœurs des sauvages Ameriquain, comparées aux mœurs des premiers temps*, 1724) 2 vols. (Toronto, 1974–7).

Lang, Andrew, *Cock-Lane and Common-sense* (London, 1894).

Custom and Myth, 1885 (Wakefield, 1974).

Modern Mythology (London, 1897).

Myth, Ritual and Religion, 2 vols. (London, 1887).

Social Origins (London, 1903).

The Making of Religion (London, 1898).

Laqueur, Thomas, 'Bodies, Death and Pauper Funerals', *Representations*, 1:1 (February 1983), 109–31.

Laurence, Margaret, *Long Drums and Cannons* (London, 1968).

'Ivory Tower or Grassroots? : The Novelist as Socio-Political Being', in *A Political Art: Essays in Honour of George Woodcock*, edited by W. H. New (Vancouver, 1978).

Lazarus, Neil, *Resistance in Postcolonial African Fiction* (London, 1990).

Le Challeux, Nicholas, *Discours de l'histoire de la Floride contenant le cruante de Espagnols* (1566).

Le Moyne De Morgues, Jacques, *Brevis Narratio eorum quae in Florida Americae provincia Gallis acciderunt, secunda in illam Navigatione, duce Renato de Laudonnière classis Praefecto* (1591).

Leach, Edmund, *Culture and Communication* (Cambridge, 1976).

(ed.), *The Structural Study of Myth and Totemism*, Association of Social Anthropologists Monograph 5 (London, 1967).

Lehmann, W. C., *Adam Ferguson and the Beginnings of Sociology* (Columbia, New York, 1930).

Lévi-Strauss, C., *Race et Histoire* (UNESCO, Paris, 1952).

Structural Anthropology (1963), translated by Claire Jacobson and Brooke Grundfest Schoepf (Harmondsworth, 1972).

Structural Anthropology 2 (1973), translated by Monique Layton (Harmondsworth, 1976).

The Scope of Anthropology (London, 1967).

Tristes Tropiques (1955), translated by John and Doreen Weightman (Harmondsworth, 1976).

Lévy-Bruhl, L., *How Natives Think* (*Les fonctions mentales dans les sociétés inférieures*, 1910) (Princeton, 1985).

The Soul of the Primitive (London, 1928).

Lewis, I. M., *Ecstatic Religion* (Harmondsworth, 1971).

Lewis, I. M. (ed.), *History and Social Anthropology*, Association of Social Anthropologists Monograph 7 (London, 1968).

Symbols and Sentiments: Cross-Cultural Studies in Symbolism (London, 1977).

Lienhardt, G., 'Anthropology and Contemporary Literature', *Journal of the Anthropological Society of Oxford*, 1974.

Lindfors, Bernth, *Folklore in Nigerian Literature* (New York, 1973).

Locke, John, *Essay Concerning Human Understanding* (1689), edited by Peter N. Nidditch (Oxford, 1979).

Two Treatises of Government (1690), edited by Peter Laslett (Cambridge, 1960).

Lockhart, J. G., *Memoirs of the Life of Sir Walter Scott, Bart.*, 7 vols. (Edinburgh, 1837–38).

Long, N., *Social Change and the Individual* (Manchester, 1968).

Loomba, Ania, *Gender, Race, Renaissance Drama* (Manchester, 1989).

Loomis, R. S., *The Development of Arthurian Romance* (London, 1963).

Lubbock, John (Lord Avebury), *Prehistoric Times* (London, 1865).

The Origin of Civilisation and the Primitive Condition of Man (1870), edited by Peter Riviere (Chicago, 1978).

Lukacs, Georg, *The Historical Novel* (1960), translated by Hannah and Stanley Mitchell (London, 1962).

Lyotard, J-F., *The Postmodern Condition* (Manchester, 1984).

Macarney, M. H. H., 'Sir Walter Scott's Use of the Preface', *Longman's Magazine*, 58 (1905).

MacDiarmid, Hugh, *Scottish Eccentrics* (1936) (London, 1972).

Macgregor, G., *The Wacousta Syndrome* (Toronto, 1985).

MacLean, Una, 'Soyinka's International Drama', *Black Orpheus*, 15 (1964).

Mafaje, A., 'The Ideology of Tribalism', *Journal of Modern African Studies*, 9 (1971), 253–61.

Maher, J. P., 'More on the History of the Comparative Method: the Tradition of Darwinism in August Schleicher's work', *Anthropological Linguistics*, 8:3:2 (1966), 1–12.

Mahood, M. M., 'Drama in New-Born States', *Présence Africaine*, 60 (1966).

Maine, Sir Henry, *Ancient Law* (London, 1861).

Majasan, I., 'Folklore as an Instrument of Education Among the Yoruba', *Folklore*, 80 (London, 1969).

Malinowski, B., *A Diary in the Strict Sense of the Term* (New York, 1967).
A Scientific Theory of Culture and Other Essays (New York, 1944).
Argonauts of the Western Pacific (London, 1922).
The Father in Primitive Psychology (London, 1927).

Mallory, J. P., 'A History of the Indo-European Problem', *Journal of Indo-European Studies*, 1:1 (1973), 21–65.

Manganaro, Marc (ed.), *Modernist Anthropology: From Fieldwork to Text* (Princeton, 1990).

Mannering, D., *The Paintings of Matisse* (London, 1989).

Manning, Patrick, *Slavery and African Life* (Cambridge, 1990).

Maranda, Pierre, and Elli Kongas Maranda, *Structural Analysis of Oral Tradition* (Philadelphia, 1971).

Marcus, George E. and Michael M. J. Fischer, *Anthropology as Cultural Critique: An Experimental Moment in the Human Sciences* (Chicago, 1986).

Marcus, G., and D. Cushman, 'Ethnographies as Texts', *Annual Review of Anthropology*, 11 (1982), 25–69.

Marsh, Peter, E. Rosser and Rom Harre, *The Rules of Disorder* (London, 1977).

Mauss, Marcel, 'A Category of the Human Mind: the Notion of Person; the Notion of Self', translated by W. D. Halls in Martin Carrithers, Steven Collins and Steven Lukes (eds.), *The Category of the Person: Anthropology, Philosophy, History* (Cambridge, 1985).

Meehan, M. F., 'Political Models in Literary Theory, 1709–1767' (unpublished PhD thesis, Cambridge University, 1977).

Meek, R. L., *Social Science and the Ignoble Savage* (Cambridge, 1976).
Turgot on Progress (Cambridge, 1973).
'The Scottish Contribution to Marxist Sociology', in J. Saville (ed.), *Democracy and the Labour Movement* (London, 1954).

Meillassoux, C., 'La farce villageoise á la ville', *Présence Africaine*, 52 (1964).

Memmi, Albert, *The Colonizer and the Colonized* (*Portrait du Colonisé précédé du Portrait du Colonisateur*, 1957), translated by Howard Greenfield with introductions by Jean-Paul Sartre and Liam O'Dowd (London, 1990).

Mémoire d'une Amerique, Musée du Nouveau Monde (La Rochelle, 1980).

Middleton, J. (ed.), *Gods and Rituals* (London, 1967).

Miles, Gary B., 'Roman and Modern Imperialism: A Reassessment', *Comparative Studies in Society and History*, 32:4 (October 1990), 629–59.

Millar, J., *Observations Concerning the Distinction of Ranks in Society* (Dublin, 1771).

Montesquieu, Charles de Secondat, Baron de, *The Spirit of Laws*, translated by T. Nugent from an edition published at Edinburgh in 1750 with the author's latest corrections, 2 vols. (Aberdeen, 1756).

Morell, K. L., *In Person: Achebe, Awonoor and Soyinka* (Seattle, 1975).

Morgan, Lewis Henry, *Ancient Society* (New York, 1877).

Morton-Williams, Peter, 'Yoruba Responses to the Fear of Death', *Africa*, 30 (1960), 34–40.

Moss, John, *Invisible in the House of Mirrors*, Canada House Lecture Series, 21 (London, 1983).

Mudimbe, V. Y., *The Invention of Africa: Gnosis, Philosophy, and the Order of Knowledge* (Indiana, 1988).

Mullaney, Steven, 'Strange Things, Gross Terms, Curious Customs: The Rehearsal of Cultures in the Late Renaissance', *Representations*, 3 (1983), 40–67.

Munro, Ian, and Reinhard Sander (eds.), *Kas-Kas, Interviews with Three Caribbean Writers*, African and Afro-American Research Institute (Austin, 1972).

Munz, Peter, *When the Golden Bough Breaks: Structuralism or Typology?* (London, 1973).

Murray, K. C., 'Ayolugba', *Nigerian Field*, 12 (1947).

'Dances and Plays', *Nigeria*, 19 (1939).

Mutiso, G-C. M., *Socio-Political Thought in African Literature* (London, 1974).

Nanen, F. G., *Revolution, Idealism and Human Freedom: Schelling, Holderlin, and Hegel and the Crisis of Early German Idealism* (The Hague, 1971).

Napier, David A., *Masks, Transformation, and Paradox* (London, 1986).

Nash, J., 'Nationalism and Fieldwork', *Annual Review of Anthropology*, 4 (1975), 225–45.

Nashe, Thomas, *The Unfortunate Traveller and Other Works* (1594) (Harmondsworth, 1972).

Needham, R., *Essential Perplexities, An Inaugural Lecture Delivered Before the University of Oxford*, 12 May 1977 (Oxford, 1978).

Right and Left: Essays on Dual Symbolic Classification (Chicago, 1973).

Neumann, J., *Le Titian Marsyas écorché vif* (Prague, 1962).

New Sum of Poetry from the Negro World, *Présence Africaine*, 57 (1966).

Ngugi Wa Thiong'o, *Decolonising the Mind* (London, 1986).

Norris, Christopher, *Deconstruction: Theory and Practice* (London, 1982).

Nussbaum, Felicity, and Laura Brown (eds.), *The New Eighteenth Century* (London, 1987).

O'Grady, Standish, *History of Ireland*, 2 vols. (Dublin, 1881).

Ogunba, Oyin, *The Movement of Transition* (Ibadan, 1975).

'The Performance of Yoruba Oral Poetry', in Wande Abimbola (ed.), *Yoruba Oral Tradition*.

'The Agemo Cult in Ijebuland', *Nigeria*, 86 (1965).

'Theatre in Nigeria', *Présence Africaine*, 58 (1966).

'Traditional Content of the Plays of Wole Soyinka', *African Literature Today*, 5 (1970).

Okpewho, Isidore, *Myth in Africa* (Cambridge, 1983).

The Epic in Africa (Columbia, 1979).

Okri, Ben, *Incidents at the Shrine* (London, 1986).

Stars of the New Curfew (London, 1988).

The Famished Road (London, 1991).

Olajubu, O., 'Iwi Egungun Chants – An Introduction', *Research in African Literature*, 5:1 (1974).

Olatunji, O., 'Yoruba Oral Poetry', *Spectrum*, 3 (1973).

Onwuachi, P. C., and A. W. Wolfe, 'The Place of Anthropology in the Future of Africa', *Human Organisation*, 25 (1966), 93–5.

Ottenberg, S., *Masked Rituals of the Afikpo* (Seattle, 1975).

Ovid, *Metamorphoses*, translated with an introduction by Mary M. Innes (Harmondsworth, 1955).

Oyebamiji, Mustapha, 'A literary appraisal of Sakava: A Yoruba traditional form of music', in Wande Abimbola (ed.), *Yoruba Oral Tradition*.

Pagden, Anthony (ed.), *The Languages of Political Theory in Early Modern Europe* (Cambridge, 1987).

Panofsky, E., *Problems in Titian: Mostly Iconographic* (London, 1969).

Panofsky, E., and F. Saxl, 'A Late Antique Religious Symbol in Works by Holbein and Titian', *The Burlington Magazine*, 49 (1926).

Parker, Andrew (ed.) *Nationalisms and Sexualities*, (London, 1992).

Parrinder, G., *West African Religion* (London, 1961).

Parry, Benita, *Conrad and Imperialism* (London, 1983).

'Problems in Current Theories of Colonial Discourse', *Oxford Literary Review*, 9:1–2, 27–58.

Parsons, A., *Belief, Magic and Anomie: Essays in Psychological Anthropology* (New York, 1969).

Payne, H., 'Malinowski's style', *Proceedings of the American Philosophical Society*, 125 (1981), 416–40.

Paz, Octavio, *Claude Lévi-Strauss: An Introduction*, 1967, translated by J. S. Bernstein and Maxine Bernstein (London, 1971).

Peacock, James L., *The Anthropological Lens: Harsh light, Soft Focus* (Cambridge, 1986).

Peel, J. D. Y., *Aladura: A Religious Movement among the Yoruba* (Oxford, 1968).

Percival, W. Keith, 'Nineteenth-Century Origins of Twentieth-Century Structuralism', *Papers from the Fifth Regional Meeting of the Chicago Linguistics Society*, 1969, edited by Robert I. Binnick et al. (Chicago, 1969), 416–20.

Philip, Marlene Nourbese, *Looking for Livingstone, An Odyssey of Silence* (Ontario, 1991).

She Tries Her Tongue, Her Silence Softly Breaks (Charlottetown, 1989).

Pinkerton, John, *Enquiry into the History of Scotland and Dissertation on the Goths*, 2 vols. (Edinburgh, 1814).

Pointon, Marcia, *Naked Authority* (Cambridge, 1990).

Povey, John, 'West African Drama in English', *Comparative Drama*, 1:2 (1967).

'Wole Soyinka and the Nigerian Drama', *Triquarterly*, 5 (1966).

'Wole Soyinka: Two Nigerian Comedies', *Comparative Drama*, 3:2 (1969).

Pratt, Mary Louise, *Imperial Eyes* (London, 1992).

Price, Sally, *Primitive Art in Civilized Places* (Chicago, 1989).

Pride, J. B., and J. Holmes, *Sociolinguistics* (Harmondsworth, 1972).

Prown, Jules David, *John Singleton Copley*, 2 vols. (Cambridge, Mass., 1966).

Puppi, Lionello, *Torment in Art: Pain, Violence and Martyrdom* (New York, 1991).

Race & Class, 'Literature: Colonial Lines of Descent', 31:1 (1989).

Radin, Paul, 'Literary Aspects of North American Mythology', *Canda Geographical Survey Museum Bulletin*, 16 (1915).

Radin, Paul, *Primitive Man as Philosopher* (London, 1927).

Primitive Religion (London, 1935).

The Trickster: A Study in American Indian Mythology, With Commentaries by C. Kerenyi and C. G. Jung (London, 1956).

Rapp, J., 'Tizians Marsyas in Kremsier', *Pantheon*, 45 (1987).

Redfield, R., *The Primitive World and its Transformations* (Cornell, 1953).

Renan, E., *De l'Origine du langage* (Paris, 1859).

Poetry of the Celtic Races and Other Studies (1896), translated by W. G. Hutchinson (New York, 1970).

Rex, John, and David Mason, *Theories of Race and Ethnic Relations* (Cambridge, 1986).

Rhees, Rush (ed.), *Recollections of Wittgenstein* (Oxford, 1984).

Rhodes, W., 'Music as an Agent of Political Expression', *African Studies Bulletins*, 5:2 (1962).

Ribault, Jean, *La complète et véridique découverte de la Terra Florida* (London, 1563).

Ricard, Alain, 'Les Paradoxes de Wole Soyinka', *Présence Africaine*, 72 (1969).

Théâtre et Nationalism (Paris, 1972).

Richards, I. A., and C. K. Ogden, *The Meaning of Meaning* (London, 1923).

Richardson, Major John, *Wacousta!* (1832), (Toronto, 1924).

Roach, A., 'The Act of Ifa Oracle', *African Arts*, 8:1 (1974).

Robertson, William, *The Situation of the World at the Time of Christ's Appearance* (Edinburgh, 1759).

Rodney, Walter, *How Europe Underdeveloped Africa* (London, 1988).

Roheim, Geza, *Psychoanalysis and Anthropology* (New York, 1950).

'Dream Analysis and Fieldwork in Anthropology', *Psychoanalysis and the Social Sciences*, 1 (1947).

Roscoe, A. A., *Mother is Gold* (Cambridge, 1971).

Roscoe, Rev. J., *The Baganda* (London, 1911).

'Notes on the Manners and Customs of the Baganda', *Journal of the Anthropological Institute*, 31 (1901), 117–30.

Immigrants and their Influence in the Lake Region of Central Africa, Frazer Lecture II (Cambridge, 1923).

'Further Notes on the Manners and Customs of the Baganda', *Journal of the Anthropological Institute*, 32 (1901), 25–80.

Roston, M., *Renaissance Perspective in Literature and the Visual Arts* (Princeton, 1987).

Rotimi, Ola, 'Traditional Nigerian Drama', in Bruce King (ed.), *Introduction to Nigerian Literature* (Lagos, 1971).

Rousseau, J-J., *The Social Contract and Discourse* (Letchworth, 1973).

Rubin, W. (ed.), *'Primitivism' in Twentieth-Century Art*, Museum of Modern Art, 2 vols. (New York, 1984).

Rushdie, Salman, *Imaginary Homelands* (London, 1991).

Sagan, Eli, *At the Dawn of Tyranny* (London, 1986).

Said, Edward, *Orientalism* (London, 1978).

'Opponents, Audiences, Constituencies and Community', in Hal Foster (ed.) *Postmodern Culture* (London, 1985).

'Orientalism Reconsidered', in *Europe and Its Others*, edited by Francis Barker et al. (Colchester, 1985).

'Representing the Colonized', *Critical Inquiry*, 15:2 (Winter 1989).

Sale, Kirkpatrick, *The Conquest of Paradise* (London, 1991).

Saussure, Ferdinand de, *Course in General Linguistics* (New York, 1959).

Sayce, A. H., *Introduction to the Science of Language*, 2 vols. (London, 1850).

Scarry, Elaine, *The Body in Pain: The Making and Unmaking of the World* (Oxford, 1985).

Scheffer, Jean-Louis, 'Thanatography, Skiagraphy' (from *Espèce de chose mélancholie*, translated with an afterword by Paul Smith, *Word and Image*, 1 (1985), 191–6.

Scholte, Bob, 'The Charmed Circle of Geertz's Hermeneutics', *Critique of Anthropology*, 6:1 (Spring 1986), 5–15.

Scott, Sir Walter, *Introductions and Notes and Illustrations to the Novels, Tales and Romances of the Author of Waverley*, 3 vols. (Edinburgh, 1833).

Letters, edited by H. J. C. Grierson, 12 vols. (London, 1932–7).

The Border Antiquities of England and Scotland, 2 vols. (Edinburgh, 1814–17).

The Centenary Edition of the Waverley Novels (Edinburgh, 1879–81).

The Letters on Demonology and Witchcraft (London, 1830).

The Minstrelsy of the Scottish Border, 1802–3, 2 vols. (Edinburgh, 1861).

The Miscellaneous Prose Works of Sir Walter Scott, 28 vols. (Edinburgh, 1834–6).

Waverley, 1814, edited by Claire Lamont (Oxford, 1981).

Sebeok, T. A., *The Play of Musement* (Bloomington, 1981).

(ed.), *Myth: A Symposium* (Bloomington, 1955).

Seidel, Michael, *Satiric Inheritance: Rabelais to Sterne* (Princeton, 1979).

Sembat, Marcel, 'The Future Moulded by Science: A Vision', translated by Sir James Frazer, *Science Progress*, 18 (July 1923), 108–12.

Shelton, A., 'Volosinov on the Ideology of Inversion', *Journal of the Anthropological Society of Oxford*, 9:3 (1978), 191–6.

Simon, Robin, *The Portrait in Britain and America: 1680–1940* (Oxford, 1982).

Sinclair, Sir J., *Statistical Accounts of Scotland*, 21 vols. (Edinburgh, 1791–9).

Singh, J. A. L., and Robert Zingg, *Wolf Children and Feral Man* (London, 1942).

Skinner, Q. (ed.), *The Return of Grand Theory in the Human Sciences* (Cambridge, 1985).

Skorupski, John, *Symbol and Theory: A Philosophical Study of Theories of Religion in Social Anthropology* (Cambridge, 1976).

Slemon, Stephen, 'Magic Realism as Post-Colonial Discourse', *Canadian Literature*, 116 (Spring 1988).

'Monuments of Empire: Allegory/Counter Discourse/Post-Colonial Writing', *Kunapipi*, 9:3 (1987).

'Revisioning Allegory: Wilson Harris' *Carnival*', *Kunapipi*, 8:2 (1986).

Smith, Adam, *Essays on Philosophical Subjects*, edited by Dugald Stewart (Dublin, 1795).

Moral and Political Philosophy, edited by H. W. Schneider (London, 1970).

Smock, G. E., 'Sir Walter Scott's Theory of the Novel' (unpublished PhD thesis, Cornell University, 1934).

Southall, A. (ed.), *Social Change in Modern Africa* (Oxford, 1961).

Soyinka, Wole, *Aké: The Years of Childhood* (London, 1981).

Collected Plays, 2 vols. (Oxford, 1973–4).

Death and the King's Horseman (London, 1975).

'Idanre' and Other Poems (London, 1967).

Isara: A Voyage Around Essay (London, 1990).

Myth, Literature and the African World (Cambridge, 1978).

Ogun Abibiman (London, 1976).

Season of Anomy (London, 1973).

The Interpreters (London, 1965).

The Man Died, 1972 (Harmondsworth, 1975).

'A Maverick in America', *Ibadan*, 21 (1966).

'Amos Tutuola on Stage', *Ibadan*, 15, 1963.

'And After the Narcissist?' *African Forum* (Spring 1966).

'Cor Teach . . .', *Ibadan*, 6 (1959).

'From a Common Back Cloth', *The American Scholar*, 32 (1963).

'Neo-Tarzanism: The Poetics of Pseudo-Tradition', *Transition*, 48 (1974).

'Towards a True Theatre', *Nigeria*, 80, 1962.

'Who's Afraid of Elesin Oba?' (unpublished conference paper delivered at University of Ibadan, 23 November 1977).

Spence, Lewis, 'Sir Walter Scott as a Student of Tradition', in H. J. C. Grierson, *Sir Walter Scott Today*.

Spenser, Edmund, *The Faerie Queene* (1590), edited by A. C. Hamilton (Harlow, 1977).

Sperber, Dan, *On Anthropological Knowledge* (*Le Savoir des Anthropologues*, 1982) (Cambridge, 1985).

Rethinking Symbolism (Cambridge, 1975).

Sperber, Dan, Oswald Ducrot, T. Todorov, Mustafa Safoun, Francois Wahl, *Qu'est ce que le structuralisme?* (Paris, 1968).

Spierenburg, Pieter, *The Spectacle of Suffering: Executions and the Evolution of Repression: From a Pre-industrial Metropolis to the European Experience* (Cambridge, 1984).

Spivak, Gayatri, *In Other Worlds* (London, 1988).

Spivak, Gayatri, and Sarah Harasym, *The Postcolonial Critic* (London, 1990).

Spurr, David, 'Colonialist Journalism: Stanley to Didion', *Raritan*, 2 (Fall 1985).

Stam, James H., *Inquiries into the Origin of Language: The Fate of a Question* (New York, 1976).

Stedman, Captain John, *A Narrative of a five years expedition against the revolted negroes, in Surinam, Guiana, on the wild coast of South America, from the year 1772–1777, elucidating the history of that country, and describing its productions, viz: quadrupeds, birds, fishes, reptiles, trees, shrubs, fruits and roots, with an account of the Indians of Guiana, and negroes of Guiana* (1796), facsimile reprint with an introduction by R. A. J. Van Lier (Barre, 1971).

The Journal of John Gabriel Stedman 1744–1797: Soldier and Author, edited by Stanhope Thompson (Mitre Press, 1962).

Stewart, Gen. David, of Garth, *Sketches of the Character, Manners and Present State of the Highlanders of Scotland*, 2 vols. (Edinburgh, 1822).

Stocking, G., 'Empathy and Antipathy in *Heart of Darkness*', in *Readings in the History of Anthropology*, edited by Regna Darnell (New York, 1974), 85–98.

Race, Culture and Evolution: Essays in the History of Anthropology (New York, 1968).

Street, Brian, *The Savage in Literature* (London, 1975).

Strong, Roy, *Art and Power* (Woodbridge, 1984).

Summers, M., *The Werewolf* (New York, 1966).

Syvret, Margaret, and Joan Stevens, *Ballière's History of Jersey* (Chichester, 1981).

Talbot, P. A., *Life in Southern Nigeria* (London, 1923).

Tannahill, Reay, *Flesh and Blood: A History of the Cannibal Complex* (New York, 1975).

Taussig, M., *Shamanism, Colonialism and the Wildman: A Study in Terror and Healing* (Chicago, 1987).

Tax, Sol, *Evolution after Darwin* (Chicago, 1960).

Terman, L. M., *The Measurement of Intelligence* (London, 1919).

Thevet, Andre, *Les singularitez de la France antartique* (1558).

Thieme, D., 'A Summary Report on the Oral Traditions of Yoruba Musicians', *Africa*, 40 (1970).

Thomas, Keith, *Religion and the Decline of Magic* (London, 1971).

Tiffin, Helen, and Stephen Slemon (eds.), *After Europe*, (Sydney, 1989).

Todorov, T., *Theories of the Symbol* (Oxford, 1982).

'Introduction à la symbolique', *Poetique*, 11 (1972).

The Topsy-Turvy World, Ausstellung des Goethe-Instituts (London, 1985).

Traore, B., *The Black African Theatre and its Social Functions* (Ibadan, 1972).

Trilling, Lionel, *Beyond Culture* (London, 1965).

Trinh T. Minh-Ha, *Framer Framed* (London, 1992).

   When The Moon Waxes Red: Representation, Gender and Cultural Politics (London, 1991).

   Woman, Native, Other: Writing Postcoloniality and Feminism (Indiana, 1989).

   'Differences', *Discourse*, 8 (1986), 11–37.

Turner, V., *The Forest of Symbols* (Cornell, 1967).

   The Ritual Process (London, 1969).

Tyler, S. A., 'The Poetic Turn in Postmodern Anthropology: The Poetry of Paul Friedrich', *American Anthropologist*, 86:2 (1984), 328–36.

Tylor, E. B., *Primitive Culture* (London, 1871).

Van Gennep, Arnold, *The Rites of Passage* (1908), translated by Marika B. Vizedom and Gabrielle L. Caffee, introduction by Solon T. Kimball (London, 1960).

   The Semi-Scholars (*Les demi-savants*, 1911), translated and edited by Rodney Needham (London, 1964).

Vickery, J. B., *The Literary Impact of 'The Golden Bough'* (Princeton, New Jersey, 1973).

Wall, Cheryl A. (ed.), *Changing Our Own Words* (London, 1989).

Wastberg, Per, (ed.), *The Writer in Modern Africa*, Proceedings of the African–Scandinavian Writers' Conference, 1967 (Uppsala, 1968).

Watson, I., 'Soyinka's Dance of the Forests', *Transition*, 27 (1966).

Webster, Steven, 'Dialogue and Fiction in Ethnography', *Dialectical Anthropology*, 7 (1982), 99–114.

   'Ethnography as Storytelling', *Dialectical Anthropology*, 8 (1983), 125–265.

   'Realism and Reification in the Ethnographic Genre', *Critique of Anthropology*, 6:1 (Spring 1986), 39–62.

Weimann, Robert, *Structure and Society in Literary History* (London, 1977).

Wescott, R. W., 'The Evolution of Language: Reopening a Closed Subject', *Studies in Language*, 19:1/4 (1967), 67–81.

White, Landeg, *For Captain Stedman* (Liskeard, 1983).

Wilden, A., *System and Structure: Essays in Communication and Exchange* (London, 1972).

Wilson, Anne, *Traditional Romance and Tale: How Stories Mean* (Ipswich, 1976).

Witney, William Dwight, 'Language and the Study of Language' (1867), in *Whitney on Language: Selected Writings of William Dwight Witney*, edited by Michael Silverstein (Cambridge, Mass., 1971).

Wittgenstein, L., *Lectures and Conversations on Aesthetics, Psychology and Religious Beliefs* (Oxford, 1967).

   Remarks on Frazer's 'The Golden Bough', edited by Rush Rhees, translated by A. C. Miles (Retford, 1979).

Wittkower, Rudolf, *Allegory and the Migration of Symbols* (London, 1977).

Yeats, W. B., *Essays and Introductions* (London, 1961).

   Ideas of Good and Evil (London, 1903).

Yemitan, E. O., trans., 'Yoruba Ijala', *Odu*, 1:1 (1964).
Young, Robert, *White Mythologies* (London, 1990).
Zeljan, Zora, 'Oxala', *Transition*, 47 (1974).
Zirimu, Pio and Andrew Gurr, *Black Aesthetics* (Nairobi, 1973).

Index

Index